Seventeenth-Century English Poetry

Seventeenth-Century English Poetry

MODERN ESSAYS IN CRITICISM

Edited by
WILLIAM R. KEAST
Cornell University

A GALAXY BOOK
New York Oxford University Press 1962

Library of Congress Catalogue Card Number: 62–16576
First Published as a Galaxy Book, 1962
Third printing, 1963

Printed in the United States of America

Preface

During the half-century since the publication of H. J. C. Grierson's edition of the poems of John Donne, seventeenth-century English poetry has been studied with intense—one might almost say relentless—interest by a succession of critics, who have often used it as the basis for the statement or illustration of critical theory and as a touchstone of literary taste. From the hundreds of critical studies which the modern interest in seventeenth-century poetry has called forth, the present book gathers together twenty-seven essays. They range in time from Grierson's influential Introduction to his 1921 anthology of *Metaphysical Lyrics & Poems* and Eliot's perhaps even more influential essay on the metaphysicals (originally published as a review of Grierson's collection), to George Williamson's recent study of the background of Donne's "Extasie." The first five essays discuss seventeenth-century poetry generally; the others deal with particular poets and poems. There are no essays on Milton because he is to have a volume to himself in this series. The essays have been chosen not only because they say illuminating things about the poetry of the period but because they provide a fairly representative sample of the different critical procedures current in recent decades. It has seemed wise to concentrate on a limited number of poets and to provide several essays on each of the more important writers, in order to permit the student to compare critical assumptions, methods, and results.

Several colleagues and friends helped by suggesting essays and by commenting on my successive attempts to make a balanced selection from the rich body of critical literature on seventeenth-century poetry. I am grateful to them.

Ithaca, New York
March 1962

William R. Keast

Contents

Seventeenth-Century English Poetry

H. J. C. GRIERSON

Metaphysical Poetry

I

Metaphysical Poetry, in the full sense of the term, is a poetry which, like that of the *Divina Commedia,* the *De Natura Rerum,* perhaps Goethe's *Faust,* has been inspired by a philosophical conception of the universe and the rôle assigned to the human spirit in the great drama of existence. These poems were written because a definite interpretation of the riddle, the atoms of Epicurus rushing through infinite empty space, the theology of the schoolmen as elaborated in the catechetical disquisitions of St. Thomas, Spinoza's vision of life *sub specie aeternitatis,* beyond good and evil, laid hold on the mind and the imagination of a great poet, unified and illumined his comprehension of life, intensified and heightened his personal consciousness of joy and sorrow, of hope and fear, by broadening their significance, revealing to him in the history of his own soul a brief abstract of the drama of human destiny. "Poetry is the first and last of all knowledge—it is as immortal as the heart of man." Its themes are the simplest experiences of the surface of life, sorrow and joy, love and battle, the peace of the country, the bustle and stir of towns, but equally the boldest conceptions, the profoundest intuitions, the subtlest and most complex classifications and "discourse of reason," if into these too the poet can "carry sensation," make of them passionate experiences communicable in vivid and moving imagery, in rich and varied harmonies.

It is no such great metaphysical poetry as that of Lucretius and

From *Metaphysical Lyrics & Poems of the Seventeenth Century* (Oxford, 1921), pp. xiii–xxxviii. Reprinted by permission of The Clarendon Press.

Dante that the present essay deals with, which this volume seeks to illustrate. Of the poets from whom it culls, Donne is familiar with the definitions and distinctions of Mediaeval Scholasticism; Cowley's bright and alert, if not profound mind, is attracted by the achievements of science and the systematic materialism of Hobbes. Donne, moreover, is metaphysical not only in virtue of his scholasticism, but by his deep reflective interest in the experiences of which his poetry is the expression, the new psychological curiosity with which he writes of love and religion. The divine poets who follow Donne have each the inherited metaphysic, if one may so call it, of the Church to which he is attached, Catholic or Anglican. But none of the poets has for his main theme a metaphysic like that of Epicurus or St. Thomas passionately apprehended and imaginatively expounded. Donne, the most thoughtful and imaginative of them all, is more aware of disintegration than of comprehensive harmony, of the clash between the older physics and metaphysics on the one hand and the new science of Copernicus and Galileo and Vesalius and Bacon on the other:

The new philosophy calls all in doubt,
The element of fire is quite put out;
The sun is lost and the earth, and no man's wit
Can well direct him where to look for it.
And freely men confess that this world's spent,
When in the planets and the firmament
They seek so many new; they see that this
Is crumbled out again to his atomies.

Have not all souls thought
For many ages that our body is wrought
Of air and fire and other elements?
And now they think of new ingredients;
And one soul thinks one, and another way
Another thinks, and 'tis an even lay.

The greatest English poet, indeed, of the century was, or believed himself to be, a philosophical or theological poet of the same order as Dante. *Paradise Lost* was written to be a justification of "the ways of God to men," resting on a theological system as definite and almost as carefully articulated in the *De Doctrina Christiana* as that which Dante had accepted from the *Summa* of Aquinas. And the poet embodied his argument in a dramatic poem as vividly and intensely conceived, as magnificently and harmoniously set forth, as the *Divina Commedia.* But in truth Milton was no philosopher. The subtleties of theological definition and inference eluded his rationalistic, practical, though idealistic, mind. He proved nothing. The definitely stated argument of the poem is an obvious begging of the question. What he did was to create, or give a new definiteness and sensible power to, a great myth which, through his poem, continued for a century or more to dominate the mind and imagination of pious protestants without many of them suspecting the heresies which lurked beneath the imposing and dazzling poem in which was retold the Bible story of the fall and redemption of man.

Metaphysical in this large way, Donne and his followers to Cowley are not, yet the word describes better what is the peculiar quality of their poetry than any other, e.g., fantastic, for poetry may be fantastic in so many different ways, witness Skelton and the Elizabethans, and Hood and Browning. It lays stress on the right things—the survival, one might say the reaccentuation, of the metaphysical strain, the *concetti metafisici ed ideali* as Testi calls them in contrast to the simpler imagery of classical poetry, of mediaeval Italian poetry; the more intellectual, less verbal, character of their wit compared with the conceits of the Elizabethans; the finer psychology of which their conceits are often the expression; their learned imagery; the argumentative, subtle evolution of their lyrics; above all the peculiar blend of passion and thought, feeling and ratiocination which is their greatest achievement. Passionate thinking is always apt to become metaphysical, probing and investigating the experience from which it takes its rise. All these qualities are in the poetry of Donne, and Donne is the great master of English poetry in the seventeenth century.

The Italian influence which Wyatt and Surrey brought into English poetry at the Renaissance gave it a more serious, a more thoughtful colour. They caught, especially Wyatt in some of the finest of his sonnets and songs, that spirit of "high seriousness" which Chaucer with all his admiration of Italian poetry had failed to apprehend. English mediaeval poetry is often gravely pious, haunted by the fear of death and the judgment, melancholy over the "Falls of Princes"; it is never serious and thoughtful in the introspective, reflective, dignified manner which it became in Wyatt and Sackville, and our "sage and serious" Spenser, and in the songs of the first group of Elizabethan courtly poets, Sidney and Raleigh and Dyer. One has but to recall "My lute, awake! perform the last," "Forget not yet the tried intent," "My mind to me a kingdom is," and to contrast them in mind with the songs which Henry VIII and Cornish were still composing and singing when Wyatt began to write, in order to realize what Italy and the Renaissance did to deepen the strain of English lyric poetry as that had flowed under French influence from the thirteenth to the sixteenth centuries. But French influence, the influence of Ronsard and his fellows, renewed itself in the seventies, and the great body of Elizabethan song is as gay and careless and impersonal as the earlier lyric had been, though richer in colour and more varied in rhythm. Then came Donne and Jonson (the schoolman and the classical scholar, one might say, emphasizing for the moment single aspects of their work), and new qualities of spirit and form were given to lyrical poetry, and not to lyrical poetry alone.

In dealing with poets who lived and wrote before the eighteenth century we are always confronted with the difficulty of recovering the personal, the biographical element, which, if sometimes disturbing and disconcerting, is yet essential to a complete understanding of their work. Men were not different from what they are now, and if there be hardly a lyric of Goethe's or Shelley's that does not owe something to the accidents of their lives, one may feel sure it was in varying degrees the same with poets three hundred years ago. Poems are not written by influences or movements or sources, but come from the living hearts of men. Fortunately, in the case of Donne, one of the most individual of poets, it is possible to some extent to reproduce the circumstances, the inner experiences from which his intensely personal poetry flowed.

He was in the first place a Catholic. Our history text-books make so little of the English Catholics that one is apt to forget they existed and were, for themselves at any rate, not a political problem, but real and suffering individuals. "I had my first breeding and conversation," says Donne, "with men of a suppressed and afflicted religion, accustomed to the despite of death and hungry of an imagined martyrdom." In these circumstances, we gather, he was carefully and religiously educated, and after some years at Oxford and Cambridge was taken or sent abroad, perhaps with a view to entering foreign service, more probably with a view to the priesthood, and visited Italy and Spain. And then, one conjectures, a reaction took place, the rebellion of a full-blooded, highly intellectual temperament against a superimposed bent. He entered the Inns of Court in 1592, at the age of nineteen, and flung himself into the life of a student and the life of a young man about town, Jack Donne, "not dissolute but very neat, a great visitor of ladies, a great frequenter of plays, a great writer of conceited verses." "Neither was it possible that a vulgar soul should dwell in such promising features." He joined the band of reckless and raffish young men who sailed with Essex to Cadiz and the Islands. He was taken into the service of Sir Thomas Egerton. Ambition began to vie with the love of pleasure, when a hasty marriage closed a promising career, and left him bound in shallows and in miseries, to spend years in the suitorship of the great, and to find at last, not altogether willingly, a haven in the Anglican priesthood, and reveal himself as the first great orator that Church produced.

The record of these early years is contained in Donne's satires—harsh, witty, lucid, full of a young man's scorn of fools and low callings, and a young thinker's consciousness of the problems of religion in an age of divided faiths, and of justice in a corrupt world—and in his Love Songs and Sonnets and Elegies. The satires were more generally known; the love poems the more influential in courtly and literary circles.

Donne's genius, temperament, and learning gave to his love poems certain qualities which immediately arrested attention and have given them ever since a power at once fascinating and disconcerting despite the faults of phrasing and harmony which, for a century after Dryden, obscured, and to some still outweigh, their poetic worth. The first of these is a depth and range of feeling unknown to the majority of Elizabethan sonneteers and song-writers. Over all the Elizabethan sonnets, in greater or less measure, hangs the suggestion of translation or imitation. Watson, Sidney, Daniel, Spenser, Drayton, Lodge, all of them, with rarer or more frequent touches of individuality, are pipers of Petrarch's woes, sighing in the strain of Ronsard or more often of Desportes. Shakespeare, indeed, in his great sequence, and Drayton in at any rate one sonnet, sounded a deeper note, revealed a fuller sense of the complexities and contradictions of passionate devotion. But Donne's treatment of love is entirely unconventional except when he chooses to dally half ironically with the convention of Petrarchian adoration. His songs are the expression in unconventional, witty language of all the moods of a lover that experience and imagination have taught him to understand—sensuality aerated by a brilliant wit; fascination and scornful anger inextricably blended:

> When by thy scorn, O murdress, I am dead
> And that thou think'st thee free
> From all solicitations from me,
> Then shall my ghost come to thy bed;

the passionate joy of mutual and contented love:

> All other things to their destruction draw,
> Only our love hath no decay;

> This no to-morrow hath nor yesterday,
> Running it never runs from us away,
> But truly keeps his first, last, everlasting day;

the sorrow of parting which is the shadow of such joy; the gentler pathos of temporary separation in married life:

> Let not thy divining heart
> Forethink me any ill,
> Destiny may take thy part,
> And may thy fears fulfil;
> But think that we
> Are but turn'd aside to sleep;
> They who one another keep
> Alive ne'er parted be;

the mystical heights and the mystical depths of love:

> Study me then you who shall lovers be
> At the next world, that is, at the next Spring:
> For I am every dead thing
> In whom love wrought new Alchemy.

If Donne had expressed this wide range of intense feeling as perfectly as he has done at times poignantly and startlingly; if he had given to his poems the same impression of entire artistic sincerity that Shakespeare conveys in the greater of his sonnets and Drayton once achieved; if to his many other gifts had been added a deeper and more controlling sense of beauty, he would have been, as he nearly is, the greatest of love poets. But there is a second quality of his poetry which made it the fashion of an age, but has been inimical to its general acceptance ever since, and that is its metaphysical wit. "He affects the metaphysics," says Dryden, "not only in his satires but in his amorous verses where nature only should reign; and perplexes the minds of the fair sex with nice speculations of philosophy when he should engage their hearts and entertain them with the softness of love." "Amorous verses," "the fair sex," and "the softness of love" are the vulgarities of a less poetic and passionate age than Donne's, but metaphysics he does affect. But a metaphysical strand, *concetti metafisici ed ideali,* had run through the mediaeval love-poetry of which the Elizabethan sonnets are a descendant. It had attained its fullest development in the poems of Dante and his school, had been subordinated to rhetoric and subtleties of expression rather than thought in

Petrarch, and had lost itself in the pseudo-metaphysical extravagances of Tebaldeo, Cariteo, and Serafino. Donne was no conscious reviver of the metaphysics of Dante, but to the game of elaborating fantastic conceits and hyperboles which was the fashion throughout Europe, he brought not only a full-blooded temperament and acute mind, but a vast and growing store of the same scholastic learning, the same Catholic theology, as controlled Dante's thought, jostling already with the new learning of Copernicus and Paracelsus. The result is startling and disconcerting—the comparison of parted lovers to the legs of a pair of compasses, the deification of his mistress by the discovery that she is only to be defined by negatives or that she can read the thoughts of his heart, a thing "beyond an angel's art"; and a thousand other subtleties of quintessences and nothingness, the mixture of souls and the significance of numbers, to say nothing of the aerial bodies of angels, the phoenix and the mandrake's root, Alchemy and Astrology, legal contracts and *non obstantes,* "late schoolboys and sour prentices," "the king's real and his stamped face." But the effect aimed at and secured is not entirely fantastic and erudite. The motive inspiring Donne's images is in part the same as that which led Shakespeare from the picturesque, natural and mythological, images of *A Midsummer-Night's Dream* and *The Merchant of Venice* to the homely but startling phrases and metaphors of *Hamlet* and *Macbeth,* the "blanket of the dark," the

fat weed
That rots itself in ease on Lethe wharf,

"the rank sweat of an enseamed bed." It is the same desire for vivid and dramatic expression. The great master at a later period of dramatic as well as erudite pulpit oratory coins in his poems many a startling, jarring, arresting phrase:

For God's sake hold your tongue and let me live:

Who ever comes to shroud me do not harm
Nor question much
That subtle wreath of hair, which crowns my arm:

I taught my silks their rustling to forbear,
Even my opprest shoes dumb and silent were.

I long to talk with some old lover's ghost
Who died before the God of love was born;

Twice or thrice had I loved thee
Before I knew thy face or name,
So in a voice, so in a shapeless flame,
Angels affect us oft and worshipped be;

And whilst our souls negotiate there
We like sepulchral statues lay;
All day the same our postures were
And we said nothing all the day.

My face and brest of haircloth, and my head
With care's harsh, sudden hoariness o'er-spread.

These vivid, simple, realistic touches are too quickly merged in learned and fantastic elaborations, and the final effect of every poem of Donne's is a bizarre and blended one; but if the greatest poetry rises clear of the bizarre, the fantastic, yet very great poetry may be bizarre if it be the expression of a strangely blended temperament, an intense emotion, a vivid imagination.

What is true of Donne's imagery is true of the other disconcerting element in his poetry, its harsh and rugged verse. It is an outcome of the same double motive, the desire to startle and the desire to approximate poetic to direct, unconventional, colloquial speech. Poetry is always a balance, sometimes a compromise, between what has to be said and the prescribed pattern to which the saying of it is adjusted. In poetry such as Spenser's, the musical flow, the melody and harmony of line and stanza, is dominant, and the meaning is adjusted to it at the not infrequent cost of diffuseness—if a delightful diffuseness—and even some weakness of phrasing logically and rhetorically considered. In Shakespeare's tragedies the thought and feeling tend to break through the prescribed pattern till blank verse becomes almost rhythmical prose, the rapid overflow of the lines admitting hardly the semblance of pause. This is the kind of effect Donne is always aiming at, alike in his satires and lyrics, bending and cracking the metrical pattern to the rhetoric of direct and vehement utterance. The result is often, and to eighteenth-century ears attuned to the clear and defined, if limited, harmony of Waller and Dryden and Pope was, rugged and harsh. But here again, to those who have ears that care to hear, the effect is not finally inharmonious. Donne's verse has a powerful and haunting harmony of its own. For Donne is not simply, no poet could be, willing to force his accent, to strain and crack a prescribed pattern; he is striving to find a rhythm that will express the passionate fullness of his mind, the fluxes and refluxes of his moods;

and the felicities of verse are as frequent and startling as those of phrasing. He is one of the first masters, perhaps *the* first, of the elaborate stanza or paragraph in which the discords of individual lines or phrases are resolved in the complex and rhetorically effective harmony of the whole group of lines:

> If yet I have not all thy love,
> Deare, I shall never have it all,
> I cannot breathe one other sigh, to move,
> Nor can entreat one other tear to fall,
> And all my treasure, which should purchase thee,
> Sighs, tears, and oaths, and letters I have spent.
> Yet no more can be due to me,
> Than at the bargain made was meant,
> If then thy gift of love was partial,
> That some to me, some shuld to others fall,
> Deare, I shall never have thee all.

> But I am none; nor will my sunne renew.
> You lovers for whose sake the lesser sunne
> At this time to the Goat is run
> To fetch new lust and give it you,
> Enjoy your summer all;
> Since she enjoys her long night's festival,
> Let me prepare towards her, and let me call
> This hour her Vigil and her Eve, since this
> Bŏth thĕ yēars | ănd thĕ dāys | dēep mīd|nĭght ĭs.

The wrenching of accent which Jonson complained of is not entirely due to carelessness or indifference. It has often both a rhetorical and a harmonious justification. Donne plays with rhythmical effects as with conceits and words and often in much the same way. Mr. Fletcher Melton's interesting analysis of his verse has not, I think, established his main thesis, which like so many "research" scholars he over-emphasizes, that the whole mystery of Donne's art lies in his use of the same sound now in *arsis*, now in *thesis;* but his examples show that this is one of many devices by which Donne secures two effects, the troubling of the regular fall of the verse stresses by the intrusion of rhetorical stress on syllables which the metrical pattern leaves unstressed, and, secondly, an echoing and re-echoing of similar sounds parallel to his fondness for resemblances in thoughts and things apparently the most remote from one another. There is, that is to say, in his verse the same blend as in his diction of the colloquial and the bizarre. He writes as one who *will* say what he has to say without regard to conventions of poetic diction or smooth verse, but what he has to say is subtle and surprising, and so are the metrical effects with which it is presented. There is nothing of unconscious or merely careless harshness in such an effect as this:

> Poor soul, in this thy flesh what dost thou know?
> Thou know'st thyself so little that thou knowst not
> How thou didst die, nor how thou wast begot.
> Thou neither know'st how thou at first camest in,
> Nor how thou took'st the poison of man's sin;
> Nor dost thou though thou know'st that thou art so
> By what way thou art made immortal know.

In Donne's pronunciation, as in southern English to-day, "thou," "how," "soul," "know," "though," and "so" were not far removed from each other in sound and the reiterated notes ring through the lines like a tolling bell. Mr. Melton has collected, and any careful reader may discover for himself, many similar subtleties of poetical rhetoric; for Donne is perhaps our first great master of poetic rhetoric, of poetry used, as Dryden and Pope were to use it, for effects of oratory rather than of song, and the advance which Dryden achieved was secured by subordinating to oratory the more passionate and imaginative qualities which troubled the balance and movement of Donne's packed but imaginative rhetoric.

It was not indeed in lyrical verse that Dryden followed and developed Donne, but in his eulogistic, elegiac, satirical, and epistolary verse. The progress of Dryden's eulogistic style is traceable from his earliest metaphysical extravagances through lines such as those addressed to the Duchess of York, where Waller is his model, to the verses on the death of Oldham in which a more natural and classical strain has entirely superseded his earlier extravagances and elegancies. In truth Donne's metaphysical eulogies and elegies and epistles are a hard nut to crack for his most sympathetic admirers. And yet they have undeniable qualities. The metaphysics are developed in a more serious, a less paradoxical, strain than in some of the songs and elegies. In his letters he is an excellent, if far from a perfect, talker in verse; and the personality which they reveal is a singularly charming one, grave, loyal, melancholy, witty. If some of the elegiac pieces are packed with tasteless and extravagant hyperboles, the *Anniversaries* (especially the second) remains, despite all its faults, one of the greatest poems on death in the language, the fullest record in our literature of the disintegrating collision in a sensitive mind of the old tradition and the new learning. Some of the invocational passages in *Of the Progresse of the Soule* are among the finest examples of his subtle and passionate thinking as well as of his most elaborate verse rhetoric.

But the most intense and personal of Donne's poems, after the love songs and elegies, are his later religious sonnets and songs; and their influence on subsequent poetry was even more obvious and potent. They are as personal and as tormented as his earlier "love-song weeds," for his spiritual Aeneid was a troubled one. To date his conversion to Anglicanism is not easy. In his satires there is a veiled Roman tone. By 1602 he disclaims to Egerton "all love of a corrupt religion," but in the autumn of the previous year he had been meditating a satire on Queen Elizabeth as one of the world's great heretics. His was not a conversion but a reconciliation, an acquiescence in the faith of his country, the established religion of his legal sovereign, and the act cost him some pangs. "A convert from Popery to Protestantism," said Dr. Johnson, "gives up so much of what he has held as sacred as anything that he retains, there is so much laceration of mind in such a conversion, that it can hardly be sincere and lasting." Something of that laceration of mind is discernible in Donne's religious verse:

> Show me dear Christ that spouse so bright and clear.

But the conflict between the old and the reformed faiths was not the only, nor perhaps the principal trouble for Donne's enlightened mind ready to recognize in all the Churches "virtual beams of one sun," "connatural pieces of one circle." A harder fight was that between the secular, the "man of the world" temper of his mind and the claims of a pious and ascetic calling. It was not the errors of his youth, as the good Walton supposed, which constituted the great stumbling block, though he never ignores these:

> O might those sighs and tears return again
> Into my breast and eyes, which I have spent,
> That I might in this holy discontent
> Mourn with some fruit, as I have mourned in vain.

It was rather the temperament of one who, at a time when a public career was more open to unassisted talent, might have proved an active and useful, if ambitious, civil servant, or professional man, at war with the claims of a religious life which his upbringing had taught him was incompatible with worldly ambition. George Herbert, a much more contented Anglican than Donne ever became, knew something of the same struggle before he bent his neck to the collar.

The two notes then of Donne's religious poems are the Catholic and the personal. He is the first of our Anglo-Catholic poets, and he is our first intensely personal religious poet, expressing always not the mind simply of the Christian as such, but the conflicts and longings of one troubled soul, one subtle and fantastic mind. For Donne's technique—his phrasing and conceits, the metaphysics of mediaeval Christianity, his packed verse with its bold, irregular fingering and echoing vowel sounds—remains what it had been from the outset. The echoing sounds in lines such as these cannot be quite casual:

> O might those *sighs* and tears return again
> Into my breast and *eyes*, which *I* have spent,
> That *I* might in this holy discontent
> Mourn with some fruit, as *I* have mourned in vain;

Puritan rebellion, whatever the indirect constitutional results, was in itself and at the moment a fanatical upheaval, successful because it also threw up the John Zizka of his age; its triumph was the triumph of Cromwell's sword:

> And for the last effect
> Still keep the sword erect.
>
> Besides the force it has to fright
> The spirits of the shady night,
> The same arts that did gain
> A power must it maintain.

To call these poets the "school of Donne" or "metaphysical" poets may easily mislead if one takes either phrase in too full a sense. It is not only that they show little of Donne's subtlety of mind or "hydroptic, immoderate thirst of human learning," but they want, what gives its interest to this subtle and fantastic misapplication of learning—the complexity of mood, the range of personal feeling which lends such fullness of life to Donne's strange and troubled poetry. His followers, amorous and courtly, or pious and ecclesiastical, move in a more rarefied atmosphere; their poetry is much more truly "abstract" than Donne's, the witty and fantastic elaboration of one or two common moods, of compliment, passion, devotion, penitence. It is very rarely that one can detect a deep personal note in the delightful love-songs with which the whole period abounds from Carew to Dryden. The collected work of none of them would give such an impression of a real history behind it, a history of many experiences and moods, as Donne's Songs and Sonnets and the Elegies, and, as one must still believe, the sonnets of Shakespeare record. Like the Elizabethan sonneteers they all dress and redress the same theme in much the same manner, though the manner is not quite the Elizabethan, nor the theme. Song has superseded the sonnet, and the passion of which they sing has lost most of the Petrarchian, chivalrous strain, and become in a very definite meaning of the words, "simple and sensuous." And if the religious poets are rather more individual and personal, the personal note is less intense, troubled and complex than in Donne's Divine Poems; the individual is more merged in the Christian, Catholic or Angelican.

Donne and Jonson are probably in the main responsible for the unconventional purity and naturalness of their diction, for these had both "shaken hands with" Spenserian archaism and strangeness, with the "rhetoric" of the sonneteers and poems like *Venus and Adonis;* and their style is untouched by any foreshadowing of Miltonic diction or the jargon of a later poetic vocabulary. The metaphysicals are the masters of the "neutral style," of a diction equally appropriate, according as it may be used, to prose and verse. If purity and naturalness of style is a grace, they deserved well of the English language, for few poets have used it with a more complete acceptance of the established tradition of diction and idiom. There are no poets till we come perhaps to Cowper, and he has not quite escaped from jargon, or Shelley, and his imagination operates in a more ethereal atmosphere, whose style is so entirely that of an English gentleman of the best type, natural, simple, occasionally careless, but never diverging into vulgar colloquialism, as after the Restoration, or into conventional, tawdry splendour, as in the century of Akenside and Erasmus Darwin. Set a poem by George Herbert beside Gray at his best, e.g.

> Sweet day so cool, so calm, so bright,
> The bridal of the earth and sky,
> The dew shall weep thy fall to-night,
> For thou must die; &c.

set that beside even a good verse from Gray, and one realizes the charm of simplicity, of perfect purity of diction:

> Still is the toiling hand of Care;
> The panting herds repose:

Yet hark how through the peopled air
 The busy murmur glows!
The insect-youth are on the wing,
Eager to taste the honied spring,
And float amid the liquid noon:
Some lightly o'er the current skim,
Some show their gaily-gilded trim
 Quick-glancing to the sun.

"The language of the age is never the language of poetry," Gray declares, and certainly some of our great poets have created for themselves a diction which was never current, but it is equally true that some of the best English poetry has been written in a style which differs from the best spoken language only as the language of feeling will naturally diverge from the language of our less exalted moods. It was in the seventeenth-century poets that Wordsworth found the best corrective to the jargon of the later eighteenth-century poetry, descriptive and reflective, which he admired in his youth and imitated in his early poems; for as Coleridge pointed out, the style of the "metaphysicals" "is the reverse of that which distinguishes too many of our most recent versifiers; the one conveying the most fantastic thoughts in the most correct language, the other in the most fantastic language conveying the most trivial thoughts."

But even the fantastic thoughts, the conceits of these courtly love poets and devout singers are not to be dismissed so lightly as a later, and still audible, criticism imagined. They played with thoughts, Sir Walter Scott complained, as the Elizabethans had played with words. But to play with thoughts it is necessary to think. "To write on their plan," says Dr. Johnson, "it was at least necessary to read and think. No man could be born a metaphysical poet, nor assume the dignity of a writer, by descriptions copied from descriptions, by imitations borrowed from imitations, by traditional imagery and hereditary similes, by readiness of rhyme and volubility of syllables." Consider a poem, *The Repulse,* by a comparatively minor poet, Thomas Stanley. That is not a mere conceit. It is a new and felicitous rendering of a real and thrilling experience, the discovery that you might have fared worse in love than not to be loved, you might have been loved and then abandoned. Carew's *Ask me no more* is a coruscation of hyperboles, but

Now you have freely given me leave to love,
 What will you do?

is a fresh and effective appeal to the heart of a woman. And this is what the metaphysicals are often doing in their unwearied play with conceits, delightfully naughty, extravagant, fantastic, frigid—they succeed in stumbling upon some conceit which reveals a fresh intuition into the heart, or states an old plea with new and prevailing force. And the divine poets express with the same blend of argument and imagination the deep and complex currents of religious feeling which were flowing in England throughout the century, institutional, theological, mystical, while in the metaphysical subtleties of conceit they found something that is more than conceit, symbols in which to express or adumbrate their apprehensions of the infinite.

The direct indebtedness of the courtly poets to Ben Jonson is probably, as Professor Gregory Smith has recently argued, small. But not only Herrick, metaphysical poets like Carew and Stanley and others owe much both of their turn of conceit and their care for form to Jonson's own models, the Latin lyrists, Anacreon, the Greek Anthology, neo-Latin or Humanist poetry so rich in neat and pretty conceits. Some of them, as Crashaw and Stanley, and not only these, were familiar with Italian and Spanish poetry, Marino and Garcilasso and their elegantly elaborated confections. But their great master is Donne. If he taught them many heresies, he instilled into them at any rate the pure doctrine of the need of passion for a lover and a poet. What the young courtiers and university wits admired and reproduced in different degrees and fashions were his sensual audacity and the peculiar type of evolution which his poems accentuated, the strain of passionate paradoxical reasoning which knits the first line to the last and is perhaps a more intimate characteristic than even the far-fetched, fantastic comparisons. This intellectual, argumentative evolution had been of course a feature of the sonnet which might fancifully be called, with its double quatrain and sestet, the poetical analogy of the syllogism. But the movement of the sonnet is slow and meditative, a single thought expanded and articulated through the triple division, and the longer, decasyllabic line is the appropriate medium:

> Then hate me when thou wilt; if ever, now;
> Now while the world is bent my deeds to cross,
> Join with the spite of Fortune, make me bow,
> And do not drop in for an after-loss;
> Ah, do not when my heart hath scaped this sorrow,
> Come in the rearward of a conquer'd woe,
> Give not a windy night a rainy morrow,
> To linger out a purpos'd overthrow.

If thou wilt leave me, do not leave me last
When other petty griefs have done their spite,
But in the onset come; so shall I taste
At first the very worst of Fortune's might;
And other strains of woe which now seem woe,
Compared with loss of thee will not seem so.

What Donne had done was to quicken this movement, to intensify the strain of passionate ratiocination, passionate, paradoxical argument, and to carry it over from the sonnet to the song with its shorter lines, more winged and soaring movement, although the deeper strain of feeling which Donne shares with Shakespeare, and with Drayton at his best, made him partial to the longer line, at least as an element in his stanzas, and to longer and more intricate stanzas. Lightening both the feeling and the thought, the courtly poets simplified the verse, attaining some of their most wonderful effects in the common ballad measure [4, 3] or the longer [4, 4] measure in couplets or alternate rhymes. But the form and content are intimately associated. It is the elaboration of the paradoxical argument, the weight which the rhetoric lays on those syllables which fall under the metrical stress, that gives to these verses, or seems to give, their peculiar *élan:*

My love is of a birth as rare
  As 'tis for object strange and high;
It was begotten by Despair
  Upon Impossibility.

The audacious hyperboles and paradoxical turns of thought give breath to and take wings from the soaring rhythm.

It is needless here to dwell at length on the several poets from whom I have selected examples of love-song and complimentary verses. Their range is not wide—love, compliment, elegy, occasionally devotion. Herrick had to leave the court to learn the delights of nature and country superstitions. Lord Herbert of Cherbury, philosopher and coxcomb, was just the person to dilate on the Platonic theme of soul and body in the realm of love on which Donne occasionally descanted in half ironical fashion, Habington with tedious thin-blooded seriousness, Cleveland and others with naughty irreverence. But Lord Herbert's *Ode,* which has been, like most of his poems, very badly edited, seems to me the finest thing inspired by Donne's *Ecstasy* and more characteristic of the romantic taste of the court of Charles. But the poetic ornament of that Court is Thomas Carew. This young careless liver was a careful artist with a deeper vein of thought and feeling in his temperament than a first reading suggests. His masque reveals the influence of Bruno. In Carew's poems and Vandyke's pictures the artistic taste of Charles's court is vividly reflected, a dignified voluptuousness, an exquisite elegance, if in some of the higher qualities of man and artist Carew is as inferior to Wyatt or Spenser as Vandyke is to Holbein. His *Ecstasy* is the most daring and poetically the happiest of the imitations of Donne's clever if outrageous elegies; Cartwright's *Song of Dalliance* its nearest rival. His letter to Aurelian Townshend on the death of the King of Sweden breathes the very enchanted air of Charles's court while the storm was brewing as yet unsuspected. The text of Richard Lovelace's *Lucasta* (1649) is frequently corrupt, and the majority of the poems are careless and extravagant, but the few good things are the finest expression of honour and chivalry in all the Cavalier poetry of the century, the only poems which suggest what "Cavalier" came to mean when glorified by defeat. His *Grasshopper* has suffered a hard fate by textual corruption and from dismemberment in recent anthologies. Only the fantastic touch about "green ice" ranks it as "metaphysical," for it is in fact an experiment in the manner of the Horatian ode, not the heroic ode, but the lighter Epicurean, meditative strain of "Solvitur acris hiems" and "Vides ut alta stet nive candidum," description yielding abruptly to reflection. A slightly better text or a little more care on the poet's part would have made it perfect. The gayest of the group is Sir John Suckling, the writer of what should be called *vers de société*, a more careless but more fanciful Prior. His beautiful *Ballad on a Wedding* is a little outside the scope of this volume. Thomas Stanley, classical scholar, philosopher, translator, seems to me one of the happiest of recent recoveries, elegant, graceful, felicitous, and if at times a little flat and colourless, not always flat like the Catholic puritan William Habington.

But the strongest personality of all is Andrew Marvell. Apart from Milton he is the most interesting personality between Donne and Dryden, and at his very best a finer poet than either. Most of his descriptive poems lie a little outside my beat, though I have claimed *The Garden* as metaphysical,

> Annihilating all that's made
> To a green thought in a green shade,

and I might have claimed *The Nymph and the Faun* had space permitted. But his few love poems and his few devotional pieces are perfect exponents of all the "metaphysical" qualities—passionate, paradoxical argument, touched with humour and learned imagery:

> As lines, so loves oblique, may well
> Themselves in every angle greet:
> But ours so truly parallel,
> Though infinite, can never meet;

and above all the sudden soar of passion in bold and felicitous image, in clangorous lines:

> But at my back I always hear
> Time's wingèd chariot hurrying near,
> And yonder all before us lie
> Deserts of vast eternity.
> Thy beauty shall no more be found;
> Nor in thy marble vault shall sound
> My echoing song: then worms shall try
> That long preserv'd virginity;
> And your quaint honour turn to dust;
> And into ashes all my lust.
> The grave's a fine and private place,
> But none I think do there embrace.

These lines seem to me the very roof and crown of the metaphysical love lyric, at once fantastic and passionate. Donne is weightier, more complex, more suggestive of subtle and profound reaches of feeling, but he has not one single passage of the same length that combines all the distinctive qualities of the kind, in thought, in phrasing, in feeling, in music; and Rochester's most passionate lines are essentially simpler, less metaphysical.

> When wearied with a world of woe,

might have been written by Burns with some differences. The best things of Donne and Marvell could only have been composed—except, as an imitative *tour de force,* like Watson's

> Bid me no more to other eyes—

in the seventeenth century. But in that century there were so many poets who could sing, at least occasionally, in the same strain. Of all those whom Professor Saintsbury's ardent and catholic but discriminating taste has collected there is none who has not written too much indifferent verse, but none who has not written one or two songs showing the same fine blend of passion and paradox and music. The "metaphysicals" of the seventeenth century combined two things, both soon to pass away, the fantastic dialectics of mediaeval love poetry and the "simple, sensuous" strain which they caught from the classics—soul and body lightly yoked and glad to run and soar together in the winged chariot of Pegasus. Modern love poetry has too often sacrificed both to sentiment.

T. S. ELIOT

The Metaphysical Poets

By collecting these poems [1] from the work of a generation more often named than read, and more often read than profitably studied, Professor Grierson has rendered a service of some importance. Certainly the reader will meet with many poems already preserved in other anthologies, at the same time that he discovers poems such as those of Aurelian Townshend or Lord Herbert of Cherbury here included. But the function of such an anthology as this is neither that of Professor Saintsbury's admirable edition of Caroline poets nor that of the *Oxford Book of English Verse.* Mr. Grierson's book is in itself a piece of criticism and a provocation of criticism; and we think that he was right in including so many poems of Donne, elsewhere (though not in many editions) accessible, as documents in the case of "metaphysical poetry." The phrase has long done duty as a term of abuse or as the label of a quaint and pleasant taste. The question is to what extent the so-called metaphysicals formed a school (in our own time we should say a "movement"), and how far this so-called school or movement is a digression from the main current.

Not only is it extremely difficult to define metaphysical poetry, but difficult to decide what poets practise it and in which of their verses. The poetry of Donne (to whom Marvell and Bishop King are sometimes nearer than any of the other authors) is late Elizabethan, its feeling often very close to that of Chapman. The "courtly" poetry is derivative from Jonson, who borrowed liberally from the Latin; it expires in the next century with the sentiment and witticism of Prior. There is finally the devotional verse of Herbert, Vaughan, and Crashaw (echoed long after by Christina Rossetti and Francis Thompson); Crashaw, sometimes more profound and less sectarian than the others, has a quality which returns through the Elizabethan period to the early Italians. It is difficult to find any precise use of metaphor, simile, or other conceit, which is common to all the poets and at the same time important enough as an element of style to isolate these poets as a group. Donne, and often Cowley, employ a device which is sometimes considered characteristically "metaphysical"; the elaboration (contrasted with the condensation) of a figure of speech to the farthest stage to which ingenuity can carry it. Thus Cowley develops the commonplace comparison of the world to a chess-board through long stanzas (*To Destiny*), and Donne, with more grace, in *A Valediction,* the comparison of two lovers to a pair of compasses. But elsewhere we find, instead of the mere explication of the content of a comparison, a development by rapid association of thought which requires considerable agility on the part of the reader.

> On a round ball
> A workman that hath copies by, can lay
> An Europe, Afrique, and an Asia,
> And quickly make that, which was nothing, All,
> So doth each teare,
> Which thee doth weare,
> A globe, yea, world by that impression grow,
> Till thy tears mixt with mine doe overflow
> This world, by waters sent from thee, my heaven dissolved so.

Here we find at least two connexions which are not implicit in the first figure, but are forced upon it by the poet: from the geographer's globe to the tear, and the tear to the deluge. On the other hand, some of Donne's most successful and characteristic effects are secured by brief words and sudden contrasts:

> A bracelet of bright hair about the bone,

where the most powerful effect is produced by the sudden contrast of associations of "bright hair" and of "bone." This telescoping of images and multiplied associations is characteristic of the phrase of some of the dramatists of the period which Donne knew: not to mention Shakespeare, it is frequent in Middleton, Webster, and Tourneur, and is one of the sources of the vitality of their language.

Johnson, who employed the term "metaphysical poets," apparently having Donne, Cleveland, and Cowley chiefly in mind, remarks of them that "the most heterogeneous ideas are yoked by violence together." The force of this impeachment lies in the failure of the conjunction, the fact that often the ideas are yoked but not united; and if we are to judge of styles of poetry by their abuse, enough examples may be found in Cleveland to justify Johnson's condemnation. But a degree of heterogeneity of material compelled into unity by the operation of the poet's mind is omnipresent in poetry. We need not select for illustration such a line as:

> Notre âme est un trois-mâts cherchant son Icarie;

we may find it in some of the best lines of Johnson himself (*The Vanity of Human Wishes*):

> His fate was destined to a barren strand,
> A petty fortress, and a dubious hand;
> He left a name at which the world grew pale,
> To point a moral, or adorn a tale.

where the effect is due to a contrast of ideas, different in degree but the same in principle, as that which Johnson mildly reprehended. And in one of the finest poems of the age (a poem which could not have been written in any other age), the *Exequy* of Bishop King, the extended comparison is used with perfect success: the idea and the simile become one, in the passage in which the Bishop illustrates his impatience to see his dead wife, under the figure of a journey:

> Stay for me there; I will not faile
> To meet thee in that hollow Vale.
> And think not much of my delay;
> I am already on the way,
> And follow thee with all the speed
> Desire can make, or sorrows breed.
> Each minute is a short degree,
> And ev'ry houre a step towards thee.
> At night when I betake to rest,
> Next morn I rise nearer my West

Of life, almost by eight houres sail,
Than when sleep breath'd his drowsy gale. . . .
But heark! My Pulse, like a soft Drum
Beats my approach, tells *Thee* I come;
And slow howe'er my marches be,
I shall at last sit down by *Thee*.

(In the last few lines there is that effect of terror which is several times attained by one of Bishop King's admirers, Edgar Poe.) Again, we may justly take these quatrains from Lord Herbert's Ode, stanzas which would, we think, be immediately pronounced to be of the metaphysical school:

So when from hence we shall be gone,
And be no more, nor you, nor I,
As one another's mystery,
Each shall be both, yet both but one.

This said, in her up-lifted face,
Her eyes, which did that beauty crown,
Were like two starrs, that having faln down,
Look up again to find their place:

While such a moveless silent peace
Did seize on their becalmed sense,
One would have thought some influence
Their ravished spirits did possess.

There is nothing in these lines (with the possible exception of the stars, a simile not at once grasped, but lovely and justified) which fits Johnson's general observations on the metaphysical poets in his essay on Cowley. A good deal resides in the richness of association which is at the same time borrowed from and given to the word "becalmed"; but the meaning is clear, the language simple and elegant. It is to be observed that the language of these poets is as a rule simple and pure; in the verse of George Herbert this simplicity is carried as far as it can go—a simplicity emulated without success by numerous modern poets. The *structure* of the sentences, on the other hand, is sometimes far from simple, but this is not a vice; it is a fidelity to thought and feeling. The effect, at its best, is far less artificial than that of an ode by Gray. And as this fidelity induces variety of thought and feeling, so it induces variety of music. We doubt whether, in the eighteenth century, could be found two poems in nominally the same metre, so dissimilar as Marvell's *Coy Mistress* and Crashaw's *Saint Teresa;* the one producing an effect of great speed by the use of short syllables, and the other an ecclesiastical solemnity by the use of long ones:

> Love, thou art absolute sole lord
> Of life and death.

If so shrewd and sensitive (though so limited) a critic as Johnson failed to defined metaphysical poetry by its faults, it is worth while to inquire whether we may not have more success by adopting the opposite method: by assuming that the poets of the seventeenth century (up to the Revolution) were the direct and normal development of the precedent age; and, without prejudicing their case by the adjective "metaphysical," consider whether their virtue was not something permanently valuable, which subsequently disappeared, but ought not to have disappeared. Johnson has hit, perhaps by accident, on one of their peculiarities, when he observes that "their attempts were always analytic"; he would not agree that, after the dissociation, they put the material together again in a new unity.

It is certain that the dramatic verse of the later Elizabethan and early Jacobean poets expresses a degree of development of sensibility which is not found in any of the prose, good as it often is. If we except Marlowe, a man of prodigious intelligence, these dramatists were directly or indirectly (it is at least a tenable theory) affected by Montaigne. Even if we except also Jonson and Chapman, these two were notably erudite, and were notably men who incorporated their erudition into their sensibility: their mode of feeling was directly and freshly altered by their reading and thought. In Chapman especially there is a direct sensuous apprehension of thought, or a recreation of thought into feeling, which is exactly what we find in Donne:

> in this one thing, all the discipline
> Of manners and of manhood is contained;
> A man to join himself with th' Universe
> In his main sway, and make in all things fit
> One with that All, and go on, round as it;
> Not plucking from the whole his wretched part,
> And into straits, or into nought revert,
> Wishing the complete Universe might be
> Subject to such a rag of it as he;
> But to consider great Necessity.

We compare this with some modern passage:

> No, when the fight begins within himself,
> A man's worth something. God stoops o'er his head,
> Satan looks up between his feet—both tug—
> He's left, himself, i' the middle; the soul wakes
> And grows. Prolong that battle through his life!

It is perhaps somewhat less fair, though very tempting (as both poets are concerned with the perpetuation of love by offspring), to compare with the stanzas already quoted from Lord Herbert's Ode the following from Tennyson:

> One walked between his wife and child,
> With measured footfall firm and mild,
> And now and then he gravely smiled.
>   The prudent partner of his blood
>   Leaned on him, faithful, gentle, good,
>   Wearing the rose of womanhood.
> And in their double love secure,
> The little maiden walked demure,
> Pacing with downward eyelids pure.
> These three made unity so sweet,
> My frozen heart began to beat,
> Remembering its ancient heat.

The difference is not a simple difference of degree between poets. It is something which had happened to the mind of England between the time of Donne or Lord Herbert of Cherbury and the time of Tennyson and Browning; it is the difference between the intellectual poet and the reflective poet. Tennyson and Browning are poets, and they think; but they do not feel their thought as immediately as the odour of a rose. A thought to Donne was an experience; it modified his sensibility. When a poet's mind is perfectly equipped for its work, it is constantly amalgamating disparate experience; the ordinary man's experience is chaotic, irregular, fragmentary. The latter falls in love, or reads Spinoza, and these two experiences have nothing to do with each other, or with the noise of the typewriter or the smell of cooking; in the mind of the poet these experiences are always forming new wholes.

We may express the difference by the following theory: The poets of the seventeenth century, the successors of the dramatists of the sixteenth, possessed a mechanism of sensibility which could devour any kind of experience. They are simple, artificial, difficult, or fantastic, as their predecessors were; no less nor more than Dante, Guido Cavalcanti, Guinizelli, or Cino. In the seventeenth century a dissociation of sensibility set in, from which we have never recovered; and this dissociation, as is natural, was aggravated by the influence of the two most powerful poets of the century, Milton and Dryden. Each of these men performed certain poetic functions so magnificently well that the magnitude of the effect concealed the absence of others. The language went on and in some respects improved; the best verse of Collins, Gray, Johnson, and even Goldsmith satisfies some of our fastidious demands better than that of Donne or Marvell or King. But while the language became more refined, the feeling became more crude. The feeling, the sensibility, expressed in the *Country Churchyard* (to say nothing of Tennyson and Browning) is cruder than that in the *Coy Mistress.*

The second effect of the influence of Milton and Dryden followed from the first, and was therefore slow in manifestation. The sentimental age began early in the eighteenth century, and continued. The poets revolted against the ratiocinative, the descriptive; they thought and felt by fits, unbalanced; they reflected. In one or two passages of Shelley's *Triumph of Life,* in the second *Hyperion,* there are traces of a struggle toward unification of sensibility. But Keats and Shelley died, and Tennyson and Browning ruminated.

After this brief exposition of a theory—too brief, perhaps, to carry conviction—we may ask, what would have been the fate of the "metaphysical" had the current of poetry descended in a direct line from them, as it descended in a direct line to them? They would not, certainly, be classified as metaphysical. The possible interests of a poet are unlimited; the more intelligent he is the better; the more intelligent he is the more likely that he will have interests: our only condition is that he turn them into poetry, and not merely meditate on them poetically. A philosophical theory which has entered into poetry is established, for its truth or falsity in one sense ceases to matter, and its truth in another sense is proved. The poets in question have, like other poets, various faults. But they were, at best, engaged in the task of trying to find the verbal equivalent for states of mind and feeling. And this means both that they are more mature, and that they wear better, than later poets of certainly not less literary ability.

It is not a permanent necessity that poets should be interested in philosophy, or in any other subject. We can only say that it appears likely that poets in our civilization, as it exists at present, must be *difficult*. Our civilization comprehends great variety and complexity, and this variety and complexity, playing upon a refined sensibility, must produce various and complex results. The poet must become more and more comprehensive, more allusive, more indirect, in order to force, to dislocate if necessary, language into his meaning. (A brilliant and extreme statement of this view, with which it is not requisite to associate oneself, is that of M. Jean Epstein, *La Poésie d'aujourd'hui.*) Hence we get something which looks very much like the conceit —we get, in fact, a method curiously similar to that of the "metaphysical poets," similar also in its use of obscure words and of simple phrasing.

> O géraniums diaphanes, guerroyeurs sortilèges,
> Sacrilèges monomanes!
> Emballages, dévergondages, douches! O pressoirs
> Des vendanges des grands soirs!
> Layettes aux abois,
> Thyrses au fond des bois!
> Transfusions, représailles,
> Relevailles, compresses et l'éternal potion,
> Angélus! n'en pouvoir plus
> De débâcles nuptiales! de débâcles nuptiales!

The same poet could write also simply:

> Elle est bien loin, elle pleure,
> Le grand vent se lamente aussi . . .

Jules Laforgue, and Tristan Corbière in many of his poems, are nearer to the "school of Donne" than any modern English poet. But poets more classical than they have the same essential quality of transmuting ideas into sensations, of transforming an observation into a state of mind.

> Pour l'enfant, amoureux de cartes et d'estampes,
> L'univers est égal à son vaste appétit.
> Ah, que le monde est grand à la carté des lampes!
> Aux yeux du souvenir que le monde est petit!

In French literature the great master of the seventeenth century—Racine—and the great master of the nineteenth—Baudelaire—are in some ways more like each other than they are like any one else. The greatest two masters of diction are also the greatest two psychologists, the most curious explorers of the soul. It is interesting to speculate whether it is not a misfortune that two of the greatest masters of diction in our language, Milton and Dryden, triumph with a dazzling disregard of the soul. If we continued to produce Miltons and Drydens it might not so much matter, but as things are it is a pity that English poetry has remained so incomplete. Those who object to the "artificiality" of Milton or Dryden sometimes tell us to "look into our hearts and write." But that is not looking deep enough; Racine or Donne looked into a good deal more than the heart. One must look into the cerebral cortex, the nervous system, and the digestive tracts.

May we not conclude, then, that Donne, Crashaw, Vaughan, Herbert and Lord Herbert, Marvell, King, Cowley at his best, are in the direct current of English poetry, and that their faults should be reprimanded by this standard rather than coddled by antiquarian affection? They have been enough praised in terms which are implicit limitations because they are "metaphysical" or "witty," "quaint" or "obscure," though at their best they have not these attributes more than other serious poets. On the other hand, we must not reject the criticism of Johnson (a dangerous person to disagree with) without having mastered it, without having assimilated the Johnsonian canons of taste. In reading the celebrated passage in his essay on Cowley we must remember that by wit he clearly means something more serious than we usually mean today; in his criticism of their versification we must remember in what a narrow discipline he was trained, but also how well trained; we must remember that Johnson tortures chiefly the chief offenders, Cowley and Cleveland. It would be a fruitful work, and one requiring a substantial book, to break up the classification of Johnson (for there has been none since) and exhibit these poets in all their difference of kind and of degree, from the massive music of Donne to the faint, pleasing tinkle of Aurelian Townshend—whose *Dialogue between a Pilgrim and Time* is one of the few regrettable omissions from the excellent anthology of Professor Grierson.

NOTE

[1] *Metaphysical Lyrics and Poems of the Seventeenth Century: Donne to Butler*. Selected and edited, with an Essay, by Herbert J. C. Grierson (Oxford: Clarendon Press).

F. R. LEAVIS

The Line of Wit

The work has been done, the re-orientation effected: the heresies of ten years ago are orthodoxy. Mr. Eliot's achievement is matter for academic evaluation, his poetry is accepted, and his early observations on the Metaphysicals and on Marvell provide currency for university lectures and undergraduate exercises. His own projected book on the School of Donne has come to seem to him unnecessary, and certainly in the last ten years much industry has been devoted to applying and expanding his hints—so that, indeed, one may well be rather shy of reverting to topics that are not, perhaps, yet exhausted. However, the appearance of an *Oxford Book of Seventeenth Century Verse* is an opportunity; an opportunity for a modest employment, over the new perspective, of the surveying and reconsidering eye.

Few who handle the new *Oxford Book* will think of reading it straight through, and fewer will actually read through it, but to persist only moderately in the undertaking is to assure oneself that one valuation at least, and that a key one, among current acceptances needs no downward revision. After ninety pages of (with some minor representation) Fulk Greville, Chapman and Drayton, respectable figures who, if one works through their allotments, serve at any rate to set up a critically useful background, we come to this:

> I wonder by my troth, what thou, and I
> Did, till we lov'd? were we not wean'd till then?

From *Revaluation: Tradition & Development in English Poetry* (London: Chatto & Windus, 1936, 1949; New York: George W. Stewart), pp. 10–36. Reprinted by permission of the publishers.

> But suck'd on country pleasures, childishly?
> Or snorted we in the seven sleepers den?
> 'Twas so; But this, all pleasures fancies bee.
> If ever any beauty I did see,
> Which I desir'd, and got, 'twas but a dreame of thee.

After this we cease reading as students, or as connoisseurs of anthology-pieces, and read on as we read the living. The extraordinary force of originality that made Donne so potent an influence in the seventeenth century makes him now at once for us, without his being the less felt as of his period, contemporary—obviously a living poet in the most important sense. And it is not any eccentricity or defiant audacity that makes the effect here so immediate, but rather an irresistible rightness.

With all that has been written of late about Donne it is still, perhaps, not altogether easy to realize how powerful an originality is represented by the stanza quoted above. In an age when music is for all classes an important part of daily life, when poets are, along with so large a proportion of their fellow-countrymen, musicians and write their lyrics to be sung, Donne uses in complete dissociation from music a stanza-form that proclaims the union of poetry and music. The dissociation is positive; utterance, movement and intonation are those of the talking voice. And consider the way in which the stress is got on "Did," and the intonation controlled, here:

> I wonder by my troth, what thou, and I
> Did, till we lov'd?

This is the spirit in which Donne uses the stanza-form—for he does indeed strictly use it: the exigencies of the pattern become means to the inevitable naturalness; they play an essential part in the consummate control of intonation, gesture, movement and larger rhythm. But that Donne is a great artist is now commonly recognized, and we are not likely to hear much more of his harsh and rugged verse and his faults of phrasing and harmony (though no doubt these could still be found). The commonplaces now regard the magnificent handling of the stanza, the building-up of varied cumulative effects within it, exemplified by (say) *The Anniversarie* and *A nocturnall upon S. Lucies day*.

There remains, perhaps, something to be said about such mastery of tone as is exhibited in (to take the example at which the book happens to be open) *Aire and Angells*—the passage from the gravely gallant and conventional exaltation of the opening to the blandly insolent matter-of-factness of the close. Indeed, the subtleties of Donne's use of the speaking voice and the spoken language are inexhaustible—or might, by a reasonable hyperbole, be called so, if we were not reminded of Shakespeare. For of Shakespeare we are, in fact, notably reminded. Whether or not Donne did actually get anything from dramatic verse can only be a matter of idle speculation, but his own verse—the technique, the spirit in which the sinew and living nerve of English are used—suggests an appropriate development of impressions that his ear might have recorded in the theatre.

And there is, of course, about Donne's characteristic poetry—in the presentment of situations, the liveliness of enactment—something fairly to be called dramatic. *Satyre iii,* which one is glad to find in this *Oxford Book,* very obviously justifies the adjective (though not, perhaps, more obviously than many of the poems in stanzas), and the handling in it of the decasyllabic line reminds us peculiarly of dramatic blank verse. Consider, for instance, the way in which Donne here, playing his sense-movement across the rimes, controls his tone and gets his key stresses, coming finally down with retarded emphasis on "damn'd":

> Are not heavens joyes as valiant to asswage
> Lusts, as earths honour was to them? Alas,
> As wee do them in meanes, shall they surpasse
> Us in the end, and shall thy fathers spirit
> Meete blinde Philosophers in heaven, whose merit
> Of strict life may be imputed faith, and heare
> Thee, whom he taught so easie wayes and neare
> To follow, damn'd?

This art has evident affinities with Shakespeare's; nevertheless Donne is writing something original and quite different from blank verse. For all their apparent casualness, the rimes, it should be plain, are strictly used; the couplet-structure, though not in Pope's way, is functional. If, for instance, "asswage" had not been a rime-word, there would not have been quite that lagging deliberation of stress upon "lusts"; just as, in the following, the riming upon the first syllable of "blindnesse" secures a natural speaking stress and intonation and an economy that is the privilege of speech (the effect is: "this state of blindness—for that's what it amounts to . . ."):

> Careless Phrygius doth abhorre
> All, because all cannot be good, as one

Knowing some women whores, dares marry none.
Gracchus loves all as one, and thinkes that so
As women do in divers countries goe
In divers habits, yet are still one kinde,
So doth, so is Religion; and this blind-
nesse too much light breeds . . .

Even so short a passage as this suggests the mimetic flexibility for which the whole piece is remarkable. The poised logical deliberation of the first three lines, suggesting the voice of invincibly rational caution, sets off the rakish levity, the bland Restoration insolence, that follows ("So doth, so is . . ."—it is an extraordinarily different logic).

But enough illustration (out of an embarrassment of choice) has been given to bring home how dramatic Donne's use of his medium can be; how subtly, in a consummately managed verse, he can exploit the strength of spoken English. But it is not enough to leave the stress there; a Donne whose art was fully represented by *Satyre iii* could not have been as important or pervasive an influence in the century as actually he was. He also wrote this:

Sweetest love, I do not goe,
For wearinesse of thee,
Nor in hope the world can show
A fitter Love for mee;
But since that I
Must dye at last, 'tis best,
To use my selfe in jest
Thus by fain'd deaths to dye.

This is not Campion, yet it is a song. And Donne's songs are, though a continuity of intermediate modes, in touch at the other end of the scale with the mode of *Satyre iii*.

Now you have freely given me leave to love,
What will you do?
Shall I your mirth or passion move,
When I begin to woo;
Will you torment, or scorn, or love mee too?

—Coming on it casually one might, at first reading, very well take this opening stanza for Donne. It is, of course, Thomas Carew—Carew who exemplifies Donne's part in a mode or tradition (or whatever other term may fitly describe that which makes the Court Poets a community) inviting to the consideration of other things besides the influence of Donne. Carew, it seems to me, has claims to more distinction than he is commonly accorded; more than he is accorded by the bracket that, in common acceptance, links him with Lovelace and Suckling. He should be, for more readers than he is, more than an anthology poet (and there is after all the cheap *Muses' Library* edition), and more of him deserves to be current than even the new *Oxford Book,* in which he has fifteen pages, gives (I should have liked to find his *In Answer of an Elegiacal Letter, upon the Death of the King of Sweden, from Aurelian Townsend, inviting me to write on that subject*). To say this is not to stress any remarkable originality in his talent; his strength is representative, and he has individual force enough to be representative with unusual vitality.

The representative quality (with the distinction he manifests in it) is well illustrated by one of his two or three best-known poems:

> Know *Celia* (since thou art so proud),
>   'Twas I that gave thee thy renown:
> Thou hadst, in the forgotten crowd
>   Of common beauties, liv'd unknown,
> Had not my verse exhal'd thy name,
> And with it ympt the wings of fame.
>
> That killing power is none of thine,
>   I gave it to thy voyce, and eyes:
> Thy sweets, thy graces, all are mine;
>   Thou art my star, shin'st in my skies;
> Then dart not from thy borrowed sphere
> Lightning on him that fixt thee there.
>
> Tempt me with such affrights no more,
>   Lest what I made, I uncreate:
> Let fools thy mystique forms adore,
>   Ile know thee in thy mortall state;
> Wise Poets that wrap'd Truth in tales,
> Knew her themselves through all her vailes.

This, in its representative quality, is a more distinguished achievement than is perhaps commonly recognized. It is not a mere charming trifle; it has in its light grace a remarkable strength. How fine and delicate is the poise it maintains may be brought out by looking through Carew's Restoration successors for a poem to compare with it. In its sophisticated gallantry there is nothing rakish or raffish—nothing of the Wild Gallant; its urbane assurance has in it nothing of the Restoration insolence. What it represents is something immeasurably finer than, after the Civil Wars and the Interregnum, was there—was there at all, by any substitution—for the mob of gentlemen who wrote with ease: it represents a Court culture (if the expression may be permitted as a convenience) that preserved, in its sophisticated way, an element of the tradition of chivalry and that had turned the studious or naively enthusiastic Renaissance classicizing and poetizing of an earlier period into something intimately bound up with contemporary life and manners—something consciously both mature and, while contemporary, traditional.

The poem under discussion is included also in Professor Grierson's *Metaphysical Lyrics and Poems of the Seventeenth Century*, and it does indeed illustrate the general debt to Donne. Yet that there is another debt is equally apparent: the "metaphysical" element is far from obtrusive, being completely subdued to the prevailing urbane elegance; and while this elegance has fairly obvious social correlations, it could not as a literary mode have been achieved by Carew (or any other of the Court group) if there had been no other major influence besides Donne's. For this influence the acclamation of the age itself leads us to Ben Jonson.

Ben Jonson, we know, is classical: "classical (Jonson, Milton, even Herrick)," say the editors of *The Oxford Book of Seventeenth Century Verse*, reminding us that there are ways and ways of being classical. How different Jonson's way is from Milton's (Herrick we may leave for a while) Mr. L. C. Knights enforces in his essay, *Tradition and Ben Jonson*,[1] stressing as he does there Jonson's rooted and racy Englishness. In considering the idiomatic quality of the Caroline lyric, its close relation to the spoken language, we do not find it easy to separate Donne's influence from Jonson's. And in considering Jonson's classicism, we cannot easily separate it from his idiomatic quality. The point is well illustrated by No. 105 in the new *Oxford Book*, the well-known song *To Celia* that takes the characteristic liberty with *Vivamus, mea Lesbia, atque amemus:*

> Come my Celia, let us prove,
> While wee may, the sports of love;
> Time will not be ours for ever:
> He, at length, our good will sever.
> Spend not then his gifts in vaine.

Sunnes that set, may rise againe:
But, if once wee lose this light,
'Tis, with us, perpetuall night.
Why should we deferre our joyes?
Fame, and rumor are but toyes.
Cannot we delude the eyes
Of a few poor household spyes?
. . . .

There is in *The Forest* another piece, *To the same,* again paying Catullus the homage of this kind of freedom:

Kiss me, Sweet: the wary lover
Can your favours keep, and cover,
When the common courting jay
All your bounties will betray.
Kiss again: No creature comes.
Kiss, and score up wealthy sums
On my lips, thus hardly sundred,
While you breathe. First give a hundred,
Than a thousand, then another
Hundred, then unto the t'other
Add a thousand, and so more:
Till you equal with the store,
All the grass that Rumney yields,
Or the sands in Chelsea fields,
Or the drops in silver Thames,
Or the stars that gild his streams,
In the silent Summer-nights,
When youths ply their stol'n delights;
That the curious may not know
How to tell 'em as they flow,
And the envious, when they find
What their number is, be pined.

This is inferior, but it exhibits very clearly the spirit in which Jonson classicized: we are reminded of the Augustan way of "translating" and "imitating" Horace and Juvenal. Jonson's effort was to feel Catullus, and the others he cultivated, as contemporary with himself; or rather, to achieve an English mode that should express a sense of contemporaneity with them. The sense itself, of course, had to be achieved by effort, and was achieved in the mode. This mode, which is sufficiently realized in a considerable body of poems, may be described as consciously urbane, mature and civilized. Whatever its relation to any Latin originals, it is indisputably *there*, an achieved actuality. It belongs, of course, to literature, and is the product of a highly refined literary sensibility; yet it is at the same time expressive, if to a large degree by aspiration only, of a way of living. In it the English poet, who remains not the less English and of his own time, enters into an ideal community, conceived of as something with which contemporary life and manners may and should have close relations.

> The direct indebtedness of the courtly poets to Ben Jonson is probably, as Professor Gregory Smith has recently argued, small. But not only Herrick, metaphysical poets like Carew and Stanley and others owe much both of their turn of conceit and their care for form to Jonson's own models, the Latin lyrists, Anacreon, the Greek Anthology, neo-Latin or Humanist poetry so rich in neat and pretty conceits.

—No higher authority in this field than Professor Grierson, from whose Introduction to *Metaphysical Lyrics and Poems of the Seventeenth Century* this comes, is to be found, which is the reason for picking the passage from an admirable essay in order respectfully to query it. If so exceptionally qualified a judge thus slights something that seems of the first importance in the poetic tradition of the century, a certain insistence may be permitted here. For the passage quoted does unmistakably suggest a failure to appreciate justly the nature of the achievement that Carew's art represents. The indebtedness to Jonson's models is of a kind that it took Jonson's genius in the first place to incur; if the later poets learnt from those models, they had learnt from Jonson how to do so.

The achievement was such as to demand all the assertive force of Jonson's genius, his native robustness. How much there was in him not immediately tending towards elegance, grace and urbanity some of the poems included in the new *Oxford Book* remind us. There are "Epigrammes" that are laboured and difficult, tough without felicity. Then there is the ode *To the immortall memorie, and friendship of that noble paire, Sir Lucius Cary and Sir H. Morison,* reminding us that Jonson's classicizing was that of a scholar, one weightily erudite and inclined to pedantry. Inclined—but there was also an inclination the other way, towards a strong idiomatic naturalness, a racy vigour: Jonson was as robustly interested in men and manners and his own talk as in literature and the poetic art. The association of these interests is apparent in the two fine *Odes* to himself; where, though there is conscious classicizing, the racy personal force has turned erudition into native sinew and the toughness is lively and English. The likeness and unlikeness to Marvell's *Horatian Ode* are, together, remarkable and significant. The Latin judicial poise and the conscious civilization are there in Ben Jonson, but curiously inseparable from a weighty and assertive personal assurance:

Come leave the loathed stage,
And the more loathsome age:
Where pride and impudence (in faction knit)
Usurpe the chaire of wit!
Indicting, and arraigning every day
Something they call a Play.
Let their fastidious, vaine
Commission of the braine
Run on, and rage, sweat, censure, and condemn:
They were not made for thee, lesse thou for them.

Say, that thou pour'st them wheat,
And they will acornes eat:
'Twere simple fury, still, thy selfe to waste
On such as have no taste!
To offer them a surfeit of pure bread,
Whose appetites are dead!
No, give them graines their fill,
Huskes, draff to drink and swill.
If they love lees, and leave the lusty wine,
Envy them not, their palate's with the swine.

. . . . . .

Leave things so prostitute,
And take the *Alcaick* lute;
Or thine own *Horace* or *Anacreons* lyre;
Warme thee by *Pindares* fire:
And though thy nerves be shrunke, and blood be cold,
Ere years have made thee old,
Strike that disdainful heate
Throughout, to their defeate:
As curious fooles, and envious of thy straine,
May, blushing, sweare no palsy's in thy braine.

But when they heare thee sing
The glories of thy *king*,
His zeale to *God*, and his just awe o'er men:
They may, blood-shaken, then,
Feele such a flesh-quake to possesse their powers
As they shall cry, "Like ours,
In sound of peace or wars,
No Harp e'er hit the stars,
In tuning forth the acts of his sweet raigne:
And raising *Charles* his chariot 'bove his *Waine*."

–His Horace and his King associate naturally: the Court culture of that "sweet reign" provided the grounding in actuality of Jonson's ideal civilization.[2]

How strong with what is behind it the urbane grace is, when achieved, comes out well in the following poem, where, in the stopping-short (as it were) on the strong side of the Caroline courtly manner, the strength asserts itself (the poem comes from *Underwoods*, and is not included in the new *Oxford Book*):

Fair friend, 'tis true your beauties move
My heart to a respect,
Too little to be paid with love,
Too great for your neglect.

I neither love, nor yet am free,
For though the flame I find
Be not intense in the degree,
'Tis of the purest kind.

It little wants of love but pain;
Your beauty takes my sense,
And lest you should that price disdain,
My thoughts to feel the influence.

'Tis not a passion's first access,
Ready to multiply;
But, like love's calmest state, it is
Possest with victory.

It is like love to truth reduced,
All the false values gone,

Which were created and induced
By fond imagination.

'Tis either fancy or 'tis fate,
To love you more than I:
I love you at your beauty's rate,
Less were an injury.

Like unstampt gold, I weigh each grace,
So that you may collect
Th' intrinsic value of your face,
Safely from my respect.

And this respect would merit love,
Were not so fair a sight
Payment enough: for who dare move
Reward for his delight?

The "tough reasonableness" of this is felt as a personal quality of Ben Jonson's, a native good sense, but it clearly has intimate relations with the impersonal urbanity and poise that we feel to be the finest fruit of his Latin studies, and the poem, though unmistakably not by one of the courtly poets, is with an equally unmistakable significance, suggestive of them. The second, fourth and sixth stanzas, indeed, might have come from a courtly Caroline; the others could not. The fifth and seventh might, considered apart, be reasonably attributed to a poet of our time who had read Donne intelligently; though they are, like the last, characteristic Jonson. It took, then, Ben Jonson's powerful genius to initiate the tradition, the common heritage, into which a line of later poets could enter, and by which a very great Augustan poet was to profit long after civilization and literary fashions had been transformed.

> It is more than a technical accomplishment, or the vocabulary or syntax of an epoch; it is, what we have designated tentatively as wit, a tough reasonableness beneath the slight lyric grace.

—This, of course, comes from Mr. Eliot's extraordinarily pregnant and decisive essay on Marvell, the very pregnancy, the suggestive compression, of which makes it desirable to try and do some disengaging and restressing. Immediately before the sentence just quoted Mr. Eliot had written:

> The wit of the Caroline poets is not the wit of Shakespeare, and it is not the wit of Dryden, the great master of contempt, or of Pope, the great master of hatred, or of Swift, the great master of disgust. What is meant is some quality which is common to the songs in *Comus* and Cowley's *Anacreontics* and Marvell's *Horatian Ode*.

—"Wit," as Mr. Eliot reminds us, is a tricky term; and, in a field as complex as that under contemplation, one can distinguish, define and fix too brutally; yet the community that associates Jonson, Carew and Marvell can with profit be more narrowly restricted, and so more sharply defined, than it is by that last sentence. The art of the songs in *Comus* has, no doubt, an affinity with the art of some of Jonson's things—an affinity, perhaps, well enough suggested by this insistence on "art"; and one may use the term "wit" to emphasize the remoteness of this art from nineteenth-century notions of the lyrical. But the songs in *Comus* have not, in or beneath their simple grace, any such subtle order of implications as leads us to call the apparently simple poise of Jonson "wit." As for Cowley, he was "Metaphysical" and, in one of many possible ways, "Horatian"; but all that he ever wrote, in any mode, proclaims him an instrument unattuned to the finenesses in question—unqualified to catch or transmit. Here is the *Anacreontic* given in the new *Oxford Book* (and the representation is fair):

> Fill the *Bowl* with rosie Wine,
> Around our temples *Roses* twine.
> And let us chearfully awhile,
> Like the *Wine* and *Roses* smile.
> Crown'd with Roses we contemn
> *Gyges'* wealthy *Diadem*.
> *To-day* is *Ours;* what do we fear?
> *To-day* is *Ours;* we have it here.
> Let's treat it kindly, that it may
> *Wish,* at least, with us to stay.
> Let's banish *Business,* banish *Sorrow;*
> To the *Gods* belongs *To-morrow.*

—This, in the comparison challenged, seems insensitive in movement and inflection, coarse in tone and heavy in touch. Where Cowley notably does not seem insensitive, in the elegy *On the Death of Mr.*

William Hervey, he suggests curiously (and significantly) at one and the same time Spenser, a more tenderly and disinterestedly elegiac Milton, and a purified elegiac strain of the eighteenth century (see Gray's sonnet on Richard West). The simple decency of sentiment, the good sense and the civilized demeanour belong to a very different order from the subtle and supremely civilized poise of Marvell's *Horatian Ode.*

In the *Dialogue between the Resolved Soul and Created Pleasure* the essential relation between this mature poise and the Caroline wit of Carew is even more obvious than in the Ode. There is a crisp gallantry about the movement; the verse carries itself with an air:

> Courage my Soul, now learn to wield
> The weight of thine immortal Shield.
> Close on thy Head thy Helmet bright.
> Ballance thy Sword against the Fight.
> See where an Army, strong as fair,
> With silken Banners spreads the air.
> Now, if thou bee'st that thing Divine,
> In this day's Combat let it shine:
> And shew that Nature wants an Art
> To conquer one resolved Heart.

The closeness of this to Carew's

> Know *Celia* (since thou art so proud),
> 'Twas I that gave thee thy renown

is plain. Marvell's theme, stated barely, is that of *Comus,* yet he can in the Choruses, while remaining a whole civilization remote from the Restoration vulgarity, heighten this conscious gallantry of bearing and gesture into something that, though so different—so fine and urbane—suggests the operatic finish of Dryden's odes:

> *Soul*
> Had I but any time to lose,
> On this I would it all dispose.
> Cease Tempter. None can chain a mind
> Whom this sweet Chordage cannot bind.
>
> *Chorus*
> *Earth cannot shew so brave a Sight*
> *As when a single Soul does fence*

The Batteries of alluring Sense,
And Heaven views it with delight.
Then persevere: for still new Charges sound:
And if thou overcom'st thou shalt be crown'd.

—That neat play on "Chordage," giving as it does a new force to the conventional figure of being held in bonds of music, reminds us that a strain of the Metaphysical is, in this mode, blent into the subtle elegance, the urbane grace. Wit, too, is plainly there in the neat, epigrammatic answers of the Soul:

If things of Sight such Heaven be,
What Heavens are those we cannot see?

Wer't not a price who'ld value Gold?
And that's worth nought that can be sold.

What Friends, if to my self untrue?
What Slaves, unless I captive you?

There is no need to explain at length why Marvell's poem produces an effect so different from that of *Comus.* Milton's moral theme is held simply and presented with single-minded seriousness; Marvell presents his in relation to a wide range of varied and maturely valued interests that are present implicitly in the wit, and his seriousness is the finer wisdom of a ripe civilization.

In Pope the line ends—the line that runs from Ben Jonson and, in the way illustrated, associates Jonson's influence with Donne's. Pope is a very varied as well as a very great poet, and the quality that relates him to Marvell may be found in different blends. Here (since one instance must suffice) we have it plain in one of the best-known of passages:

She comes! she comes! the sable Throne behold
Of *Night* primaeval and of *Chaos* old!
Before her, *Fancy's* gilded clouds decay,
And all its varying Rain-bows die away.
Wit shoots in vain its momentary fires,
The meteor drops, and in a flash expires.
As one by one, at dread Medea's strain,
The sick'ning stars fade off th' ethereal plain;
As Argus' eyes by Hermes' wand oppress,
Clos'd one by one to everlasting rest;

Thus at her felt approach, and secret might,
Art after *Art* goes out, and all is Night.
See skulking *Truth* to her old cavern fled,
Mountains of Casuistry heap'd o'er her head!
Philosophy, that lean'd on Heav'n before,
Shrinks to her second cause, and is no more.
Physic of *Metaphysic* begs defence,
And *Metaphysic* calls for aid on *Sense!*
See *Mystery* to *Mathematics* fly!
In vain! they gaze, turn giddy, rave, and die.
Religion blushing veils her sacred fires,
And unawares *Morality* expires.
For *public* Flame, nor *private*, dares to shine;
Nor *human* Spark is left, nor Glimpse *divine!*

—The affinity with the mode of Marvell's Dialogue should be fairly obvious. The weight behind that concluding passage of the *Dunciad* is greater than Marvell could supply and the urbanity has a different inflection, but the relation between wit and solemnity (Pope is deeply moved by his vatic nightmare—that is, by his positive concern for civilization) is essentially that of the Dialogue.

The line, then, runs from Ben Jonson (and Donne) through Carew and Marvell to Pope. But, in spite of the recent readjustment of perspective, Mr. Waller's service in reforming our numbers still distracts from the recognition of this line, and the succession Waller-Denham-Dryden-Pope still commonly gets the stress. And this succession does of course represent a decisive development in the century—the development that makes Cowley seem a significant figure (he was found a great poet by his own age) and, in his very insufficiency, more representative than Marvell. The last point may be best enforced, not by enlisting Dr. Johnson and bringing up examples of Cowley's "Metaphysical" extravagance, but by turning to the poem *Of Wit*, which exemplifies Cowley's essential good sense. In that poem he discusses and expounds wit in a manner and spirit quite out of resonance with the Metaphysical mode—quite alien and uncongenial to it; with a reasonableness that has little to do with the "tough reasonableness" underlying Marvell's lyric grace (a grace of which Cowley has nothing). It is a spirit of good sense, of common sense; appealing to criteria that the coming age will refine into "Reason, Truth and Nature." The verse-mode implicitly desiderated, as it were, is a polite one, intimately related to manners and a social code: it is that, in short, with the initiation of which the Augustans credited Mr. Waller.

The suave refinement of the polite mode represented by Waller is in its very nature something less fine and sensitive (the inferiority is immediately apparent in the movement and texture of the verse) than the urbane grace of Carew (to make him representative). The taste to which it appeals has limitations of the general kind intimated by "fine ear" as used in this sentence from the Preface to the new *Oxford Book:* "Palgrave's chief and best guide was Tennyson, on whose fine ear the metres of the 'metaphysicals' must have grated as did those of his friend Browning. . . ."

Dryden's genius, it is true, comes out in a certain native English strength; the strength that led Hopkins to say of him: "He is the most masculine of our poets; his style and his rhythms lay the strongest stress of all our literature on the naked thew and sinew of the English language. . . ."[3] Though Hopkins, I think, overstates, that kind of strength is certainly there. Yet the kind of inferiority referred to strikes us at once if we compare Dryden's verse with Pope's. Pope's greater strictness of versification is popularly supposed to mean greater monotony; actually, manifesting as it does a much greater fineness and profundity of organization, a much greater intensity of art, it is the condition of a much, an immeasurably, greater variety. This superiority of Pope establishes itself incontestably if we place alongside the passage of the *Dunciad* quoted above for its affinity with Marvell the opening of *Mac Flecknoe* (the comparison may not seem fair, but would it, whatever passage of Dryden were chosen?) Above every line of Pope we can imagine a tensely flexible and complex curve, representing the modulation, emphasis and changing tone and tempo of the voice in reading; the curve varying from line to line and the lines playing subtly against one another. The verse of *Mac Flecknoe*, in the comparison, is both slack and monotonous; again and again there are awkward runs and turns, unconvinced and unconvincing, requiring the injected rhetorical conviction of the declaimer to carry them off.

The comparison, of course, *is* unfair: Dryden's effects are all for the public ear—for the ear in public (so to speak). And this is true not only of his pamphleteering verse, but also (for instance) of his blank verse in *All for Love* when compared with Shakespeare's: appropriately true, it might be said, for what more can one demand of dramatic verse than that it should be good verse of the theatre, giving nothing more than, well declaimed, can be appreciated on a first hearing? So Dryden's satiric pamphlets were, we can see, magnificently effective for their purpose; and, read in the appropriate spirit, they are magnificently effective now. But the appropriate spirit is not that which

Pope demands; we are not to strain the inner ear (if the convenient expression may be allowed to pass) as if, behind the immediate effect, there were a fine organization.

The point about Dryden, the great representative poet of the later seventeenth century, may be brought out by comparing him, in what might for the immediate purpose be called the social quality of his verse, with Ben Jonson. The community to which Jonson as a poet belongs is, though (as we have seen) brought into relation with the life and manners of his time, predominantly ideal; membership is the achievement of creative effort. Jonson's greater fineness and his more assertive robustness go together. The community to which Dryden belongs as a poet is that in which he actually lives, moves, eats and talks; and he belongs to it so completely and, with its assurance of being sophisticated and civilized (it is on the point of considering itself truly Augustan—that is, as attaining and realizing afresh a kind of absolute of civilization), it is so completely engrossing that he has no ear, no spiritual antennae, for the other community. One has more conviction in calling him a great representative poet than in calling him a great poet, for he is certainly a great representative. He may be a greater poet than Marvell, but he did not write any poetry as indubitably great as Marvell's best.

Pope's peculiar greatness is that he can be a complete Augustan, realizing in his poetry the strength of that actual concentrated civilization immediately around him, and at the same time, as we have seen, achieve a strength so closely related to Marvell's. And it is a very great poet indeed of whom we can say that, writing under George I, he is very much closer to Donne than Dryden is.

Some of the considerations above have touched fairly directly on that now familiar topic, the "dissociation of sensibility." Something that might well be covered by the phrase is the development, in the spirit of Waller's "reform," of a verse that, as was loosely said, appeals only to the public—or, it might be better to say, social—ear. Mr. Eliot, who put the phrase into currency, ascribed the dissociation very largely to the influence of Dryden and Milton. Dryden is the voice of his age and may be said to have, in that sense, responsibility. And even without reference forward to the eighteenth century the coupling of his name with Milton's can be readily justified. Dryden's admiration for Milton and the proofs offered in Dryden's verse of the sincerity and practical force of that admiration are significant: he is truly representative, and in admiring Milton's magniloquence (as Mr. Eliot calls it) he is indicating what sort of taste for the exalted will complement the taste that sees in Mr. Waller the discoverer of the poetic norm.

The Restoration itself has Dryden's odes and heroic plays: it is left for the eighteenth century to derive its exalted public decorum of poetry from Milton (who in Gray's Pindaric odes is inseparable from Dryden).

A serious attempt to account for the "dissociation of sensibility" would turn into a discussion of the great change that came over English civilization in the seventeenth century—the change notably manifested in the decisive appearance of modern English prose during the early years of the Restoration. Social, economic and political history, the Royal Society, Hobbes, intellectual and cultural history in general—a great and complex variety of considerations would be involved. Regarding the decay of the Caroline courtly tradition some obvious reflections present themselves—for it is patently decay that any representative handful of Restoration lyrics illustrates. Charles II was a highly intelligent man of liberal interests, and his mob of gentlemen cultivated conversation and the Muses. But that the old fine order, what was referred to above as the "Court culture," did not survive the period of disruption, exile and "travels" is apparent even in the best things of Etherege, Sedley, Rochester and the rest: the finest specimens of the tenderly or cynically gallant and polite lack the positive fineness, the implicit subtlety, examined above in Carew. The cheaper things remind us forcibly that to indicate the background of Restoration poetry we must couple with the Court, not as earlier the country house, but the coffee-house, and that the coffee-house is on intimate terms with the Green Room.

We are given a good view of this background in Professor Pinto's book on Rochester,[4] and the background explains, perhaps, why we have to disagree with Professor Pinto's estimate of Rochester as a poet: "If Milton is the great poet of belief in the seventeenth century, Rochester is the great poet of unbelief." Rochester is not a great poet of any kind; yet he certainly had uncommon natural endowments, which, it is reasonable to suggest, he might have done much more with had he been born thirty years earlier. As it is, his few best lyrics are peculiarly individual utterances, with no such relation to convention or tradition as is represented by Carew or Marvell—a point that Professor Grierson makes in his introduction to *Metaphysical Lyrics and Poems of the Seventeenth Century* when he says (p. xxxviii)

"When wearied with a world of woe,

might have been written by Burns with some differences." It is in his satires that Rochester belongs decidedly to a tradition; they are very striking at their best and plainly stand on a line leading from the Metaphysicals to Pope.

As for the tradition of wit and grace in the lyric, after Etherege, Sedley and Rochester (contemporaries, it may be significantly noted, of Dryden, Tom D'Urfey and Aphra Behn) we get Prior. And if we compare Prior's *To a Child of Quality* (No. 423 in *The Oxford Book of English Verse*) with Marvell's *The Picture of little T. C. in a Prospect of Flowers* we realize how great was the loss when the tradition died—died so completely—into the modes, into the conventions of sentiment and expression, of a new age.

The impression of the period as an incomparably rich one is strongly confirmed by the survey. Donne, Ben Jonson, Herbert, Milton, Marvell, Dryden it is a matchless array; and the lesser figures show, by their number and quality, how remarkably favourable to the development of its talent the century was. To start with Donne and Ben Jonson together was luck indeed; either was qualified to be a decisive force. Without Jonson behind him what would Herrick (still an overrated figure) have been? The point of the instance lies in the very triviality of Herrick's talent, which yet produced something not altogether negligible (beside him Carew looks like a major poet). Herrick, too, in his trivially charming way, illustrates the advantages poetry enjoyed in an age in which a poet could be "classical" and in touch with a living popular culture at the same time.

In both parts of the century the poet was practising an art that had important social functions, recognizable as such by the many (there are Dryden's verse pamphlets to be remembered here as well as Jacobean drama).

NOTES

[1] See *Scrutiny*, September, 1935.

[2] The opening stanza of the other *Ode* illustrates well the kind of imagery that, going with Jonson's idiomatic manner, helps him, as an influence, to blend so easily with Donne:

> Where do'st thou careless lie
> Buried in ease and sloth:
> Knowledge, that sleepes, doth die;
> And this Securitie,
> It is the common Moth,
> That eats on wits, and Arts, and destroyes them both.

[3] *The Letters of Gerard Manley Hopkins to Robert Bridges*, CLV.

[4] *Rochester: Portrait of a Restoration Poet* by V. de Sola Pinto.

HELEN GARDNER

The Metaphysical Poets

The term "metaphysical poets" came into being long after the poets to whom we apply it were dead. Samuel Johnson, who coined it, did so with the consciousness that it was a piece of literary slang, that he was giving a kind of nickname. When he wrote in his *Life of Cowley* that "about the beginning of the seventeenth century appeared a race of writers that may be termed the metaphysical poets," his "may be termed" indicates that he did not consider that these poets had the right to be called "metaphysical" in the true sense. He was adapting a witty sally from Dryden who, writing in 1693, said of Donne:

> He affects the metaphysics, not only in his satires, but in his amorous verses, where nature only should reign; and perplexes the minds of the fair sex with nice speculations of philosophy, when he should engage their hearts, and entertain them with the softnesses of love. In this . . . Mr Cowley has copied him to a fault.

Between Dryden and Johnson comes Pope, who is reported by Spence to have remarked that "Cowley, as well as Davenant, borrowed his metaphysical style from Donne." But the only writer I know of before Dryden who spoke as if there were a "metaphysical school" is Drummond of Hawthornden (1585–1649) who, in an unfortunately undated letter, speaks of poets who make use of "Metaphysical *Ideas* and *Scholastical Quiddities.*"

From *The Metaphysical Poets* (Oxford, 1961), pp. xix-xxxiv. Reprinted by permission of The Clarendon Press.

What we call metaphysical poetry was referred to by contemporaries as "strong lines," a term which calls attention to other elements in metaphysical poetry than its fondness for indulging in "nice speculations of philosophy" in unusual contexts. The term is used in connexion with prose as well as with verse—indeed the earliest use I know of is by a prose writer—and so invites us to look at metaphysical poetry in a wider context. Like the later term "metaphysical," the term "strong-lined" is a term of disapprobation. It too is a kind of slang, a phrase which would seem to have been coined by those who disliked this way of writing. Thus Burton, in the preface to *The Anatomy of Melancholy* (1621), contrasts his own "loose free style" with "neat composition, strong lines, hyperboles, allegories," and later speaks disparagingly of the "affectation of big words, fustian phrases, jingling termes, strong lines, that like *Acastes* arrows caught fire as they flew"; and Quarles, in the preface to *Argalus and Parthenia* (1629), declares:

> I have not affected to set thy understanding on the Rack, by the tyranny of *strong lines*, which (as they fabulously report of *China* dishes) are made for the third *Generation* to make use of, and are the meere itch of wit; under the colour of which, many have ventured (trusting to the *Oedipean* conceit of their ingenious Reader) to write *non-sense*, and felloniously father the created expositions of other men; not unlike some painters, who first make the picture, then, from the opinions of better judgments, conclude whom it resembles.

These are complaints against an established manner in prose and verse. It is a manner which developed in the last decade of the sixteenth century with the cry everywhere for "More matter and less words." In prose, Cicero, the model for the sixteenth century, was dethroned in favor of the Silver Latin writers, Seneca and Tacitus. Recommending Sir Henry Savile's translation of Tacitus in 1591, Anthony Bacon commends Tacitus because he "hath written the most matter with the best conceit in the fewest words of any Historiographer," and adds "But he is hard. *Difficilia quæ pulchra;* the second reading will please thee more than the first, and the third than the second." The same conception that difficulty is a merit is applied to poetry in Chapman's preface to *Ovid's Banquet of the Sense* (1595), where he declares that poetry, unlike oratory, should not aim at clarity: "That Poetry should be as pervial as oratory and plainness her special ornament, were the plain way to barbarism." Poetry, like prose, should be close-packed and dense with meaning, something to be "chewed and digested," which will not give up its secrets on a first reading. In the 1590's also formal satire first appeared in English, and the satirists took as their model Persius, the most obscure of Roman satirists, and declared that satire should be "hard of conceit and harsh of style." The same period sees the vogue of the epigram and the great popularity of Martial.

What came to be called by its denigrators the "strong-lined" style had its origins in this general desire at the close of Elizabeth's reign for concise expression, achieved by an elliptical syntax, and accompanied by a staccato rhythm in prose and a certain deliberate roughness in versification in poetry. Along with this went admiration for difficulty in the thought. Difficulty is indeed the main demerit in this way of writing for those who dislike it, and the constant complaint of its critics is that it confuses the pleasures of poetry with the pleasures of puzzles. It is one of its merits for those who approve it. Jasper Mayne, in his elegy on Donne, put his finger on one of the delights of reading "strong-lined" verse when he said

> Wee are thought wits, when 'tis understood.

It makes demands upon the reader and challenges him to make it out. It does not attempt to attract the lazy and its lovers have always a certain sense of being a privileged class, able to enjoy what is beyond the reach of vulgar wits. The great majority of the poets included in this book did not write to be read by all and sundry. Few of them published their poems. They were "Chamber poets," as Drayton, with the jealousy of the professional for the amateur, complains. Their poems passed from hand to hand in manuscript. This is a source of both weakness and strength. At times the writing has the smell of a coterie, the writer performing with a self-conscious eye on his clever readers. But at its best it has the ease and artistic sincerity which comes from being able to take for granted the understanding of the audience for whom one writes.

The first characteristic that I shall isolate in trying to discuss the admittedly vague and, it is often thought, unsatisfactory term "metaphysical poetry" is its concentration. The reader is held to an idea or a line of argument. He is not invited to pause upon a passage, "wander with it, and muse upon it, and reflect upon it, and bring home to it, and prophesy upon it, and dream upon it" as a "starting-post towards all the 'two-and-thirty Palaces.'" Keats's advice can be followed profitably with much poetry, particularly with Elizabethan and Romantic poetry; but metaphysical poetry demands that we pay attention and read on. For this reason I have resisted the temptation to print excerpts from longer poems. It is, of course, possible and pleasurable to linger over passages of striking beauty and originality, but, on the whole, I think that to do so is to miss the special pleasure that metaphysical poetry has to give. It does not aim at providing, to quote Keats again, "a little Region to wander in," where lovers of poetry "may pick and choose, and in which images are so numerous that many are forgotten and found new in a second Reading." A metaphysical poem tends to be brief, and is always closely woven. Marvell, under the metaphor of a garland, characterizes his own art finely in "The Coronet" when he speaks of a "curious frame" in which the flowers are "set with Skill and chosen out with Care." And Donne in a sermon, speaking of the Psalms as especially dear to him in that they were poems, stresses the same elements of deliberate art (curiosity), and economy of language, when he defines psalms as

> Such form as is both curious, and requires diligence in the making, and then when it is made, can have nothing, no syllable taken from it, nor added to it.

Concentration and a sinewy strength of style is the mark of Ben Jonson as well as of Donne, and such adjectives as "strenuous" and "masculine" applied to him by his admirers point to a sense in which he too was in some degree a "strong-lined" man, and explain why so many younger writers were able to regard both him and Donne as equally their masters. Behind both, as behind much of the poetry of their followers, lies the classical epigram, and there is some truth in saying that a metaphysical poem is an expanded epigram. Almost all the poets in this collection exercised their skill in the writing of epigrams. Their efforts make on the whole very dreary reading; but the vogue of the epigram helped to form the taste for witty poetry. The desire for concentration and concision marks also the verse forms characteristic of seventeenth-century lyric. It appears in the fondness for a line of eight syllables rather than a line of ten, and in the use of stanzas employing lines of varying length into which the sense seems packed, or of stanzas built on very short lines. A stanza of Donne or Herbert is not, like rhyme royal or a Spenserian stanza, an ideal mould, as it were, into which the words have flowed. It is more like a limiting frame in which words and thought are compressed, a "box where sweets compacted lie." The metaphysical poets favoured either very simple verse forms, octosyllabic couplets or quatrains, or else stanzas created for the particular poem, in which length of line and rhyme scheme artfully enforced the sense. In a poem not included here, "The Triple Foole," Donne suggests, in passing, this conception of the function of rhyme and metre:

> I thought, if I could draw my paines,
> Through Rimes vexation, I should them allay,
> Griefe brought to numbers cannot be so fierce,
> For, he tames it, that fetters it in verse.

The second characteristic of metaphysical poetry, its most immediately striking feature, is its fondness for conceits, and here, of course, Jonson and Donne part company. A conceit is a comparison whose ingenuity is more striking than its justness, or, at least, is more immediately striking. All comparisons discover likeness in things unlike: a comparison becomes a conceit when we are made to concede likeness while being strongly conscious of unlikeness. A brief comparison can be a conceit if two things patently unlike, or which we should never think of together, are shown to be alike in a single point in such a way, or in such a context, that we feel their incongruity. Here a conceit is like a spark made by striking two stones together. After the flash the stones are just two stones. Metaphysical poetry abounds in such flashes, as when Cartwright in his New Year's poem, promising to be a new man, declares that he will not be new as the year is new when it begins again its former cycle, and then thinks of two images of motion without progression, the circulation of the blood and a mill:

> Motion as in a Mill
> Is busie standing still.

The wit of this depends on our being willing to suppress our memory of other features of mills, and particularly on our not allowing ourselves to think that mills are very usefully employed grinding corn while "standing still." Normally metaphor and simile allow and invite the mind to stray beyond the immediate point of resemblance, and in extended or epic simile, which is the diametrical opposite of the conceit, the poet himself expatiates freely, making the point of comparison a point of departure. In an extended conceit, on the other hand, the poet forces fresh points of likeness upon us. Here the conceit is a kind of "hammering out" by which a difficult join is made. I borrow the phrase from Shakespeare's poet-king Richard II, who occupies himself in prison composing a conceited poem:

> I have been studying how I may compare
> This prison where I live unto the world:
> And for because the world is populous,
> And here is not a creature but myself,
> I cannot do it; yet I'll hammer it out.
> My brain I'll prove the female to my soul . . .

Longer conceits set themselves to "prove" likeness. They may, as here, start from a comparison which the speaker owns is far from obvious and then proceeds to establish. Or they may start from one that is immediately acceptable generally and then make us accept further resemblances in detail after detail. Thus nobody, I imagine, would think Lady Macbeth is being particularly ingenious when she compares the troubled face of her husband to a book in which men may "read strange matters." She leaves our imaginations to give further content to this comparison of finding meaning in a book and meaning in a face and to the deliberately imprecise words "strange matters." But when Lady Capulet takes up the same comparison to urge Juliet to wed Count Paris she expands the comparison for us in detail after detail so that it becomes a conceit, and most people would add a very tasteless and ineffective one.

> Read o'er the volume of young Paris' face
> And find delight writ there with beauty's pen;
> Examine every married lineament,
> And see how one another lends content;
> And what obscur'd in this fair volume lies
> Find written in the margent of his eyes.
> This precious book of love, this unbound lover,
> To beautify him, only lacks a cover. . . .
> That book in many eyes doth share the glory
> That in gold clasps locks in the golden story:
> So shall you share all that he doth possess,
> By having him making yourself no less.

Elizabethan poetry, dramatic and lyric, abounds in conceits. They are used both as ornaments and as the basis of songs and sonnets. What differentiates the conceits of the metaphysicals is not the fact that they frequently employ curious learning in their comparisons. Many of the poets whom we call metaphysical, Herbert for instance, do not. It is the use which they make of the conceit and the rigorous nature of their conceits, springing from the use to which they are put, which is more important than their frequently learned content. A metaphysical conceit, unlike Richard II's comparison of his prison to the world, is not indulged in for its own sake. It is used, as Lady Capulet uses hers, to persuade, or it is used to define, or to prove a point. Ralegh's beautiful comparison of man's life to a play is a good example of a poem which seems to me to hover on the verge of becoming a metaphysical poem. Its concision and completeness and the ironic, colloquially made point at the end—"Onely we dye in earnest, that's no Jest"—bring it very near, but it remains in the region of the conceited epigram and does not cross the border. On the other hand, Lady Capulet's conceit fails to be metaphysical in another way. She does not force us to concede the justness of her initial comparison by developing it, she merely argues from various arbitrarily chosen points of comparison between a book and a bachelor. In a metaphysical poem the conceits are instruments of definition in an argument or instruments to persuade. The poem has something to say which the conceit explicates or something to urge which the conceit helps to forward. It can only do this if it is used with an appearance of logical rigour, the analogy being shown to hold by a process not unlike Euclid's superimposition of triangles. I have said that the first impression a conceit makes is of ingenuity rather than of justice: the metaphysical conceit aims at making us concede justness while admiring ingenuity. Thus, in one of the most famous of all metaphysical conceits, the comparison of the union in absence of two lovers with the relation between the two legs of a compass, Donne sustains the comparison through the whole process of drawing a circle, because he is attempting to give a "proof by analogy" of their union, by which he can finally persuade his mistress not to mourn. In another of his unfortunately rare asides on the art of poetry, Donne, again speaking of the Psalms, said:

> In all Metricall compositions . . . the force of the whole piece is for the most part left to the shutting up; the whole frame of the Poem is a beating out of a piece of gold, but the last clause is as the impression of the stamp, and that is it that makes it currant.

We might expand this by saying that the brilliant abrupt openings for which metaphysical poetry is famous, are like the lump of gold flung down on the table to be worked; the conceits are part of the beating out by which the metal is shaped to receive its final stamp, which is the point towards which the whole has moved.

Argument and persuasion, and the use of the conceit as their instrument, are the elements or body of a metaphysical poem. Its quintessence or soul is the vivid imagining of a moment of experience or of a situation out of which the need to argue, or persuade, or define arises. Metaphysical poetry is famous for its abrupt, personal openings in which a man speaks to his mistress, or addresses his God, or sets a scene, or calls us to mark this or see that. A great many of the poems in this collection are inspired by actual occasions either of personal, or, less often, public interest. The great majority postulate an occasion. We may not accept that Donne's "Good Friday" was actually "made as I was riding westward that day," as a heading in some manuscripts tells us, but we must accept as we read the poem that he is riding westward and thinking as he rides. Marvell calls us to look at little T.C. in her garden. The child of one of Marvell's friends, Theophila Cornewall, bore the same beautiful name as her elder sister who had died two days after her baptism, a name which has a foreboding ring since the proverb says that the "Darlings of the Gods" die young. This lovely poem would seem to have arisen from thoughts suggested by the name and family history of a friend's child. Whether Marvell actually caught sight of her in a garden we have no means of knowing. But he does not convey to us his sense of the transience of spring and the dangerous fragility of childhood through general reflections on human life. He calls us to watch with him a child "in a Prospect of Flowers." Equally, when his subject belongs to the ideal world of pastoral, not the world of daily life, his nymph is set before us complaining for her fawn while the little beast's life-blood is ebbing away. She tells of her betrayal in love as the tears are running down her cheeks in mourning for the creature who consoled her for that betrayal. Even poems of generalized reflection are given the flavour of spontaneous thought, as when Herbert opens his poem "Man" with "My God, I heard this day . . . ," and thus gives the poem the air of having sprung from the casual overhearing of a chance remark.

The manner of metaphysical poetry originates in developments in prose and verse in the 1590's. The greatest glory of that decade is that it saw the flowering of the drama. Metaphysical poetry is the poetry of the great age of our drama. Its master John Donne was, we are told, "a great frequenter of plays" in his youth. As an ambitious young man of social standing he would not have considered writing for the players, and his work is too personal, wilful, and idiosyncratic for us to imagine him doing so with any success. But his strong dramatic imagination of particular situations transforms the lyric and makes a metaphysical poem more than an epigram expanded by conceits.

I have begun this volume a little before Donne with poems which in some ways anticipate the metaphysical manner: Ralegh's fine passionate conceit of a pilgrimage, written when he was under sentence of death, some specimens of Fulke Greville's "close, mysterious and sentencious way of writing," Southwell's meditations, Shakespeare's strange celebration of married chastity in the most "strong-lined" of all poems, if "strong lines" are riddles, Alabaster's attempts at the concise expression of theological paradox, Wotton's laconic comment on the greatest scandal of the age. But the minute the reader reaches Donne, he will have the same sense of having arrived as when, in a collection of pre-Shakespearian plays, we hear the voice of Marlowe. Ralegh is too discursive, Greville too heavy and general, Southwell too dogged in his conceits and in his verse, one line padding at the same pace after another, Shakespeare too remote, and too symbolic, creating a static world where Love and Constancy are deified. The vehement, colloquial tone of the Satire "Of Religion" creates the sense of an actual historical situation in which urgent choices present themselves. In the three splendid Elegies a man is speaking to a woman at a moment when all the faculties are heightened, as in drama, by the thought of what impends. He is about to go to the wars—what will she say to him when he returns, perhaps mutilated? He has to travel and she wants to come with him as his page—he is horrified at the thought of such romantic folly and implores her to be his true mistress and "home of love." With the tide of passion rising in him, impatient for the moment when she will be his, he watches her undressing for bed. The sense of the moment gives Donne's wit its brilliance and verve, the aptness and incongruity of the comparisons being created by their contexts. Without this, as in some of his complimentary pieces, he labours to be witty and never becomes "airborne." The fading of this desire to make poems out of particular moments, made imaginatively present rather than remembered, and played over by wit rather than reflected upon, is apparent towards the end of this volume. The metaphysical style peters out, to be replaced by the descriptive and reflective poetry of the eighteenth century, a century which sees the rise of the novel and has virtually no drama.

The strong sense of actual and often very ordinary situations which the metaphysical poets convey makes me agree with Grierson in thinking that words such as "conceited" or "fantastic" do not sum up their quality at all. A reader may at times exclaim "Who would ever think such a thought in such a situation?" He will not exclaim "Who can imagine himself in such a situation?" Dryden praised Donne for expressing deep thoughts in common language. He is equally remarkable for having extraordinary thoughts in ordinary situations. The situations which recur in seventeenth-century lyric are the reverse of fantastic, and often the reverse of ideal or romantic situations. Thus, a very favourite topic is the pleasure of hearing a beautiful woman sing or play. This domestic subject is, of course, a favourite on the Continent, and not merely with the poets, but with the painters. Such poems usually go beyond compliment to create a sense of the occasion; as Waller, in praising Lady Isabella Rich, whom Dorothy Osborne described as "Lady Isabella that speaks and looks and plays and sings and all so prettily," expresses exactly the delight which we receive during an actual performance from artistry:

> Such moving sounds from such a careless touch,
> So unconcern'd her selfe, and we so much!

Again there are a great many poems which arise out of the common but unromantic situation of love between persons of very different ages. A mature man may rather ruefully complain to "a very young Lady"

> That time should mee so far remove
> From that which I was borne to love.

This Horatian theme of the charm of young girls to older men is given various twists. The situation is reversed when Cartwright persuades his Chloe not to mind being older than he is; and at the end of the period Rochester gives us a fresh variation on the theme that age and youth are not so incompatible as the romantics claim by writing a song for "A Young Lady to her Ancient Lover."

The most serious and impassioned love poetry of the century argues, or assumes as a base for argument, that love is a relation between two persons loving—"It cannot *be* love till I love her that loves me." The poems which Donne wrote on the experience of loving where love is returned, poems in which "Thou" and "I" are merged into "We," are his most original and profound contributions to the poetry of human love. It is not possible to find models for such poems as "The Good-Morrow," "The Anniversarie," "The Canonization," and, less perfect but still wonderful, "The Extasie." These poems have the right to the title metaphysical in its true sense, since they raise, even when they do not explicitly discuss, the great metaphysical question of the relation of the spirit and the senses. They raise it not as an abstract problem, but in the effort to make the experience of the union of human powers in love, and the union of two human beings in love, apprehensible. We never lose our sense of a "little roome" which love has made "an every where." In the lighter verses of Donne's followers this theme that love is the union of two human beings, not the service of a votarist to a goddess, is handled with a mixture of gallantry, sensibility and good sense that has a peculiar charm:

> 'Tis not how witty, nor how free,
> Nor yet how beautifull she be,
> But how much kinde and true to me.

This is a very characteristic note. There are plenty of high and chivalrous fancies, and the Platonic ideal of love as the union of souls casts its spell; but the tone of the bargain scene in *The Way of the World* is anticipated in many lyrics in which the speaker sets forward the terms on which he is willing to make the "world without end bargain" of love. The question "What shall I do if she does not love me?" is often handled and usually with a glance at the old chivalric answer. Suckling's impudent "The devil take her" is flat blasphemy against the religion of love. King's exquisite "Tell me no more how fair she is" is chivalrous enough, as is Waller's "It is not that I love you less"; but earlier servants of love would not, I think, have shown so stoical an acceptance of the fact that their love was hopeless, nor been so sensible in resolving not to keep their wounds green by hearing the lady's praises or by haunting her company. In one of his beautifully tempered songs of love unreturned, Godolphin seriously considers what creates the obligation to constancy. Parting for the wars, or parting to go abroad, or the final parting of death, actual or anticipated, are also favourite subjects. They too inspire poems which are metaphysical in both senses, as lovers ponder such questions as "Can love subsist without the things that elemented it?" and "Shall we meet in another world, and, if so, shall we know each other?"

The seventeenth century was, as Cowley said, "a warlike, various and tragical age." A glance at the biographical notes will show how many of the poets included in this book at one time or another "trailed a pike" or "raised a troop of horse," or went on missions abroad, or played a part in public affairs. They were for the most part men of the world who knew its ways. Their wit, high-flown and extravagant though it is, goes with a strong sense of the realities of daily life, the common concerns of men and women. And in spite of Johnson's accusation of pedantry, it has the flavour of the wit of conversation between friends who urge each other on to further flights. Donne perhaps meant what he said when, in the stanza of "The Will" in which he restores gifts to those from whom he had received them, he leaves

> To Nature, all that I in Ryme have writ;
> And to my company my wit.

"I know the world and believe in God" wrote Fulke Greville, a Calvinist who was well acquainted with the winding stair of politics. Donne might have said the same, and Herbert has no need to tell us that he knows the ways of Learning, Honour, and Pleasure; it is apparent in all his poetry that he was not unworldly because of lack of knowledge of the world. The strength of the religious poetry of the metaphysical poets is that they bring to their praise and prayer and meditation so much experience that is not in itself religious. Here too the poems create for us particular situations out of which prayer or meditation arises: Donne riding westward, or stretched out upon his deathbed; Herbert praying all day long "but no hearing," or noting his own whitening hair, or finding, after a night of heaviness, joy in the morning; Vaughan walking to spend his hour, or sitting solitary at midnight thinking of departed friends. Even with Crashaw, where this sense of the poet's own situation is unimportant, how vividly he dramatizes, rather than narrates, the story of St. Teresa, and invokes the weeping Magdalen; and how vigorously he urges the hesitant Countess of Denbigh against delay.

Much stress has been laid recently upon the strongly traditional element in the conceits of metaphysical religious poetry. A good deal that seems to us remote, and idiosyncratic, the paradoxes and the twistings of Scripture to yield symbolic meanings, reaches back through the liturgy and through commentaries on Scripture to the Fathers and can be paralleled in medieval poetry. It is also true that the metaphysical manner of setting a subject, "hammering it out," and then "shutting it up" is closely allied to the method of religious meditation and that many metaphysical poems are poetical meditations. And yet, as strongly—or even more strongly—as in reading the secular poetry, the more we suggest common qualities and the more we set the poets in a tradition, the more strongly we are aware of their intensely individual treatment of common themes. How individually, for instance, Herbert treats the old theme of the stages of human life and the traditional lesson of the *Ars Moriendi* in "Mortification." Who else but Herbert would, with compassionate irony in place of the usual gloom of the moralist, show man as unconsciously amassing at each stage what he needs for his burial? And how tenderly and sympathetically he epitomizes each stage of our strange eventful pilgrimage, catching its very essence: the dreamless sleep of boyhood, the retraction of energies and interests in middle age, and the pathos of old age, unable to speak for rheum. The comparison of sleep to death, and of a bed to a grave, is stock enough. It is transformed by the further haunting image

> Successive nights, like rolling waves,
> Convey them quickly, who are bound for death.

The poem concludes with an old moral for its "shutting up"; but the moral is made new by the time we reach it, because Herbert has so expanded our understanding of our dying life. The metaphysical style heightens and liberates personality. It is essentially a style in which individuality is expressed. The best pupils in the school of Donne learned from their master how to speak their own minds in their own voices.

For this reason I have contented myself with describing some of the characteristics of metaphysical poetry and have not attempted to construct a definition of "a metaphysical poem." Such definitions do not seem to me very profitable, since none of these poets ever thought of himself as writing such a thing, and they usually lead their creators to finding fault with this or that poet for not conforming to the critic's definition. I am aware that I have included in this collection some poems whose presence under its title may be challenged. If I had the space I could defend them all on one ground or another, though my defence would of course have to take the form of "All these poems are metaphysical, but some are more metaphysical than others." I am more concerned that readers should find them beautiful and interesting than that they should approve or disapprove of them as conforming or not conforming to the idea of a metaphysical poem. All of them have a certain pungency in their thought, or in their turns of phrase, which makes them, whether profound or flippant, deserve the praise of being "fine and wittie."

JOSEPH ANTHONY MAZZEO

A Critique of Some Modern Theories of Metaphysical Poetry

Numerous theories of "metaphysical" poetry have been advanced ever since the appearance of Sir Herbert Grierson's great edition of Donne's poems in 1912 initiated the modern revaluation of the "metaphysical" poets. However, few of these theories seem to have approached the problem from the perspectives offered by sixteenth- and seventeenth-century literary critics themselves. One of the reasons for this oversight is the curious fact that there is no body of critical literature in English on the metaphysical movement written when that movement, under various names, such as "Concettismo," "Marinismo," and "Gongorismo," was flourishing throughout Europe. Another reason is that we seem to have forgotten that the word "conceit," "concetto," or "concepto" also meant metaphor as well as "conceit" in the sense in which Dr. Johnson used the word. This is especially surprising when we consider that many modern critics find the most striking characteristic of the metaphysical poet to be his desire to extend the range and variety of metaphorical expression.

Giordano Bruno, the first critic to attempt a conceptual formulation of "concettismo," as the "metaphysical" style was known in Italy, began his argument to *De gli eroici furori* with an attack on the Petrarchan theory of poetic inspiration. For the older notion of "amore" directed toward personal beauty, Bruno attempted to substitute the idea of "heroic love" directed toward the universe. This second kind

From *Modern Philology,* L (1952), pp. 88–96. Reprinted by permission of The University of Chicago Press.

of love he interprets as the gift which both the philosopher and the poet have for perceiving the unity of dissimilars or, in other terms, for making heterogeneous analogies. Thus, for Bruno, "metaphysical" poetry was essentially concerned with perceiving and expressing the universal correspondences in his universe.

This conception of the poet as one who discovers and expresses the universal analogies binding the universe together was later developed by the theorists of the conceit in the seventeenth century, the most familiar of whom are Baltasar Gracián in Spain and Emmanuele Tesauro in Italy, and was made the basis for a poetic of "concettismo" or, as I have called it elsewhere, "a poetic of correpondences." [1]

One of the cardinal tenets of the critics of the conceit is that the conceit itself is the expression of a correspondence which actually obtains between objects and that, since the universe is a network of universal correspondences or analogies which unite all the apparently heterogeneous elements of experience, the most heterogeneous metaphors are justifiable. Thus the theorists of the conceit justify the predilection of the "school of wit" for recondite and apparently strained analogies by maintaining that even the more violent couplings of dissimilars were simply expressions of the underlying unity of all things.

It is, of course, true that analogical thought is a fundamental property of the human mind in any age and that the notion of universal analogy has a long history which reaches back to Plato. The important point is that Bruno and the theorists of the conceit employed the principle as the basis of a poetic for the first time. The fact that they did so does not "explain" metaphysical poetry any more than Aristotle's *Poetics* "explains" Sophocles. This is not the function of a poetic or a theory of poetry. Rather, it formulates conceptually a concrete body of literature already in existence. As Hegel put it in his preface to *The Philosophy of Right*, "When philosophy paints its gray in gray, a shape of life has grown old . . . it cannot be rejuvenated but only understood. The owl of Minerva spreads its wings at twilight."

What a poetic can do, however, is make explicit the cultural presuppositions which may underlie a particular body of literature, a style, or a genre. That Bruno and the theorists of the conceit should have based their poetic on the principle of universal analogy meant that they wished to justify and formulate philosophically the actual practice of metaphysical poets in making recondite and heterogeneous analogies and in using mundane and "learned" images.

The principle of universal analogy as a poetic, or the poetic of correspondences, offers, in my opinion, a theory of metaphysical poetry which is simpler, in greater harmony with the evidence, and freer from internal contradictions than the major modern theories that have yet been formulated. It is in the light of this theory, contemporary to the metaphysical movement, that I propose to review the various modern theories.

One popular modern theory derives "metaphysical" poetry from the Petrarchan and troubadour traditions and describes it as a decadent and exaggerated version of these earlier traditions.[2] If this is so, we can hardly understand the deliberately "irregular" versification of many of the greatest "metaphysical" poets, such as Donne; the colloquial tone and the homely and technical imagery characteristic of "concettismo"; the fact that Bruno, a "concettista" himself and the probable founder of Neapolitan "concettismo," began his *De gli eroici furori* with an attack on the Petrarchan and troubadour conventions and offered a clear and determined substitute theory. He, at least, was certain that he was doing something else, and the poetic creations of the "metaphysicals" are sufficient evidence that he was. We can avoid this conclusion only if we insist on regarding the conceit as merely an odd or unusual image, in which case we can find it everywhere (and therefore nowhere) and even take its origin back to Martial. But it is clear that literary history cannot be made from superficial similarities and that the historian of taste must seek and determine the different cultural presuppositions that underlie the creations of minds as diverse as Bruno and Arnaut Daniel, without, at the same time, swallowing up the individual uniqueness and greatness of every great artist and work of art in the general historical categories we construct for them.

Another theory would attribute the "metaphysical" style to the influence of Ramistic logic, but it seems to me that this view raises more questions than it answers. Norman E. Nelson has made an acute criticism of the confusion between poetry, rhetoric, and logic that the defenders of the Ramistic theory are involved in.[3] It is at least questionable whether any system of inference or any empirical construction like rhetoric can have the kind of effect on a culture that Miss Tuve, the originator of this theory, describes. If her almost deterministic view of the influence of logic and rhetoric were true, she would still have to explain away the fact that Milton, who wrote a Ramist logic and defended Ramist theories, was surely no "metaphysical" poet. The connection between "concettismo" and Ramism, if one can be established, is not a causal relationship. Rather, they are both expressive, in different ways, of what we might call the "rhetoricizing" tendency of Renaissance humanism, the belief shared with Ramus by Valla and others that literature or rhetoric, rather than the old scholastic logic, revealed the true path which the mind must take in its quest for truth.[4] It would seem that the confusion of logic and poetry characteristic of our modern "Ramists" is a result of the current use of the term "logical image" to refer to the kind of expanded metaphor characteristic of much "metaphysical" poetry. It is, of course, clear that the "logic" of development of an expanded metaphor has often very little to do with the logic of a syllogism or system of inference and is, indeed, directed toward a different end.

Another group of scholars relates the "metaphysical" style to the baroque, but variously, sometimes completely identifying it with the baroque and sometimes distinguishing the two. Croce, for example, calls "concettismo" a baroque phenomenon but considers anything baroque a negative aspect of Renaissance history whose only excuse for existence was to purge Western civilization from medievalism. It is otherwise with Hatzfeld, who, distinguishing "concettismo" and baroque, gives the honors to the latter, of which the conceit and its uses are, at most, a degenerate parody.[5] It is difficult to discuss the views of this group, since the term "baroque" itself is, like "Renaissance" and "Romantic," so variable in reference. However, the notion has been applied with greatest success to the study of the visual arts, where it is at least referable to specific techniques. I do not propose to complicate further this already complex problem, but it would seem desirable to keep the characteristics of baroque painting, sculpture, and architecture firmly in mind when we extend this term to other cultural spheres and not allow ourselves to be misled by chronological simultaneity alone. The original fruitful use of the concept of the baroque with reference to the plastic arts suggests that Cassirer's category of "form" and the principle of universal analogy might well be kept separated and that true "concettismo" belongs to the latter, while the baroque, as Croce suggested, is best understood as the transformation of the Renaissance interest in "form" into a preoccupation with "ornament" and in a weakening of the distinctions between the arts.

Perhaps the most widespread theory of the "metaphysical" style is the emblem theory. This view, establishing a causal connection between the emblem movement or "emblem habit" and the conceit which is purportedly its result, is usually expressed in terms of a baroque theory of the "metaphysical" style. Mario Praz, the foremost representative of this group, bases his analysis on Croce's, without assuming the latter's negative attitude toward either the baroque or the "metaphysical" styles. However, his study of the actual creations of this literary movement leads him to a view of the conceit and the emblem which might be called the "game" theory, a position he assumes when he says of the conceit and emblem that they are of the nature of the charade or riddle—the by-products of an amusing, lighthearted (perhaps perverse?) verbal and pictorial game.[6] This is surely an astonishing description of a style in which some of the greatest religious poetry of all time was written, and it is, in effect, denied by the sensitivity of Praz's concrete criticism of John Donne and Richard Crashaw.

I believe that this conclusion is a consequence of Praz's insistence on the intimate relationship between emblem and conceit and between the mass of different styles, some of them quite perverse, which went under the name of "Marinismo," "Gongorismo," "Seicentismo," "Euphuism," etc. However, not only are the resemblances between Donne and Lyly superficial at best, but the easy application of some notion of strangeness or eccentricity in style will find resemblances where none exist and lead to false or useless descriptions of cultural phenomena. Praz seems closer to a working definition of the conceit when he says that it is to poetry what the illusory perspective is to art, although, in the light of both the theory and the practice of the "metaphysical" style, this insight is of somewhat limited utility and best describes a style like Crashaw's.

Praz makes much of the fact that the emblem was usually accompanied by an epigram, and, since he seems to hold that emblem and "metaphysical" poem are related to each other as cause and effect, he concludes that the epigram is the genre most characteristic of "concettismo." This conclusion, in turn, leads to his placing great emphasis on the diffusion of the *Greek Anthology* during the Renaissance as one of the important influences on the growth of the "metaphysical" movement.[7] However, while the *Greek Anthology* stimulated many imitators, it seems to have had little effect on the best of the poets of wit. The long and "conceited" works of Marino, Gongora, Donne, and others preclude accepting this view, at least in the form in which it is stated. Praz's stress on the epigram also leads him to emphasize brevity as the most desirable quality of a good conceit, a quality which presumably helped make it "sharp" or "pointed." Brevity in the conceit was commended by the theorists of the conceit themselves, but they also recognized what we would today call the "expanded metaphor," and they often seem to mean by "brevity" a quality opposed to the Ciceronian notion of *copia*. There is, of course, no reason why an epigram should not have conceits, but there is also no apparent reason to establish a determined relationship between "concettismo" and epigram and, via the epigram, between "concettismo" and the emblem. I shall take up the more fundamental inadequacies of the emblem theory in detail when I discuss the views of Austin Warren below, since he presents this theory in purer form than does Praz. In the latter's version the emblem plays an important role, but mediately, through the epigram, which had to be brief, playful, and puzzling and was analogous to illusory perspective in the arts. However, while this analysis is true of certain individual works, especially of some productions of the school of Marino, it is inadequate to the movement as a whole and gives no real clue to the *forma mentis* of a "concettista."

Indeed, this theory of the conceit was implicitly rejected by the seventeenth-century theorists of the conceit in whose works the emblem and *impresa,* as well as the epigram or "arte lapidaria," are treated as incidental topics involved in the analysis of conceit or metaphor. They were fully aware that any theory of the conceit had to be a theory of metaphor or analogy, not a theory of genres. Emmanuele Tesauro, for example, analyzed all genres, literary and artistic, as forms of "acutezze" or types of metaphorical expression by extending the categories of rhetoric to include all literary and figurative creations.[8] Thus Tesauro himself realized that the roots of "concettismo" lay deeper than any classification of genres and were rooted in the nature of expression itself. Not only the epigram but all genres, including the lyric itself, had become "metaphysical."

Austin Warren, as I observed above, shares some of Praz's conceptions about the emblem to an even greater degree. He says:

> The connection of the emblem with poetry was, from the start, close: indeed the term often transferred itself from the picture to the epigram which ordinarily accompanied it. . . . Thus the arts reinforced one another. The influence on poetry was not only to encourage the metaphorical habit but to impart to the metaphors a hardness, a palpability which, merely conceived, they were unlikely to possess. And yet the metaphors ordinarily analogized impalpabilities—states of the soul, concepts, abstractions. . . . Many emblems owe their undeniable grotesqueness to the visualization of metaphors, often scriptural, which were not intended so to be visualized.[9]

In this particular passage, I take it that Warren means by "hardness" a kind of precision and by "palpability" a strong visual or sensuous element in the image. In any case the "metaphysical" image purportedly acquired these properties from the "emblem habit," which helped to develop metaphorical habits of mind and, presumably, habits for making recondite metaphors instead of commonplace ones.

However, as I have already explained, the theorists of the conceit either do not deal with the emblem at all or treat it merely as one aspect of the general theory of wit, making no direct connection between emblem and conceit. Taking our cue from them once more, we might observe that the qualities of precision and the strong sensuous element to be found in much "metaphysical" poetry can be accounted for, to the degree that any poetic "accounts for" a living and creative poetic tradition, by their theory of wit (*ingegno, ingenio, esprit*) as the faculty which, like Bruno's *genio,* finds and expresses the universal analogies latent in the data of experience. The desire to draw correspondences between heterogeneous things and thereby reveal the unity of what appears fragmentary and the desire to develop these correspondences are bound to give to the resultant imagery some of those qualities Warren discerns in the poets of wit.

From a more general critical point of view, the "palpability" or "hardness" of an image is, after all, a function of what the poet wishes to say and can say. In its own way Dante's imagery is as "hard" and "palpable" as one could wish. What the poet can say and the way he can say it are in part given by his culture, in so far as the culture makes him a man of a particular place, time, and environment, and in large part by his imaginative power, which enables him to "inform" and universalize his cultural and personal experience. No poetic has yet explained the secret of his power, although a poetic which is true to the concrete works of art it attempts to describe theoretically can give us insight into the nature of the imagination by telling us what it did with what it worked with. Universal analogy and its later formulation as a poetic can thus tell us something about the Renaissance imagination and throw light on Donne, Marino, Crashaw, and others, in spite of their differences. In this light, it would seem to be an error to attribute a movement such as "concettismo" to some secondary cultural phenomenon such as the "emblem habit" or Ramist logic and try, by so doing, to obliterate the differences between poets by swallowing them up in an influence.

Warren's version of the emblem theory of "metaphysical" poetry is based on a general theory of imagery involving the nature of the analogues in a metaphor:

> All imagery is double in its reference, a composite of perception and conception. Of these ingredients, the proportions vary. The metaphorist can collate image with image, or image with concept, or concept with image, or concept with concept.[10]

After discussing the series of combinations according to which the "ingredients" of an image may be arranged, he continues:

> Then too, the metaphorists differ widely in the degree of visualization for which they project their images. The epic simile of Homer and of Spenser is fully pictorial; the intent, relative to the poet's architecture, is decorative. On the other hand, the "sunken" and the "radical" types of imagery—the conceits of Donne and the "symbols" of Hart Crane—expect scant visualization by the senses.[11]

This passage is especially important because the author is here distinguishing between those poets called "metaphysical" (he also seems to include the modern "neo-metaphysicals") and all others. However, in this passage Warren is not analyzing the school of wit and its imagery in terms of "palpability" or "hardness" purportedly derived from the emblem; indeed, he seems to be saying that the Donnean conceit is capable of "scant visualization." It would therefore lack the properties which the emblem supposedly gave to the conceit. In the passage previously cited, Warren closely connected the emblem to the conceit, while in this passage the conceit is completely severed from those properties which it was supposed to have derived from the emblem.

It is clear that we are involved in a contradiction. Unintentionally, Warren is pointing out one important thing about "metaphysical" poetry and about poetic imagery in general. The qualities of the "metaphysical" image seem to have nothing to do with whether or not it can be visualized or with the sensory content of the image itself, although it may be prominent. The qualities of the "metaphysical" image are a function of the *manner* in which the analogues are related, and it is this very point that the theorists of the conceit make when they insist that the wit is in the "form" of the conceit and not in the "matter."

A further reason for the inevitable inadequacy of the emblem theory is the historical fact that the emblem movement, initiated by the introduction of the *Hieroglyphica* of Horapollo to Renaissance Europe, is a cultural phenomenon distinct from the poetry of wit and has other cultural presuppositions. Although emblem and conceit were later found together, they are found together at a relatively late date and usually in minor authors like Quarles, who gave emblems already in existence a verse commentary.[12] Granted that a poet might find an emblem suggestive of some image or another, the vast bulk of the creations of the school of wit do not seem to be related to the emblem literature in any intrinsic way. The very grotesqueness of many of the emblems is testimony to the fact that the conceit preceded—and was therefore independent of—its graphic expression. If anything, it was the conceit which made the emblem grotesque rather than the emblem making the conceit "harder" and more "palpable." Emblems drawn to many of the conceits of Donne or Crashaw or to much of the so-called "decorative imagery" of Homer would all be equally grotesque.

Perhaps the basic unexamined assumption in this whole theory is that there is a radical distinction in kinds of imagery. The sharp cleavage between what are called "decorative" imagery and "functional" imagery needs to be closely examined. We might begin by asking in what sense the imagery of Homer can be said to be decorative. It is clear even from a cursory reading of the *Iliad* that many of Homer's analogues for the events of battle are drawn from the world of peaceful endeavor. One of the obvious functions of these analogues is to heighten the pitch of the battle scenes and to bring the "great" world of peace into relationship with the "little" world of war. In this sense the *Iliad* is as much about peace as about war; metaphor is the link between these two worlds, revealing the nature of war through analogy with the events and experiences of peace. It follows that the poet's "choice" of analogues depends upon what he wants to say, upon what elements in the world of men he wishes to bring into the world of his poem. This is at least one sense in which the microcosm-macrocosm analogy is still profoundly vital.

When Homer compares an attacking army to a huge wave breaking on a beach, he would, in the opinion of some, be making a fully pictorical metaphor. However, all the reader has to do is to try to think of the various ways in which an emblem might be constructed to represent this metaphor to see how grotesque the results could be. Two *separate* pictures could be drawn, and they could be quite photographic. But this would not result in the creation of an emblem, for the emblem would have to embody the whole metaphor at once in one representation. We must bear in mind that the metaphor is part identity and part difference. What Homer wants us to see is the way in which a wave under certain conditions is like an army under certain other conditions. By joining these two particular analogues, he selects those qualities of waves which can be transferred to armies. The pictorial quality is not in the whole metaphor or in the identity but in each analogue separately as a kind of sensuous residue remaining after the identity has been established, and as such it is part of the total effect of the image. Thus the pictorial quality remains precisely that aspect of the image which cannot be transferred from one analogue to the other.

It follows from this analysis that, when we speak of "pictorial imagery," we cannot mean that the metaphor can necessarily be absorbed into a pictorial representation or that, conversely, it was necessarily created by a graphic representation. Both historical evidence and theoretical necessity, therefore, require abandoning the emblem theory of "metaphysical" poetry. The emblem movement is more closely related to the tendency in the baroque plastic arts toward breaking down the barriers between the arts in the effort to create a universal art which would somehow combine all of them. Its great vogue was largely the work of the Jesuits, who found the emblem a useful pedagogic device for propagating the faith.

The failure to see the way in which the emblem is related and the extent to which it is not related to the conceit can lead to some further misinterpretations. Praz, for example, derives the limbeck image as used in the writings of the spiritual alchemists from the emblem tradition and believes that this image is a mere "conceit" or witticism.[13] But it was part of the religious and symbolic vocabulary derived from the symbols of empirical alchemy by application of the principle of universal analogy whereby they were extended to apply to all levels of existence. The limbeck was thus no mere suggestive and fanciful image but the symbol of a process that was recapitulated in every order of a universe seen *sub specie alchemiae*. The failure to realize the nature of this image leads Praz to misunderstand the significance of the work of Michael Maier, the alchemist who published an alchemical work containing both emblems and music to be sung to the various stages of the alchemical process, as a very strange example of baroque sensibility or "concettismo." [14] However, what Maier did was to use the emblems for their pedagogic value, much as a chemistry textbook might have illustrations and equations. Music as a necessary part of the alchemical process was a characteristic result of the conviction that all things are universally related and affect each other through correspondences.

Although, as Warren maintains, "both the emblem and the conceit proceed from wit," they do not proceed from the same kind of wit, or in the same way.[15] The relationship is not, above all, filial but, at most, cousinly. Our own time is less "witty" than the time of Donne, and universal analogy has passed out of existence as a common habit of thought; the difficulty we have in penetrating this view of the world from within and somehow understanding it as "natural" and not "perverse" is, perhaps, the most important reason of all for the confusion about the nature of the poetry of wit. Many students of the movement have been aware that what may impress us as perverse, shocking, or recondite need not have had the same effect on contemporaries. This has sometimes been attributed to habitual usage and "taste." However, the "metaphysical" poets and their contemporaries possessed a view of the world founded on universal analogy and derived habits of thought which prepared them for finding and easily accepting the most heterogeneous analogies.[16]

NOTES

[1] Giordano Bruno, *Opere italiane,* ed. Giovanni Gentile, Vol. II (Bari, 1927). I refer the reader to two articles of mine: "A Seventeenth-Century Theory of Metaphysical Poetry," *RR,* XLII (1951), 245–55, and "Metaphysical Poetry and the Poetic of Correspondences," *JHI,* XIV (1953), 221–34.

[2] Helmut Hatzfeld, "A Clarification of the Baroque Problem in the Romance Literatures," *Comparative Literature,* I (1949), 115–16.

[3] This theory is advanced primarily by Rosemond Tuve, *Elizabethan and Metaphysical Imagery* (Chicago, 1946). Nelson's article on *Peter Ramus and the Confusion of Logic, Rhetoric and Poetry* is in the series "University of Michigan Contributions in Modern Philology," No. 2 (April, 1947).

[4] This view was characteristic of many humanists who were also nominalists and who therefore banished all previous metaphysical assumptions from logic. The new rhetoric-logic was to teach men how to follow in their voluntary thinking the same "natural" laws that were followed in involuntary thinking. Hence the numerous literary examples to be found in Ramist logics. However, although Ramus abandoned the old metaphysical assumptions, he reintroduced the old categories, arranging them by dichotomies in a purely arbitrary and empirical order.

[5] See René Wellek, "The Concept of Baroque in Literary Scholarship," *Journal of Aesthetics,* V (1946), 77–109, for a discussion of the concept of baroque and for a bibliography on the subject. The following treat the "metaphysical" movement or "concettismo" as a manifestation of the baroque: Benedetto Croce, *Storia della eta' barocca in Italia* (2d ed.; Bari, 1946); *Problemi di estetica* (4th ed.; Bari, 1949); *Saggi sulla letteratura italiana del seicento* (2d ed.; Bari, 1924); *Nuovi saggi sulla letteratura italiana del seicento* (Bari, 1931). Mario Praz, *Seicentismo e marinismo in Inghil-terra: John Donne—Richard Crashaw* (Florence, 1925). The studies of the two poets were reprinted separately in 1945. Also Praz, *Studies in Seventeenth-Century Imagery* (London, 1939, an Italian version of which last appeared as *Studi sul concettismo* (Florence, 1946). A companion volume to the English version of this book consisting of a bibliography of emblem books appeared in London in 1947 as Vol. II of the same title. Also see Marcellino Menéndez y Pelayo, *Historia de las ideas estéticas en España* (4th ed.; Madrid, 1928–33), Vol. II, Part II.

[6] Praz, *John Donne,* p. 7. Other works in support of the emblem theory are Rosemary Freeman, *English Emblem Books* (London, 1948); Austin Warren, *Richard Crashaw: A Study in Baroque Sensibility* (University, La., 1939); Ruth Wallerstein, *Studies in Seventeenth-Century Poetic* (Madison, 1950). Miss Wallerstein also agrees with Miss Tuve on the influence of Ramist logic.

[7] Praz, *Richard Crashaw,* pp. 114 ff. This desire to force "influences" leads Praz to find it strange that metaphysical poetry should have flourished in England, although the emblem did not have a very wide vogue there (cf. *Studi dul concettismo,* p. 202).

[8] Emmanuele Tesauro, *Il Cannochiale Aristotelico* (2d ed., 1663), chaps. xiv, xv. In these two chapters Tesauro sketched the outline of his generalized theory of wit. Cf. Croce, *Problemi di estetica,* pp. 313 ff.

[9] Warren, pp. 73–4.

[10] Ibid., p. 177.

[11] Ibid.

[12] Cf. *The Hieroglyphics of Horapollo,* trans. George Boas (New York, 1950). Mr. Boas' introduction is quite valuable. The standard work on the emblem movement is by Ludwig Volkmann, *Bilderschriften der Renaissance: Hieroglyphik und Emblematik in ihren Beziehungen und Fortwirkungen* (Leipzig, 1923). A typical late Renaissance edition of Horapollo is the work of Nicolao Caussino, *Symbolica Aegyptiorum sapientia,* together with a *Polyhistor symbolicus* (Paris, 1647). These two works, consisting of the text and translation of Horapollo, an anthology of classical remarks on symbols and hieroglyphics, and a hieroglyphic bestiary, constitute a kind of encyclopedia. The hieroglyphic-emblem movement seems to have been in part a continuation of the tradition of medieval exemplarism, especially zoölogical exemplarism. It is in this enriched form that the emblem movement reached Quarles: "Before the knowledge of letters, God was known by *Hieroglyphicks;* And, indeed, what are the Heaven, and Earth, nay every Creature, but *Hieroglyphicks* and *Emblems* of his glory" (see Francis Quarles, *Emblemes* [London, 1635], "To the Reader").

[13] Praz, *Studi sul concettismo,* pp. 49–50 n., 199–200.

[14] Michael Maier, *Atalanta fugiens* (Oppenheim, 1618). Also John Read, *Prelude to Chemistry* (New York, 1937), Chap. VI, which is on Maier. Some samples of his music in modern notation are appended to the work. For spiritual alchemy see H. Brémond, *Histoire littéraire du sentiment religieux en France* (Paris, 1925), Vol. VII, Part II, chap. v.; and Evelyn Underhill, *Mysticism* (16th ed.; New York, 1948), pp. 140 ff.

[15] Warren, p. 75.

[16] Ibid., p. 173.

J. B. LEISHMAN

Donne and Seventeenth-Century Poetry

In the historical consideration of literature there are three dangers against which we should be continually on our guard: the danger that we may lose sight of the larger differences and distinctions through concentrating too much attention upon the subsidiary ones; the danger that we may pervert these subsidiary distinctions into antitheses; the danger that within these subsidiary distinctions we may insist too much upon identity and too little upon difference. In the present field of study we have, on the one hand, heard perhaps too much of a School of Jonson and a School of Donne, of the classical and the so-called metaphysical strains in seventeenth-century poetry, and not enough of those larger differences between the characteristic non-dramatic poetry of the Age of Elizabeth and that of the Jacobean and Caroline periods, differences in which both Jonson and Donne equally share; while, on the other hand, we have had, perhaps, too many generalizations about the so-called metaphysical poets and not enough insistence on the very important differences between them. It is, indeed, easier to perceive certain obvious differences between the poetry of Donne and Jonson than to perceive certain important resemblances, just as it is easier to perceive certain superficial resemblances between, say, Donne and Crashaw than to become aware of their fundamental differences. The ultimate purpose of such generalizations, classifications and distinctions is to increase awareness, to enable us, by analysis and comparison, to achieve a clearer recog-

From *The Monarch of Wit: An Analytical and Comparative Study of the Poetry of John Donne* (London, 1951; 3rd ed., 1957), pp. 9–26. Reprinted by permission of The Hutchinson Publishing Group.

nition, a more intense appreciation, of the peculiar virtue, the essential *thisness*, of whatever literature we may be studying; this, though, is a strenuous task, and most of us, I fear, tend unconsciously to manipulate these generalizations, classifications and distinctions, disregarding here, over-emphasizing there, until we have spread over everything a veil of custom and a film of familiarity which shall save us as much as possible from the insupportable fatigue of thought. Donne has been too often considered as a so-called metaphysical poet and too little as a seventeenth-century poet (many characteristic seventeenth-century poets began to write during the reign of Elizabeth); let us begin, then, by trying to reach some not too inadequate conception of the characteristics of seventeenth-century poetry in general and of the principal differences and varieties within that fundamental identity.

That such a conception is both real and necessary is proved by the fact that the poetry of those two very individual and very different poets, Ben Jonson and John Donne, who are commonly regarded as the founders of two different schools, has many important characteristics in common. They were—to begin with an important fact which has received too little attention—they were both, in a sense, coterie-poets, poets who made their initial impact not upon the common reader but upon comparatively small circles of intellectuals and literary amateurs. Apart from his contributions to the facetious commendations of Thomas Coryat in the latter's *Crudities* (1611) and to the elegies on Prince Henry in *Lachrymae Lachrymarum* (1613), the only poems Donne printed during his life-time were the two *Anniversaries* upon the religious death of Mistris Elizabeth Drury, in 1611 and 1612. The first collected edition of his poems was not published until 1633, two years after his death, and his great reputation as a poet during his life-time was gained entirely through the circulation of his poems in manuscript. Jonson, it is true, was a much more public poet than Donne: he wrote plays, which were not only acted, but published, under very careful supervision, by himself. Nevertheless, the great body of his non-dramatic verse was not published until after his death, and he too, though less exclusively and remotely than Donne, was the master, the *arbiter elegantiarum*, of a circle, of a coterie, of various young Templars and Courtiers who gathered round him in taverns, hung upon his words, begged copies of his verses, and were proud to be known as his sons.

When we speak, as we often do, of Jonson and Donne as the two great influences on the non-dramatic poetry of the first half of the seventeenth century, and when we think, as we often do, of that poetry chiefly in its relation to either or both of them, we should not forget that we are speaking and thinking only of that portion of seventeenth-century poetry which we now chiefly read and remember, and that much even of this poetry, easy, familiar, *harmlos* (to borrow a German word) as it now seems to us, may well have seemed quite exceptionally choice and sophisticated to its writers and first readers. There are many seventeenth-century poems which may seem to us only very superficially like Donne's, but which at the time may well have seemed astonishingly *dernier cri* and quite beyond the reach of simple-minded admirers of Forests of Arden and Bowers of Bliss. Both Jonson and Donne were superior persons, and both seem to have been well aware of their superiority, but Donne, though far more urbane, was a much more superior person than Jonson, and, except superficially, much less imitable. Contemporary allusions to his poetry are few and far between, and even quite advanced men seem to have remained ignorant of it for an incredibly long time.[1] In the various miscellanies published between 1640 and 1660, whose contents seem to have been derived partly from printed texts and partly from manuscript commonplace books, and which may be regarded as reflecting fairly accurately the taste of the average cultivated gentleman of the time of Charles I, both the number of Donne's poems included and any obvious traces of his influence are remarkably small. The influence of Jonson, the epigrammatic rather than the moral Jonson, the Jonson of "Still to be neat, still to be drest," "Come my Celia, let us prove," and "If I freely may discover," is far more striking. It is in the wittily, often impudently, argumentative love-poem, and in the indecently, sometimes obscenely, witty "elegy," epigram, or paradox, that Donne's influence upon the secular poetry of the seventeenth century is chiefly apparent.[2] Such poems, though, are more frequent in the published works of particular poets (Carew, Suckling, Lovelace, Cowley), and in certain manuscript collections, than in the miscellanies, where the persistence both of the hearty Elizabethan song and of the Elizabethan pastoral tradition is far more noticeable. In the main, Donne's dialectic is simplified and his wit coarsened by his imitators. One wonders what Donne thought of them. (It must sometimes have been an embarrassment to him that, at the time when he was preaching in St. Paul's, various obscene epigrams were being handed about and attributed to "Dr. Donne.") Jonson, so often prickly and dogmatic, was probably a more indulgent parent: when he declared that "my son Cartwright writes all like a man," the modern reader finds it hard to know just what he meant, and will perhaps reflect that, after all, it's a wise father who knows his own children.

William Drummond of Hawthornden, a disciple of Spenser and of the Italians, has recorded that when Ben Jonson visited him in 1619 he told him that his poems "were all good . . . save that they smelled too much of the Schooles, and were not after the fancie of the tyme." Jonson, no doubt, was speaking for himself and for those who agreed with him, but it is really impossible to know just how many did agree with him, or to form even a rough estimate of the proportion of then readers of English poetry who shared this "fancie of the tyme." [3] In saying that the poetry of Jonson and of Donne was in a sense coterie poetry, I want to insist upon the fact that it is almost impossible to know just how far the coterie extended, whom it included, who, so to speak, were in the inner circle and who were merely on the fringe. Where fashion and mode are active the detection and disintrication of "influences" become formidably difficult. Milton admired Homer and Virgil and Ovid, Tasso and della Casa, not because anyone had told him to do so, but because he believed that was how great poetry should be written: one often feels, though, that many of his contemporaries admired Donne because to admire Donne was the done thing. Similarly, although to-day one constantly hears it said that contemporary English poets have been greatly influenced by Hopkins, by Mr. Eliot, and even by Rilke, it may well be that future generations will find the business of detecting these "influences" a most baffling task. Generalizations even about those seventeenth-century poets whose work is available in modern editions can at best be tentative. Not even the well-known poets will fit neatly into categories: even in them we encounter all manner of paradoxes and tergiversations. Cowley has related that it was the discovery of a volume of Spenser in his mother's parlour that made him irrecoverably a poet; when, however, he went out into the world he discovered that not Spenser but Donne was the man, and set himself to imitate Donne—"to a fault," as Dryden said, who himself confessed that Cowley had been the darling of his youth. When, though, one turns from the poets whose works are available in modern editions to the miscellanies and manuscript commonplace books of the age, the task of generalizing about seventeenth-century poetry, seventeenth-century taste, and seventeenth-century sensibility seems almost impossible. If I am now attempting to generalize myself, it is with an almost overwhelming conviction of the vanity of dogmatizing.

Each of these two very characteristic seventeenth-century poets, Jonson and Donne, was born during the reign of Elizabeth, and each had begun to establish his reputation during the last decade of the sixteenth century. Nevertheless, great as are the differences between them, the poetry of each has more in common with that of the other than it has with the poetry of Spenser, or of the Sonneteers, or with the lyrics in the song-books, or with such poems as *Venus and Adonis* and *The Rape of Lucrece*. On the one hand, neither Jonson nor Donne seems ever to have shared the ambition of Spenser and of several of Spenser's disciples to write a large-scale heroic or narrative poem. On the other hand, they both took the short poem more seriously than the typical Elizabethan poets did. Even if one leaves out of account the great mass of utterly undistinguished Elizabethan lyric, where the same rhymes, phrases, and properties appear over and over again with wearisome iteration, where nymphs and swains on the plains trip at leisure in a measure, view with pleasure Flora's treasure in meadows fresh and gay where fleecy lambs do play, weave in bowers crowns of flowers, or where fountains spring from mountains sigh and languish in their anguish—even if one forgets what the great majority of the poems (including Spenser's and Sidney's) in say, *Englands Helicon,* are really like—even if one confines oneself to the long-sifted contents of modern anthologies, one often feels that even the best Elizabethan poets just tossed off their delightful lyrics: partly, perhaps, because they were generally intended to be sung and therefore ought not to be too weighty or condensed. And one's general impression of the Elizabethan sonneteers is that they wrote too many sonnets and wrote them too easily. Jonson's foolish Matheo in *Every Man in His Humour* would, when melancholy, "write you your halfe score or your dozen of sonnets at a sitting." Both Jonson and Donne seem to have set a new fashion of writing short but very concentrated poems—Donne's always and Jonson's often intended to be handed round in manuscript and admired by connoisseurs. For it cannot be too strongly insisted that most of what we now chiefly remember of the non-dramatic poetry of the first half of the seventeenth century was poetry that for years had been circulating in manuscript before it finally found its way into print, while most of the non-dramatic poets who were publishing were either belated Elizabethans or pertinacious disciples of Spenser, and were regarded by the young intellectuals of the Court, the Inns of Court, and the Universities as old-fashioned and out of date. (One can go a good way towards "placing" the younger Milton among his contemporaries by saying that for him neither the *Faerie Queene* nor Ovid's *Metamorphoses* was out of date.) It is significant and almost symbolic that that grand old Elizabethan, Michael Drayton, who was born a year earlier than Shakespeare and who lived and wrote and published until 1631, should have twice rather bitterly and contemptuously protested against this new fashion for short poems circulated in manuscript. In 1612, in the Preface to the first part of his immense *Poly-olbion,* that "chorographical description of all the tracts, rivers, mountains, forests, and other parts of this renowned isle of Great Britain," he declared that

> in publishing this Essay of my Poeme, there is this great disaduantage against me; that it commeth out at this time, when Verses are wholly deduc't to Chambers, and nothing esteem'd in this lunatique Age, but what is kept in Cabinets, and must only passe by Transcription;

and in his *Epistle to Henry Reynolds, Esquire, of Poets and Poesie,* published in 1627, after reaching the end of his description of English poets from Chaucer to the two Beaumonts and William Browne, he added that he was not concerned with those poets who were too proud to publish and who chose to be known only through the circulation of their poems in manuscript.

Jonson, as I have admitted, was a less exclusive, a more public, poet than Donne, but he too wrote what he most valued for an audience fit though few. Spenser, one might almost say, wrote for all who cared for poetry at all; both Jonson and Donne wrote very emphatically for those who knew what was what. There is some analogy, though only a slight one, between the literary situation then and that which exists to-day; there was something, though only something, of the same gulf between "serious" and "popular" poetry. The position of Spenser had been in some ways similar to that of Tennyson; the position of Jonson and Donne was in some ways similar to that of Mr. Eliot. The Jacobean intellectuals, or some of them, reacted against the Elizabethans somewhat as the inter-war intellectuals did against the Victorians. This analogy, though, must not be pressed too far: [4] it is sufficient to insist that much of the most memorable non-dramatic poetry of the first half of the seventeenth century, a poetry very greatly influenced by the example of either Jonson or Donne or both, is a more exclusive and critical and intellectual kind of poetry than that which is typically Elizabethan. The phrase "strong-lined" is often used by seventeenth-century writers to describe the new qualities which they admired in the poetry both of Jonson and of Donne: something close-packed and strenuous, requiring some effort and connoisseurship to appreciate it, as distinguished from the easily appreciated, "the soft, melting and diffuse style of the Spenserians." [5] The facts, not merely that no one has ever thought of calling Jonson a metaphysical poet, but that his poetry shares many typical seventeenth-century characteristics with

Donne's, should suggest to us that it is worth while to try to consider Donne more as a typical seventeenth-century or "strong-lined" poet, and less as a so-called metaphysical one.

Jonson addressed two very encomiastic epigrams to Donne (xxiii and xcvi), as well as one (xciv) commending a manuscript of his Satires to the Countess of Bedford, and Donne, who never condescended to praise any other contemporary poet, contributed some very flattering Latin verses to the quarto edition of Jonson's *Volpone*. They had, indeed, much in common. Both, one might almost say, wrote as though Spenser had never lived: Spenser's national and patriotic strain, his Platonic idealism, his elaborate description, his amplification and ornamentation—all these find no place in their verse. They rejected too what one may call the Petrarchan tradition, the too often merely extravagant and conventional adoration of the sonneteers, and they rejected the elaborate and mainly frigid decoration of such poems as *Venus and Adonis* and *The Rape of Lucrece*. Both insisted on what Jonson called "language such as men do use," and would have disagreed with Gray and agreed with Wordsworth (in theory, though not always in practice) that there should be no essential difference between the diction of poetry and that of conversation. Both wrote much poetry that was satirical and realistic. Both—a very notable characteristic of the typical seventeenth-century as distinguished from the typical Elizabethan lyrist—stamped an image of themselves upon nearly all they wrote; for, while one of the chief characteristics of the Elizabethan lyric is a certain anonymousness, the song rather than the singer, seventeenth-century lyrists, as Professor Moorman has observed, lyrists otherwise so different as Crashaw, Vaughan, Suckling or Herrick, "whether their poetry be intense or not, stand revealed to us in what they write." Finally—to conclude this brief review of affinities—both Jonson and Donne wrote poems more sequacious, organic and untransposable than their predecessors, although with Donne this new sense of structure seems to have been stimulated by scholastic logic, with Jonson by the example of the classical lyric.

Seventeenth-century poetry, then, or much of seventeenth-century poetry, is colloquial in diction, undecorative and untraditional in imagery, dispensing with what Carew, in his elegy on Donne, called

> the goodly exil'd traine
> Of gods and goddesses, which in thy just raigne
> Were banish'd nobler Poems,

personal in tone and logical in structure. In these respects both Jonson and Donne are characteristic seventeenth-century poets. "But," some readers may be inclined to ask at this point, "what about Donne's metaphysics, what about his famous metaphysical wit?" In the pages that follow I shall hope to demonstrate, among other things, first, that Donne is certainly not a metaphysical poet in the wider sense of being a philosophic one; secondly, that although, in the narrower sense which Dryden had in mind when he declared that Donne "affected the metaphysics," he does indeed occasionally draw illustrations and analogies from the realms of philosophy, theology, and popular science, what, probably, most readers have in mind when they call him a metaphysical poet is an often syllogistic argumentation and argumentativeness which might, however, be more appropriately called scholastic or dialectical than metaphysical; thirdly, that in almost all Donne's best poetry there is a dramatic element, an element of personal drama, which is no less characteristic than the argumentative, scholastic or dialectical strain; and fourthly, closely connected with this element of drama, that there is in many of his poems a very strong element of sheer wit and paradox. Now if one regards Donne's poetry chiefly in this way, as what I have called the dialectical expression of personal drama, one will, I think perceive more clearly what are the really important resemblances and differences, on the one hand, between his poetry and that of other so-called metaphysical poets, and, on the other hand, between his poetry and that of Jonson and of poets who are commonly regarded as belonging to the School of Jonson. What, looked at in one way, seem differences in kind appear, when looked at in another way, to be rather differences in degree. The important thing, perhaps, is to decide which is the right way of looking, which is the viewpoint which will enable us to distinguish rightly between differences in degree and differences in kind, and to decide precisely at what point differences which at first seem merely differences in degree pass into differences in kind.

Consider, for example, the stylistic relationship between Herbert and Donne: the best poetry of both might equally well be described as the dialectical expression of personal drama. Herbert, like Donne, can make the purest poetry out of almost bare argument, and Herbert's expression of his relationship to God is no less dramatic than Donne's expression of various imaginary relationships with women and of his actual relationship with his wife; true though it be that Donne's dialectic is more ingenious than Herbert's and his analogies more various and, as it often seems to us, more far-fetched, and although in much of Donne's poetry there is an element of sheer invention, sheer wit and sheer paradox which we do not find in Herbert's. How much of the poetry of other so-called metaphysical poets may be appropriately described as the dialectical expression of personal drama? Certainly Marvell's *To his Coy Mistress* and *The Definition of Love,* although in most of Marvell's poetry the dialectical element is more apparent than the dramatic, and although the *Horatian Ode* is nearer to Jonson's kind of poetry than to Donne's. Crashaw's poetry is personal and often dramatic, but is it dialectical? Vaughan's poetry is personal, but less intimately so than Herbert's; dialectical, but less tightly and consistently so than Herbert's; occasionally, but not pervasively, dramatic, and with a strong element of vision and visual imagery that is found neither in Herbert's poetry nor in Donne's.

Now, on the other hand, between Donne's kind of poetry and Jonson's, which are the differences in degree and which are the differences in kind? Although the differences between Donne's kind of poetry and Jonson's are greater than those between Donne's kind of poetry and Herbert's, although very little, if any, of Jonson's poetry could be described as the dialectical expression of personal drama, and although the element of sheer wit is as absent from Jonson's poetry (though Jonson could admire it in Donne's) as it is from Herbert's, there still remain many differences which may perhaps be profitably regarded as differences within a fundamental identity, that, namely, of seventeenth-century poetry in general, differences in degree rather than in kind. Both Donne's language and Jonson's language is colloquial, "language such as men do use," but Donne's is more defiantly and resolutely colloquial. Jonson's poetry, in comparison with the typical Elizabethan lyric or with Spenser or with the sonneteers, is free from decoration, but Jonson does not exile the gods and goddesses so rigorously or reject the whole apparatus of classical mythology and allusion so utterly and consistently as Donne. Jonson's lyrics, in comparison with typical Elizabethan lyrics, are organic and untransposable, but they are seldom so rigorously logical, so capable of prose-analysis, as Donne's, Donne's dialectical method here introducing what almost amounts to a difference in kind. And although, in comparison with the anonymity of the typical Elizabethan lyric, Jonson's lyrics are personal and individual, they are so rather in the way in which Horace's Odes are so than in the way in which Donne's poems are. The style and tone are individual, but, as with Horace, never, or very seldom, eccentrically and unclassically individual, and the matter, as with Horace, is essentially public, "what oft was thought, though ne'er so well expressed."

Indeed, the idea or ideal of the kind of poetry that Jonson most wanted to write and was continually trying to write, a poetry memorably expressing that "high and noble matter" of which he spoke in his

Epistle *To Elizabeth Countesse of Rutland,* has been, I cannot but think, most perfectly realized in some of Horace's Odes. Were I limited to the choice of one ode which should represent as completely as possible both the manner and the matter of the graver Horace, I think I should choose the sixteenth of his Second Book, of which I here offer a translation "according to the Latin measure, as near as the language will permit":

Peace is what one, caught on the open sea, will
beg of heav'n above when the sombre storm clouds
hide the moon, and stars are no longer certain
guides for the sailor.

Peace the savage fighters of Thracia pray for,
peace, the Mede resplendent with broidered quiver,
peace, unbought, dear Grosphus, with proffered gold or
purple or jewels.

Ah, for neither treasure nor lictors bearing
rods before a Consul can check the spirit's
wretched civil strife or the cares that circle
costliest ceilings.

Well can fare on little, his humble table's
brightest piece of plate the ancestral salt-dish
one of whose light sleep not a fear or sordid
wish has deprived him.

Why, with such short span, do we so contend for
large possessions? Why do we seek for countries
warmed with other suns? Has an exile ever
quitted himself then?

Sickly Care can clamber aboard the brass-bound
galleys, keep abreast of the knightly riders,
swifter far than stags or the cloud-compelling
easterly breezes.

Let the soul, content with the present, scorn to
reck what lies beyond, and with smiles attemper
things that taste but sourly. From ev'ry aspect
nothing is perfect.

Early death removed the renowned Achilles,
age prolonged left little to cheer Tithonus;
me perhaps some blessing denied to you some
hour will have granted.

Flocks in hundreds bleat and Sicilian cattle
low around your folds, in the stables whinny
chariot-racing horses, and doubly-dyed in
African purple

glows the wool you're clad with; to me, with small
domain, the subtle spirit of Grecian Muses
came as Fate's mixed gift, and a soul aloof from
envious throngers.

It was, I say, towards poetry of this kind, individual indeed, but both in manner and in matter essentially public and classical, a poetry of statement and of weighty generalization, that Jonson was continually striving. I need not multiply examples: consider the concluding lines of *To the World: A farewell for a Gentle-woman, vertuous and noble:*

My tender, first, and simple yeeres
  Thou did'st abuse, and then betray;
Since stird'st vp iealousies and feares,
  When all the causes were away.
Then, in a soile hast planted me,
  Where breathe the basest of thy fooles;
Where enuious arts professed be,
  And pride, and ignorance the schooles,
Where nothing is examin'd, weigh'd,
  But, as 'tis rumor'd, so beleeu'd:
Where euery freedome is betray'd,
  And euery goodnesse tax'd, or grieu'd.
But, what we'are borne for, we must beare:
  Our fraile condition it is such,
That, what to all may happen here,
  If't chance to me, I must not grutch.
Else, I my state should much mistake,
  To harbour a diuided thought
From all my kinde: that, for my sake,
  There should a miracle be wrought.
No, I doe know, that I was borne

To age, misfortune, sicknesse, griefe:
But I will beare these, with that scorne,
As shall not need thy false reliefe.
Nor for my peace will I goe farre,
As wandrers doe, that still doe rome,
But make my strengths, such as they are,
Here in my bosome, and at home.

Or consider one of the most Horatian, I might almost say, one of the most Roman, things Jonson ever wrote, the verses *To Sir Robert Wroth,* penetrated with that characteristically Roman reverence for the traditional pursuits and festivals of the countryman which recurs so often, and with equal spontaneity, in the poems of Jonson's disciple Herrick. After describing, in magnificently animated and colourful verse, the varied activities of the estate and the hospitality of its owner, Jonson concludes with a passage which, in part at any rate, is no less Virgilian than Horatian, and which was probably inspired by some famous lines at the end of Virgil's second Georgic:

Let others watch in guiltie armes, and stand
The furie of a rash command,
Goe enter breaches, meet the cannons rage,
That they may sleepe with scarres in age.
And shew their feathers shot, and cullors torne,
And brag, that they were therefore borne.
Let this man sweat, and wrangle at the barre,
For euery price, in euery iarre,
And change possessions, oftner with his breath,
Then either money, warre, or death:
Let him, then hardest sires, more disinherit,
And each where boast it as his merit,
To blow vp orphanes, widdowes, and their states;
And thinke his power doth equall *Fates*.
Let that goe heape a masse of wretched wealth,
Purchas'd by rapine, worse then stealth,
And brooding o're it sit, with broadest eyes,
Not doing good, scarce when he dyes.
Let thousands more goe flatter vice, and winne,
By being organes to great sinne,
Get place, and honor, and be glad to keepe
The secrets, that shall breake their sleepe:
And, so they ride in purple, eate in plate,

Though poyson, thinke it a great fate.
But thou, my WROTH, if I can truth apply,
Shalt neither that, nor this enuy:
Thy peace is made; and, when man's state is well,
'Tis better, if he there can dwell.
God wisheth, none should wracke on a strange shelfe:
To him, man's dearer then t'himselfe.
And, howsoeuer we may thinke things sweet,
He alwayes giues what he knowes meet;
Which who can vse is happy: Such be thou.
Thy morning's and thy euening's vow
Be thankes to him, and earnest prayer, to finde
A body sound, with sounder minde;
To doe thy countrey seruice, thy selfe right;
That neither want doe thee affright,
Nor death; but when thy latest sand is spent,
Thou maist thinke life, a thing but lent.

It is in what may be called, in a wide sense, his moral poetry, that portion of his non-dramatic verse which is still far less widely known than it deserves to be, that Jonson is most fundamentally akin to Horace and, at the same time, most representative of one of the most characteristic strains in seventeenth-century and Augustan verse. From Wotton's

How happy is he born and taught
That serveth not another's will

to the youthful Pope's

Happy the man whose wish and care
A few paternal acres bound,
Content to breathe his native air
In his own ground

how much of the morality, one might almost say, how much of the religion, of English poets seems almost indistinguishable from that blend of Stoicism and Epicureanism which has been so perfectly expressed by Horace! How often we find it, the disintrication of the mean from its extremes, the exposure and rebuke of immoderate ambitions and desires and of every kind of too-muchness, the praise of moderate hospitality, of good talk and good wine, of the healthfulness of country life as distinguished from that of the city and the court, the celebration of antique virtue and simplicity—these, together with exhortations not to be too cast down by grief or ill-fortune, but to recognize and accept the conditions of human life.[6]

Although they both share in varying degrees those common characteristics of seventeenth-century poetry in general which I have tried to indicate, there is a very great difference, a difference not merely in degree but in kind, between Donne's exercises in sheer wit, Donne's dialectical expression of personal drama, and that essentially classical and public poetry towards which Jonson was always striving. Jonson's most memorable lines (often adapted from classical authors) are weighty and general:

> Men have beene great, but never good by chance.[7]
>
> Man may securely sinne, but safely never.[8]
>
> A good *Poet's* made, as well as borne.[9]
>
> 'Tis wisdom, and that high,
> For men to use their fortune reverently,
> Even in youth.[10]

Donne's most memorable lines are personal and dramatic:

> I wonder by my troth, what thou, and I
> Did, till we lov'd? [11]
>
> For Godsake hold your tongue, and let me love.[12]
>
> If yet I have not all thy love,
> Deare, I shall never have it all.[13]

Donne's style and manner are not only individual, but, in comparison with Horace's or Jonson's, eccentrically and unclassically individual. And as for the matter of his poetry, where he is being mainly witty and paradoxical, it is public only in the sense that we can imagine its being publicly recited and enjoyed in companies whose conceptions of wit, whose tastes, in comparison with Horace's or Pope's or Dr. Johnson's (for Ben Jonson, although his own practice was very different, could admire Donne's wit), were eccentric and unclassical. Where, on the other hand, Donne is being serious, or mainly serious, the matter of his poetry, in comparison with that of Ben Jonson or Horace, is essentially private, not "What oft was thought, though ne'er so well expressed," but something "seldom thought and seldom so expressed." A. N. Whitehead once defined religion as "What the individual does with his own solitariness": [14] nearly all Donne's serious poetry, his love-poetry no less than his religious poetry, and nearly all Herbert's poetry and Vaughan's, is in this sense essentially, not merely nominally, religious, is a record of what the poet has been doing with his solitariness. This solitariness, this privateness, this self-containedness, this, together with the often dialectical and dramatic expression of it, is, it seems to me, the most important difference between the serious poetry of Donne and the so-called Metaphysical School and that of Jonson and the Classical or Horatian School.

NOTES

[1] All hitherto known contemporary allusions to Donne's poetry have recently been collected (together with many discoveries of his own) by Mr. W. Milgate in a series of articles now appearing in *Notes and Queries* (27th May, 10th June, 8th July, 1950). Perhaps the most remarkable result of these investigations is their revelation of the extreme scarcity and comparative lateness of any definite allusions to Donne's lyrics. Round about 1606 or 1608 Francis Davison, editor of the *Poetical Rapsody* (1602), was compiling a list of "Manuscripts to gett," and he noted, among other things, "Satyres, Elegies, Epigrams etc. by John Don. q[re]. some from Eleaz. Hodgson, and Ben: Johnson." Thus as late as 1606 or 1608 even so enthusiastic a poetry-lover as Francis Davison does not seem to have known (except, possibly, as an "etc.") that Donne had written lyrics. The first certainly dateable evidence that Donne's lyrics were in circulation is a setting of *The Expiration* in Alfonso Ferrabosco's *Book of Ayres,* 1609; the first reference to a (manuscript) "book" of "Jhone Dones lyriques" occurs in a list made by William Drummond of Hawthornden of books read by him during the year 1613. It was, as might be expected, for his Satires and Epigrams, those of his poems least unlike what many of his contemporaries were doing, and, to a lesser extent, for his Elegies (for which, it may be suggested, Marlowe's translation of Ovid's *Amores* had prepared the ground) that Donne was first admired. No surviving manuscript collection of his poetry bears an earlier date than 1620. Indeed, it was during the late 1620's and the 1630's that most of the surviving seventeenth-century manuscript commonplace books (private anthologies, one might call them), which in various ways owe so much to Donne, were put together. It would seem to have been during those years that the change of taste rather splenetically alluded to by Drayton in the Preface to the first part of his *Poly-olbion* (1612) became really widely diffused, at any rate among courtiers and university men, and that Ben Jonson was being in some sort its spokesman when, in 1619, he told Drummond that his poems were "not after the fancie of the tyme." It would seem to have been during these years that, among what one may call the literary amateurs, Donne's reputation and influence were at their height. Nevertheless, in discussing seventeenth-century poetic taste and the history of poetic reputations during that period, it seems necessary to make some distinction between what I have called literary amateurs and common readers. In a very important letter to the *Review of English*

Studies (January, 1946), occasioned by Dr. Percy Simpson's review of Professor G. E. Bentley's *Shakespeare and Jonson. Their Reputations in the Seventeenth Century Compared,* Dr. W. W. Greg suggested that, if the bibliographical evidence were placed beside that of literary allusion, the conclusion would seem to be that, while writers praised Jonson, readers read Shakespeare. In these matters it is very necessary to know, not merely who is speaking, but who he is speaking *for*. The great admirers of Donne were nearly all men who were accustomed to write a little poetry themselves, even if no more than an occasional eulogy or elegy.

[2] His influence in a narrower and more specialized field, that of eulogy and funeral elegy (or, as he himself would have called it, "epicede"), was perhaps still more immediate and decisive. Poems of this kind, though, are more frequent in the manuscript commonplace books than in the miscellanies, except in such essentially academic miscellanies as *Parnassus Biceps.*

[3] In an undated letter to the physician and celebrated Latin poet, Dr. Arthur Johnston, published in the folio edition of his *Works* (1711, p. 143), Drummond has expressed his own opinion of a certain "fancie of the tyme." Although (as we shall see later) he admired Donne as an "epigrammatist" and praised his Second Elegy, *The Anagram,* it is almost impossible not to suppose that Drummond is here alluding to Donne and to some of Donne's imitators. The letter begins abruptly with a Sidneian encomium on the antiquity and dignity of poetry, and then proceeds as follows: "In vain have some Men of late (Transformers of every Thing) consulted upon her Reformation, and endeavoured to abstract her to *Metaphysical* Idea's, and *Scholastical* Quiddities, denuding her of her own Habits, and those Ornaments with which she hath amused the World some Thousand Years. *Poesy* is not a Thing that is yet in the finding and search, or which may be otherwise found out, being already condescended upon by all Nations, and as it were established *jure Gentium,* amongst *Greeks, Romans, Italians, French, Spaniards.* Neither do I think that a good Piece of *Poesy,* which *Homer, Virgil, Ovid, Petrarch, Bartas, Ronsard, Boscan, Garcilasso* (if they were alive, and had that Language) could not understand, and reach the Sense of the Writer. Suppose these Men could find out some other new *Idea* like *Poesy,* it should be held as if Nature should bring forth some new *Animal,* neither Man, Horse, Lyon, Dog, but which had some Members of all, if they had been proportionably and by right Symmetry set together. What is not like the Ancients and conform to those Rules which hath been agreed unto by all Times, may (indeed) be something like unto *Poesy,* but it is no more *Poesy* than a Monster is a Man. Monsters breed Admiration at the First, but have ever some strange Loathsomness in them at last." Milton would probably have subscribed to every word of this.

[4] The chief danger of such analogies is that they tend to make us forget what I may call the Elizabethan time-scale and the fact that scarcely anything of what now seems to us most memorable in Elizabethan poetry

and drama had been published or acted before the last decade of the sixteenth century. So far as we know, with the possible exception of Kyd's *Spanish Tragedy,* Marlowe's *Tamburlaine* (1587) was the first serious blank-verse drama to be acted on a public stage: some ten years later Shakespeare, who, like so many others, had begun by not very successfully attempting to imitate the "mighty line" and the "great and thundering speech," was already parodying them through the mouth of Ancient Pistol. When we speak of a "reaction" against Spenser or against the sonneteers we tend, perhaps, to convey the impression that Jonson and Donne had been brought up on the *Faerie Queene* and on sonnet-sequences, had been cloyed and surfeited with them, whereas in fact it was rather a case of dislike at first sight. The first three books of the *Faerie Queene* were not published until 1590, and the remaining three books not until 1596. The first Elizabethan sonnet-sequence, Thomas Watson's Ἑκατομπαθία, containing a hundred eighteen-line "sonnets," was published in 1582, but sonnet-sequences did not become the rage or the fashion until the publication of Sidney's *Astrophel and Stella* in 1591; then followed (to mention only the most famous) Daniel's *Delia* and Constable's *Diana* in 1592, Drayton's *Idea* in 1594, Spenser's *Amoretti* in 1595.

One may perhaps describe the situation with some approximation to truth by saying that the poetry of Spenser, of Jonson and of Donne and of their several disciples and imitators was all simultaneously competing for public favour, but that during the first half of the seventeenth century, among the more intellectual and sophisticated, the examples of Jonson and of Donne on the whole prevailed.

When we speak of nineteenth- or twentieth-century literary "movements" or "reactions," we are generally thinking in terms of generations; if we transfer these phrases to the Elizabethan literary scene we must learn to think in terms of a few years, or even, sometimes, of a few months.

[5] See an article by G. Williamson, "Strong Lines," in *English Studies,* 1936, 152 ff.

[6] There is, of course, another way of looking at the matter, which may be suggested by the following entry in the Diary of John Manningham, of the Middle Temple, under 12th February, 1602: "Ben Jonson the poet nowe lives upon one Townesend and scornes the world. (*Tho: Overbury.*)" ed. Bruce, Camden Society, p. 130.

[7] *An Epistle to Sir Edward Sacvile,* l. 124.

[8] *Epode,* "Not to know vice at all."

[9] *To the Memory of my beloved, the Author Mr. William Shakespeare.*

[10] *An Ode,* "High-spirited friend."

[11] *The good-morrow.*

[12] *The Canonization.*

[13] *Lovers infinitenesse.*

[14] *Religion in the Making,* 1927, p. 6.

C. S. LEWIS

Donne and Love Poetry in the Seventeenth Century

Little of Manfred (but not very much of him)
W. S. GILBERT.

I have seen an old history of literature in which the respective claims of Shelley and Mrs. Hemans to be the greatest lyrist of the nineteenth century were seriously weighed; and Donne, who was so inconsiderable fifty years ago, seems at the moment to rank among our greatest poets.

If there were no middle state between absolute certainty and what Mr. Kellett calls the whirligig of taste, these fluctuations would make us throw up criticism in despair. But where it is impossible to go quite straight we may yet resolve to reel as little as we can. Such phenomena as the present popularity of Donne or the growing unpopularity of Milton are not to be deplored; they are rather to be explained. It is not impossible to see why Donne's poetry should be overrated in the twentieth and underrated in the eighteenth century; and in so far as we detect these temporary disturbing factors and explain the varying appearances of the object by the varying positions of the observers, we shall come appreciably nearer to a glimpse of Donne *simpliciter*. I shall concern myself in what follows chiefly with his love poetry.

In style this poetry is primarily a development of one of the two

From *Seventeenth Century Studies Presented to Sir Herbert Grierson* (Oxford, 1938), pp. 64–84. Reprinted by permission of The Clarendon Press.

styles which we find in the work of Donne's immediate predecessors. One of these is the mellifluous, luxurious, "builded rhyme," as in Spenser's *Amoretti:* the other is the abrupt, familiar, and consciously "manly" style in which nearly all Wyatt's lyrics are written. Most of the better poets make use of both, and in *Astrophel and Stella* much of Sidney's success depends on deliberate contrast between such poetry as

> That golden sea whose waves in curls are broken

and such poetry as

> He cannot love: no, no, let him alone.

But Wyatt remains, if not the finest, yet much the purest example of the plainer manner, and in reading his songs, with their conversational openings, their surly (not to say sulky) defiances, and their lack of obviously poetic ornament, I find myself again and again reminded of Donne. But of course he is a Donne with most of the genius left out. Indeed, the first and most obvious achievement of the younger poet is to have raised this kind of thing to a much higher power; to have kept the vividness of conversation where Wyatt too often had only the flatness; to sting like a lash where Wyatt merely grumbled. The difference in degree between the two poets thus obscures the similarity in kind. Donne has so far surpassed not only Wyatt but all the Elizabethans in what may be called their Wyatt moments, and has so generally abstained from attempting to rival them in their other vein, that we hardly think of him as continuing one side of their complex tradition; he appears rather as the innovator who substituted a realistic for a decorated kind of love poetry.

Now this error is not in itself important. In an age which was at all well placed for judging the comparative merits of the two styles, it would not matter though we thought that Donne had invented what in fact he only brought to perfection. But our own age is not so placed. The mellifluous style, which we may agree to call Petrarchan though no English poet is very like Petrarch, has really no chance of a fair hearing. It is based on a conception of poetry wholly different from that of the twentieth century. It descends from old Provençal and Italian sources and presupposes a poetic like that of Dante. Dante, we may remember, thinks of poetry as something to be made, to be "adorned as much as possible," to have its "true sense" hidden beneath a rich vesture of "rhetorical colouring." The "Petrarchan" sonneteers are not trying to make their work sound like the speaking voice. They are not trying to communicate faithfully the raw, the merely natural, impact of actual passion. The passion for them is not a specimen of "nature" to be followed so much as a lump of ore to be refined: they ask themselves not "How can I record it with the least sophistication?" but "Of its bones what coral can I make?", and to accuse them of insincerity is like calling an oyster insincere because it makes its disease into a pearl. The aim of the other style is quite different. It wishes to be convincing, intimate, naturalistic. It would be very foolish to set up these two kinds of poetry as rivals, for obviously they are different and both are good. It is a fine thing to hear the living voice, the voice of a man like ourselves, whispering or shouting to us from the printed page with all the heat of life; and it is a fine thing, too, to see such life—so pitiably like our own, I doubt not, in the living—caught up and transfigured, sung by the voice of a god into an ecstasy no less real though in another dimension.[1] There is no necessary quarrel between the two. But there are many reasons why one of them should start with overwhelming odds in its favour at the present moment. For many years our poetics have been becoming more and more expressionistic. First came Wordsworth with his theory, and we have never quite worked it out of our system; even in the crude form that "you should write as you talk," it works at the back of much contemporary criticism. Then came the final break-up of aristocracy and the consequent, and still increasing, distaste for arduous disciplines of sentiment —the wholesale acceptance of the merely and unredeemedly natural. Finally, the psychological school of criticism overthrew what was left of the old conception of a poem as a construction and set up instead the poem as "document." In so far as we admire Donne for being our first great practitioner in one of the many possible kinds of lyric, we are on firm ground; but the conception of him as liberator, as one who substituted "real" or "live" or "sincere" for "artificial" or "conventional" love lyric, begs all the questions and is simply a prejudice *de siècle*.

But of course when we have identified the Wyatt element in Donne, we have still a very imperfect notion of his manner. We have described "Busie old foole" and "I wonder by my troth" and "For Godsake hold your tongue, and let me love"; but we have left out the cleaving remora, the triple soul, the stiff twin compasses, and a hundred other things that were not in Wyatt. There were indeed a great many things not in Wyatt, and his manly plainness can easily be over-praised— "pauper videri Cinna vult et est pauper." If Donne had not reinforced the style with new attractions it would soon have died of very simplicity. An account of these reinforcements will give us a rough notion of the unhappily named "metaphysical" manner.

The first of them is the multiplication of conceits—not conceits of any special "metaphysical" type but conceits such as we find in all the Elizabethans. When Donne speaks of the morning coming from his mistress's eyes, or tells how they wake him like the light of a taper, these fanciful hyperboles are not, in themselves, a novelty. But, side by side with these, we find, as his second characteristic, what may be called the difficult conceit. This is clearly a class which no two readers will fill up in quite the same way. An example of what I mean comes at the end of *The Sunne Rising* where the sun is congratulated on the fact that the two lovers have shortened his task for him. Even the quickest reader will be checked, if only for an infinitesimal time, before he sees how and why the lovers have done this, and will experience a kind of astonished relief at the unexpected answer. The pleasure of the thing, which can be paralleled in other artistic devices, perhaps in rhyme itself, would seem to depend on recurrent tension and relaxation. In the third place, we have Donne's characteristic choice of imagery. The Petrarchans (I will call them so for convenience) had relied for their images mainly on mythology and on natural objects. Donne uses both of these sparingly—though his sea that "Leaves embroider'd works upon the sand" is as fine an image from nature as I know—and taps new sources such as law, science, philosophy, and the commonplaces of urban life. It is this that has given the Metaphysicals their name and been much misunderstood. When Johnson said that they were resolved to show their learning he said truth in fact, for there is an element of pedantry, of dandyism, an *odi profanos* air, about Donne—the old printer's address not to the *readers* but to the *understanders* is illuminating. But Johnson was none the less misleading. He encouraged the idea that the abstruse nature of some of Donne's similes was poetically relevant for good or ill. In fact, of course, when we have once found out what Donne is talking about—that is, when Sir Herbert Grierson has told us—the learning of the poet becomes unimportant. The image will stand or fall like any other by its intrinsic merit—its power of conveying a meaning "more luminously and with a sensation of delight." The matter is worth mentioning only because Donne's reputation in this respect repels some humble readers and attracts some prigs. What is important for criticism is his avoidance of the obviously poetical image; whether the intractable which he is determined to poetize is fetched from Thomas Aquinas or from the London underworld, the method is essentially the same. Indeed it would be easy to exaggerate the amount of learned imagery in his poems and even the amount of his learning. He knows much, but he seems to know even more because his knowledge so seldom overlaps with our own;

and some scraps of his learning, such as that of angelic consciousness or of the three souls in man, come rather too often—like the soldiers in a stage army, and with the same result. This choice of imagery is closely connected with the surprising and ingenious nature of the connexions which Donne makes between the image and the matter in hand, thus getting a double surprise. No one, in the first place, expects lovers to be compared to compasses; and no one, even granted the comparison, would guess in what respect they are going to be compared.

But all these characteristics, in their mere enumeration, are what Donne would have called a "ruinous anatomie." They might all be used—indeed they all are used by Herbert—to produce a result very unlike Donne's. What gives their peculiar character to most of the *Songs and Sonets* is that they are dramatic in the sense of being addressed to an imagined hearer in the heat of an imagined conversation, and usually addresses of a violently argumentative character. The majority of lyrics, even where nominally addressed to a god, a woman, or a friend, are meditations or introspective narratives. Thus Herbert's "Throw away thy rod" is formally an apostrophe; in fact, it is a picture of Herbert's own state of mind. But the majority of the *Songs and Sonets,* including some that are addressed to abstractions like Love, present the poet's state of mind only indirectly and are ostensibly concerned with badgering, wheedling, convincing, or upbraiding an imagined hearer. No poet, not even Browning, buttonholes us or, as we say, "goes for" us like Donne. There are, of course, exceptions. *Goe and catche a falling starre*, though it is in the form of an address, has not this effect; and *Twicknam Garden* or the *Nocturnall* are in fact, as well as in pretension, soliloquies. These exceptions include some of Donne's best work; and indeed, one of the errors of contemporary criticism, to my mind, is an insufficient distinction between Donne's best and Donne's most characteristic. But I do not at present wish to emphasize this. For the moment it is enough to notice that the majority of his love lyrics, and of the *Elegies,* are of the type I have described. And since they are, nearly always, in the form of arguments, since they attempt to extort something from us, they are poetry of an extremely exacting kind. This exacting quality, this urgency and pressure of the poet upon the reader in every line, seems to me to be the root both of Donne's weakness and his strength. When the thing fails it exercises the same dreadful fascination that we feel in the grip of the worst kind of bore—the hot-eyed, unescapable kind. When it succeeds it produces a rare intensity in our enjoyment—which is what a modern critic meant (I fancy) when he claimed that Donne made all other poetry sound less "serious." The point is worth investigation.

For, of course, in one sense these poems are not serious at all. Poem after poem consists of extravagant conceits woven into the preposterous semblance of an argument. The preposterousness is the point. Donne intends to take your breath away by the combined subtlety and impudence of the steps that lead to his conclusion. Any attempt to overlook Donne's "wit" in this sense, or to pretend that his rare excursions into the direct expression of passion are typical, is false criticism. The paradox, the surprise, are essential; if you are not enjoying these you are not enjoying what Donne intended. Thus *Womans Constancy* is of no interest as a document of Donne's "cynicism"—any fool can be promiscuously unchaste and any fool can say so. The merit of the poem consists in the skill with which it leads us to expect a certain conclusion and then gives us precisely the opposite conclusion, and that, too, with an appearance of reasonableness. Thus, again, the art of *The Will* consists in keeping us guessing through each stanza what universal in the concluding triplet will bind together the odd particulars in the preceding six lines. The test case is *The Flea*. If you think this very different from Donne's other poems you may be sure that you have no taste for the real Donne. But for the accident that modern cleanliness by rendering this insect disgusting has also rendered it comic, the conceit is exactly on the same level as that of the tears in *A Valediction: of weeping*.

And yet the modern critic was right. The effect of all these poems is somehow serious. "Serious" indeed is the only word. Seldom profound in thought, not always passionate in feeling, they are none the less the very opposite of gay. It is as though Donne performed in deepest depression those gymnastics which are usually a sign of intellectual high spirits. He himself speaks of his "*concupiscence* of wit." The hot, dark word is well chosen. We are all familiar—at least if we have lived in Ireland—with the type of mind which combines furious anger with a revelling delight in eloquence, nay grows more rhetorical as anger increases. In the same way, wit and the delight in wit are, for Donne, not only compatible with, but actually provoked by, the most uneasy passions—by contempt and self-contempt and unconvinced sensuality. His wit is not so much the play as the irritability of intellect. But none the less, like the angry Irishman's *clausulae,* it is still enjoyed and still intends to produce admiration; and if we do not hold our breaths as we read, wondering in the middle of each complication how he will resolve it, and exclaiming at the end "How ever did you think of *that*?" (Carew speaks of his "fresh invention"), we are not enjoying Donne.

Now this kind of thing can produce a very strong and a very peculiar pleasure. Our age has nothing to repent of in having learned to relish it. If the Augustans, in their love for the obviously poetical and harmonious, were blind to its merits, so much the worse for them. At the same time it is desirable not to overlook the special congeniality of such poetry to the twentieth century, and to beware of giving to this highly specialized and, in truth, very limited kind of excellence, a place in our scheme of literary values which it does not deserve. Donne's rejection of the obviously poetical image was a good method—for Donne; but if we think that there is some intrinsic superiority in this method, so that all poetry about pylons and *non obstantes* must needs be of a higher order than poetry about lawns and lips and breasts and orient skies, we are deceived—deceived by the fact that we, like Donne, happen to live at the end of a great period of rich and nobly obvious poetry. It is natural to want your savoury after your sweets; but you must not base a philosophy of cookery on that momentary preference. Again, Donne's obscurity and occasional abstruseness have sometimes (not always) produced magnificent results, and we do well to praise them. But, as I have hinted, an element of dandyism was present in Donne himself—he "would have no such readers as he could teach"—and we must be very cautious here lest shallow call to shallow. There is a great deal of dandyism (largely of Franco-American importation) in the modern literary world. And finally, what shall we say of Donne's "seriousness," of that persistency, that nimiety, that astringent quality (as Boehme would have said) which makes him, if not the saddest, at least the most uncomfortable, of our poets? Here, surely, we find the clearest and most disturbing congeniality of all. It would be foolish not to recognize the growth in our criticism of something that I can only describe as literary Manichaeism—a dislike of peace and pleasure and heartsease simply as such. To be bilious is, in some circles, almost the first qualification for a place in the Temple of Fame.[2] We distrust the pleasures of imagination, however hotly and unmerrily we preach the pleasures of the body. This seriousness must not be confused with profundity. We do not like poetry that essays to be wise, and Chaucer would think we had rejected "doctryne" and "solas" about equally. We want, in fact, just what Donne can give us—something stern and tough, though not necessarily virtuous, something that does not conciliate. Born under Saturn, we do well to confess the liking complexionally forced upon us; but not to attempt that wisdom which dominates the stars is pusillanimous, and to set up our limitation as a norm—to believe, against all experience, in a Saturnocentric universe—is folly.

Before leaving the discussion of Donne's manner I must touch, however reluctantly, on a charge that has been brought against him from the time of Ben Jonson till now. Should he, or should he not, be hanged for not keeping the accent? There is more than one reason why I do not wish to treat this subject. In the first place, the whole nature of Donne's stanza, and of what he does within the stanza, cannot be profitably discussed except by one who knows much more than I do about the musical history of the time. *Confined Love,* for example, is metrically meaningless without the tune. But I could make shift with that difficulty: my real trouble is of quite a different kind. In discussing Donne's present popularity, the question of metre forces me to a statement which I do not make without embarrassment. Some one must say it, but I do not care for the office, for what I have to say will hardly be believed among scholars and hardly listened to by any one else. It is simply this—that the opinions of the modern world on the metre of any poet are, in general, of no value at all, because most modern readers of poetry do not know how to scan. My evidence for this amazing charge is twofold. In the first place I find that very many of my own pupils—some of them from excellent schools, most of them great readers of poetry, not a few of them talented and (for their years) well-informed persons—are quite unable, when they first come to me, to find out from the verse how Marlowe pronounced Barabas or Mahomet. To be sure, if challenged, they will say that they do not believe in syllable-counting or that the old methods of scansion have been exploded, but this is only a smoke screen. It is easy to find out that they have not got beyond the traditional legal fiction of longs and shorts and have never even got so far: they are in virgin ignorance. And my experience as an examiner shows me that this is not peculiar to my own pupils. My second piece of evidence is more remarkable. I have heard a celebrated belle-lettrist—a printed critic and poet—repeatedly, in the same lecture, so mispronounce the name of a familiar English poem as to show that he did not know a decasyllabic line when he met it. The conclusion is unavoidable. Donne may be metrically good or bad, in fact; but it is obvious that he might be bad to any degree without offending the great body of his modern admirers. On that side, his present vogue is worth precisely nothing. No doubt this widespread metrical ignorance is itself a symptom of some deeper change; and I am far from suggesting that the appearance of *vers libre* is simply a result of the ignorance. More probably the ignorance, and the deliberate abandonment, of accentual metres are correlative phenomena, and both the results of some revolution in our whole sense of rhythm—a revolution of great importance reaching deep down into the unconscious and even perhaps into the blood. But that is not our business at the moment.

The sentiment of Donne's love poems is easier to describe than their manner, and its charm for modern readers easier to explain. No one will deny that the twentieth century, so far, has shown an extraordinary interest in the sexual appetite and has been generally marked by a reaction from the romantic idealization of that appetite. We have agreed with the romantics in regarding sexual love as a subject of overwhelming importance, but hardly in anything else. On the purely literary side we are wearied with the floods of uxorious bathos which the romantic conception undoubtedly liberated. As psychologists we are interested in the new discovery of the secreter and less reputable operations of the instinct. As practical philosophers we are living in an age of sexual experiment. The whole subject offers us an admirable field for the kind of seriousness I have just described. It seems odd, at first sight, that a sixteenth-century poet should give us so exactly what we want; but it can be explained.

The great central movement of love poetry, and of fiction about love, in Donne's time is that represented by Shakespeare and Spenser. This movement consisted in the final transmutation of the medieval courtly love or romance of adultery into an equally romantic love that looked to marriage as its natural conclusion. The process, of course, had begun far earlier—as early, indeed, as the *Kingis Quhair*—but its triumph belongs to the sixteenth century. It is most powerfully expressed by Spenser, but more clearly and philosophically by Chapman in that under-estimated poem, his *Hero and Leander*. These poets were engaged, as Professor Vinaver would say, in reconciling Carbonek and Camelot, virtue and courtesy, divine and human love; and incidentally in laying down the lines which love poetry was to follow till the nineteenth century. We who live at the end of the dispensation which they inaugurated and in reaction against it are not well placed for evaluating their work. Precisely what is revolutionary and creative in it seems to us platitudinous, orthodox, and stale. If there were a poet, and a strong poet, alive in their time who was failing to move with them, he would inevitably appear to us more "modern" than they.

But was Donne such a poet? A great critic has assigned him an almost opposite role, and it behoves us to proceed with caution. It may be admitted at once that Donne's work is not, in this respect, all of a piece; no poet fits perfectly into such a scheme as I have outlined—it can be true only by round and by large. There are poems in which Donne attempts to sing a love perfectly in harmony with the moral law, but they are not very numerous and I do not think they are usually his best pieces. Donne never for long gets rid of a medieval sense of the sinfulness of sexuality; indeed, just because the old conventional division between Carbonek and Camelot is breaking up, he feels this more continuously and restively than any poet of the Middle Ages.

Donne was bred a Roman Catholic. The significance of this in relation to his learned and scholastic imagery can be exaggerated; scraps of Calvin, or, for that matter, of Euclid or Bacon, might have much the same poetical effect as his scraps of Aquinas. But it is all-important for his treatment of love. This is not easily understood by the modern reader, for later-day conceptions of the Puritan and the Roman Catholic stand in the way. We have come to use the word "Puritan" to mean what should rather be called "rigorist" or "ascetic," and we tend to assume that the sixteenth-century Puritans were "puritanical" in this sense. Calvin's rigorist theocracy at Geneva lends colour to the error. But there is no understanding the period of the Reformation in England until we have grasped the fact that the quarrel between the Puritans and the Papists was not primarily a quarrel between rigorism and indulgence, and that, in so far as it was, the rigorism was on the Roman side. On many questions, and specially in their view of the marriage bed, the Puritans were the indulgent party; if we may without disrespect so use the name of a great Roman Catholic, a great writer, and a great man, they were much more Chestertonian than their adversaries. The idea that a Puritan was a repressed and repressive person would have astonished Sir Thomas More and Luther about equally. On the contrary, More thought of a Puritan as one who "loved no lenten fast nor lightly no fast else, saving breakfast and eat fast and drink fast and luske fast in their lechery"—a person only too likely to end up in the "abominable heresies" of the Anabaptists about communism of goods and wives. And Puritan theology, so far from being grim and gloomy, seemed to More to err in the direction of fantastic optimism. "I could for my part," he writes, "be very well content that sin and pain and all were as shortly gone as Tindall telleth us: but I were loth that he deceved us if it be not so." More would not have understood the idea, sometimes found in the modern writers, that he and his friends were defending a "merry" Catholic England against sour precisions; they were rather defending necessary severity and sternly realistic theology against wanton labefaction—penance and "works" and vows of celibacy and mortification and Purgatory against the easy doctrine, the mere wish-fulfilment dream, of salvation by faith. Hence when we turn from the religious works of More to Luther's *Table-talk* we are at once struck by the geniality of the latter. If Luther is right, we have waked from nightmare into sunshine: if he is wrong, we have entered a fools' paradise. The burden of his charge against the Catholics is that they have needlessly tormented us with scruples; and, in particular, that "Antichrist will regard neither God nor the love of women." "On what pretence have they forbidden us marriage? 'Tis as though we were forbidden to eat, to drink, to sleep." "Where women are not honoured, temporal and domestic government are despised." He praises women repeatedly: More, it will be remembered, though apparently an excellent husband and father, hardly ever mentions a woman save to ridicule her. It is easy to see why Luther's marriage (as he called it) or Luther's "abominable bichery" (if you prefer) became almost a symbol. More can never keep off the subject for more than a few pages.

This antithesis, if once understood, explains many things in the history of sentiment, and many differences, noticeable to the present day, between the Protestant and the Catholic parts of Europe. It explains why the conversion of courtly love into romantic monogamous love was so largely the work of English, and even of Puritan, poets; and it goes far to explain why Donne contributes so little to that movement.

I trace in his poetry three levels of sentiment. On the lowest level (lowest, that is, in order of complexity), we have the celebration of simple appetite, as in *Elegy XIX*. If I call this a pornographic poem, I must be understood to use that ugly word as a descriptive, not a dyslogistic, term. I mean by it that this poem, in my opinion, is intended to arouse the appetite it describes, to affect not only the imagination but the nervous system of the reader.[3] And I may as well say at once—but who would willingly claim to be a judge in such matters? —that it seems to me to be very nearly perfect in its kind. Nor would I call it an immoral poem. Under what conditions the reading of it could be an innocent act is a real moral question; but the poem itself contains nothing intrinsically evil.

On the highest, or what Donne supposed to be the highest, level we have the poems of ostentatiously virtuous love, *The Undertaking*, *A Valediction: forbidding mourning*, and *The Extasie*. It is here that the contrast between Donne and his happier contemporaries is most marked. He is trying to follow them into the new age, to be at once passionate and innocent; and if any reader will make the experiment of imagining Beatrice or Juliet or Perdita, or again, Amoret or Britomart, or even Philoclea or Pamela, as the auditress throughout these poems, he will quickly feel that something is wrong. You may deny, as perhaps some do, that the romantic conception of "pure" passion has any meaning; but certainly, if there is such a thing, it is not like this. It does not prove itself pure by talking about purity. It does not keep on drawing distinctions between spirit and flesh to the detriment of the latter and then explaining why the flesh is, after all, to be used. This is what Donne does, and the result is singularly unpleasant. The more he labours the deeper "Dun is in the mire," and it is quite arguable that *The Extasie* is a much nastier poem than the nineteenth *Elegy*. What any sensible woman would make of such a wooing it is difficult to imagine—or would be difficult if we forgot the amazing protective faculty which each sex possesses of not listening to the other.

Between these two extremes falls the great body of Donne's love poetry. In certain obvious, but superficial, respects, it continues the medieval tradition. Love is still a god and lovers his "clergie"; oaths may be made in "reverentiall feare" of his "wrath"; and the man who resists him is "rebell and atheist." Donne can even doubt, like Soredamors, whether those who admit Love after a struggle have not forfeited his grace by their resistance, like

> Small townes which stand stiffe, til great shot
> Enforce them.

He can personify the attributes of his mistress, the "enormous gyant" her Disdain and the "enchantress *Honor*," quite in the manner of *The Romance of the Rose*. He writes *Albas* for both sexes, and in the *Holy Sonnets* repents of his love poetry, writing his palinode, in true medieval fashion. A reader may wonder, at first, why the total effect is so foreign to the Middle Ages: but Donne himself has explained this when he says, speaking of the god of Love,

> If he wroung from mee a teare, I brin'd it so
> With scorne or shame, that him it nourish'd not.

This admirable couplet not only tells us, in brief, what Donne has effected but shows us that he knew what he was doing. It does not, of course, cover every single poem. A few pieces admittedly express delighted love and they are among Donne's most popular works; such are *The Good-morrow* and *The Anniversarie*—poems that again remind us of the difference between his best and his typical. But the majority of the poems ring the changes on five themes, all of them grim ones—on the sorrow of parting (including death), the miseries of secrecy, the falseness of the mistress, the fickleness of Donne, and finally on contempt for love itself. The poems of parting stand next to the poems of happy love in general popularity and are often extremely affecting.

We may hear little of the delights of Donne's loves, and dislike what we hear of their "purity"; the pains ring true. The song *Sweetest love, I do not goe* is remarkable for its broken, but haunting, melody, and nowhere else has Donne fused argument, conceit, and classical imitation into a more perfect unity. *The Feaver* is equally remarkable, and that for a merit very rare in Donne—its inevitability. It is a single jet of music and feeling, a straight flight without appearance of effort. The remaining four of our five themes are all various articulations of the "scorne or shame" with which Donne "brines" his reluctantly extorted tributes to the god of Love; monuments, unparalleled outside Catullus, to the close kinship between certain kinds of love and certain kinds of hate. The faithlessness of women is sometimes treated, in a sense, playfully; but there is always something—the clever surprise in *Womans Constancy* or the grotesque in *Goe and catche a falling starre*—which stops these poems short of a true anacreontic gaiety. The theme of faithlessness rouses Donne to a more characteristic, and also a better, poetry in such a hymn of hate as *The Apparition*, or in the sad mingling of fear, contempt, and self-contempt in *A Lecture upon the Shadow*. The pains of secrecy give opportunity for equally fierce and turbulent writing. I may be deceived when I find in the sixteenth *Elegy*, along with many other nauseas and indignations, a sickened male contempt for the whole female world of nurses and "midnight startings" and hysterics; but *The Curse* is unambiguous. The ending here is particularly delicious just because the main theme—an attack on *Jalosie* or the "lozengiers"—is so medieval and so associated with the "honour of love." Of the poet's own fickleness one might expect, at last, a merry treatment; and perhaps in *The Indifferent* we get it. But I am not sure. Even this seems to have a sting in it. And of *Loves Usury* what shall I say? The struggle between lust and reason, the struggle between love and reason, these we know; but Donne is perhaps the first poet who has ever painted lust holding love at arm's length, in the hope "that there's no need to trouble himself with any such thoughts yet"—and all this only as an introduction to the crowning paradox that in old age even a reciprocated love must be endured. The poem is, in its way, a masterpiece, and a powerful indirect expression of Donne's habitual "shame and scorne." For, in the long run, it must be admitted that "the love of hatred and the hate of love" is the main, though not the only, theme of the *Songs and Sonets*. A man is a fool for loving and a double fool for saying so in "whining poetry"; the only excuse is that the sheer difficulty of drawing one's pains through rhyme's vexation "allays" them. A woman's love at best will be only the "spheare" of a man's—inferior to it as the heavenly spheres are to their intelligences or air to angels. Love is a spider that can transubstantiate all sweets into bitter: a devil who differs from his fellow devils at court by taking the soul and giving nothing in exchange. The mystery which the Petrarchans or their medieval predecessors made of it is "imposture all," like the claims of alchemists. It is a very simple matter (*foeda et brevis voluptas*), and all it comes to in the end is

> that my man
> Can be as happy as I can.

Unsuccessful love is a plague and tyranny; but there is a plague even worse–Love might try

> A deeper plague, to make her love mee too!

Love enjoyed is like gingerbread with the gilt off. What pleased the whole man now pleases one sense only–

> And that so lamely, as it leaves behinde
> A kinde of sorrowing dulnesse to the minde.

The doctors say it shortens life.

It may be urged that this is an unfair selection of quotations, or even that I have arrived at my picture of Donne by leaving out all his best poems, for one reason or another, as "exceptions," and then describing what remains. There is one sense in which I admit this. Any account of Donne which concentrates on his love poetry must be unfair to the poet, for it leaves out much of his best work. By hypothesis, it must neglect the dazzling sublimity of his best religious poems, the grotesque charm of *The Progresse of the Soule,* and those scattered, but exquisite, patches of poetry that appear from time to time amidst the insanity of *The First and Second Anniversaries.* Even in the *Epistles* there are good passages. But as far as concerns his love poetry, I believe I am just. I have no wish to rule out the exceptions, provided that they are admitted to be exceptions. I am attempting to describe the prevailing tone of his work, and in my description no judgement is yet implied.

To judgement let us now proceed. Here is a collection of verse describing with unusual and disturbing energy the torments of a mind which has been baffled in its relation to sexual love by certain temporary and highly special conditions. What is its value? To admit the "unusual and disturbing energy" is, of course, to admit that Donne is a poet; he has, in the modern phrase, "put his stuff across." Those who believe that criticism can separate inquiry into the success of communication from that into the value of the thing communicated will demand that we should now proceed to evaluate the "stuff"; and if we do so, it would not be hard to point out how transitory and limited and, as it were, accidental the appeal of such "stuff" must be. But something of the real problem escapes under this treatment. It would not be impossible to imagine a poet dealing with this same stuff, marginal and precarious as it is, in a way that would permanently engage our attention. Donne's real limitation is not that he writes *about,* but that he writes *in,* a chaos of violent and transitory passions. He is perpetually excited and therefore perpetually cut off from the deeper and more permanent springs of his own excitement. But how is this to be separated from his technique—the nagging, nudging, quibbling stridency of his manner? If a man writes thus, what can he communicate but excitement? Or again, if he finds nothing but excitement to communicate, how else should he write? It is impossible here to distinguish cause from effect. Our concern, in the long run, must be with the actual poetry (the "stuff" *thus* communicated, this communication of *such* "stuff") and with the question how far that total phenomenon is calculated to interest human imagination. And to this question I can see only one answer: that its interest, save for a mind specially predisposed in its favour, must be short-lived and superficial, though intense. Paradoxical as it may seem, Donne's poetry is too simple to satisfy. Its complexity is all on the surface—an intellectual and fully conscious complexity that we soon come to the end of. Beneath this we find nothing but a limited series of "passions"—explicit, mutually exclusive passions which can be instantly and adequately labelled as such—things which can be readily talked about, and indeed, must be talked about because, in silence, they begin to lose their hard outlines and overlap, to betray themselves as partly fictitious. That is why Donne is always arguing. There are puzzles in his work, but we can solve them all if we are clever enough; there is none of the depth and ambiguity of real experience in him, such as underlies the apparent simplicity of *How sleep the brave* or *Songs of Innocence,* or even Αἰαι Λειψύδριον.[4] The same is true, for the most part, of the specifically "metaphysical" comparisons. One idea has been put into each and nothing more can come out of it. Hence they tend to die on our hands, where some seemingly banal comparison of a woman to a flower or God's anger to flame can touch us at innumerable levels and renew its virginity at every reading. Of all literary virtues "originality," in the vulgar sense, has, for this reason, the shortest life. When we have once mastered a poem by Donne there is nothing more to do with it. To use his own simile, he deals in earthquakes, not in that "trepidation of the spheres" which is so much less violent but "greater far."

Some, of course, will contend that his love poems should interest me permanently because of their "truth." They will say that he has shown me passion with the mask off, and catch at my word "uncomfortable" to prove that I am running away from him because he tells me more truth than I can bear. But this is the mere frenzy of anti-romanticism. Of course, Donne is true in the sense that passions such as he presents do occur in human experience. So do a great many other things. He makes his own selection, like Dickens, or Gower, or Herrick, and his world is neither more nor less "real" than theirs; while it is obviously less real than the world of Homer, or Virgil, or Tolstoy. In one way, indeed, Donne's love poetry is less true than that of the Petrarchans, in so far as it largely omits the very thing that all the pother is about. Donne shows us a variety of sorrows, scorns, angers, disgusts, and the like which arise out of love. But if any one asked "What is all this *about*? What is the attraction which makes these partings so sorrowful? What is the peculiarity about this physical pleasure which he speaks of so contemptuously, and how has it got tangled up with such a storm of emotions?", I do not know how we could reply except by pointing to some ordinary love poetry. The feeblest sonnet, almost, of the other school would give us an answer with coral lips and Cupid's golden wings and the opening rose, with perfumes and instruments of music, with some attempt, however trite, to paint that iridescence which explains why people write poems about love at all. In this sense Donne's love poetry is parasitic. I do not use this word as a term of reproach; there are so many good poets, by now, in the world that one particular poet is entitled to take for granted the depth of a passion and deal with its froth. But as a purely descriptive term, "parasitic" seems to me true. Donne's love poems could not exist unless love poems of a more genial character existed first. He shows us amazing shadows cast by love upon the intellect, the passions, and the appetite; to learn of the substance which casts them we must go to other poets, more balanced, more magnanimous, and more humane. There are, I well remember, poems (some two or three) in which Donne himself presents the substance; and the fact that he does so without much luxury of language and symbol endears them to our temporarily austere taste. But in the main, his love poetry is *Hamlet* without the prince.

Donne's influence on the poets of the seventeenth century is a commonplace of criticism. Of that influence at its best, as it is seen in the great devotional poetry of the period, I have not now to speak. In love poetry he was not, perhaps, so dominant. His *nequitiae* probably encouraged the cynical and licentious songs of his successors, but, if so, the imitation is very different from the model. Suckling's impudence, at its best, is light-hearted and very unlike the ferocity of Donne; and Suckling's chief fault in this vein—a stolid fleshliness which sometimes leads him to speak of his mistress's body more like a butcher than a lecher—is entirely his own. The more strictly metaphysical elements in Donne are, of course, lavishly reproduced; but I doubt if the reproduction succeeds best when it is most faithful. Thus Carew's stanzas *When thou, poor Excommunicate* or Lovelace's *To Lucasta, going beyond the Seas* are built up on Donne's favourite plan, but both, as it seems to me, fail in that startling and energetic quality which this kind of thing demands. They have no edge. When these poets succeed it is by addding something else to what they have learned from Donne—in fact by reuniting Donne's manner with something much more like ordinary poetry. Beauty (like cheerfulness) is always breaking in. Thus the conceit of asking where various evanescent, beautiful phenomena go when they vanish and replying that they are all to be found in one's mistress is the sort of conceit that Donne might have used; and, starting from that end, we could easily work it up into something tolerably like bad Donne. As thus:

Oh fooles that aske whether of odours burn'd
The seminall forme live, and from that death
Conjure the same with chymique arte—'tis turn'd
To that quintessence call'd her Breath!

But if we use the same idea as Carew uses it we get a wholly different effect:

Ask me no more where Jove bestows
When June is past, the fading rose:
For in your beauty's orient deep
These flowers, as in their causes, sleep.

The idea is the same. But the choice of the obvious and obviously beautiful rose, instead of the recondite seminal form of vegetables, the great regal name of Jove, the alliteration, the stately voluptuousness of a quatrain where all the accented syllables are also long in quantity (a secret little known)—all this smothers the sharpness of thought in sweetness. Compared with Donne, it is almost soporific; compared with it, Donne is shrill. But the conceit is there; and "as in their causes, sleep" which looks at first like a blunder, is in fact a paradox that Donne might have envied. So again, the conceit that the lady's hair outshines the sun, though not much more than an Elizabethan conceit, might well have appeared in the *Songs and Sonets;* but Donne would neither have wished, nor been able, to attain the radiance of Lovelace's

> But shake your head and scatter day!

This process of enchanting, or, in Shakespeare's sense, "translating" Donne was carried to its furthest point by Marvell. Almost every element of Donne—except his metrical roughness—appears in the *Coy Mistress.* Nothing could be more like Donne, both in the grimness of its content and in its impudently argumentative function, than the conceit that

> worms shall try
> That long preserved virginity.

All the more admirable is the art by which this, and everything else in that poem, however abstruse, dismaying, or sophistical, is subordinated to a sort of golden tranquillity. What was death to Donne is mere play to Marvell. "Out of the strong," we are tempted to say, "has come sweetness," but in reality the strength is all on Marvell's side. He is an Olympian, ruling at ease for his own good purposes, all that intellectual and passionate mobility of which Donne was the slave, and leading Donne himself, bound, behind his chariot.

From all this we may conclude that Donne was a "good influence"—a better influence than many greater poets. It would hardly be too much to say that the final cause of Donne's poetry is the poetry of Herbert, Crashaw, and Marvell; for the very qualities which make Donne's kind of poetry unsatisfying poetic food make it a valuable ingredient.

NOTES

[1] Those who object to "emotive terms" in criticism may prefer to read ". . . used by an accomplished poet to produce an attitude relevant not directly to outer experience but to the central nucleus of the total attitude-and-belief-feeling system." It must not be supposed, however, that the present writer's theory of either knowledge or value would permit him, in the long run, to accept the restatement.

[2] In this we have been anticipated. See *Emma,* Chap. 25: "I know what worthy people they are. Perry tells me that Mr. Cole never touches malt liquor. You would not think it to look at him, but he is bilious—Mr. Cole is very bilious."

[3] The restatement of this in terms acceptable to the Richardian school (for whom all poetry equally is addressed to the nervous system) should present no difficulty. For them it will be a distinction between parts, or functions, of the system.

[4] The superficial simplicity here is obvious; the deeper ambiguity becomes evident if we ask whether Lipsydrion is an object of detestation or of nostalgic affection.

JOAN BENNETT

The Love Poetry of John Donne
A Reply to Mr. C. S. Lewis

In that brilliant and learned book *The Allegory of Love* Mr. Lewis writes, "cynicism and idealism about women are twin fruits on the same branch—are the positive and negative poles of a single thing." Few poets provide a better illustration of this than John Donne. These *Songs and Sonets* and *Elegies* which, Mr. Lewis would have us believe, never explain "why people write poems about love at all," are the work of one who has tasted every fruit in love's orchard, from that which pleased only while he ate it—

> And when hee hath the kernell eate
> Who doth not fling away the shell?—

to that which raised a thirst for even fuller spiritual satisfaction, so that he wrote:

> Here the admyring her my mind did whett
> To seeke thee God.

How is it then that distinguished critics wonder what it is all about; that Dryden declares "Donne perplexes the minds of the fair sex with nice speculations of philosophy, when he should engage their hearts and entertain them with the softness of love"; and that Mr. Lewis

From *Seventeenth Century Studies Presented to Sir Herbert Grierson* (Oxford, 1938), pp. 85–104. Reprinted by permission of The Clarendon Press.

wonders "what any sensible woman can make of such love-making"? A part of the trouble is, I believe, that they are accustomed to, or that they prefer, another kind of love poetry, in which the poet endeavours to paint the charms of his mistress:

> Some asked me where Rubies grew
>   And nothing I did say:
> But with my finger pointed to
>   The lips of Julia.
> Some asked how Pearls did grow and where?
>   Then spoke I to my Girle,
> To part her lips and show them there
>   The Quarelets of Pearl.

Donne tells us very little about that beauty of "colour and skin" which he describes in *The Undertaking* as "but their oldest clothes." He writes almost exclusively about the emotion, and not about its cause; he describes and analyses the experience of being in love, if I may use that word for the moment to cover his many kinds of experience which range from the mere sensual delight presupposed in *Elegy XIX* to the "marriage of true minds" celebrated in *The Good-morrow,* or in *The Valediction: forbidding mourning.* In *Elegy XIX,* for instance, Donne is writing of the same kind of experience as that of which Carew writes in *The Rapture.* But Carew expends his poetic gifts in description of the exquisite body of the woman, so that the reader can vicariously share his joys. Donne, on the other hand, gives two lines to description, and even so they are not really about what he sees; he is content to suggest by analogy the delight of the eye when the woman undresses:

> Your gown going off, such beauteous state reveals,
> As when from flowry meads th' hills shadow steales.

The poem is not about her exquisite body, but about what he feels like when he stands there waiting for her to undress. Now it may be that "any sensible woman" would rather be told of

> Thy bared snow and thy unbraided gold,

but I am not sure. She can see that in her looking-glass, or she may believe she sees these things reflected in the work of some painter, for the painter's art can show such things better than any words. It may interest her more to know what it feels like to be a man in love. In any case, it is of that that Donne chooses to write. He is not incapable of describing physical charms; his description of a blush in *The Second Anniversary:*

> her pure, and eloquent blood
> Spoke in her cheekes, and so distinctly wrought,
> That one might almost say, her body thought;

is better, in my judgement, than Spenser's

> And troubled bloud through his pale face was seene
> To come and goe with tydings from the hart.[1]

Or again, Mr. Lewis speaks of the radiance of Lovelace's line,

> But shake your head and scatter day,

which was anticipated, and perhaps suggested, by Donne's

> Ev'ry thy haire for love to worke upon
> Is much too much, some fitter must be sought;
> For, nor in nothing, nor in things
> Extreme, and scatt'ring bright, can love inhere.

But the fact remains that such touches of description are very rare in Donne's poetry. His interest lay elsewhere, namely in dramatizing, and analysing, and illustrating by a wealth of analogy the state, or rather states, of being in love.

But what does he mean by love? We have the whole mass of Donne's poems before us, thrown together higgledy-piggledy with no external evidence as to when or to whom any one of them was written. And in some of them love is "imposture all," or "a winter-seeming summers night"; in others physical union is all in all so that two lovers in bed are a whole world; and elsewhere we are told that

> Difference of sex no more wee knew
> Than our Guardian Angells doe.

And elsewhere again:

> Our bodies why doe wee forbeare?
> They are ours, though they are not wee, Wee are
> The intelligences, they the spheare.
> We owe them thankes because they thus

Did us, to us, at first convay,
Yeelded their forces, sense, to us,
Nor are drosse to us, but allay.

The temptation to assign each poem to a particular period and to associate each with a particular woman is very strong. It has been yielded to again and again, not only in Sir Edmund Gosse's biography, but much more recently. Yet it must be resisted for two reasons: first because we have no evidence as to when any one of the *Songs and Sonets* was written, and secondly because we cannot know how far the experience of which any one of them treats was real or imaginary. Mr. Lewis is very well aware of these things. But it is no less misleading to go to the other extreme and read them as though they were all written at one time, or all with equal seriousness and sincerity. We have some important facts to guide us. Between the years 1597 and 1601 Donne fell in love with Anne More. He married her in 1601, as Walton puts it, "without the allowance of those friends whose approbation always was, and ever will be necessary, to make even a virtuous love become lawful." He had nine children by her, and watched over them with her when they were sick, and suffered with her when some of them died. He had been married seven years when he wrote a letter headed "From mine hospital at Mitcham," in which he says:

> I write from the fire-side in my parlour, and in the noise of three gamesome children, and by the side of her whom, because I have transplanted to such a wretched fortune, I must labour to disguise that from her by all such honest devices, as giving her my company and discourse.

Three years later, in 1611, Donne is reluctant to leave home and travel with his patron Sir Robert Drury, because his wife, who was then with child, "professed an unwillingness to allow him any absence from her saying her divining soul boded her some ill in his absence." The wording of that sentence, quoted by Walton, is heard again in one of Donne's loveliest songs, but the sense is reversed. Experience tells us that when we are afraid to let a loved one go it is not, as a rule, because *we* may come to harm in his absence. It is much more probable that Anne Donne was afraid for her husband on those dangerous seas to which his poetry so often refers, and that he then wrote the lyric for her, which pleads:

Let not thy divining heart
Forethinke me any ill,

Destiny may take thy part,
And may thy feares fulfill;
But thinke that wee
Are but turn'd aside to sleepe;
They who one another keepe
Alive n'er parted bee.

This is of course conjecture, and I claim no more than a strong probability. It was on this journey with Sir Robert, which Donne finally and reluctantly undertook, that he saw that "vision of his wife with a dead child in her arms" that Walton so convincingly describes. I am not concerned with the authenticity or otherwise of the vision, but with the direction of Donne's thoughts. In 1614, thirteen years after his marriage, we have further evidence of the constancy and of the quality of Donne's love for his wife. In a letter to Sir Robert More, on 10 August of that year, he again explains why he cannot and will not leave Anne in solitude:

> When I begin to apprehend that, even to myself, who can relieve myself upon books, solitariness was a little burdensome, I believe it would be much more so to my wife if she were left alone. So much company therefore, as I am, she shall not want; and we had not one another at so cheap a rate as that we should ever be weary of one another.

Such words need no comment. But if any more evidence is required as to the nature and endurance of Donne's love for his wife, we have *Holy Sonnet XVII*, written after her death in 1617:

Since she whom I lov'd hath payd her last debt
To Nature, and to hers, and my good is dead,
And her Soule early into heaven ravished,
Wholly on heavenly things my mind is sett.
Here the admyring her my mind did whett
To seeke thee God; so streames do shew their head.

Without claiming any knowledge as to the dates of particular poems, we are bound to recognize that seventeen years of married love will have taught Donne something he did not know when he wrote, for instance, *Elegy VII*. And we do, in fact, find that the poems express views of love which could scarcely all have been held at the same time.

Mr. Lewis, of course, recognizes that Donne's love poetry is "not all of a piece." "There are poems," he admits, "in which Donne attempts to sing of a love perfectly in harmony with the moral law, but they are not very numerous and I do not think they are usually among his best pieces." That judgement seems to me very odd, but it is impossible to discuss it without first deciding of what "moral law" we are thinking. The moral law governing sexual relations has been very differently conceived of in different periods of the world's history. No one has expounded the medieval view more clearly than Mr. Lewis himself in *The Allegory of Love* where he explains [2] that, for the medieval Church,

> love itself was wicked and did not cease to be wicked if the object of it were your own wife. . . . The views of the medieval churchman on the sexual act within marriage are limited by two complementary agreements. On the one hand nobody ever asserted that the act was intrinsically sinful. On the other hand all were agreed that some evil element was present in every concrete instance of it since the Fall.

Mr. Lewis believes that Donne never for long freed himself from this "medieval sense of the sinfulness of sexuality." Born a Roman Catholic, and deeply read in the Fathers of the Church, he must of course have considered it. But does his poetry support the belief that he continued to accept it? The value of Donne's love poetry largely depends upon the answer. "The great central movement of love poetry in Donne's time," Mr. Lewis reminds us, was at variance with the medieval view. It was now believed that marriage sanctified sexual love; and for Spenser, once the marriage ceremony is over, the sexual act is its proper consummation and the chaste moon bears witness to it in the *Epithalamion:*

> Who is the same, which at my window peepes?
> Or whose is that faire face that shines so bright?
> Is it not Cinthia, she that never sleepes,
> But walkes about high heaven al the night?
> O fayrest goddesse, do thou not envy
> My love with me to spy:
> For thou likewise didst love, though now unthought,
> And for a fleece of wooll, which privily
> The Latmian shepherd once unto thee brought,
> His pleasure with thee wrought.

Therefore to us be favorable now;
And sith of womens labours thou hast charge,
And generation goodly dost enlarge,
Encline thy will t'effect our wishful vow,
And the chaste wombe informe with timely seed,
That may our comfort breed:
Till which we cease our hopeful hap to sing,
Ne let the woods us answere, nor our Eccho ring.

On the other hand, in Chapman's *Hero and Leander,* to which Mr. Lewis especially invites our attention, we have the reverse aspect of this view of the morality of love. The sexual act before marriage, albeit the expression of true love, is not in harmony with the moral law:

By this the Sovereign of Heavens golden fires,
And young *Leander,* Lord of his desires,
Together from their lovers armes arose:
Leander into Hellespontus throwes
His Hero-handled bodie, whose delight
Made him disdaine each other Epithete,
And as amidst the enamoured waves he swims,
The God of gold of purpose guilt his lims,
That this word guilt, including double sence,
The double guilt of his *Incontinence,*
Might be exprest, that had no stay t'employ
The treasure which the Love-God let him joy
In his deare Hero, with such sacred thrift,
As had beseemed so sanctified a gift:
But like a greedie vulgar Prodigall
Would on the stock dispend, and rudely fall
Before his time, to that unblessed blessing,
Which for lusts plague doth perish with possessing.

Where does Donne stand in relation either to this belief that marriage, and marriage alone, sanctifies the sexual act, or to the medieval view that it is alike sinful within or without the marriage bond? If I read the poetry aright, he accepts neither view, or rather he totally rejects the second and does not consider the first. The purity or otherwise of the act depends for him on the quality of the relation between the lovers. We have in *The Sunne Rising* a celebration of the same event as in the stanza quoted from *Epithalamion;* but the difference in treatment is noteworthy. Donne is joyously impudent to the sun, whereas

Spenser is ceremoniously respectful to the moon, and (which is the point here relevant), in Donne's poem we neither know nor care whether the marriage ceremony has taken place. For Donne, if delight in one another is mutual, physical union is its proper consummation; but, if the lovers are not "inter-assuréd of the mind," then "the sport" is "but a winter-seeming summers night," and

> at their best
> Sweetnesse and wit they are but *mummy* possest.

There are a number of poems in which Donne is writing about love which has not reached physical consummation, but there is only one, *The Undertaking,* in which he writes as though this state of affairs were satisfactory. Elsewhere he makes it plain that he has merely acquiesced, not without protest, in the human laws that forbade what he holds to be the natural expression of human loves. This reluctant obedience to the rules is most clearly stated in *The Relique,* where he explains precisely how he and the woman behaved, and makes known in a parenthesis what he thinks of the law that inhibited them:

> Comming and going, wee
> Perchance might kisse, but not between those meales;
> Our hands ne'er toucht the seales,
> Which nature, injur'd by late law, sets free.

Donne's poetry is not about the difference between marriage and adultery, but about the difference between love and lust. He does not establish the contrast between them in any one poem, but we arrive at his views by submitting ourselves to the cumulative evidence of all his poetry and, in so far as they are relevant, of his prose and of his life as well. The most important part of this evidence is the violent contrast between his cynical poems and those in which he celebrates

> our waking souls
> Which watch not one another out of feare.

In order to establish that contrast I must, unfortunately, refer to the vexed question of Donne's rhythm. Mr. Lewis assures us that "most modern readers do not know how to scan." However that may be, unless they can hear the difference between quick and slow movements, or between smooth and staccato, and unless they can submit to the rhythm sufficiently to throw the emphasis precisely where Donne has arranged for it to fall, they cannot understand his poetry. If they can hear these things they will be aware of the difference between the bored, flippant tone of

> Will no other vice content you?
> Will it not serve your turn to do, as did your mothers?
> Or have you all old vices spent, and now would finde out others?
> Or doth a feare, that men are true, torment you?
> Oh we are not, be not you so,
> Let mee, and doe you, twenty know;

and the tone of angry scorn in

> Must I alas
> Frame and enamell Plate, and drinke in Glasse?
> Chase waxe for others seales? breake a colts force
> And leave him then, beeing made a ready horse;

and, so utterly remote from either, the controlled emotion in

> I scarce believe my love to be so pure
> As I had thought it was,
> Because it doth endure
> Vicissitude, and season, as the grasse;
> Methinks I lyed all winter when I swore,
> My love was infinite, if spring make' it more.

The greatness of Donne's love poetry is largely due to the fact that his experience of the passion ranged from its lowest depths to its highest reaches. No one, not even Shakespeare, knew better than he that

> The expense of spirit in a waste of shame
> Is lust in action; and till action, lust
> Is perjured, murderous, bloody, full of blame,
> Savage, extreme, rude, cruel, not to trust;
> Enjoy'd no sooner but despised straight;
> Past reason hunted; and no sooner had,
> Past reason hated.

Many of the *Songs and Sonets* and the *Elegies* dramatize the experience which Shakespeare here describes. But Donne came to know also the "marriage of true minds," and many of his poems are about that experience. Nor does he repent of this love poetry in the *Holy Sonnets;* on the contrary, he expressly states that love for his wife led directly to the love of God. He does not even overlook his grosser experiences, but is prepared to use "prophane love" to illustrate his faith in Christ's pity:

> No, no, but as in my idolatrie
> I said to all my profane mistresses
> Beauty, of pitty, foulnesse only is
> A signe of rigour: so I say to thee,
> To wicked spirits are horrid shapes assign'd
> This beauteous forme assures a piteous minde.

There is no note of shame here, neither wallowing self-abasement nor a hiding or forgetting of the past. He is simply using, characteristically, just what is relevant for his present purpose. Physical beauty, which his poetry so seldom describes, he nevertheless accepts as a type of the soul's beauty:

> For though mind be the heaven where love doth sit
> Beauty a convenient type may be to figure it.

Donne never despised the flesh. Even in a Lenten sermon he asks his hearers "what Christian is denied a care of his health and a good habitude of body, or the use of those things which may give a cheerfulness to his heart and a cheerfulness to his countenance," and in his *Litany* he prays

> From thinking us all soule, neglecting thus
> Our mutuall duties, Lord deliver us.

Mr. Lewis's objections to *The Extasie* depend upon Donne's treatment of the relation between soul and body, and it is therefore important to discover what in fact Donne thought about this. "Love does not," writes Mr. Lewis, "prove itself pure by talking about purity. It does not keep on drawing distinctions between spirit and flesh to the detriment of the latter and then explaining that the flesh is after all to be used." I must admit that I find this rather perplexing. Perhaps nothing can be proved by talking about it, neither the purity of love nor the purity of Donne's poetry. But language is the poet's only means of communication, and if Chapman is allowed to express his conception of the immorality of premarital relations by talking about it, why may not Donne, by the same means, express his belief that

As our blood labours to beget
  Spirits as like soules as it can,
Because such fingers need to knit
  That subtile knot that makes us man:
So must pure lovers soules descend
  T'affections, and to faculties,
Which sense may reach and apprehend,
  Else a great Prince in prison lies.

On what grounds does Mr. Lewis object to Donne "drawing distinctions between spirit and flesh to the detriment of the latter"? What else could he do? Could a man of his time and of his religion have thought of the flesh either as equal to or as indistinguishable from the spirit? Donne, like any man of his time, and, I suppose, any Christian of any time, thinks of the body as inferior to the soul, although it can be the "temple of the Holy Ghost." He is not singular in supposing that, in this life, the soul can and must express itself through the body. Milton goes so far as to assert that even the Angels need some equivalent for this means of expression:

Whatever pure thou in the body enjoy'st
(And pure thou wert created,) we enjoy
In eminence; and obstacle find none
Of membrane, joint, or limb, exclusive bars;
Easier than air with air, if Spirits embrace,
Total they mix, union of pure with pure
Desiring, nor restrain'd conveyance need,
As flesh to mix with flesh, or soul with soul.[3]

Donne, in *The Extasie,* is attempting (by his usual means of employing a series of analogies) to explain that the union of spirit with spirit expresses itself in the flesh, just as the soul lives in the body and, in this world, cannot exist without it. The passage quoted above includes one of these analogies, an obscure one for modern readers because it depends on contemporary physiology. Sir Herbert Grierson supplies a quotation from Burton's *Anatomy of Melancholy* which gives the explanation:

The spirits in a man which are the thin and active part of the blood, and so are of a kind of middle nature, between soul and body, those spirits are able to doe, and they doe the office, to unite and apply the faculties of the soul to the organs of the body, and so there is a man.

Sir Herbert also refers us to Donne's twenty-sixth sermon which throws yet more light on the notion to which the poem refers:

> As the body is not the man [writes Donne], nor the soul is not the man, but the union of the soul and the body, by those spirits through which the soul exercises her faculties in the organs of the body, makes up the man; so the union of the Father and the Son to one another, and of both to us, by the Holy Ghost, makes up the body of the Christian religion.

There are, I suppose, three possible views of the relation between soul and body: the Manichaean view that the body is the work of the Devil; the materialist view that "explains all psychical processes by physical and chemical changes in the nervous system," and so makes the soul non-existent; and the orthodox Christian view that the body and the soul are both from God and therefore both good. We seem to have wandered far from Donne's *Extasie,* and if Mr. Lewis is right in thinking it a "nasty" poem, these philosophical considerations are irrelevant, and these theological considerations even worse. But is he right? The point Donne wishes to make in *The Extasie,* as in so many of his serious love poems, is that a man and a woman united by love may approach perfection more nearly than either could do alone:

> A single violet transplant
>   The strength, the colour, and the size,
> (All which before was poore, and scant,)
>   Redoubles still, and multiplies.
> When love, with one another so
>   Interinanimates two soules,
> That abler soule, which thence doth flow,
>   Defects of lonelinesse controules.

I have tried to show that Donne was very far from retaining "the medieval view of the sinfulness of sex"; but Mr. Lewis has yet another accusation to bring, equally incompatible with my own belief that Donne is one of the greatest love poets in the English language. Contempt for women seems to him to permeate the poetry. Once again I shall be forced to assume that readers are more sensitive to rhythm than Mr. Lewis supposes, for I am going to quarrel with Mr. Lewis's interpretation of *Elegy XVI* largely by appealing to the reader's ear. He admits that he "may be deceived" when he finds here "a sickened male contempt for the whole female world of nurses and 'midnight startings'." Most certainly he is deceived, and the varied rhythms of that poem are an important index of the extent of that deception. One of the most remarkable things about the poem is the contrast between the solemn, tender music of the verse whenever Donne addresses the woman, and the boisterous staccato in which he describes the foreign lands to whose dangers she will be exposed if she insists upon following him abroad. I must beg leave to quote the poem at sufficient length to illustrate the nature and extent of this difference.

> By our first strange and fatall interview,
> By all desires which thereof did ensue,
> By our long starving hopes, by that remorse
> Which my words masculine perswasive force
> Begot in thee, and by the memory
> Of hurts, which spies and rivals threatned me,
> I calmly beg: But by thy fathers wrath,
> By all paines, which want and divorcement hath
> I conjure thee, and all the oathes which I
> And thou have sworne to seale joynt constancy,
> Here I unsweare, and overswear them thus,
> Thou shalt not love by wayes so dangerous.
> Temper, O faire love, loves impetuous rage,
> Be my true Mistris still, not my faign'd Page.

It is tempting to quote even more of this melodious pleading, but this is enough to illustrate the liturgical music of his address to this beloved of whom Mr. Lewis can think Donne is contemptuous. When, in the same poem, he wants to express contempt, his music is very different:

> Men of France, changeable Camelions,
> Spittles of diseases, shops of fashions,
> Loves fuellers, and the rightest company
> Of Players, which upon the worlds stage be,
> Will quickly know thee, and no lesse, alas!
> Th'indifferent Italian, as we passe
> His warme land, well content to thinke thee Page,
> Will hunt thee with such lust, and hideous rage,
> As *Lots* faire guests were vext.

And now, in case the point is not yet proven, let us hear how he speaks of her "midnight startings," and how the rhythm changes once again as she comes back into the picture:

When I am gone, dreame me some hapinesse,
Nor let thy lookes our long hid love confesse,
Nor praise, nor dispraise me, nor blesse, nor curse
Openly loves force, nor in bed fright thy Nurse
With midnight startings, crying out oh, oh
Nurse, O my love is slaine, I saw him goe
O'r the white Alpes alone; I saw him I,
Assail'd, fight, taken, stabb'd, bleed, fall, and die.
Augure me better chance, except dread *Jove*
Thinke it enough for me to'have had thy love.

I said I would argue my case "almost" solely on the grounds of rhythm, but in case Mr. Lewis is right in thinking modern readers are for the most part impervious to the music of verse, they will, I trust, be convinced that the mere prose sense of the last line is incompatible with contempt for the woman.

No one will deny that at one period of his life Donne wrote of women with contempt. At this time he despised them equally for yielding to his lust or for denying themselves to him. There is nothing to choose between his contempt for the woman whom he addresses as "Nature's lay Idiot" in *Elegy VII* and his contempt for the woman who has refused him, and to whom he addresses that brilliant piece of vituperation *The Apparition*. (Whether either situation had its exact counterpart in real life is beside the point, the contempt in the poems is real enough.) At this time he treats with equal scorn the whore, both

Her whom abundance melts and her whom want betraies,

and the "fain'd vestall," and the woman who

will bee
False e'er I come, to two or three.

But the measure of his contempt for easy virtue, coyness, and faithlessness is the measure of his admiration when he finds a woman to whom he can say

So thy love may be my love's sphere.

But to Mr. Lewis that, too, sounds contemptuous; and as *Aire and Angels* has been variously understood, it is worth while to pause and examine the sentence in its context. The poem is an account of Donne's search for, and final discovery of, the true object of love. It begins with much the same idea as he expresses in the first stanza of *The Good-morrow:*

> If ever any beauty I did see,
> Which I desired, and got, 'twas but a dream of thee.

In *Aire and Angels:*

> Twice or thrice had I loved thee,
> Before I knew thy face or name;
> So in a voice, so in a shapelesse flame,
> *Angells* affect us oft, and worship'd bee;
> Still when, to where thou wert, I came
> Some lovely glorious nothing I did see.

And here, as so often elsewhere in the *Songs and Sonets,* Donne asserts his belief that "pure lovers soules" must "descend t'affections, and to faculties":

> But since my soule, whose child love is,
> Takes limmes of flesh, and else could nothing doe,
> More subtile than the parent is,
> Love must not be, but take a body too.

And at first he imagines that the physical beauty of the loved woman is the object of his search:

> And therefore what thou wert, and who,
> I bid love aske, and now
> That it assume thy body, I allow,
> And fix it selfe in thy lip, eye, and brow.

So far the progress is one to which we are accustomed, both in the literature of love and in experience; from a general reaching out after beauty to a particular worship of one person who sums up and over-reaches all that had seemed fair in others. So Romeo catches sight of Juliet and forgets Rosalind:

> Did my heart love till now? forswear it, sight!
> For I ne'er saw true beauty till this night.

But Donne is not satisfied. There is no rest for his love in the bewildering beauty of his mistress:

> Whilst thus to ballast love, I thought,
> And so more steddily to have gone,
> With wares that would sinke admiration,
> I saw, I had loves pinnace overfraught,
> Ev'ry thy haire for love to worke upon
> Is much too much, some fitter must be sought;
> For, nor in nothing, nor in things
> Extreme, and scatt'ring bright, can love inhere.

The search is not yet over. But it is to end in a discovery surely more pleasing to any woman in love than would be the mere worship of her beauty. Beauty is transient, but love can last if it be for something which, though expressed in the body, is yet not the body:

> Then as an Angell, face and wings
> Of aire, not pure as it, yet pure doth weare,
> So thy love may be my loves spheare.

The doctrine of St. Thomas Aquinas, about the Angels assuming a body of air, provided Donne with the analogy he wanted:

> Et sic Angeli assumunt corpora ex aere, condensando ipsum virtute divina, quantam necesse est ad corporis assumendi formationem.

So much is necessary; the point of the image for Donne is that the air-body of the Angels is neither nothing, nor too much, but just sufficient to confine a spirit on earth. So the woman's love for him is a resting-place for his spirit. It is, of course, the final couplet of the poem that has led to mis-understanding. Dr. Leavis, in *Revaluations*,[4] speaks of "the blandly insolent matter-of-factness of the close" of *Aire and Angels;* and, isolated from its context, that is how it sounds:

> Just such disparitie
> As is twixt Aire and Angells puritie,
> 'Twixt womens love, and mens will ever bee.

There are two possible ways of reading this. The way which I am combating supposes that Donne, reversing the sentiment of the rest of the poem, throws out a contemptuous generalization about the impurity of woman's love in comparison with man's. My own view is that Donne, satisfied with the logical aptness of his image, is, characteristically, indifferent to the associations of the word "purity," whose meaning is, to his mind, made sufficiently clear by the context. The air-body is only less pure than the angel in so far as it can exist on earth and so enable a spirit to appear to men. A woman's love is only less pure than a man's in so far as it is focused upon a single object and does not continually reach out towards "some lovely glorious nothing." I would support this view by referring the reader to other instances in which Donne shows a similar indifference to the irrelevant associations his words may suggest. The use of the word "pure" in *Loves Growth* is similarly circumscribed by its context:

> I scarce believe my love to be so pure
> As I had thought it was,
> Because it doth endure
> Vicissitude, and season as the grasse.

The sense in which it is not so pure is explained in the next stanza:

> Love's not so pure, and abstract, as they use
> To say, which have no Mistresse but their Muse,
> But as all else, being elemented too,
> Love sometimes would contemplate, sometimes do.

Donne is not saying that love is unclean, or less clean than he had supposed; we have already seen that he does not think of the flesh as impure in that sense, but that, like everything else on earth, it is composed of diverse elements. He is arguing that the quickening of love in the springtime is not an increase, since his love was complete before,

> And yet no greater, but more eminent
> Love by the spring is growne;
> As, in the firmament,
> Starres by the sunne are not inlarg'd, but showne;

and, to make his meaning clear, Donne adds three more images or illustrations:

> Gentle love deeds, as blossomes on a bough,
> From loves awakened root do bud out now.
> If, as in water stir'd more circles bee

Produc'd by one, love such additions take,
Those like so many spheares, but one heaven make,
For, they are all concentrique unto thee.

And finally, the "blandly matter-of-fact" image:

As princes doe in times of action get
New taxes, but remit them not in peace.

Here, however, the last line of the poem,

No winter shall abate this spring's increase,

prevents the reader from supposing that the prosaic image implies a reversal of the emotional tone of the poem. The point relevant to my argument about *Aire and Angels* is that Donne always trusts the reader to ignore irrelevant associations. The political image here is logically apt; and that is a sufficient reason for him to use it. In a sermon on *The Nativity* he develops at some length an image in which the Saviour is likened to a good coin with which man's debt to God is paid:

> First he must pay it in such money as was lent; in the nature and flesh of man; for man had sinned and man must pay. And then it was lent in such money as was coined even with the image of God; man was made according to his image: that image being defaced, in a new mint, in the womb of the blessed Virgin, there was new money coined; the image of the invisible God, the second person in the Trinity, was imprinted into the human nature. And then, that there might be all fulness, as God, for the payment of this debt, sent down in bullion, and the stamp, that is, God to be conceived in man, and as he provided the mint, the womb of the blessed Virgin, so hath he provided an exchequer, where this money is issued; that in his church, where his merits should be applied to the discharge of particular consciences.

No one, I suppose, will imagine that because Donne uses this mundane imagery he is speaking irreverently of God, of the Virgin Mary, of Christ, and of the Church. He chooses the image, here as elsewhere, because it provides him with an apt analogy.

I hope I may have persuaded some readers that Donne did not think sex sinful, and that contempt for women is not a general characteristic of his love poetry. But Mr. Lewis brings yet one more accusation against him: "He is perpetually excited and therefore perpetually cut off from the deeper and more permanent springs of his own excitement." Now one way of answering this would be to say that love is an exciting experience, and that great love poetry is therefore bound to communicate excitement. But with this I am not quite content. Love is exciting, but it is also restful. Unreciprocated love is a torment of the spirit, but reciprocated love is peace and happiness. In the astonishment and uncertainty of the early stages of love there is excitement and there is also fear, but there comes a time when there is confidence and a sense of profound security. Donne is a great love poet because his poetry records and communicates these diverse experiences. He would be less great if it were true that he is "perpetually excited." The truth is that, just as his early contempt for women is the measure of his later reverence for one woman, so his vivid experience of the torment of insecure love has made him the more keenly relish the peace of a love

inter-assured of the mind.

He tells in *The Good-morrow* of lovers who

Watch not one another out of feare;

and in *The Anniversarie* the final glory of a well-spent year is the sense of safety with which it has endowed the lovers:

Who is so safe as wee? Where none can doe
Treason to us except one of us two.

In *The Canonization* he tells us that future lovers will address him and his mistress as

You to whom love was peace, that now is rage.

And in *The Dissolution* we read of a love so secure that the "elements" of love, "fire of Passion, sighs of ayre, water of teares and earthly sad despaire" were "ne'ere worne out by loves securitie." There are two alternative readings of this line; it may be "ne'ere worne out" (never) or "neere worne out" (nearly). The former seems to me the more probable reading, since Donne is arguing that he is now overburdened with elements, which he is more likely to be if they had not been spent. Moreover, in "loves securitie," "fire of Passion, sighs of ayre, water of teares and earthly sad despaire" are not "worne out" (such love does not call for the expense of spirit); "never" fits the sense better than "nearly," but, for my present argument, it is not of vital importance which reading we choose, the significant word is "securitie." Nor does Donne merely tell us of the fearlessness, safety, peace, and security that love may give; the serenity of which he speaks is reflected in the movement of his verse, the quiet speaking voice is heard in the rhythm of *The Good-morrow,* and in *A Valediction: forbidding mourning,* and quiet pleading in the last stanza of *A Valediction: of weeping:*

> O more then Moone,
> Draw not up seas to drowne me in thy spheare,
> Weepe me not dead, in thine armes but forbeare
> To teach the sea, what it may do too soone;
> Let not the winde
> Example finde,
> To doe me more harme, than it purposeth;
> Since thou and I sigh one another's breath,
> Who e'r sighs most, is cruellest, and hasts the others death;

and in that gracious lyric, "Sweetest love I do not goe."

Since writing the above I have read Professor Crofts's article on John Donne in *Essays and Studies,* vol. xxii, in which he presents much the same case against the love poetry as Mr. Lewis. Their hostility to Donne springs from the same causes. Both are unable to believe that a poet so brilliantly cynical is to be taken seriously when he is reverent or tender. Yet this very diversity of experience and feeling is among Donne's singular merits. Professor Crofts complains (p. 131) that for Donne "Love when it comes is not an experience which . . . wipes away the trivial, fond records of youthful apostasy." And that is true; the memory of trivial and bitter moments was clear enough for him to draw upon them for analogies even in the *Holy Sonnets;* whether this is regrettable or no is a matter of taste. There is no doubt, however, that Donne's habit of drawing upon all and any of his past experience bewilders some readers; it is not customary. Equally unusual is the absence of description which vexes both Mr. Lewis and Professor Crofts. "He cannot see her—does not apparently want to see her; for it is not of her that he writes but of his relation to her." That also is perfectly true; the only question is whether good love poetry need be descriptive.

But, in addition to these matters of taste and opinion, Professor Crofts adduces two matters of fact in opposition to the view that Donne's conception of love was altered by his relations with Anne More. The first is Ben Jonson's remark in the *Conversations with Drummond* that "all his best pieces were written ere he was twenty five years of age." But we neither know which poems Jonson had read when he made this remark, nor which he thought were the best. The second fact is that the *Metempsychosis* was dated by Donne himself Aug. 1601, four months before his marriage, and it contains cynical generalizations about women. As it is a fragment of a bitter satire against Queen Elizabeth, prompted by the sacrifice of Essex, that is not surprising. Moreover, is it so strange to be contemptuous of many, or even of most women and to love and reverence a few? The love and friendships which Donne enjoyed did not expunge his former experiences, but they enlarged his understanding so that the body of his poetry has a completeness which it could not otherwise have had. He had felt almost everything a man can feel about a woman, scorn, self-contempt, anguish, sensual delight, and the peace and security of mutual love. And he shapes such poems out of all this that we are, as Professor Crofts says, "aware of the man speaking in a manner and to a degree hardly to be paralleled in our reading of lyric poetry. Every word is resonant with his voice, every line seems to bear the stamp of his peculiar personality." Is this not enough to set him among the great love poets?

NOTES

[1] *The Faerie Queene,* I, ix, 51.
[2] On page 14.
[3] *Paradise Lost,* Bk. viii, 622–9.
[4] P. 12.

GEORGE WILLIAMSON

The Convention of *The Extasie*

Since Pierre Legouis challenged Grierson's interpretation of "The Extasie" and argued that it should be read as a poem of seduction, it has attracted more attention than any other poem by Donne. Merritt Y. Hughes, in reply, has tried to establish its Platonic lineage by means of Castiglione's *Courtier*.[1] But the problem raised by Legouis has a framework that has not been examined in subsequent discussion.

Long ago Morris W. Croll suggested this when he pointed to the original pattern for Fulke Greville's *Caelica* 75 in Sidney's Eighth Song of *Astrophel and Stella:*

> The two poems have in common the description of a May landscape, the walk of two lovers through "an enamel'd meade" (in Greville), in "a grove most rich of shade" (in Sidney), the long silence of both, with nice analysis of their emotions, finally a long casuistic dialogue on love, in which the ardor of the lover is restrained by the prudence of his mistress, or, in Greville's case, by her anger.[2]

For this pattern Janet G. Scott, in *Les Sonnets Elisabéthains,* found no precise antecedent, but a relation that lends support to Legouis:

> La chanson VIII a quelque ressemblance avec ces Chants de Mai ou "Reverdies" composés par les Trouvères et les Troubadours lorsqu'un souffle d'amour venait les troubler au

From *Seventeenth Century Contexts* (London: Faber & Faber; Chicago: The University of Chicago Press, 1960, 1961), pp. 63–77. Reprinted by permission of the publishers.

> printemps. L'oeuvre de la Pléiade est remplie de similaires invitations à l'amour, mais le dialogue du poète anglais avec Stella introduit quelques différences non sans originalité.[3]

Yet what Croll calls the "casuistic dialogue on love" is a crucial difference in Sidney's invitation to love, and removes it equally from Marlowe's *Passionate Shepherd to his Love* or its successors.

In 1903 Croll outlined the "convention" begun by Sidney in a footnote to his comparison of the imitation by Fulke Greville:

> Poems following this convention are numerous in later poets. Compare Donne's *The Ecstacy,* Lord Herbert's *Ode on a Question moved whether Love should continue forever,* Wither's *Fair-Virtue, The Mistress of Phil'arete,* Sonnet 3. In Donne's poem by a characteristic subtlety the dialogue is reduced to a monologue spoken by the undistinguished soul of the two lovers. There may be an original in some foreign literature, or Sidney's Song may have suggested the rest. Sedley shows the abuse of the form in various poems and Cartwright protests against the Platonism which found expression in it in his *No Platonic Love.*

Various signs point to Sidney as the exemplar for the English poets, but his verse form undergoes some modification in the later poets. The popularization of Platonic theories, Miss Scott reminds us, was "due à des ouvrages comme les *Asolani* de Bembo, et le *Cortegiano* de Castiglione." Obviously Platonism is not the only love casuistry that finds expression in this convention. The variety of poets who employ this convention is in itself enough to challenge our interest, and more than enough to destroy some of our preconceptions. The probable chronological order of their poems is Sidney, Greville, Donne, Wither, and Lord Herbert. However, we shall examine their use of this convention not in chronological order but rather in that of complication: Sidney, Greville, Wither, Herbert, Donne. Various new elements or alterations of the old will enter into this complication.

Sidney's Song begins with a pastoral setting:

> In a Grove most rich of shade,
> Where Birds wanton musique made,
> *May,* then young, his pyed weedes showing,
> New perfum'd, with flowers fresh growing,
> *Astrophell* with *Stella* sweete,
> Did for mutuall comfort meete . . .

Theirs is an unhappy, forbidden love: "Him great harmes had taught much care,/ Her faire necke a foul yoake bare." Now they find solace for their grief in each other's company,

> While their eyes by Love directed,
> Enterchangeably reflected . . .
> But their tongues restrain'd from walking,
> Till their harts had ended talking.

Finally, "Love it selfe did silence breake," and Astrophell began a "blazon" of her beauties leading to a request, which is suggested by the lines, "*Stella,* in whose body is/Writ each Character of blisse." Fearing to put his request directly, he asks on his knees, "That not I, but since I love you,/Time and place for me may move you." Then all the elements of place and season conspire to preach love, "And if dumbe things be so wittie,/Shall a heavenly grace want pittie?" Finally his hands "Would have made tongues language plaine," but her hands "Gave repulse, all grace excelling." His argument has been based on the analogies of nature suggested by the pastoral setting.

Then Stella's argument begins, "While such wise she love denied,/As yet love she signified." Asking him to "Cease in these effects to prove" her love, she answers in terms of her situation, her "foule yoake." Thus she finds her only comfort in him, and swears her faith by the eyes he praised; in short, she gives all her love and faith, but not her body. For she is restrained by honour and would remain free of shame.

> There-with-all, away she went,
> Leaving him to passion rent:
> With what she had done and spoken,
> That there-with my Song is broken.

She can say "Tirant honour dooth thus use thee" because of the foul yoke which she wears, not because Stella herself would refuse him. Thus she does not argue in terms of the pastoral setting, but in terms of their social condition. These restraints lend vehemence to her vows.

In Greville's imitation of Sidney the brief setting is made more suggestive:

> In the time when herbs and flowers,
> Springing out of melting powers,
> Teach the earth that heate and raine
> Doe make *Cupid* live againe:
> Late when *Sol,* like great hearts, showes
> Largest as he lowest goes,
> *Caelica* with *Philocell*
> In fellowship together fell.

Her hair, however, is made suggestive of mourning, "Of hopes death which to her eyes,/Offers thoughts for sacrifice." The love of Philocell and the scorn of Caelica are then analysed as "Through enamel'd Meades they went,/Quiet she, he passion rent." Here the echo of Sidney leads into a reversal of roles in which Philocell protests his love when at length "His despaire taught feare thus speake":

> You, to whom all Passions pray,
> Like poore Flies that to the fire,
> Where they burne themselves, aspire . . .

These resemblances to Donne's "Canonization" begin a long appeal of the forlorn lover to the cruel mistress. Her cold answers show, says Greville, "How self-pitties have reflexion,/Backe into their owne infection." For she replies that her love is dead and advises him to "let Reason guide affection,/From despaire to new election." Now Philocell begs for pity, but implies doubt of Caelica; whereupon "His eyes great with child with teares/Spies in her eyes many feares." In fury she tells him to be gone, that men are full of contradictions, that he has imposed on her enough, and finally, "I will never rumour move,/At least for one I doe not love."

Then Greville takes up the defence of Philocell against Caelica:

> Shepheardesses, if it prove,
> *Philocell* she once did love,
> Can kind doubt of true affection
> Merit such a sharpe correction?

Thus Greville begins to elaborate the love casuistry as he spells out the argument, which involves Philocell's jealousy and Caelica's wrong. He argues that the nature of love excuses and explains its abuses, and that Philocell will remain faithful to his martyrdom. Greville concludes, "Here my silly Song is ended," but hastens to assure the nymphs that they can find faith in men if they will be constant.

In Greville the seductive element is almost lost in the extension and complication of the love casuistry. Sidney's descriptive praise of the lady is greatly reduced, and the pastoral setting finds no place in the love casuistry. While a more hopeless Petrarchan atmosphere is developed, the poem ends with a real problem in love casuistry and thus justifies the argumentative resolution. Sidney's Song was broken by an action which also completed its argument.

Wither's Sonnet 3 of *Fair Virtue* begins with the familiar setting:

> When Philomela with her strains
> The spring had welcomed in,
> And Flora to bestrow the plains

With daisies did begin,
My love and I, on whom suspicious eyes
Had set a thousand spies,
To cozen Argus strove;
And seen of none
We got alone
Into a shady grove.

Here "The earth, the air, and all things did conspire/To raise contentment higher"; so that if the lovers had "come to woo," nothing would have been lacking. Hand in hand they walked, and talked "Of love and passions past." Their "souls infus'd into each other were" and shared each other's sorrow. But then their bodies begin to betray their souls:

Her dainty palm I gently prest,
And with her lips I play'd;
My cheek upon her panting breast,
And on her neck I laid.
And yet we had no sense of wanton lust . . .

Soon their passions overpower them:

But kissing and embracing we
So long together lay,
Her touches all inflamed me,
And I began to stray.
My hands presum'd so far, they were too
bold . . .

As Wither makes this turn upon Sidney, his lover's virtue is "put to flight," and his lady in tears begins to plead with him not to spot their "true love," protesting "Whilst thee I thus refuse/In hotter flames I fry." Her Platonic lament increases in vehemence:

Are we the two that have so long
Each other's loves embraced?
And never did affection wrong,
Nor think a thought unchaste?

Her argument now involves a line used by Sidney: "I should of all our passions grow ashamed,/And blush when thou art named." But her reasons are quite different, for those "who are to lust inclin'd,/Drive love out of the mind." And she is no Stella:

No vulgar bliss I aimed at
When first I heard thee woo;
I'll never prize a man for that
Which every groom can do.

While she speaks he regains control of himself because in her

Those virtues shine
Whose rays divine
First gave desire a law.

Thus the blush of shame returns to him, for his "soul her light of reason had renew'd." Then he preaches to "wantons" contempt of the body, "Since every beast/In pleasure equals you." And because the conquest of evil brings "peace without compare." But lest the wantons still think his conquest slight, he puts it beyond the labours of Hercules and the chastity of Diana. Whether this persuaded the wantons of his higher love seems at best doubtful.

Wither has certainly made the Sidney convention a vehicle for a prurient Platonism. Nature conspires with the body, not the soul, but the argument turns against nature in the conclusion. When the rescued lover expresses the moral of Platonic love, he counts its dividends too much in the old currency to establish the new. Altogether the pastoral framework is at odds with the Platonism, and matters are not improved by mixing mythology into the realism of the poem.

Lord Herbert's "Ode upon a Question moved, whether Love should continue for ever?" has the most elaborate pastoral setting of all. Nature in flower waits for the sun, "the wish'd Bridegroom of the earth." Birds, wind, brook, lovers, all "An harmony of parts did bind." The lovers walked "towards a pleasant Grove" and reposed on the grass,

Long their fixt eyes to Heaven bent,
Unchanged, they did never move,
As if so great and pure a love
No Glass but it could represent.

Then Celinda raises the question of love's end at death, and does so in stanzas that are a temptation to quote, asking whether if love's fire is kindled with life, it will not go out with life. Since this also raises the problem of sense in love, Melander answers that their love is beyond but not above sense, and that they must reach toward the invisible through the visible.

Rephrasing her question, he answers that since their "virtuous habits" are born of the soul, they "Must with it evermore endure." In Herbert's *De Veritate* (ed. Carré, p. 123) this argument rests upon this proposition: "It is then reasonable to believe that the faculties with which we are born do not perish at death." If sin's guilt never dies, the joy of virtuous love is still more certain of survival. Otherwise Heaven's laws would be vain, "When to an everlasting Cause/They gave a perishing Effect." Where God admits the fair, he does not exclude love; nor does he exclude sense if bodies rise again:

> For if no use of sense remain
> When bodies once this life forsake,
> Or they could no delight partake,
> Why should they ever rise again?

The final postulate here alters the statement in *De Veritate* (p. 124): "When that which is corruptible in us is separated from what is incorruptible, which I hold to be the great unceasing work of nature, it is not the faculties which fall into decay, but the sense-organs." And if love is the end of knowledge here in imperfection, how much more perfect will it be in perfection. Then his argument takes its final turn: "Were not our souls immortal made,/Our equal loves can make them such." Although this suggests the end of Donne's "Good morrow," it turns toward propagation as a final answer to the question moved:

> So when one wing can make no way,
> Two joyned can themselves dilate,
> So can two persons propagate,
> When singly either would decay.

In this persuasive figure their relation to heaven is not forsaken as "Each shall be both, yet both but one." Indeed, her eyes "look up again to find their place":

> While such a moveless silent peace
> Did seize on their becalmed sense,
> One would have thought some influence
> Their ravish'd spirits did possess.

Thus Herbert exhibits no such dislocation of the Platonic mode as we find in Wither. But it is not quite so simple as saying that since their love is of the soul and the soul is immortal, therefore their love is immortal. For body is involved in this awareness, and so it becomes the last resort in persuasion and fulfilment, because God is best known and loved in his creatures.

Herbert's argument, however, needs to be understood not simply as Platonism but in terms of his *De Veritate*. It may be judged by this summary of his remarks on love (pp. 196–8): "Consequently, though our mind can become immersed in physical feelings while it concerns itself with the common good, yet I place love among the intellectual and spiritual faculties, because lust and similar cravings can be found in a plethoric body apart from love. . . . As for the objects of the intellectual and spiritual faculties, there are two kinds, namely, particular and general. In this respect they are also distinguished from the physical faculties, which seem only to have particular objects. The particular objects of the internal intellectual faculties are the divine attributes, while the common objects are physical objects. . . . Love was the first of the inner emotions. This faculty is above all sensitive to the divine beauty and goodness and afterwards to all the divine attributes. . . . The common object of this faculty is physical love. For this reason the feeling which relates to the perpetuation of the species, so long as it is not infected with unlawful lust or concupiscence, is humane and may spring from the faculty which seeks the general good."

While the final statement in this summary gives another dimension to the conclusion of his *Ode*, the relation between the physical and intellectual in love explains the form which his answer takes in arguing "that the faculties with which we are born do not perish at death." Once this has been said, however, one must return to the poetic cogency of the *Ode* which may be illuminated but cannot be replaced by the structure of *De Veritate*. The ambiguity of the conclusion to the *Ode* appears more clearly by virtue of our comparison, but we have to take care not to lose the meaning of the physical because of its intellectual implication, or else we will transform the primary impact of the poem and blunt the surprise of its ending. For the conclusion seems both to consummate their love and to compromise his answer. But even the beauty of stanzas like

> This said, in her up-lifted face,
> Her eyes which did that beauty crown,
> Were like two starrs, that having faln down,
> Look up again to find their place:

may owe something to the idea in Plato's *Timaeus* that souls, before their human birth, were in the stars. And Herbert's final turn gives a rarefied air to the conclusion of "The Extasie."

Donne, like Herbert, is interested less in the moral casuistry of love than in the philosophical questions provoked by it. Hence the debate in "The Extasie" may involve body and soul rather more than two lovers. Croll has said that "In *Astrophel and Stella* and the *Arcadia* the prevailing idea is the contrast between the abstract spiritual ideals which appeal to the soul alone and the concrete forms on which ordinary human desire is fixed." But he adds that the Platonic mode of thought is used by Sidney rather as a literary convention than as a serious philosophy. Obviously it is not a part of the convention of physical love introduced by Sidney's Eighth Song, which is more properly described as an invitation to love.

This convention may be restated for "The Extasie" as follows: description of the burgeoning of nature; description of lovers and their emotions; their absorption in the rapture of love; their relationship to some problem arising from this state of rapture; its investigation and solution; relation of the solution to their initial rapture.

The pastoral setting of "The Extasie" is reduced to the shortest and most carnally suggestive form yet found in this convention:

> Where, like a pillow on a bed,
> A Pregnant banke swel'd up, to rest
> The violets reclining head,
> Sat we two, one anothers best.

Hands and eyes as yet were "all the meanes to make us one,"

> And pictures in our eyes to get
> Was all our propagation.

In Sidney, it may be remembered, their eyes "Enterchangeably reflected." The last line sounds as if Donne were beginning where Herbert concluded, but it simply introduces the consummation of physical union toward which they seem bent. This consummation, however, remains uncertain because it must be decided by the souls, "which to advance their state" had left the bodies, their prisons. Now they "hung 'twixt her, and mee," preventing consummation until they have negotiated an agreement; meanwhile the bodies lie inanimate, like statues. Now this negotiation involves a discovery about the nature of their love, but it can be understood only by one refined enough by love to understand the language of the soul. Hence the character of the invoked witness and yet his inability to distinguish voices in a union of minds. For they discover that it was not sex but a mingling of souls that moved them to love. At this point it seems as if their original physical means to union have been completely invalidated. But a violet from the pastoral setting provides an analogy to show how transplanted souls also redouble in the abler soul of love.

> Wee then, who are this new soule, know,
>   Of what we are compos'd, and made,
> For, th' Atomies of which we grow,
>   Are soules, whom no change can invade.

And so their love acquires the superior powers that belong to the soul, and the negotiations would seem to have gone against the bodies, if it were not for the fact that the violet helped to elucidate the mystery of their love. Even so the shift to the voice of feeling takes us by surprise:

> But O alas, so long, so farre
>   Our bodies why doe wee forbeare?

We might suppose that isolated superiority is too much for them, or that some "defects of lonelinesse" are not controlled by their souls. But of course their ecstasy had a physical origin, and their negotiation requires some solution for the problem of the bodies.

In this argument the apology for body now begins. The bodies are not the souls, but their senses first brought the souls together. As sphere to intelligence, or as air to heaven, the body is the agent or medium of the soul. As blood ascends to spirits to unite body and soul, so even pure lovers' souls must descend to affections and faculties which sense may reach, or else the living soul is locked in a bodily prison, except in ecstasy.

> To' our bodies turne wee then, that so
>   Weake men on love reveal'd may looke;
> Loves mysteries in soules doe grow,
>   But yet the body is his booke.

Weak men require physical revelation, but initiates in love's mysteries, who do not, will see small change when their spiritual unity is manifested in the physical. Thus their original physical union may be consummated without spiritual adulteration, for the bodies are not "drosse to us, but allay." Thus the problem of the physical in love posed by the original situation has been solved by inclusion, not by rejection. Again the hypothetical listener—for the souls are still speaking—is called to witness the final turn of the argument.

Only the rejection of the physical would have saved "The Extasie" from any suggestion of an invitation to love, but even its inclusion probably did not assure its success for Dryden because it still "perplexes the minds of the fair sex with nice speculations of philosophy." And this philosophical turn is given form by Croll's observation: "In Donne's poem by a characteristic subtlety the dialogue is reduced to a monologue spoken by the undistinguished soul of the two lovers." And the reason for this form is that there is no contrariety between the lovers but only in the subject of their discourse. Hence the monologue is instrumental to the philosophy, and Donne uses the ecstasy for this mingling of souls or rise to the Platonic level. He does not, like Bembo in Castiglione's *Courtier*, make a kiss the cause of this mingling of souls, though "one alone so framed of them both ruleth (in a manner) two bodies" in his poem. But he did use the ecstasy as an expressive device in *Ignatius his Conclave:*

> I was in an *Extasie*, and
> *My little wandring sportful Soule,*
> *Ghest, and Companion of my body*
> had liberty to wander through all places . . .

Here of course it is a satiric device, not a Platonic device. In Donne's poem it becomes a means arising from the rapture of love by which to analyse that rapture in terms of the nature of man. In a subtler form this poem is a debate between the soul and body or an analysis of love in these terms without the sharp oppositions found in "A Valediction: of the booke" or "A Valediction: forbidding mourning."

Thus into a convention of physical love Donne introduces the Platonic convention as a means to investigate the nature of love. Up to a point the steps in both conventions coincide, but the conclusion denies and harmonizes the extremes of both. The physical convention is clear from the beginning; the Platonic is introduced by the ecstasy. The former includes the latter and is modified by it. The sensual, idyllic convention, united with the Platonic, issues in a mediate or combined position; but while posing the carnal versus spiritual contention, the poem never surrenders the primacy of the spiritual, nor ever rejects or condemns the carnal like Wither.

Donne's poetry runs the gamut of love described by Bembo on the basis of his analysis of man in Castiglione's *Courtier:*

> And because in our soule there be three manner waies to know, namely, by sense, reason, and understanding: of sense there ariseth appetite or longing, which is common to us with

> brute beastes: of reason ariseth election or choice, which is proper to man: of understanding, by the which man may be partner with Angels, ariseth will.

Donne is more likely to base his analysis on the three souls mentioned in "A Valediction: of my name, in the window":

> Then, as all my soules bee,
> Emparadis'd in you, (in whom alone
> I understand, and grow and see,) . . .

Here the three souls are named by their major faculties in this order: rational, vegetable, animal or sensitive. But whichever scale is used, Donne treats the various kinds of love and lovers described by Bembo. On the sensual level it is bound by the limitations of the senses; on the Platonic level it is a relation of souls or mind, unaffected by the physical and its limitations of time and space. The problem of absence is usually solved on this level. But Donne is seldom a pure Platonist; he usually inhabits the region of "The Extasie," occasionally ascending higher on the scale or descending lower. He even has moments of scorn for "That loving wretch that sweares,/'Tis not the bodies marry, but the mindes," but it never reaches the mockery of Cartwright's "Tell me no more of minds embracing minds." Nevertheless, Bembo's discussion in the *Courtier* is the best introduction to Donne's treatment of love.

The study of this convention gives us a concrete lesson in the kind of literary continuity and change that took place between Elizabethan and Jacobean times. It also provides us with some insight into the relations between tradition and the individual talent in these poets. Of course the poems are not equally representative of their poets; but since the broad form is dictated by the convention, their own formal powers, both poetic and metrical, can be measured comparatively within a limited area. If such a comparison is thought to be altogether unfair, perhaps we could agree that this convention does not provide easy examples by which to illustrate the decline of poetry in Jacobean times. And possibly also that the usual course of such conventions is towards decline rather than the reverse. I do not think Donne and Herbert need to fear the verdict, and I find Greville worthy of more serious interest than either Sidney or Wither.

NOTES

[1] *Modern Language Review*, Vol. 27, No. 1.

[2] *The Works of Fulke Greville*, Philadelphia, 1903, p. 9.

[3] Paris, 1929, p. 47.

LOUIS L. MARTZ

John Donne in Meditation: the *Anniversaries*

> Beare not therefore with her losses, for shee is won for ever, but with the momentary absence of your most happy sister: yea it can not iustly bee called an absence, many thoghts being daily in parlee with her, onely mens eyes and eares unwoorthy to enioy so sweet an obiect, have resigned their interest, and interested this treasure in their hearts, being the fittest shrines for so pure a Saint, whome, as none did know but did love, so none can nowe remember [but] with devotion. Men may behold hir with shame of their former life, seeing one of the weaker sexe honour her weaknesse wyth such a trayne of perfections. Ladies may admire her as a glorie to their degree, in whom honour was portraied in her full likenesse, grace having perfited Natures first draught with all the due colours of an absolute vertue: all women accept her as a patterne to immitate her gifts and her good partes.
>
> Robert Southwell, *The Triumphs over Death* (in memory of Margaret Sackville), 1595

I

From the early days of Donne's Satire 3, where meditation struggles to convert the methods of Roman satire, down to the late days of his

From *The Poetry of Meditation: A Study in English Religious Literature of the Seventeenth Century* (New Haven: Yale University Press; London: Oxford University Press, 1954), pp. 211–48. Reprinted, by permission of the publishers, with emendations from the 2nd edition (paperback, 1962).

"Hymne to God the Father," where he seems to transform the refrain of Wyatt's love-lament,[1] the distinctive note of Donne is always his ground-tone of religious quest, even when the overt mode of the poem is one of mockery. His search for the One underlies and explains his discontent with the fluctuations of transitory passion, as he makes clear in the *Second Anniversary:*

> But pause, my soule; And study, ere thou fall
> On accidentall joyes, th'essentiall.
> Still before Accessories doe abide
> A triall, must the principall be tride.
> And what essentiall joy can'st thou expect
> Here upon earth? what permanent effect
> Of transitory causes? Dost thou love
> Beauty? (And beauty worthy'st is to move)
> Poore cousened cousenor, *that* she, and *that* thou,
> Which did begin to love, are neither now;
> You are both fluid, chang'd since yesterday;
> Next day repaires, (but ill) last dayes decay.
> Nor are, (although the river keepe the name)
> Yesterdaies waters, and to daies the same.
> So flowes her face, and thine eyes, neither now
> That Saint, nor Pilgrime, which your loving vow
> Concern'd, remaines; but whil'st you thinke you bee
> Constant, you'are hourely in inconstancie. (383–400)

Consequently, in his "Songs and Sonets" the central power arises from the way in which, along with his insistence on the physical, he grips the thin Petrarchan affirmation of spiritual love, and builds it up on every side with theological proofs and profound religious images.

Thus readers have disagreed over whether "The Extasie" is a poem of seduction or a deep theological and philosophical exploration of the relationship between body and soul: [2] for it is all these things, simultaneously. The wit of the title depends upon the double reference to "sensuall Extasie" and mystical *extasis;* the whole poem develops from the physical desires implied in the curious "composition of place" with which the poem opens:

> Where, like a pillow on a bed,
> A Pregnant banke swel'd up . . . .

Those desires, then, after long intellectual analysis of human love, are finally reconciled with the spiritual in an exhortation that involves the theological concepts of incarnation and revelation:

To'our bodies turne wee then, that so
Weake men on love reveal'd may looke;
Loves mysteries in soules doe grow,
But yet the body is his booke.

Likewise, the somber tradition of meditation on death lies behind "The Funerall," with its half-mocking transformation of a symbol of physical lust into a religious "mystery":

Who ever comes to shroud me, do not harme
Nor question much
That subtile wreath of haire, which crowns my arme;
The mystery, the signe you must not touch,
For 'tis my outward Soule,
Viceroy to that, which then to heaven being gone,
Will leave this to controule,
And keepe these limbes, her Provinces, from dissolution.

Or, more violently, in "Twicknam garden" the tears and sighs of the traditional lover are converted into agony by a bitter play upon religious images:

But O, selfe traytor, I do bring
The spider love, which transubstantiates all,
And can convert Manna to gall,
And that this place may thoroughly be thought
True Paradise, I have the serpent brought.

In his love-poems, then, the central wit consists in this: in taking up the religious motifs conventionally displayed in Petrarchan verse, and stressing them so heavily that any one of three results may be achieved. Sometimes the effect is one of witty blasphemy, as in "The Dreame," where he deifies his lady by attributing her arrival in his bedroom to her Godlike power of reading his mind. Sometimes, as in "The Extasie," the poem maintains a complex tone in which the playful and the solemn, the profane and the sacred, are held in a perilous poise:

As 'twixt two equall Armies, Fate
Suspends uncertaine victorie . . . .

And at other times human love is exalted to the religious level, notably in "A nocturnall upon S. Lucies day," where, in accordance with the ancient ecclesiastical usage of the term "nocturnal," or "nocturne,"

Donne presents a midnight service, a "Vigill," commemorating the death of his beloved—his saint. He recalls the passionate fluctuations of their worldly career, in terms that suggest a long period of frustrated spiritual devotion:

> Oft a flood
> Have wee two wept, and so
> Drownd the whole world, us two; oft did we grow
> To be two Chaosses, when we did show
> Care to ought else; and often absences
> Withdrew our soules, and made us carcasses.

But with her death his physical life has died, and he is "re-begot Of absence, darkenesse, death": in him love has "wrought new Alchimie" by expressing "A quintessence even from nothingnesse." His only life now lies in the spiritual realm where she now lives:

> You lovers, for whose sake, the lesser Sunne
> At this time to the Goat is runne
> To fetch new lust, and give it you,
> Enjoy your summer all;
> Since shee enjoyes her long nights festivall,
> Let mee prepare towards her, and let mee call
> This houre her Vigill, and her Eve, since this
> Both the yeares, and the dayes deep midnight is.

Surely Mr. Murray is right in arguing that this poem deals with Donne's love for his wife; [3] its conclusion seems to point the way toward the opening lines of Holy Sonnet 17:

> Since she whom I lov'd hath payd her last debt
> To Nature, and to hers, and my good is dead,
> And her Soule early into heaven ravished,
> Wholly on heavenly things my mind is sett.

It seems to me quite possible that Donne wrote the "Nocturnall" after his wife's death in 1617; though it might have been composed on some occasion of severe illness, such as one recorded in a letter by Donne (1606?), where he speaks of a certain "paper" written during a night of his wife's severe labor:

> It is (I cannot say the waightyest, but truly) the saddest lucubration and nights passage that ever I had. For it exer-

> cised those hours, which, with extreme danger to her, whom I should hardly have abstained from recompensing for her company in this world, with accompanying her out of it, encreased my poor family with a son. Though her anguish, and my fears, and hopes, seem divers and wild distractions from this small businesse of your papers, yet because they all narrowed themselves, and met in *Via regia,* which is the consideration of our selves, and God, I thought it time not unfit for this despatch.[4]

In any case, the "Nocturnall" vividly illustrates the way in which Donne's poetry, throughout his career, moves along a Great Divide between the sacred and the profane, now facing one way, now another, but always remaining intensely aware of both sides. In his love-poetry the religious aspects are frequently so strong that they seem to overwhelm the fainter religious themes of Petrarchan poetry; while in six of the "Holy Sonnets" (3, 13, 14, 17, 18, 19) the memories and images of profane love are deliberately used in love-sonnets of sacred parody. One must observe, then, the greatest possible caution in considering the relation between the "profane" and the "religious" in Donne's work: individual poems will not fall easily into such categories; nor can the poems be safely dated by assumptions about the more religious, and the less religious, periods of his life.

II

Donne may well have written some of his love-songs and some of his "Holy Sonnets" during the same periods of his life: one of the most dubious assumptions in modern studies of Donne has been the universal acceptance of Gosse's dating of all the "Holy Sonnets" in 1617 or after, simply because one of the sonnets refers to the death of Donne's wife.[5] Grierson accepted this dating, and thereby gave it currency, along with the view that Donne's religious poems "fall into two groups": those written before his ordination, which are marked by a more intellectual style, and those written after his ordination and after the death of his wife, which are of a more passionate quality. But such distinctions are at best hazardous with a personality so paradoxical as Donne's; moreover, as I have suggested in the case of "La Corona," differences in style may also be explained by differences in the meditative traditions which Donne is following in certain poems. Grierson's examination of the manuscripts does not support the above dating of the "Holy Sonnets." He points out, for example, that in the

Harleian manuscript they bear the heading: "Holy Sonnets: written 20 yeares since." After this general heading the manuscript then gives, under the special heading, "La Corona," the seven sonnets properly belonging to that sequence. "Thereafter follow," Grierson adds, "without any fresh heading, twelve of the sonnets belonging to the second group, generally entitled *Holy Sonnets*." Noting that the date 1629 is given to other poems in this manuscript, Grierson adds that this would bring us back to the year 1609, a dating which he is inclined to accept for "La Corona." But, as Grierson says, "the question is, did the copyist [of this manuscript] intend that the note should apply to all the sonnets he transcribed or only to the *La Corona* group?" Having already accepted Gosse's dating, he is forced to rule out the second group; yet the sonnet on Donne's wife is not among these twelve, and indeed the fact that only twelve of the sonnets occur here may suggest that the nineteen "Holy Sonnets" were not necessarily all written in the same period, as Gosse assumes. Grierson himself notes that he "cannot find a definite significance in any order," and that "each sonnet is a separate meditation"; this would seem to destroy the basis for Gosse's dating.[6]

Furthermore, it is a curious fact that Donne's "Elegie on Mistris Boulstred," who died on August 4, 1609,[7] seems unquestionably to represent a recantation of his famous sonnet:

> Death be not proud, though some have called thee
> Mighty and dreadfull, for, thou art not soe,
> For, those, whom thou think'st, thou dost overthrow,
> Die not, poore death, nor yet canst thou kill mee.

The opening lines of the elegy seem explicitly to answer this opening of the sonnet:

> Death I recant, and say, unsaid by mee
> What ere hath slip'd, that might diminish thee.
> Spirituall treason, atheisme 'tis, to say,
> That any can thy Summons disobey.

Lines 9–10 appear to reinterpret lines 7–8 of the sonnet:

> And soonest our best men with thee doe goe,
> Rest of their bones, and soules deliverie.

> Now hee will seeme to spare, and doth more wast,
> Eating the best first, well preserv'd to last.

And indeed all the first half of the elegy (1–34) amounts to a denial of the sonnet's ending, "death, thou shalt die." We have the parenthesis, "were Death dead" (15); and the exclamations, "O strong and long-liv'd death" (21), "How could I thinke thee nothing" (25), "O mighty bird of prey" (31). The conclusion seems inevitable that Holy Sonnet 10 must have been written before August 4, 1609. If this is so, could it not also be true of other "Holy Sonnets"?

The conjecture is supported by the evidence of Donne's painful letters from Mitcham, where he frequently speaks of his "meditation," [8] and by Grierson's dating of "La Corona" (1607–9), "The Annuntiation and Passion" (March 25, 1608), and "The Litanie" (1609–10).[9] Everything that we know of Donne indicates that, during the years from his marriage in 1601 down through the time of his ordination in 1615, he was engaging in the most fervent and painful self-analysis, directed toward the problem of his vocation. The crisis and culmination of these efforts, I believe, is represented in the two *Anniversaries*, both of which, surprisingly enough, may have been written in the year 1611. (See Appendix 2.) Thus they seem to come immediately before the first clear announcement by Donne, in his letter of c. 1612, that he has decided to enter the ministry: "having obeyed at last, after much debatement within me, the Inspirations (as I hope) of the Spirit of God, and resolved to make my Profession Divinitie . . . ." [10] The relationship of the *Anniversaries* to these "debatements" is reinforced by the very close verbal and thematic similarities, pointed out by Mrs. Simpson, between these poems and Donne's *Essayes in Divinity:* those "Several Disquisitions, Interwoven with Meditations and Prayers," which "were the voluntary sacrifices of severall hours, when he had many debates betwixt God and himself, whether he were worthy, and competently learned to enter into Holy Orders." [11]

The *Anniversaries,* along with his other meditations of this period —including, perhaps, many of the "Holy Sonnets"—may be seen as part of the spiritual exercises which Donne was performing in the effort to determine his problem of "election": the term which St. Ignatius Loyola gave to that crucial portion of his *Exercises* of the Second Week (pp. 54–60), where the exercitant is faced with the problem of deciding upon a way of life, "as for example an office or benefice to be accepted or left." One of the problems here described by the *Exercises* is one that, according to Walton, troubled Donne when Morton in the year 1607 urged Donne to accept an office in the Church: "there are others that first desire to possess benefices and then to serve God in them. So these do not go straight to God, but wish God to come straight to their inordinate affections; thus they make of the end a means, and of the means an end; so that what they ought to take first they take last." [12] Among the Jesuit methods for "making a sound and good election" in such matters, it is interesting —with the "Holy Sonnets" in mind—to notice that meditations on the love of God, on death ("as if I were at the point of death"), and on the Day of Judgment are especially recommended, along with another method that may have some relation to the poem which Donne later wrote "To Mr Tilman after he had taken orders": "The second rule is to place before my eyes a man whom I have never seen or known, and to consider what I, desiring all perfection for him, would tell him to do and choose for the greater glory of God our Lord, and the greater perfection of his soul; and acting so, to keep the rule which I lay down for another." For these methods of "election" might be used to confirm a decision made, as well as to make the original decision. Finally, it is worth noting that among the various "methods of prayer" recommended in the *Spiritual Exercises,* there is one that is similar to the method followed by Donne in "The Litanie": it consists "in considering the signification of each word" in a public, liturgical prayer, and in dwelling "on the consideration of this word, so long as he finds meanings, comparisons, relish, and consolation in thoughts about this word." (p. 80)

The *Anniversaries,* then, were composed during a period when Donne appears to have been utilizing all the modes of meditation and self-analysis that he knew, in the effort to make the crucial decision of his life. It was a period when his weighing of the sacred and profane tendencies within himself must have reached a climax of intensity; and this, I believe, is why the two poems represent Donne's most elaborate examples of the art of sacred parody and his most extensive efforts in the art of poetical meditation.

Yet the *Anniversaries* are not usually treated as whole poems. For one thing, the biographical facts underlying these poems lead readers to approach them with suspicion, since they were written in memory of the daughter of Donne's generous patron, Sir Robert Drury—a girl who died in her fifteenth year, and whom Donne admits he never saw.[13] As a result, the elaborate eulogies of Elizabeth Drury are frequently dismissed as venal and insincere, while interest in the poems centers on those passages which reflect Donne's awareness of the "new philosophy," on explicitly religious portions, or on any portions which provide illustrative quotations for special studies of Donne and his period.

Such fragmentary appreciation of the poems has, I think, hampered an understanding of their full significance. For each poem is carefully designed as a whole, and the full meaning of each grows out of a deliberately articulated structure. Furthermore, a close reading of each poem shows that the two *Anniversaries* are significantly different in structure and in the handling of Petrarchan imagery, and are consequently different in value. The *First Anniversary*, despite its careful structure, is, it must be admitted, successful only in brilliant patches; but I think it can be shown that the *Second Anniversary*, despite some flaws, is as a whole one of the great religious poems of the seventeenth century.

III

Let us look at the structure of the *First Anniversary: An Anatomie of the World. Wherein, By occasion of the untimely death of Mistris Elizabeth Drury, the frailty and the decay of this whole World is represented.* The poem is divided into an Introduction, a Conclusion, and five distinct sections which form the body of the work. Each of these five sections is subdivided into three sections: first, a meditation on some aspect of "the frailty and the decay of this whole world"; second, a eulogy of Elizabeth Drury as the "Idea" of human perfection and the source of hope, now lost, for the world; third, a refrain introducing a moral:

> Shee, shee is dead; shee's dead: when thou knowest this,
> Thou knowest how poore a trifling thing man is.
> And learn'st thus much by our Anatomie . . . .

In each section the second line of this refrain is modified so as to summarize the theme of the whole section; in the following outline of the poem I use part of the second line of each refrain as the heading for each section:

Introduction, 1–90. The world is sick, "yea, dead, yea putrified," since she, its "intrinsique balme" and "preservative," its prime example of Virtue, is dead.

Section I, 91–190: "how poore a trifling thing man is."

1. Meditation, 91–170. Because of Original Sin man has decayed in length of life, in physical size, in mental capacity.
2. Eulogy, 171–82. The girl was perfect virtue; she purified herself and had a purifying power over all.
3. Refrain and Moral, 183–90. Our only hope is in religion.

Section II, 191–246: "how lame a cripple this world is."

1. Meditation, 191–218. The "universall frame" has received injury from the sin of the Angels, and now in universe, in state, in family, " 'Tis all in peeces, all cohaerence gone."
2. Eulogy, 219–36. Only this girl possessed the power which might have unified the world.
3. Refrain and Moral, 237–46. Contemn and avoid this sick world.

Section III, 247–338: "how ugly a monster this world is."

1. Meditation, 247–304. Proportion, the prime ingredient of beauty, no longer exists in the universe.
2. Eulogy, 305–24. The girl was the "measure of all Symmetrie" and harmony.
3. Refrain and Moral, 325–38. Human acts must be "done fitly and in proportion."

Section IV, 339–76: "how wan a Ghost this our world is."

1. Meditation, 339–58. "Beauties other second Element, Colour, and lustre now, is as neere spent."
2. Eulogy, 359–68. The girl had the perfection of color and gave color to the world.
3. Refrain and Moral, 369–76. There is no pleasure in an ugly world; it is wicked to use false colors.

Section V, 377–434: "how drie a Cinder this world is."

1. Meditation, 377–98. Physical "influence" of the heavens upon the earth has been weakened.
2. Eulogy, 399–426. The girl's virtue has little effect on us now because of this weakened "correspondence" between heavens and earth; in fact the world's corruption weakened her effect while she lived.
3. Refrain and Moral, 427–34. Nothing "Is worth our travaile, griefe, or perishing," except the joys of religious virtue.

Conclusion, 435–74.

It seems clear that the religious motifs in Petrarchan lament, found at their best in Petrarch's poems "To Laura in Death," have here combined with strictly religious meditation to produce a poem which derives its form, fundamentally, from the tradition of spiritual exercises. The Jesuit exercises, we recall, normally involve a series of five exercises daily for a period of about a month, each meditation being precisely divided into points, usually into three points.

At the same time it is important to recall the ways of celebrating the Ideal Woman—the "Type, or an Idaea of an Accomplisht piety" [14] —represented in the meditations of the rosary which have been discussed in Chapter 2. The divisions of the Dominican rosary fall into three series of five meditations each, while, in Loarte's *Instructions*, every meditation "is distinguished into three pointes." (f.6v.) Meditation on only five of these mysteries at a time was quite common: the name "rosary," says Worthington, is "used sometimes largely, and sometimes strictly"; "largely" it contains fifteen mysteries; "strictly" it contains five, "as it is commonly ment, when one is appointed for penance, or for pardon, or for other like cause to say a Rosarie." (preface) Thus the number five becomes associated with the celebration of the Virgin: the five-petaled Rose becomes her flower.[15] This, evidently, is what lies behind Donne's treatment of the five-petaled flower in his poem, "The Primrose":

> Live Primrose then, and thrive
> With thy true number five;
> And women, whom this flower doth represent,
> With this mysterious number be content . . . .

With this symbolic number in mind, it is even more suggestive to consider the Jesuit Puente's directions for using the rosary to meditate upon the virtues of Mary. "The principall thing wherein wee are to manifest our devotion, towards the Virgin," says Puente, is "the imitation of her heroicall virtues, wherunto it will greatly ayd, to meditate them in the recitall of the Rosarie, in every tenne Ave Maries, one virtue." And in doing this, we are to follow a threefold procedure: "fixing the eyes and intention upon three things."

> 1. Upon the heroicall acts which the Virgin exercised about that virtue . . . admiring her sanctitie, reioycing therin, glorifying God, who gave it unto her, and exulting for the reward which he hath given for such a virtu. 2. To fixe mine eyes upon the wante which I have of that virtu, and upon the contrary faults and defects wherinto I fall, sorrowing for them with great confusion and humiliation . . . . 3. To make some stedfast purposes, with the greatest stabilitie that I can, to imitate the B. Virgin in these acts of virtue, assigning to this effect some particular virtue, trusting in the favor of this pious Mother, that shee will assist me to performe the same. (2, 587)

Such a threefold division of meditation, within a larger fivefold structure, has a long tradition, as Wilmart has shown by his publication of the meditations of Stephen of Salley, an English Cistercian of the early thirteenth century.[16] Stephen gives fifteen meditations on the Joys of the Virgin, divided into three series of fives; the most interesting aspect of them here is the subdivision of each meditation into three parts: (1) *Meditatio*, on the mystery itself; (2) *Gaudium*, a summary of the "Joy"; (3) *Peticio*, prayer to the Virgin invoking her assistance in the achievement of Christian perfection—the whole meditation ending with the refrain of an Ave Maria.

Meditation on the Virgin might easily influence Petrarchan eulogy; in fact Petrarch himself suggests such an influence by concluding his sequence to Laura with a *canzone* to the Virgin Mary. His previous treatment of Laura is different only in degree, not in kind. Thus in a poem describing what Donne calls "the Idea of a Woman," some connotations of Mary would appear to be almost inevitable for a poet of Donne's background. At any rate, in Donne's Introduction to his *Anatomie,* along with Petrarchan hyperbole, we find Elizabeth Drury treated in terms which seem to adumbrate the practice of meditating on Mary: she is a "Queene" ascended to Heaven, attended by Saints; her Name has a mysterious power: [17]

> Her name defin'd thee [the world], gave thee forme, and frame,
> And thou forgett'st to celebrate thy name.

She is "A strong example gone, equall to law," she was "The Cyment which did faithfully compact, And glue all vertues." Nothing remains for us, in this dying world, but to arouse our souls to imitate her; such memory of her

> Creates a new world, and new creatures bee
> Produc'd: the matter and the stuffe of this,
> Her vertue, and the forme our practice is.

Yet we cannot sustain ourselves in this new "dignitie" without some defense against the assaults of the world upon us, and against that presumption which destroys the self-righteous:

> Yet, because outward stormes the strongest breake,
> And strength it selfe by confidence growes weake,
> This new world may be safer, being told
> The dangers and diseases of the old:

For with due temper men doe then forgoe,
Or covet things, when they their true worth know.

The twofold aim of religious meditation is suggested in the last two lines. Meditation on the sinfulness of the "old man" and on the corruption of the world will teach men to "forgoe" the things of this world; and, conversely, meditation on the Example of Virtue will lead men to "covet" the imitation of the perfect soul.

In this twofold purpose of meditation lies another aspect of spiritual exercises which deserves consideration: the practice of dividing meditations into two sequences according to the seven days of the week, with two kinds of meditation each day.[18] Thus, in general, the exercitant alternates meditation leading to contempt of the world and of self with consolatory and uplifting meditation on Christ. As Juan de Avila explains,

> They who are much exercised in the *knowledge* of themselves, (in respect that they are continually viewing their defects so neer at hand) are wont to fall into great sadnes, and disconfidence, and pusillanimity; for which reason, it is necessary that they do exercise themselves also in another *knowledge,* which giveth comfort, and strength, much more then the other gave discouragement . . . .
>
> It is therefore fit for thee, after the exercise of the *knowledge of thy selfe* to imploy thy mind, upon the *knowledge of Christ Iesus our Lord.*[19]

This widespread use of contrasting meditations is also given thorough development in an English work contemporary with the *Anniversaries:* Nicholas Breton's *Divine Considerations of the Soule* (1608). Breton gives two series of seven meditations, one on "the excellencie of God," the other on "the vilenesse of man," to be used in this manner:

> Looke then upon the greatnes of God and the smalnesse of man; the goodnes of God, and the vilenesse of man; the wisdome of God, and the folly of man; the love of God, and the hate of man; the grace of God, and the disgrace of man; the mercy of God, and the tyranny of man; and the glory of God, and the infamy of man: and fixing the eye of the heart upon the one and the other, how canst thou but to the glory of God, and shame of thy selfe . . . cry with the Prophet David, *Oh Lord what is man that thou doest visit him?*[20]

Donne's *Anatomie* seems clearly to fall into such a mold, with its alternation of contempt (Meditation) and glorification (Eulogy), Donne's Moral merely serves to draw a brief conclusion from this contrast.

These examples are, I hope, sufficient to suggest the various and flexible relationships that exist between Donne's *Anatomie* and the tradition of methodical meditation. In particular, his fivefold sequence and his alternation of contempt and praise within each section mark the poem as a spiritual exercise. But the ultimate question remains and has no doubt already been suggested by the above parallels: is it valid to write in such a tradition when the pattern of virtue is, literally taken, only a girl? Certainly the chief problem in evaluating the poem has been very shrewdly put in the blunt objection of Ben Jonson: "That Donne's Anniversary was profane and full of blasphemies; that he told Mr. Donne, if it had been written of the Virgin Mary it had been something; to which he answered that he described the Idea of a Woman and not as she was." [21]

IV

When does laudation of an Ideal Woman become thus objectionable in poetry with a strong religious note? It has not been generally considered so in Dante and Petrarch. Is it objectionable in Donne? An answer, so far as this poem is concerned, may be suggested by noting Petrarch's general treatment of Laura in Death. Petrarch has successfully combined eulogy with religious themes by keeping his sequence always focused on his central symbol of perfection: the *contemptus mundi,* the hyperbole of the world's destruction, the praise of Laura in Heaven, are all justified by maintaining Laura as the origin and end of the poems' emotions, and thus making her the First Cause of the sequence.

> The chosen angels, and the spirits blest,
> Celestial tenants, on that glorious day
> My Lady join'd them, throng'd in bright array
> Around her, with amaze and awe imprest.
> "What splendour, what new beauty stands confest
> Unto our sight?"—among themselves they say;
> "No soul, in this vile age, from sinful clay
> To our high realms has risen so fair a guest."
> Delighted to have changed her mortal state,
> She ranks amid the purest of her kind;

And ever and anon she looks behind,
To mark my progress and my coming wait;
Now my whole thought, my wish to heaven I cast;
'Tis Laura's voice I hear, and hence she bids me haste.[22]

Donne's *Anatomie* has no such focus: it has instead a central inconsistency which defeats all Donne's efforts to bring its diverse materials under control. For it is not correct to say, as Empson says, that "the complete decay of the universe" is presented as having been caused by the death of Elizabeth Drury. If this were so, the poem might achieve unity through supporting a dominant symbol of virtue's power, and one might be able to agree with Empson that the "only way to make the poem sensible is to accept Elizabeth Drury as the Logos."[23] But, after the Introduction has elaborately presented this hyperbole, one discovers in the first Meditation that Elizabeth Drury has, basically, nothing to do with the sense of decay in the poem. The whole first Meditation is strictly in the religious tradition; it meditates the decline of man through sin from God's original creation:

There is no health; Physitians say that wee,
At best, enjoy but a neutralitie.
And can there bee worse sicknesse, then to know
That we are never well, nor can be so?
Wee are borne ruinous . . . .
For that first marriage was our funerall:
One woman at one blow, then kill'd us all . . . .
(91–106)

The meditation opens with an echo of the general confession in the *Book of Common Prayer*—"there is no health in us"—a theme developed by St. Bernard and countless others:

Engendered in sin, we engender sinners; born debtors, we give birth to debtors; corrupted, to the corrupt . . . . We are crippled souls from the moment when we enter into this world, and as long as we live there, and we shall still be so when we leave it; from the sole of our foot to the crown of our head there is no health in us.[24]

Continuing with a descant on traditional conceptions of the decay of man from his first grandeur,[25] the meditation comes to a full climactic close as (in St. Bernard's terminology) the indestructible

Image of God within man makes its traditional judgment of the ruined Likeness:

> Thus man, this worlds Vice-Emperour, in whom
> All faculties, all graces are at home . . .
> This man, so great, that all that is, is his,
> Oh what a trifle, and poore thing he is! (161–70)

The first Meditation thus forms a unit in itself; it strikes one as having no fundamental relation to the preceding account of the destruction of the world by the girl's death.

Then, clumsily and evasively, the poem comes back to the girl and to the Petrarchan hyperbole of the world's death:

> If man were any thing, he's nothing now:
> Helpe, or at least some time to wast, allow
> T'his other wants, yet when he did depart
> With her whom we lament, hee lost his heart.
> (171–4)

The Eulogy is being tacked on; and soon the difficulty of including this hyperbole in the poem becomes embarrassingly obvious:

> shee that could drive
> The poysonous tincture, and the staine of *Eve,*
> Out of her thoughts, and deeds; and purifie
> All, by a true religious Alchymie;
> Shee, shee is dead; shee's dead: when thou knowest this,
> Thou knowest how poore a trifling thing man is.
> (179–84)

But we have known it before, and not for these reasons; thus the section comes to a flat and forced conclusion. We pause, and begin the second section almost as if the Eulogy and Moral had never intervened:

> Then, as mankinde, so is the worlds whole frame
> Quite out of Joynt, almost created lame:
> For, before God had made up all the rest,
> Corruption entred, and deprav'd the best:
> It seis'd the Angels, and then first of all
> The world did in her cradle take a fall . . . .
> (191–6)

This second Meditation includes the famous passage beginning "And new Philosophy calls all in doubt," where Donne sardonically turns the optimism of the scientists into proof of pessimism:

> And freely men confesse that this world's spent,
> When in the Planets, and the Firmament
> They seeke so many new; they see that this
> Is crumbled out againe to his Atomies. (209–12)

But this is not related to "the untimely death of Mistris Elizabeth Drury." The passage on the new philosophy is an integral part of a meditation on the effects of sin; the effects of the new philosophy represent the final stages in a long and universal sequence of decay.

The second Eulogy reveals an even further split in the poem. Instead of pursuing the explicitly religious imagery of the first Eulogy, Donne here attempts to secularize the compliments, at the same time using images traditionally associated with Mary:[26]

> She whom wise nature had invented then
> When she observ'd that every sort of men
> Did in their voyage in this worlds Sea stray,
> And needed a new compasse for their way;
> She that was best, and first originall
> Of all faire copies, and the generall
> Steward to Fate; she whose rich eyes, and brest
> Guilt the West Indies, and perfum'd the East . . . .
> (223–30)

The traditional religious feelings which have thus far been growing in the poem are here balked, particularly by the references to "wise nature" and "Fate." The poem has broken apart, and the break is not mended by the blurred imagery one finds in the following Moral and in the transition to Section III (lines 237–50). Here Donne presents the imagery of "this worlds generall sicknesse" with an imprecise and damaging ambiguity. What is the "feaver," the "consuming wound"? Is it that conventional one described in the Introduction as the result of the girl's death? Or is it the infection of Original Sin? The vague and general imagery tries to include both elements, but it will not do. The last words of the transition—"ages darts"—tell us clearly that the third and fourth Meditations, on loss of proportion and color, deal with the results of sin, not with emotions related to the poem's alleged protagonist.

The remaining Eulogies and the Conclusion try desperately to maintain something of the introductory hyperbole, but it cannot be done. The poem does not justify the elaborate imagery with which Donne attempts to transmute the girl into a symbol of virtue's power. The imagery seems extravagant—even blasphemous—not because of what we know about the circumstances of the poem's composition, but because the imagery is not supported by the poem as a whole.

The very fact that the poem is rigidly divided into sections and subsections gives us another aspect of its failure. Nearly all the joints between sections and subsections are marked by strong pauses or by clumsy transitions; while the Morals are strained in an attempt to bring Meditation and Eulogy into some sort of unity. The parts will not fuse into an imaginative organism. One can omit all the rest of the poem and simply read through the Meditations consecutively; the sequence is consistent and, with a brief conclusion, would form a complete—and a rather good—poem.

We should not leave the *Anatomie* without noticing in some detail the richness with which Donne develops these strictly religious aspects of the work. Let us look for a moment at the third Meditation, as complex a passage as Donne ever wrote. It works by a fusion of two main ideas. Astronomical observations seem to prove that the universe is decaying as a result of sin, for it seems to have lost its spherical, circular nature, the sign of immutable perfection. At the same time the passage mocks the vanity and presumption of man in attempting to understand and control God's mysterious universe. The irony of such attempts is that they only reveal—in two ways—the corruption of all things. Nevertheless man persists in the intellectual, Abelardian effort to comprehend the unknowable or inessential, persists in the *curiositas* which St. Bernard denounced as the father of pride.

Donne begins (251 ff.):

> We thinke the heavens enjoy their Sphericall,
> Their round proportion embracing all.
> But yet their various and perplexed course,
> Observ'd in divers ages, doth enforce
> Men to finde out so many Eccentrique parts,
> Such divers downe-right lines, such overthwarts,
> As disproportion that pure forme:

"Perplexed" is the central word here. The course of the heavenly bodies is so involved, so tangled, that man cannot follow it and is "enforced" to discover, or to invent ("finde out"),[27] fantastically complicated scheme of the universe which serves to "disproportion that pure forme," but never surely hits the truth of things. We may also take "perplexed" in another sense: the heavenly bodies themselves seemed to be confused about their course.

> It teares
> The Firmament in eight and forty sheires,
> And in these Constellations then arise
> New starres, and old doe vanish from our eyes:
> As though heav'n suffered earthquakes, peace or war,
> When new Towers rise, and old demolish't are.

"It," grammatically, seems to refer to the heavens' "perplexed course." But in this context "It" may also refer by implication to the science of Astronomy which invented the forty-eight constellations; thus, when man's "knowledge" has settled things by violence ("teares"), erratic heaven refuses to conform. Nevertheless, presumptuous men

> have impal'd within a Zodiake
> The free-borne Sun, and keepe twelve Signes awake
> To watch his steps; the Goat and Crab controule,
> And fright him backe, who else to either Pole
> (Did not these Tropiques fetter him) might runne:

The Goat and Crab are ugly symbols of sensuality, and will the Sun obey such commanders? Apparently so; yet the Sun is full of guile that may deceive us:

> For his course is not round; nor can the Sunne
> Perfit a Circle, or maintaine his way
> One inch direct; but where he rose to-day
> He comes no more, but with a couzening line,
> Steales by that point, and so is Serpentine:
> And seeming weary with his reeling thus,
> He meanes to sleepe, being now falne nearer us.

The sun is degenerate, having fallen nearer to the sphere of corruption—serpentine in his winding and in his wiliness, and, like a drunken man, reeling toward a "lethargy" like that which has overtaken earth.

> So, of the Starres which boast that they doe runne
> In Circle still, none ends where he begun.

> All their proportion's lame, it sinkes, it swels.
> For of Meridians, and Parallels,
> Man hath weav'd out a net, and this net throwne
> Upon the Heavens, and now they are his owne.
> Loth to goe up the hill, or labour thus
> To goe to heaven, we make heaven come to us.
> We spur, we reine the starres, and in their race
> They're diversly content t'obey our pace.

Here the complex feelings of the Meditation reach a climax. All man's hubristic attempts have resulted only in a deceptive "mastery" of corruption. Man's claims to worldly power and knowledge mean only that he refuses to undergo the spiritual discipline necessary for his salvation.

The remainder of this third Meditation is not of such sustained power, and indeed goes to pieces in its last ten lines. A discussion of the earth's solidity interrupts the theme of proportion, and a shift to abstract morality at the close is too abrupt. The best of the poem is over.

V

The full title of Donne's *Second Anniversary* itself suggests the possibilities of a unity not achieved in the earlier poem: *Of the Progresse of the Soule. Wherein, By occasion of the Religious death of Mistris Elizabeth Drury, the incommodities of the Soule in this life, and her exaltation in the next, are contemplated.* Here, clearly, is an "occasion" to use Mistress Drury as a symbol naturally integrated with the traditional matter of religious meditation: a "Religious death" (not the "untimely death" of the *Anatomie's* title) is the ultimate aim in this life for all the devout. The poem's structure indicates that Donne is indeed moving throughout with the imaginative ease that marks the management of a truly unified conception.

The *Progresse* consists of an Introduction, only half as long as the Introduction to the preceding poem; a Conclusion, less than half as long; and seven sections which constitute the body of the work. These proportions, in a poem over fifty lines longer, indicate an important shift in emphasis. The Introduction and Conclusion to the *Anatomie*, with their emphasis on hyperbolic praise of the dead girl, make up a quarter of that poem; whereas these portions make up only about an eighth of the *Progresse*. Each section of the *Progresse* is subdivided in a manner reminiscent of the *Anatomie*. The first section contains (1) a Meditation on contempt of the world and one's self; (2) a

Eulogy of the girl as the pattern of Virtue; (3) a Moral, introduced by lines which recall the refrain of the preceding poem:

> Shee, shee is gone; she is gone; when thou knowest this,
> What fragmentary rubbidge this world is
> Thou knowest, and that it is not worth a thought;
> He honors it too much that thinkes it nought.

But, as the following outline shows, the "refrain" does not appear hereafter, and of the remaining sections, only the second concludes with a distinct Moral; in the rest the moral is absorbed into the Eulogy:

Introduction, 1–44.
Section I, 45–84.
1. Meditation, 45–64.
2. Eulogy, 65–80.
3. Refrain and Moral, 81–4.

Section II, 85–156.
1. Meditation, 85–120.
2. Eulogy, 121–46.
3. Moral, 147–56.

Section III, 157–250.
1. Meditation, 157–219.
2. Eulogy, 220–50.

Section IV, 251–320.
1. Meditation, 251–300.
2. Eulogy, 301–20.

Section V, 321–82.
1. Meditation, 321–55.
2. Eulogy, 356–82.

Section VI, 383–470.
1. Meditation, 383–446.
2. Eulogy, 447–70.

Section VII, 471–510.
1. Meditation, 471–96.
2. Eulogy, 497–510.

Conclusion, 511–28.

This gradual modification of the strict mold which marked the sections of the *Anatomie* suggests a creative freedom that absorbs and transcends formal divisions. The first striking indication that this is true is found in the ease of the reader's movement from part to part. We are freed from the heavy pauses that marked the close of each section in the *Anatomie:* omission of the refrain and, above all, omission of the flat, prosy Morals, makes possible an easy transition from section to section; the only heavy pause occurs at the close of the long Moral in Section II. We are always aware that a new sequence is beginning: it is essential that we feel the form of the poem beneath us. But each new sequence, with the above exception, follows inevitably from the close of the preceding one, as at the close of the first section, where the words of the very brief Moral, "thought" and "thinkes," lead directly to the dominant command of the second Meditation: "Thinke then, my soule, that death is but a Groome . . . Thinke thee laid on thy death-bed . . . Thinke . . . Thinke . . ."; the traditional self-address of religious meditation.

The transition within each section from Meditation to Eulogy is even more fluent; we do not find here the sharp division of meaning which marked these two elements in the *Anatomie*. In the previous poem every Meditation was strictly a scourging of the world and of man, every Eulogy the picture of a lost hope. But in the *Progresse* every Meditation, together with this scourging, includes the hope of salvation which is imaged in the Eulogy, and in every Meditation except the first, this hope, this upward look, is stressed in the latter part of the Meditation, with the result that the reader is carried easily into the realm where the symbol of perfect virtue now lives.

In Sections III and V the distinction between Meditation and Eulogy is even further modified, for the Meditation itself falls into two contrasting parts. In Section III we have first (157–78) a meditation on the loathsomeness of the body, which "could, beyond escape or helpe," infect the soul with Original Sin. But Donne does not dwell long on this; he lifts his eyes from these "ordures" to meditate, in a passage twice as long (179–219), his soul's flight to heaven after death—a flight that leads directly to the Eulogy. Likewise, in Section V, after meditating the corrupt company kept on earth (321–38), Donne lifts his eyes to meditate (339–55) the soul's "conversation" with the inhabitants of Heaven—a theme which leads naturally into the Eulogy of Heaven's new inhabitant.

Fundamentally, the union of Meditation with Eulogy is due to a difference in Donne's treatment of the Eulogies in this poem. Here he has avoided a clash between eulogy and religious meditation by giving up, except in the brief Introduction and first Eulogy, the Petrarchan hyperbole which in parts of the *Anatomie* attributed the decay of the world to the girl's death. This hyperbole, together with the single reminder of the refrain, appears to be brought in at the beginning of the *Progresse* to link this poem with its predecessor, in line with Donne's original plan of writing a poem in the girl's memory every year for an indefinite period. The labored Introduction to the *Progresse* is certainly a blemish on the poem; yet it may be said that the reminiscences of the *Anatomie* are functional: they suggest that the negative "anatomizing" of the other poem may be taken as a preparation for the positive spiritual progress to be imaged in the second poem. At any rate, Donne does not use this hyperbole in the six later Eulogies, nor in the brief Conclusion, of the second poem. Instead, he consistently attempts to transmute the girl into a symbol of virtue that may fitly represent the Image and Likeness of God in man, recognition of which is, according to St. Bernard, the chief end and aim of religious meditation.

Thus Juan de Ávila's *Audi Filia* begins its section on self-knowledge with a chapter (57) summarizing the command to "know thyself" which St. Bernard found in the famous verse of his beloved *Canticle:* "Si ignoras te, O pulchra inter mulieres, egredere, et abi post greges sodalium tuorum . . . ."[28] If the soul, the intended Bride, does not know herself—that is, does not know whence she comes, where she is, and whither she is going—she will live forever in the "Land of Unlikeness," that land of sin and disorder in which man forgets that he was made in God's Image and Likeness, and thus lives in a state of exile where the Image is defaced and the Likeness lost. As Gilson explains, "Man is made to the image of God in his free-will, and he will never lose it; he was made to the likeness of God in respect of certain virtues, enabling him to choose well, and to do the good thing chosen; now these he has lost" by sin. But the central fact is that the Image—free will—is indestructible; and hence "to know ourselves is essentially," in St. Bernard's view, "to recognize that we are defaced images of God."[29] Take care, says St. Bernard, "now thou art sunk into the slime of the abyss, not to forget that thou art the image of God, and blush to have covered it over with an alien likeness. Remember thy nobility and take shame of such a defection. Forget not thy beauty, to be the more confounded at thy hideous aspect."[30]

In accordance with the twofold aim of meditation implied in the last sentence, Donne's *Second Anniversary* presents seven Meditations which may be called, for the most part, a description of the "defaced image," the Land of Unlikeness; while the seven Eulogies, for the most part, create a symbol of the original Image and Likeness, the lost beauty and nobility that must not be forgotten. That is not to say that Donne gives up Petrarchan imagery; not at all—but this imagery is now attuned to the religious aims of the poem. The Eulogies are sometimes too ingenious; yet the excessive ingenuity remains a minor flaw: it does not destroy the poem's unity.

The fifth Eulogy is a good example:

> Shee, who being to her selfe a State, injoy'd
> All royalties which any State employ'd;
> For shee made warres, and triumph'd; reason still
> Did not o'rthrow, but rectifie her will:
> And she made peace, for no peace is like this,
> That beauty, and chastity together kisse:
> She did high justice, for she crucified
> Every first motion of rebellious pride:
> And she gave pardons, and was liberall,
> For, onely her selfe except, she pardon'd all . . . .
> (359–68)

The hyperbole is here so tempered, so controlled, by interpretation in terms of the virtue essential to a restored Likeness, that the more extravagant images which follow become acceptably symbolic of the importance of such virtue in the world: it is the one thing needful:

> Shee coy'nd, in this, that her impressions gave
> To all our actions all the worth they have:
> She gave protections; the thoughts of her brest
> Satans rude Officers could ne'r arrest.
> As these prerogatives being met in one,
> Made her a soveraigne State; religion
> Made her a Church; and these two made her all.
> (369–75)

Thus throughout the *Progresse* Meditation and Eulogy combine to present its central theme: the true end of man.

Let us look now at the whole movement of the poem; we can then see that this central theme is clearly introduced at the beginning of the first Meditation, carried to a climax in the fourth and fifth sections, and resolved in the Eulogy of Section VI. There is no flagging of power in this poem: it is a true progress. After the labored Introduction, Donne strikes at once into the heart of his theme:

> These Hymnes, thy issue, may encrease so long,
> As till Gods great *Venite* change the song. [end of Intro.]
> Thirst for that time, O my insatiate soule,

And serve thy thirst, with Gods safe-sealing Bowle.
Be thirstie still, and drinke still till thou goe
To th' only Health, to be Hydroptique so. (43–8)

The "Bowle" is the Eucharist, a "seale of Grace," as Donne calls it in his sermons.[31] One thinks of the "Anima sitiens Deum" in St. Bernard—the Soul, the Bride, which thirsts for God, desiring a union of will between herself and God, that union which at last results in Perfect Likeness after death.[32] This imagery is then supported in Section II by the line, "And trust th' immaculate blood to wash thy score" (106); as well as by the lines of Section III (214–15) where Donne refers to death as the soul's "third birth," with the very significant parenthesis, "Creation gave her one, a second, grace." One needs to recall that at the close of the *Anatomie* Donne has said that he

Will yearely celebrate thy second birth,
That is, thy death; for though the soule of man
Be got when man is made, 'tis borne but than
When man doth die. (450–3)

The omission of Grace may be said to indicate the fundamental flaw of the *First Anniversary:* it lacks the firm religious center of the *Progresse.*

This promise of salvation is the positive aspect of the soul's progress; but, as Gilson says, "By this thirst for God we must further understand an absolute contempt for all that is not God."[33] This complementary negative aspect is consequently introduced immediately after the above lines on the Eucharist:

Forget this rotten world; And unto thee
Let thine owne times as an old storie bee.
Be not concern'd: studie not why, nor when;
Doe not so much as not beleeve a man. (49–52)

Donne is taking as his prime example of vanity that curiosity which forms the first downward step in St. Bernard's Twelve Degrees of Pride—curiosity, which occurs, St. Bernard tells us, "when a man allows his sight and other senses to stray after things which do not concern him."

> So since it [the soul] takes no heed to itself it is sent out of doors to feed the kids. And as these are the types of sin, I may quite correctly give the title of "kids" to the eyes and

> the ears, since as death comes into the world through sin, so does sin enter the mind through these apertures. The curious man, therefore, busies himself with feeding them, though he takes no trouble to ascertain the state in which he has left himself. Yet if, O man, you look carefully into yourself, it is indeed a wonder that you can ever look at anything else.[34]

This theme of curiosity remains dormant until Section III of the poem, where it emerges gradually from Donne's magnificent view of his own soul's flight to Heaven after death. It is important to note that this is not, strictly speaking, "the flight of Elizabeth Drury's soul to Heaven," as most commentators describe it.[35] It is Donne's own soul which here is made a symbol of release, not only from physical bondage, but also from that mental bondage which is the deepest agony of the greatest souls:

> she stayes not in the ayre,
> To looke what Meteors there themselves prepare;
> She carries no desire to know, nor sense,
> Whether th' ayres middle region be intense;
> For th' Element of fire, she doth not know,
> Whether she past by such a place or no;
> She baits not at the Moone, nor cares to trie
> Whether in that new world, men live, and die.
> *Venus* retards her not, to 'enquire, how shee
> Can, (being one starre) *Hesper*, and *Vesper* bee.
> (189–98)

In the last two lines Donne is renouncing one of his own witty *Paradoxes and Problems;* in the earlier part he is renouncing the astronomical curiosity which had drawn his scorn in the greatest passage of the *Anatomie*. Here, however, as Coffin has well shown (pp. 171, 185–92), there is a much stronger emphasis on problems such as "fire" and the moon which were being debated in Donne's own day. From all such vain controversies the soul is now freed and

> ere she can consider how she went,
> At once is at, and through the Firmament.
> (205–6)

It is not until Section IV that this theme reaches its full, explicit development. Turning here from the heavens, Donne scourges the search for physical understanding of earth and its creatures; yet, as before, the very flagellation suggests an almost indomitable curiosity, and shows a mind that has ranged through all the reaches of human learning:

> Wee see in Authors, too stiffe to recant,
> A hundred controversies of an Ant;
> And yet one watches, starves, freeses, and sweats,
> To know but Catechismes and Alphabets
> Of unconcerning things, matters of fact—
> (281–85)

matters which do not concern the true end of man, as implied in the following lines:

> When wilt thou shake off this Pedantery,
> Of being taught by sense, and Fantasie?
> Thou look'st through spectacles; small things seeme great
> Below; But up unto the watch-towre get,
> And see all things despoyl'd of fallacies: [36]
> Thou shalt not peepe through lattices of eyes,
> Nor heare through Labyrinths of eares, nor learne
> By circuit, or collections to discerne.
> In heaven thou straight know'st all, concerning it,
> And what concernes it not, shalt straight forget.
> (291–300)

All worldly philosophy is vain, for essential truth, says Donne, cannot be learned through sense-impressions of external things, nor through that "Fantasie" which transmits sense-impressions to the intellect. Such philosophy is the way of pride; true knowledge comes only through humility, as Donne, echoing St. Bernard, declares in a significant passage of his *Essayes:*

> It is then humility to study God, and a strange miraculous one; for it is an ascending humility, which the Divel, which emulates even Gods excellency in his goodnesse, and labours to be as ill, as he is good, hath corrupted in us by a pride, as much against reason; for he hath fill'd us with a descending pride, to forsake God, for the study and love of things worse then our selves.
> (pp. 3–4)

True knowledge lies within and leads to virtue, the fourth Eulogy explains:

> Shee who all libraries had throughly read
> At home in her owne thoughts, and practised
> So much good as would make as many more:
> Shee whose example they must all implore,
> Who would or doe, or thinke well . . .
> She who in th' art of knowing Heaven, was growne
> Here upon earth, to such perfection,
> That she hath, ever since to Heaven she came,
> (In a far fairer print,) but read the same. . . .
> (303–14)

Religious virtue creates, or rather *is*, the restored Likeness which, according to St. Bernard, makes possible some knowledge of God; with St. Bernard, as Gilson says, "the resemblance of subject and object is the indispensable condition of any knowledge of the one by the other." [37] This is made plain in the sixth Eulogy, which provides the resolution of the whole poem by obliterating all traces of Petrarchan compliment and giving explicitly in the terms of St. Bernard a definition of the soul's perfection on earth. The sixth Meditation leads the way into this Eulogy by an abstract definition of "essential joy":

> Double on heaven thy thoughts on earth emploid;
> All will not serve; Only who have enjoy'd
> The sight of God, in fulnesse, can thinke it;
> For it is both the object, and the wit.
> This is essentiall joy, where neither hee
> Can suffer diminution, nor wee. (439–44)

God is both the object of knowledge and the means of knowing; though this full knowledge and joy can never be achieved on earth, we can, the Eulogy explains, come closest to it by striving to restore the Divine Likeness, as did she,

> Who kept by diligent devotion,
> Gods Image, in such reparation,
> Within her heart, that what decay was growne,
> Was her first Parents fault, and not her owne:
> Who being solicited to any act,
> Still heard God pleading his safe precontract;

> Who by a faithfull confidence, was here
> Betroth'd to God, and now is married there . . .
> Who being here fil'd with grace, yet strove to bee,
> Both where more grace, and more capacitie
> At once is given . . . . (455–67)

Compare the words of St. Bernard, speaking of that conformity between the soul's will and God's which leads to mystic ecstasy:

> It is that conformity which makes, as it were, a marriage between the soul and the Word, when, being already like unto Him by its nature, it endeavours to show itself like unto Him by its will, and loves Him as it is loved by Him. And if this love is perfected, the soul is wedded to the Word. What can be more full of happiness and joy than this conformity? what more to be desired than this love? which makes thee, O soul, no longer content with human guidance, to draw near with confidence thyself to the Word, to attach thyself with constancy to Him, to address Him with confidence, and consult Him upon all subjects, to become as receptive in thy intelligence, as fearless in thy desires. This is the contract of a marriage truly spiritual and sacred. And to say this is to say too little; it is more than a contract, it is a communion, an identification with the Beloved, in which the perfect correspondence of will makes of two, one spirit.[38]

The "faithfull confidence" of Donne's poem is akin to the "confidence" (*fiducia*) of St. Bernard, an attribute of the soul which has passed beyond fear of divine punishment and stands on the threshold of mystic ecstasy.[39] This recognition of the end of man on earth and in Heaven is the fulfillment of the poem; the brief remainder is summary and epilogue.

In such a poem of religious devotion the sevenfold division of sections assumes a significance beyond that of the fivefold division of the *Anatomie*. Seven is the favorite number for dividing religious meditations: into those *semaines* and *septaines* that were characteristic of the "New Devotion" in the Low Countries; [40] or into the contrasting meditations for each day of the week that formed the basis of popular daily exercises throughout Europe. A glance at the summary of the latter exercises, as presented by Fray Luis (see above, Chap. 1, sec. 1), will show that Donne is following closely their general tenor and development: from thoughts of sin, death, and the miseries of this life, to thoughts of happy "conversation" with the blessed in Heaven, of "essentiall joy" and "accidentall joyes."[41] But the sevenfold division of this poem suggests more than a relation to the practice of methodical meditation. As Donne says in his *Essayes*, "*Seven* is ever used to express infinite." (p. 129) It is the mystic's traditional division of the soul's progress toward ecstasy and union with the Divine. St. Augustine thus divides the progress of the soul into seven stages,[42] and anyone familiar with mystical writings will realize how often the division has been used by later mystics, as in St. Teresa's *Interior Castle*. Thus Donne's *Progresse* uses both mystical structure and mystical imagery to express a goal: the Infinite, the One.

This does not mean that Donne's *Progresse* is, properly speaking, a mystical poem, even though he uses in his title the mystical term "contemplate," and in the poem cries, "Returne not, my Soule, from this extasie" (321). The next line after this—"And meditation of what thou shalt bee"—indicates that the ecstasy is metaphorical only. "Meditation" is always discursive, always works through the understanding; it is only the preparation for ascent to the truly mystical state now generally understood in the term "contemplation," which St. Bernard defines as "the soul's true unerring intuition," "the unhesitating apprehension of truth."[43] Donne's use of the word "contemplate" in the title of his *Progresse* may indicate a higher spiritual aim than the "represent" of the *Anatomie's* title, but his *Progresse* remains a spiritual exercise of the purgative, ascetic life. It represents an attempt to achieve the state of conversion best described by Donne himself in a prayer at the close of his *Essayes in Divinity:*

> Begin in us here in this life an angelicall purity, an angelicall chastity, an angelicall integrity to thy service, an Angelical acknowledgment that we alwaies stand in thy presence, and should direct al our actions to thy glory. Rebuke us not, O Lord, in thine anger, that we have not done so till now; but enable us now to begin that great work; and imprint in us an assurance that thou receivest us now graciously, as reconciled, though enemies; and fatherly, as children, though prodigals; and powerfully, as the God of our salvation, though our own consciences testifie against us.

NOTES

[1] See the epigraphs to Part 2; *Tottel's Miscellany*, ed. Rollins, 1, 62–3.

[2] See the controversy stirred up by Pierre Legouis' remarks in *Donne the Craftsman* (Paris, Henri Didier, 1928), pp. 61–9; cf. Merritt Hughes,

"The Lineage of 'The Extasie,' " *MLR,* 27 (1932), 1–5; Frank A. Doggett, "Donne's Platonism," *Sewanee Review,* 42 (1934), 274–92; George Reuben Potter, "Donne's *Extasie,* Contra Legouis," *PQ,* 15 (1936), 247–53. For a striking treatment of the contrast between "sensuall Extasie" and spiritual ecstasy, see St. François de Sales, *Love of God,* Bk. 7, Chap. 4.

[3] W. A. Murray, "Donne and Paracelsus: An Essay in Interpretation," *RES,* 25 (1949), 115–23. One must, I think, discard Grierson's hesitant suggestion (*Poems of Donne,* 2, xxii, 10) that the poem may have been addressed to Lucy, Countess of Bedford; for the imagery of the "Saint Lucies night," which occurs also in the *Second Anniversary* (line 120), provides its own metaphorical occasion (St. Lucy's Day, Dec. 13, "being the shortest day," according to the old calendar). See the interesting discussion of this problem by J. B. Leishman, *The Monarch of Wit* (London, Hutchinson's University Library, 1951), pp. 170–73. Leishman tends to feel that the "Nocturnall" deals with Donne's wife, but finds it hard to believe that Donne wrote the poem "after the actual death of his wife in 1617, when he had been two years in orders." But if the poem is fundamentally religious, the difficulty seems to lessen.

[4] Donne, *Letters,* pp. 126–7; cf. Edmund Gosse, *The Life and Letters of John Donne* (2 vols., London, Heinemann, 1899), 1, 154. Gosse says the letter "seems to refer to the birth of Francis Donne, baptized at Mitcham on the 8th of January 1607."

[5] Gosse, 2, 106. This assumption has now been effectively questioned by Miss Helen Gardner, in her recent edition of the *Divine Poems.* Her discussion of the dating of the "Holy Sonnets" (pp. xxxvii–l) seems to be absolutely convincing. She dates six of the sonnets between February and August, 1609, and most of the others shortly after; her printing of the sonnets in groups of twelve, four, and three is surely the right way to present them.

[6] *Poems of Donne,* ed. Grierson, 2, 225–9, 231; and the textual notes for the sonnets, 1, 317–31. Miss Helen Gardner has called my attention to the fact that Grierson's description of the appearance of the "La Corona" sonnets in the Harleian manuscript is not quite accurate. He says (2, 227) that the general heading "is followed at once by 'Deign at my hands,' and then the title *La Corona* is given to the six sonnets which ensue." But all seven sonnets appear under this title, as I have since observed.

[7] Idem, 2, 212. Miss Gardner (*Divine Poems,* pp. xlvii–xlviii) also discusses the significance of this recantation; she points out that E. K. Chambers, in his pioneer edition of Donne's poems (1896), had observed the relationship between this Elegy and Holy Sonnet 10 and suggested the priority of the sonnet.

[8] See Gosse, 1, 174, 190, 195.

[9] *Poems of Donne,* ed. Grierson, 2, 225–9, 238–9; Rhodes Dunlap (*Modern Language Notes,* 63 [1948], 258–9) has shown that the occasion of the second of these poems must be March 25, 1608, the first day of the year, old style. To all such evidence of Donne's meditation during this period

we should add the verse-letter to Rowland Woodward cited in Chap. 3 above, for Grierson (*Poems of Donne, 2,* 146–8) conjectures that this was written between 1602–8. Donne's advice here with regard to "Blowing our sparkes of vertue" reminds one of similar references to Donne's exercises in self-analysis that occur in a letter printed by Evelyn Simpson in *A Study of the Prose Works of John Donne* (2d ed., Oxford: Clarendon Press, 1948), pp. 313–14; the letter seems to date from sometime around 1600. For the importance of such introspection in Donne's middle years see George Reuben Potter, "John Donne's Discovery of Himself," *University of California Publications in English, 4* (1934), 3–23.

[10] Gosse, *2,* 20; Simpson, *Prose Works,* p. 29.

[11] John Donne, *Essayes in Divinity,* London, 1651: title-page and note "To the Reader." See the excellent edition of this work by Evelyn Simpson (Oxford: Clarendon Press, 1952), pp. xiii–xvii; and Simpson, *Prose Works,* pp. 207–11.

[12] Cf. Walton, *Lives,* p. 34: " 'And besides, whereas it is determined by the best of *Casuists,* that *Gods Glory should be the first end, and a maintenance the second motive to embrace that calling;* and though each man may propose to himself both together; yet the first may not be put last without a violation of Conscience, which he that searches the heart will judge. And truly my present condition is such, that if I ask my own Conscience, whether it be reconcileable to that rule, it is at this time so perplexed about it, that I can neither give my self nor you an answer.' " See Gosse, *1,* 157–62.

[13] Donne, *Letters,* p. 219. For the interpretations of the *Anniversaries* recently advanced by Marjorie Nicolson and Marius Bewley, see my Appendix 2.

[14] Stafford, p. 219; see above, Chap. 2, sec. 5.

[15] See also the use of the number five in Ben Jonson's "Ghyrlond of the blessed Virgin Marie": "Here, are five letters in this blessed Name,/ Which, chang'd, a five-fold mysterie designe . . . ." (*Ben Jonson,* ed. C. H. Herford, Percy and Evelyn Simpson [11 vols., Oxford: Clarendon Press, 1925–52], *8,* 412). The poem was first published in Stafford's *Femall Glory.*

[16] A. Wilmart, *Auteurs Spirituels et Textes Dévots du Moyen Age Latin* (Paris, 1932), pp. 317–60.

[17] For devotion to the Name of Mary see Puente, *1,* 263–4.

[18] See above, Chap. 1, sec. 1.

[19] Juan de Ávila, *Audi Filia* ([St. Omer], 1620), pp. 336–8; the translation is attributed to Donne's friend, Sir Tobie Matthew.

[20] Nicholas Breton, *Works,* ed. A. B. Grosart (2 vols., Edinburgh, 1879), *2,* 23.

[21] "Conversations with Drummond," *Ben Jonson,* ed. Herford and Simpson, *1,* 133 (modernized).

[22] *Rime* 346 in the translation by John Nott: *The Sonnets, Triumphs and other poems of Petrarch,* trans. "various hands," London: G. Bell and

Sons, 1907 (there printed as Sonnet 75 of the sequence "To Laura in Death"). For Petrarch's use of the hyperbole of the world's destruction see *Rime* 268, 326, 338, 352; by Donne's time this had evidently become a convention of compliment, as in Donne's love-poem, "A Feaver," and in a sonnet by Sannazaro pointed out by Mario Praz: see *A Garland for John Donne,* ed. Theodore Spencer (Cambridge: Harvard University Press, 1931), pp. 66–9.

[23] William Empson, *English Pastoral Poetry* (New York: W. W. Norton, 1938), p. 84.

[24] St. Bernard, *Sermones de Diversis,* 42. 2; *Patrologiae cursus completus . . . Series* [*latina*], ed. Jacques Paul Migne (221 vols., Paris, 1844–65), *183,* 662. I quote the translation by Downes in Gilson's study of St. Bernard, p. 46 (see below, sec. 5, n. 2).

[25] See St. Cyprian, *Liber ad Demetrianum,* secs. 3, 4; *Patrologiae cursus completus, 4,* 564–7. One finds here the germ of many of Donne's comments on the world's decay throughout the *Anatomie.*

[26] Cf. Southwell's poem on the Virgin's Nativity: "Load-starre of all inclosed in worldly waves,/The car[d] and compasse that from ship-wracke saves." The imagery is based, of course, on the "Ave maris stella" and the interpretation of the name Mary as meaning "Star of the Sea": cf. Puente, *1,* 263: "Shee is the Starre of the sea, for that shee is the light, consolation, and guide of those, that sayle in the sea of this worlde, tossed with the greate waves, and tempestes of temptations . . . ." Cf. also Southwell's poem on the death of the Virgin, cited earlier, Chap. 2, sec. 6.

[27] See *OED,* "find," *v.,* 2, 15; 4, 20. Charles Monroe Coffin gives an interesting discussion of this whole Meditation in a different context: *John Donne and the New Philosophy* (New York: Columbia University Press, 1937), pp. 181–2.

[28] This quotation from the *Canticle* (1.7) is given in the version cited by St. Bernard in his *Sermones in Cantica Canticorum,* 34. 1; *Patrologiae cursus completus, 183,* 959; it differs from the modern Vulgate reading.

[29] Étienne Gilson, *The Mystical Theology of Saint Bernard,* trans. A. H. C. Downes (New York: Sheed and Ward, 1940), pp. 225 (n. 45), 70.

[30] St. Bernard, *Sermones de Diversis,* 12. 2; *Patrologiae cursus completus, 183,* 571. I quote the translation by Downes in Gilson's above study, p. 71.

[31] See Itrat Husain, *The Dogmatic and Mystical Theology of John Donne* (London: S.P.C.K., 1938), pp. 30–31.

[32] Gilson, *Saint Bernard,* pp. 111–12.

[33] Idem, p. 238, n. 161.

[34] St. Bernard, *The Twelve Degrees of Humility and Pride,* pp. 6, 55–6. See Gilson, *Saint Bernard,* Appendix I, on the importance of *curiositas* in St. Bernard's thought, where "kids" is shown to be another reference to the *Canticle,* 1.7: "Si ignoras te . . . ."

[35] Charles Monroe Coffin has made some helpful comments on this passage in a letter which he kindly allows me to quote: "in the imagined progress

of his own soul, he has implied the felicitous passage of hers . . . . There is, to me at least, a rather certain ambiguity in the situation, as I think there should be, and the momentary assimilation of the vision of his own progress into that which has 'exalted' E.D. into heaven seems appropriate and, I should say, inevitable."

[36] Cf. Francisco de Osuna, p. 201: "Sion means 'a watchtower,' that is, the grace received by the heart during its recollection, whence much knowledge of God can be discerned."

[37] Gilson, *Saint Bernard*, p. 148.

[38] St. Bernard, *Sermons on the Song of Songs*, 83, 3; *Life and Works of Saint Bernard*, trans. Samuel J. Eales (London, 1889–96), 4, 508.

[39] Gilson, *Saint Bernard*, pp. 24, 113, 138n.

[40] See Debongnie, pp. 168, 170–71, 184–7, 209–11; and H. Watrigant, "La Méditation Méthodique et l'École des Frères de la Vie Commune," *Revue d' Ascétique et de Mystique*, 3 (1922), 134–55. See also Puente, 1, 43 f.

[41] With the latter part of the *Second Anniversary* compare Loarte, *Exercise*, pp. 92–3:

> Secondly, ponder what a comfort and sweete delight it shal-be, to be in that blessed societie of so many Angels, Saintes, Apostles, Martyrs, Confessors, Virgins, al of them being so bright and beautiful? what shal it be to see the sacred humanitie of Christ, and of his blessed mother? howe shal a man be ravished with the hearing of the sweet harmonie and melodious musicke that shal be there, and to enjoye so sweete a conversation everlastingly.
>
> Thirdly consider howe yet besides these, ther shal be another glorye muche more excellent, and surpassinge all humane capacitie: which shal be, to see God face to face, wherin consisteth our essential beatitude. For that al other thinges, what soever may be imagined, be but accidental glorie: which being so exceeding great and incomparable, what shal the essential be?

[42] See St. Augustine, *De Quantitate Animae*, with trans. by F. E. Tourscher (Philadelphia: Peter Reilly, 1933), Chaps. 33–5.

[43] St. Bernard, *On Consideration*, trans. George Lewis (Oxford: Clarendon Press, 1908), p. 41.

RALPH S. WALKER

Ben Jonson's Lyric Poetry

It has become almost a point of etiquette, in writing of Ben Jonson, to begin by deploring the lack of genuine critical appreciation of his work which nineteenth century criticism reveals. In drama, criticism, poetry and prose, he holds a position in the development of English literature, so influential that it has become a matter of urgency to inquire into the causes of his eclipse. Surely there is something wrong with the critical faculty of an age which fails to appreciate the works of a writer who so profoundly influenced his successors for two hundred years. The discrepancy between Ben Jonson's literary prestige in the seventeenth and eighteenth centuries and his place in the general estimation of to-day requires to be accounted for in the interests of critical balance.

And it might, of course, be urged in explanation, that influence and merit need not be proportionate. If this were so, Waller, in virtue of the respect in which he was held by the early eighteenth century, ought to shine more brilliantly than he does among the fixed stars, and even Bowles, perhaps, because Coleridge extolled him to the nineteenth, ought to gain thereby a lustre which we cannot recognize in him. But these were reputations based on some particular merit which had a temporal appeal out of proportion to its permanent value. In Waller it was mastery of a specific metre; in Bowles it was a freedom from the particular type of artificiality which was stifling contemporary poetry. In comparison Ben Jonson's influence was lasting

From *Criterion,* XIII (1933–34), pp. 430–48. Reprinted by permission of Faber & Faber, Ltd.

and profound, not confined to any specific quality in literature, and not even confined to any single branch of it. Waller and Bowles have sunk contentedly into their appropriate niches: Ben Jonson seems to hover, in an unexplained, unsatisfactory way, between supreme greatness and comparative insignificance.

Much has been written in the past about his drama, though not always in terms so glowing as Dryden's. If his criticism is beyond reproach, it is seldom referred to, on the score that it consists for the most part in mere translation. But of all his literary activities his lyrical poetry has had least critical attention paid to it. The lavish encomiums of the seventeenth century, since they are themselves lyrical in form, are perhaps of doubtful validity as criticism. Shirley, Marmion, Herrick, and a host of minor poets paid tribute to Ben Jonson, as to their spiritual father, but the nineteenth century chose to see his merit in their productions rather than in his own. Symonds, for instance, after much searching for the qualities it lacks, dismisses his lyric verse with: "For Jonson's fame it is quite enough to point out that these, rather than Shakespeare's lyrics, struck the keynote of the seventeenth century." Gregory Smith "hesitates when he comes to consider Jonson as a poet," and expresses, "with a farmerly touch of annoyance," his surprise at the indefinability of his lyric success. Saintsbury is no less troubled by "the anomalous and seemingly contradictory power" of his lyrical "grace and sweetness," and Swinburne pauses, in the course of a lengthy pæan of praise for his lyric verse, to indicate "its crowning and damning defect."

And it is true that Ben Jonson, besides producing a number of shining successes, in more than one of the departments of literature towards which he directed his efforts, wrote a great deal in all of them that is unimpressive. For the onus of origination weighed heavily upon him. It is a frequently made and misleading implication that the greatest poets are necessarily the greatest originators. As a rule it is the lesser poets, towards the end of a period of decadence, who shoulder the burden of preparing for a new and great poetic achievement. Coming in the dawn of a new era, they feel in them the stirrings of a new attitude to life which cannot be expressed in outworn literary forms. And the great poet, coming with the new age, is relieved of the hard spadework—is left to gather up and mould and modify their experiments into a final perfection. The real originators are the Cowpers who prepare the ground and make straight the way for the Wordsworths. And in doing so—who knows?—perhaps they dissipate much of the creative energy which might have made them major poets, had they come at a time when a suitable "idiom," in all its component elements, was waiting—suspended in the literature of the past—for the fusing influence of their individuality. But Ben Jonson was his own experimenter. He was not only, in a sense, more original than Blake, but he was even more consciously so. His whole development as a literary artist resolves itself into a huge struggle to give utterance to the peculiar harmony, which he felt within him, between emotional inspiration and intellectual conviction—for this harmony produced in Ben Jonson a "sensibility" radically different from any that had previously found expression in English literature. But he won his victory—or rather a number of brief victories—and the fruits are most plainly to be seen among his lyric poems.

It would be a mistake to trace out his development as if it were a single, evolutionary process, concurrent with the ascertained events of his life. This method has played havoc with too much criticism in the past. And nobody has suffered more from the prominence of biography in critical literature than Ben Jonson. Even the obviousness of the errors in which a taste for biography involved Dr. Johnson's critical acumen has not since served to relegate it to its proper sphere. Biography cannot reveal a character in its entirety; it can only create an imaginary one based on a selection of known facts. The Ben Jonson of biography is almost as much of an imaginary figure as one of the "humorous" characters of his own comedy. He has risen up, with his "mountain belly and his rocky face," his pig-headedness, his bluntness and pedantry, and come between the critics and his works—overwhelmed them, by the sheer force of his personality, into dumbness and stupidity. Criticism has really nothing to do with this fleshly ghost, in spite of its strange fascination. Ben Jonson, bricklayer's apprentice, military adventurer, social lion and oracle of his age, must be "depersonalized" and considered merely as the writer of certain tragedies and comedies, masques, poems and critical statements, if his works are to be approached in a reasonably critical frame of mind, free from irrelevant preconceptions as to the nature of the man.

This Scylla of the biographic method, which has already wrecked so many of his critics, has a Charybdis for the present-day critic of Ben Jonson in the shape of a temptation to defend him against the tacit or implied detraction of the nineteenth century. But there is no need to champion him: "I will have no man addict himself to me." He has been defrauded of nothing; any loss that may have been incurred has been the unappreciative critic's, not Ben Jonson's. Ever since Plato sent forth a challenge with his, the tendency of criticism to degenerate into dialectic has been its most fatal characteristic. When Swift wrote his *Battle of the Books,* without perhaps realizing how fundamental his diagnosis was, he laid bare the principal cause of the sterility of criticism, not only in his own day but in the two thousand years between Aristotle and Coleridge. The taint of the polemical has rendered far too much criticism abortive, and where the temptation to forsake the bench for the bar is as strong as it is in discussing Ben Jonson's work, it is more than ever necessary to guard against it.

But the undeclared antagonism of the nineteenth century towards Ben Jonson is, after all, not difficult to understand. Having once adopted the "divine afflatus" theory of poetic inspiration, with the swing of the pendulum of taste away from eighteenth century artificiality, Ben Jonson became an enigma, and a disturbing one at that. For if poetic achievement was to be gauged solely by a scale of values based on the apparent spontaneity of the emotion expressed in poetry, there could be no accounting for the obviously conscious art of Ben Jonson—an art which never denied its consciousness, but which nevertheless succeeded in expressing beauty and emotion. And furthermore, as avowed opponents of eighteenth century pseudo-classicism, the romantic and Victorian schools were bound to regard Ben Jonson with some severity, as the fountain-head of all they held most antagonistic to their own view of art—the spring and origin of the great classical movement in English literature. And, had they reflected on the matter at all, the bitterest pill for them would have been the incontrovertible fact of his lyric success—for the lyric was then generally believed to be, as Pater says, "the highest and most complete form of poetry," and the romantics held it as their own especial province. And so, without conscious malevolence, they seem to have ignored Ben Jonson as a poet, and to have accepted him simply as a dramatist—for as such they found him more easily vulnerable, and more readily explained away by the dwarfing process of comparison with Shakespeare.

As a dramatist he has at last received a measure of understanding appreciation from Mr. T. S. Eliot, who points out that a comparison between Shakespeare and Ben Jonson is simply misleading unless it is used to emphasize their essential difference of intention, and the consequent incommensurability of their achievement. But even when it is realized that the beauty and emotional impulse of "Catiline" and "Volpone" are revealed less in detail than in the structure of the play as a finished entity—a significant point in the understanding of Ben Jonson's art in all its branches—it remains true that his most complete, most impeccable and most influential successes were not in the realm of drama at all. In spite of *Epicœne* and *The Alchemist*, and in spite of *Bartholomew Fair*, it is in the lesser products of his genius, the poems, that Ben Jonson's originality achieves its most triumphant expression.

His plays are all, in a sense, experimental. Each and all have their significance as manifestations of the general conception of beauty and art which underlay his practice, but they do not in any single case afford more than a partial outlet for its expression. In no single play are the peculiar elements which go to the making of Ben Jonson's individual sensibility synthesized and brought to a perfect fruition. They are dispersed among the plays, but in the perfect lyrics alone they blend into a harmony which permits of full and satisfactory self-expression. And it is because no critic hitherto seems to have recognized in these lyrics a form of self-expression, of a profound and fundamental kind, that they have appeared so unaccountable in their perfection, have given rise to so much hedging on the part of commentators, and have proved a source, not of genuine pleasure, but of uneasiness and mystification.

If his drama is experimental, the majority of his poems, in their conscious striving after form, are of that nature too. But they represent a more sustained current of experimentation than do the plays. Yet, even in Ben Jonson's lyric style, there is no normal evolutionary growth from one phase to another of lessening imperfection. Success is occasional and spasmodic. His artistic development is not a systematic progression, partly because it is not a mere subconscious urge. It is not what is last in point of time that is best. Dryden was right when he called his later comedies "his dotages." His poetic sensibility, seeking adequate expression, is for ever pushing towards the surface, first in one direction and then, meeting some repulse, in another. From the parent trunk various branches spring and rebranch, and the finest flowers are not necessarily at the tip of the uttermost twig. But, with Ben Jonson, it is the lyric stem which is most prolific in the finest flowers.

And having said this, it has to be admitted that the supreme lyric success of Ben Jonson, as far as bulk goes, is small. Some scattered lyrics in the plays and masques, a very few in the *Forest* and *Underwoods*, make up the total score. He very seldom attains to that poise between endeavour and achievement which allows an unimpeded precipitation of artistic emotion. The onus of origination takes its toll, for the conflict is for ever in progress between a longing to fall back upon the fully developed style ready to his hand, and the stern realization that it cannot express his idea of beauty, and therefore cannot possibly provide his genius with an adequate medium. Again and again he returns to dabble in the Elizabethan mode, only, as with the *Sad Shepherd*, to relinquish it unsatisfied. And the astonishing feature of this inner conflict of Ben Jonson, the artist, is the complete intellectual comprehension which accompanies it. He is simultaneously critic and poet: conscious and unconscious artistic intention are consistent in him. He does not experiment merely from a subconscious impulse; he consciously aims at the accomplishment of an artistic ideal. And he is so thoroughly aware of his intention that he can formulate his ideal in prose and propagandize for it in his conversation. He is perhaps the first Englishman—one is not sure of Sidney or Ascham—to have a clear conception of art as a living process, dependent for its welfare on the service and devotion of its practitioners. Side by side with Ben Jonson's conscientious dedication to an ideal, goes the creative urgency towards the formation of an individual mode of expression; but, though the two forces—intellectual and emotional if you will, or conscious and subconscious—are complementary products of the same essential being, they do not often move directly and unerringly towards their mutual end. A defect of will in Ben Jonson, a readiness to despair at times, baulked them, it seems, of utterance in perfect harmony. But now and then the blending did occur, and it is just there, at the point of fusion, that Ben Jonson touches the peak of success in his lyric utterance.

It is where Ben Jonson's ideal of beauty finds for itself an expression which perfectly agrees with his ideal of art that this fusion takes place. The two become one and indivisible. To the romantic, beauty reveals itself in strangeness, in excess, and it tends to make its first appeal by way of sensuous apprehension. Contrast the poetry of Keats with that of Ben Jonson and it becomes apparent that the æsthetic perception actuating the two is fundamentally different. From the velvety woodbines and sleek marigolds of Keats, to turn to this:

> So love emergent out of chaos brought
> The world to light,
> And gently moving on the waters wrought
> All forms to sight

is like turning from some warm, lush meadow of actual experience, to a cool, paved terrace, erected, not in the outer world, but in the stillness of the mind. Ben Jonson's conception of beauty does not to the same extent involve appreciation of external phenomena: his themes are not evoked through an emotional sympathy with the autumn sky or the nightingale's song. Instead of springing from the contemplation of variety and diversity in man and nature, his beauty belongs to the apprehension of their underlying symmetry. It is the harmony and finish of the scheme of things which is beautiful to Ben Jonson, and not any incidental development in nature. His idea of beauty is intimately connected with the balance of the universe, the order and rhythm of the spheres, the perfection of adjustment underlying the irregularity of outward forms.

But the abstract idea of this symmetry is not in itself the inspiration of Ben Jonson's poetry, so much as the idea made manifest in the ordered working of a finished creation. It is as if the poet saw the world as an architect might see a cathedral, impressed not so much by its surface beauties, its carvings and its gargoyles, nor yet concerned with its original conception as an idea, or a plan on paper, but moved to exultation at the mathematical precision of design revealed in the perfect structure. The mystic sees in every form of outward manifestation only an imperfect shadow of the idea behind it. But for Ben Jonson it is "love emergent out of chaos" which brings the world to light. The unfulfilled idea with all its possibilities is to him a thing of imperfection. It is not perfect or complete till it has found expression. Ben Jonson's highest beauty is a beauty of completion—"it might be" is beautiful only when it has become "it is." And, because his ideal beauty is thus intimately linked with the creative act, where it finds adequate expression it does so in a finished and conscious art.

All the qualities of Ben Jonson's lyric success demonstrate, in their own particular, the essential components of his ideal of beauty:

> It was a beauty that I saw,
> so pure, so perfect.

The all-pervading restraint of *An Hymn to Diana*, the simple economy of utterance in the verses *To the Author of "The Touchstone of Truth,"* the even movement, unswerving directness of language and naked dignity of style towards which he strives and which at times he achieves, together with the ordered management, and finished execution which give to his stanzas their effect of balanced finality—all these are expressions of those central principles of purity and perfection which comprise Ben Jonson's idea of beauty.

Possibly all this implies little more than that Ben Jonson was classically-minded. But if such a beauty is essentially that of the "classic" as opposed to the "romantic," in poetry, it is doubtful whether it has found anywhere in English literature such complete expression as in the lyric of Ben Jonson. It recurs in the poetry of his seventeenth century successors, but in a modified and derivative form. Pope and the eighteenth century Augustans were pseudo-classicists of a Frenchified and modernized type. Herford is mistaken when he calls Ben Jonson "a precursor of the Augustans, imperfectly grasping the ideals they were destined to achieve." The Elizabethan renaissance writers, again, were Italianate and essentially romantic, despite their superficial devotion to the classics. Only in Ben Jonson is there a complete absorption of the abstract and indefinable spirit usually indicated by the epithet "classical."

And because it is probable that Ben Jonson, to a great extent, "absorbed" his mental attitude through constant and devoted study of the classical poets, there are those who would deny his originality. Some of his successful lyrics are directly inspired by Horace, Catullus and the Greek anthology—"you may track him everywhere in their snow." But except by means of imitation and absorption, there can be no originality. The great originators are those with the longest tradition behind their art. It is only through a reverent absorption of the spirit and wisdom of the past that originality is achieved, and the more complete the absorption the more fundamental the originality. The unoriginal poet is the poet who accepts without absorption, whose expression lacks individuality because it is of shallow root and imperfectly realized.

Ben Jonson, steeped in the spirit of a refined and purified classicism, was faced with the necessity of developing a new and individual mode of expression. To his indebtedness to the classics he owed that supreme originality which rendered him more clearly aware than his contemporaries of the tawdriness and insincerity of the overhandled Elizabethan style. He set himself to evolve a new and original style, but he did so because he had something new to express, an ideal of beauty never before expressed in English poetry.

Those who deny originality to Ben Jonson are generally those who most admire his less original work. Had he lingered only where:

> In the stocks of trees white faies do dwell,
> And spanlong elves that dance about a pool
> With each a little changeling in their arms,

had he relied for inspiration on his invocation to Fancy:

> Break, Phant'sie, from thy cave of cloud,
> And spread thy purple wings;
> Now all thy figures are allowed,
> And various shapes of things;
> Create of airy forms a stream . . .

And though it be a waking dream,
Yet let it like an odour rise
To all the senses here,
And fall like sleep upon their eyes,
Or music in their ear,

he would have attained a certain minor success in the Elizabethan tradition. But he seldom rises to any considerable height on these borrowed "purple wings." And it is the constant lament of his nineteenth century critics that he did not assume them oftener. "That singing power," says Swinburne, "hardly now and then could his industry attain to it by some exceptional touch of inspiration or of luck." Gregory Smith finds him "rarely, if indeed ever, possessed by compelling song. He has no passion." There is more penetration in Symond's verdict: "If the haunting evanescent exquisiteness of Shakespeare's song is absent, we have not the right to demand this from a singer of so different a mould." His Elizabethan poems are, as a rule, unsatisfactory, because of the sense of insecurity, the half-insincerity, which pervades them and gives them what Coleridge might have called their "inconstancy." When he weaves a gauzy fabric of romance with borrowed silks, he is apt to tear it suddenly and brutally, as if impatient at his own pretence. For this Scott dubbed him "coarse." The unexpected relapse into an incongruous key is typical of his experiments in the purely Elizabethan, is paralleled by his inclusion of the Maudlin-Lorel dialogue in the *Sad Shepherd*, and indicates the unsuitability of the medium to his needs. It can be illustrated in the song just quoted from the *Vision of Delight*, whose sixth line, omitted above, runs:

It must have blood and nought of phlegm.

That Ben Jonson constantly returned to essay the Elizabethan mode was partly due, perhaps, to the desire for appreciation which is never wholly absent from the creative mind, however stern its dedication to a higher end. And to write an Elizabethan pastoral was to make a stronger bid for popular applause than to write *Sejanus*. Nor are the opening lines of the *Sad Shepherd* without their own beauty:

Here she was wont to go! and here! and here!
Just where those daisies, pinks and violets grow:
The world may find the spring by following her,
For other print her airy steps ne'er left.

But they represent a mere reorganization of exhausted elements according to a recognized formula. The freshness is due to a momentary recapturing of the *Midsummer Night's Dream* atmosphere, a fleeting glimpse which is gone as quickly as it came. And the masques, though they possess their own peculiar merit, contain little poetry apart from the occasional isolated lyrics which stand out from their framework like precious stones in a setting of tinsel.

The "done-to-order" artificiality of Ben Jonson's masque style is essentially different from the art of his lyric style. Emotional impulse and craftsmanship are inextricably combined in the pre-eminently successful lyrics like the *Song to Celia* or the *Hymn to Diana.* The beauty expressed in the finished lyric is a beauty which belongs to, and cannot be expressed otherwise than in craftsmanship. The conscious artistry of Ben Jonson's lyric style is a cause and a result of his poetic emotion. And so his rarest singing lyrics make no attempt to disown their conscious engineering of design. The complicated internal balance of the *Triumph of Charis,* the careful and almost monosyllabic simplicity of *An Hymn to God the Father:*

> If thou hadst not
> Been stern to me,
> But left me free,
> I had forgot
> Myself and Thee. . . .

are essential products of that restraint and finish which belong to Ben Jonson's art. If his lyrics have a frigid and translucent beauty like that of a crystal cameo, they are like a cameo also in their unashamed avowal of the carver's hand. The form of the finished lyric is itself an emotional product, for form and system are intrinsic factors in Ben Jonson's ideal of beauty. His lyric at its best possesses a peculiar integrity of its own, it seems to express nothing beyond or behind itself, but, in its final state, to be itself the idea which it expresses.

It is this fact which must inevitably baulk romantic criticism in any effort to appreciate Ben Jonson. It can appreciate the frame of mind which gave birth to a penitential poem like *An Hymn to God the Father,* or the pathos of the *Epitaph on Salathiel Pavy;* it can acclaim the occasional liberation of emotion from its framework which occurs in lines like these:

> O had I now your manner, mastery, might,
> Your power of handling shadow, air and spright,
> How I would draw, and take hold and delight!

But it cannot take the hint which is contained in the substance of these lines. It cannot account for lyrics like the *Vision of Beauty* or the *Birth of Love* or the song beginning:

O do not wanton with those eyes.

For expression, to a romantic poet like Shelley, is always imperfect—always embodying something which it is inadequate to contain. And, to a critic possessed of such a theory as to the function of form in poetry, it is only natural to suspect in Ben Jonson's best work an element of insincerity. But there is a difference between attempting to express a preconceived state of consciousness and evolving an emotional state by expressing it. Different standards have to be applied to poetry which is a means, like that of Shelley, and poetry which is an end, like that of Ben Jonson. In its very skilfulness Ben Jonson's poetry is eminently sincere, and its craft-consciousness is not something over which Symonds, Swinburne and Gregory Smith need be disparaging or even apologetic.

The formal nature of Ben Jonson's subconscious ideal of beauty belongs equally to his conscious ideal for art—an ideal which becomes apparent in his critical utterances. It has often been said that Ben Jonson made no original contribution to Renaissance criticism, that he merely restated a position fully formulated in the writings of critics like Sidney, Webbe and Puttenham. They, too, had been concerned about the prevalence of poetastry, and had seen salvation for the "rakehelly rout of ragged rhymesters" and "pottical, poetical heads" in a redisciplining of art on classical lines. Moreover, Ben Jonson's "Discoveries," like his lyrics, very largely consist of free translations from Greek and Latin. But his originality in criticism, as in poetry, is an originality of absorption and comprehension which finds an outlet in practice as well as in theory. Much more than any of his predecessors, he bound over his whole being to the accomplishment of his artistic ideal, and to its furthering in English literature.

The state of poetry which roused such a vigorous reforming zeal in Ben Jonson was a decadent one—that is to say its conventions had become outworn, and were no longer applicable to the changed attitude of men towards their changed conditions. As Young Lorenzo puts it, in *Every Man in his Humour,* poetry seemed now

Patched up in remnants and old worn rags,
Half starved for want of her peculiar food.

The bastard classical tradition, which English literature inherited from Renaissance Italy, had provided an ideal outlet for the exuberant vitality of an awakening world. The youthful overflow of Elizabethan spirits had found artistic expression in extreme naïveté, and in extreme artificiality; for the simplicity and affectation of Elizabethan poetry are both, in their opposite ways, effects of that comparative immaturity of mind which marks the age. But the clear-eyed simplicity of a lyric by Peele was too genuine a thing to outlast its incentive. Its freshness belonged to the dawn and could not survive it. The Golden Pomp, abandoning simplicity, sought to express itself in rhetoric and rhodomontade. But, with the decline of that spirit of boundless optimism which could put genuineness into the rant of a Marlowe, the sustaining fabric of sincerity dwindled and the empty shell of affectation remained. Artfulness in phraseology, from being a tenderly nourished acquisition, became almost an unnatural passion.

> Taffeta phrases, silken terms precise,
> Three-piled hyperboles, spruce affectation,
> Figures pedantical; these summer flies

blew the style of Lyly's euphuistic imitators "full of maggot ostentation." The pursuit of literature degenerated into a scramble after "archaic, inkhorn, oversea" phraseology. Bacon could diagnose "the distemper of learning" as consisting in "the whole inclination of the times . . . rather towards copy than weight," Shakespeare could parody the mannerisms of the day in the absurd effusion of Holofernes, and Ben Jonson was moved to indignation at the "greedy fry" too easily

> Taken with false baits
> Of worded balladry.

The deepening cast of thought which characterises the Jacobean period, rendered it impossible for poetry to seek salvation in any effort to exchange its artificiality for the graceful carelessness of the early Elizabethan style. Past methods were too flimsy to express the new complexities of a maturer age. Thought tended to become increasingly subjective, and elation of the senses was no longer a sufficient impetus to verse-writing. The lyric, to survive, must prepare to convey more strenuous experiences than it had previously done, must adapt itself to bear a new intensity of meaning, and to express a more personal and reflective mood. Ben Jonson's lyric style at its height does not fulfil these temporal demands upon the genre, although it furthers their fulfilment. It is peculiar in its lack of any profound or even apparent moral value, since it is not, to a normal extent, inspired by a personal experience previous to its embodiment in a poem, but seems somehow to spring directly out of the experience of creation. But Ben Jonson was well aware of the tendency of the times towards increased profundity of thought, and of the incapacity of existing poetic conventions to cope with the new depth of consciousness which ensued. The style of his "occasional" verse, compliment, epitaph and epigram, is an effect of this awareness. And, as a critic, he saw in himself a Horace, and in his contemporaries the infatuated sons of Pompilius: "What is so furious and Bedlamlike as a vain sound of chosen and excellent words without any subject of sentence or science mixed?"

More alive than Webbe to "the cankered enmity of curious custom," more aware than Harvey of what constitutes a "right artificiality," Ben Jonson applies to the prevalent disease a panacea compounded of simplicity and restraint, craftsmanship, sincerity and wit. His real and infinite debt to the classics is not to be gauged by uncovering the sources of his adaptations. It is to be found in his recognition, brought about by acquaintance with the classics, that true wit does not consist in mere word-play and that decadent Elizabethan verse-craftsmanship was a craftsmanship wrongly applied and of a self-destructive nature. By his frankness, his directness of style and his glorification of "good sense," he seeks to confound the mishandlers of the Petrarchian involution and exalt that "language such as men do use" which is commended in the prologue to *Every Man in his Humour*. And he supports his practice by many a frontal assault on meaningless verbal sensationalism: it is for trafficking in such verbiage that Crispinus is punished in the *Poetaster*.

The reaction against the Spenserian tradition in lyric poetry was not due in its inception solely to Ben Jonson. Reaction against excess in any one direction may take the form of a reversion to normality; more often it develops into a violent swing in an opposite direction. Both these tendencies are visible in Jacobean poetry, and it is perhaps because Donne's influence was, in a sense, eccentric, that it was more immediate, but less enduring than Ben Johnson's. Ben Jonson's influence is formal in the widest sense. It takes account of the needs of poetry as an evolutionary force. It is not primarily concerned with the temporary situation, but reaches out to what is permanent in art. To Donne, poetic form is something of an encumbrance, an intractable medium which must be controlled lest it control. For, before Donne seized and wrested it victoriously to his needs, the lyric had not passed through any phase of preparation for his coming. The very suddenness of the change it had to undergo in his hands lessened the enduring effect of his influence. Ben Jonson, although "he esteemeth John Donne the first poet in the world, in some things," believed "that Donne himself, for not being understood, would perish." And it is true that, in comparison with an impersonal poet like the Ben Jonson of

Queen and huntress, chaste and fair,

Donne's appeal was very largely to the specific in his age. Hence eighteenth and nineteenth century indifference, and hence the new appreciation of Donne's poetry which results from a certain similarity in the outlooks of the seventeenth and twentieth centuries.

But Donne's immediate influence was profound, and, since it served to deepen the scope of the lyric, it was complementary to the influence of Ben Jonson—in spite of the seeming antagonism which drew from Ben Jonson his "Donne for not keeping of accent deserves hanging." Ben Jonson's insistence on the classic and permanent virtues of restraint, simplicity, decorum and good workmanship, was valuable as a corrective to the bad effect which such an individual style as Donne's might have had on its imitators. Both helped to bring a new sincerity into the lyric, Ben Jonson by dispensing with the vain conceit, Donne by developing a new conceit, possessed of a new personal urgency, and capable of expressing genuine, if highly intellectualized, emotion. Together they opposed Spenserian facility and Petrarchian affectation.

To follow out exhaustively the influence of Ben Jonson's lyric style on seventeenth century poetry, would be unprofitable and, in fact, impossible. There is no extricating the two dominating influences of Donne and Ben Jonson from their interplay throughout the period. The metre of Herrick's *Night Piece,* the movement of Carew's *Secrecy Protested,* the design of Suckling's *False One,* are obviously derived directly from Ben Jonson's verse. But, had his example produced nothing but surface imitation of this kind, it would have been of doubtful benefit. His influence is far more penetrating, more all-pervading, and is less concerned with superficialities than with the promotion, in the work of his successors, of the fundamental qualities which went to make his own supreme lyric success.

Compared to that of Donne or Milton, Ben Jonson's originality was of a more impersonal type, less occupied in the creation of a purely or exclusively individual mode of utterance. The great individualists among the poets are a danger to their imitators. A Shakespearian or a Miltonic inflection may prove stifling to a lesser poet. But Ben Jonson, through his absorption of the classic ideal, achieved an unusual negation of the accidentally personal. And his lyric style, in which alone he attains to perfect self-expression, exerts a force which, instead of overwhelming his followers in its personality, in its impersonality acts only on their art. It is this truth which becomes obscured if the Ben Jonson of biography, a forceful individual, arrogant, exclusive, sensitive to personal affront, is allowed to wield an undue influence on the critic of his art. And it is because this has been so in the past, to such a great extent, that so little genuine criticism has been brought to bear on it.

His influence on the eighteenth century was probably wider and more general, if less direct, than it had been on the seventeenth. He had prepared English poetry for the coming of the age of reason; he had done much towards enabling it to fulfil its new requirements; he had been the voice crying in the wilderness. And, to the first genuine classic lyricist of English poetry the debt of the English neo-classic lyric is naturally inestimable. But the eighteenth century, like the seventeenth, never fully realized the significance of Ben Jonson's lyric success—never achieved his peculiar virtue of self-absorption in art, the perfect harmony between emotion and the process of creation which Ben Jonson derived from his clearer conception of the underlying ideal of classic art.

Sometimes his poetry expresses a preconceived emotion; sometimes it embodies a conception of beauty which is typically Elizabethan; sometimes it employs the "idiom of wit." But these are not intrinsic factors in his highest lyric success, and his poetry should not be valued merely, or chiefly, on their account. Prejudiced criticism detaches fragments illustrative of these qualities for special commendation, just as it concentrates on isolated passages of a similar kind in the plays, ignoring the essential artistic intention from which they are accidental divergences. It is of the utmost importance that Ben Jonson's poetry should be judged as what it is, and by what it tries to be—not as something wholly different. Ben Jonson's peculiar lyric achievement is a poetry which is, in its own way, "absolute." It cannot be considered as the product of an emotional mood detachable from itself; nor does it arouse one. The touchstone of "high seriousness" does not apply. The "subject," although it forms an integral part of the finished lyric, is not the predominant or determining factor in its composition. It is not what it says, but what it is, that matters. To this extent the philosophic meaning is irrelevant—let it be derived from Philostratus, from Catullus, or from chance. In its construction there is not the normal opposition between art and inspiration—for art is its inspiration. And it is because this truth has never hitherto been duly recognized, that Ben Jonson's poetry has been so long a stumbling block for criticism—its success the cause of insincere applause, its influence a mystery.

GEOFFREY WALTON

The Tone of Ben Jonson's Poetry

It is well known that Pope imitated the opening couplet of Jonson's *Elegie on the Lady Jane Pawlet, Marchion: of Winton:*

> What gentle ghost, besprent with *April* deaw,
> Hayles me, so solemnly, to yonder Yewgh?

in his own opening couplet of the *Elegy to the Memory of an Unfortunate Lady:*

> What beck'ning ghost, along the moonlight shade
> Invites my steps, and points to yonder glade?

The similarity and the difference between the grand style of Pope and the slightly Spenserian language of Jonson on this occasion are obvious. I have chosen to begin with a reference to this piece of plagiarism, however, because these two poems may be taken to mark, in so far as there are any beginnings and ends in literature, the limits of my study, and because the debt draws pointed attention to the dignified and courteous tone of Jonson's poetry, especially in his occasional verses. Several lines of elegy, which often intersect and blend, run between Jonson's epitaphs and formal eulogies and Pope's poem, which seems to gather up into itself all the various threads, the earlier Metaphysical and philosophic meditation of Donne, the formality of Cowley on Crashaw, the tenderness of Cowley on Hervey, the satire of Dryden in

From *Metaphysical to Augustan: Studies in Tone and Sensibility in the Seventeenth Century* (London: Bowes & Bowes, 1955), pp. 23–44. Reprinted by permission of the publishers.

the ode on Anne Killigrew and the elegiac of Milton on the same Lady Jane.[1] Pope inherited a large measure of Metaphysical wit coming from Donne, but the predominant aspect of his genius, the Augustan decorum, can be traced back to Donne's contemporary, Jonson.

Although Jonson's greatness as a poet is generally recognized, very little has been written on his lyric and other non-dramatic poems. There is room for a detailed consideration of certain aspects of this work and for some redirection of attention towards poems hitherto neglected. Making a limited approach, I want to try to locate and define as clearly as possible his characteristic tone and civilized quality.

One often finds oneself trying, with a certain sense of frustration, to reconcile Professor C. H. Herford's morose rough diamond "with no native well-spring of verse music" and the kind of seventeenth-century Mallarmé implied by Mr. Ralph Walker.[2] The coarse side of Jonson must not be forgotten. He was rooted in the English life of tavern and workshop in his life and in his art, besides being the friend of Selden and Lord Aubigny. We have to take into account *The Voyage* as well as the *Hymn to Diana,* and remember the last line of *A Celebration of Charis*. Dr. Leavis places the odes to himself at the central point, as showing us both the independent, forthright working dramatist and the learned Horatian who brought out his plays annotated in folio.[3]

I disagree with Dr. Leavis about the odes. "The racy personal force" and the "weighty and assertive personal assurance" are indeed present. The poems are eminently successful in the sense that they communicate their content without hesitation or vagueness. One can accept and applaud the fiercely contemptuous satire on dullness and ill will, but the final effect, I think, embarrasses still, as it seems to have embarrassed the "Tribe" and as the author in person had earlier embarrassed Drummond of Hawthornden.[4] These odes are too personal and self-regarding. It is not the self-pity of a Shelley that is forced upon us, but self-assertion and unseemly pride:

> 'Twere simple fury still thyselfe to waste
> On such as have no taste. . . .
>
> 'Tis crowne enough to vertue still, her owne applause.

This is not redeemed by the finer aspiration of:

> Strike that disdaine-full heate
> Throughout, to their defeate,
> As curious fooles, and envious of thy straine,
> May, blushing, sweare no palsey's in thy braine.

Though Cartwright, Randolph and Cleveland approved, one can sympathize with that excellent literary critic, Thomas Carew, when he expostulates:

> 'Tis true (dear Ben) thy just chastizing hand
> Hath fixed upon the sotted Age a brand
> To their swolne pride, and empty scribbling due . . .
> . . . but if thou bind,
> By Citie custome, or by *Gavell-kind*,
> In equall shares thy love on all thy race,
> We may distinguish of their sexe and place;
> Though one hand form them and though one brain strike
> Souls into all, they are not all alike.
> Why should the follies then of this dull age
> Draw from thy Pen such an immodest rage,
> As seems to blast thy (else immortall) Bayes,
> When thine owne hand proclaims thy ytch of praise?
> The wiser world doth greater Thee confesse
> Than all men else, than Thyself only lesse.

Along with his mastery of the irregular Donnean couplet, Carew shows here a fineness of feeling and a regard for his poetic father, a polish of tone and an integrity of character, which represent all that was best in the class and way of life from which he came. Carew feels that the great intellectual leader has been ungentlemanly in a very deep sense; that ideal demanded a measure of humility; it was something rooted in the traditional code and which became obliterated in the more superficial, if more formally polite, Augustan age. In an ode on the same theme, not published until the present century, Jonson expresses a proud but far more admirable attitude towards the public:

> Yet since the bright and wise
> *Minerva* deignes
> Uppon this humbled earth to cast hir eyes,
> Wee'l rip our ritchest veynes
> And once more strike the Eare of tyme with those fresh straynes:
> As shall besides delight
> And Cuninge of their grounde
> Give cause to some of wonder, some despight;
> But unto more despaire to imitate their sounde. . . .
>
> Cast reverence if not feare
> Throughout their generall brests

And by their taking let it once appeare
Who worthie come, who not, to be witts Pallace guests.

However, the point to be emphasized is that Jonson at his best has a superlatively civilized tone, and it was, in fact, in him that Carew found models for the expression of such a tone in poetry. In Jonson it springs, of course, mainly from his classical culture, that culture which Carew and his class shared in a way corresponding to Jonson's participation in the social activities which produced the manners and the tone of their world. The tone which issues in Jonson's poetry from this double source is best exemplified in the following ode:

High-spirited friend,
I send nor Balmes, nor Cor'sives to your wound,
Your fate hath found
A gentler, and more agile hand, to tend
The Cure of that, which is but corporall,
And doubtful Dayes, (which were nam'd *Criticall,*)
Have made their fairest flight,
And now are out of sight.
Yet doth some wholesome Physick for the mind,
Wrapt in this paper lie,
Which in the taking if you misapply
You are unkind.

Your covetous hand,
Happy in that faire honour it hath gain'd
Must now be rayn'd.
True valour doth her owne renowne command
In one full Action; nor have you now more
To doe, then to be husband of that store.
Thinke but how deare you bought
This same which you have caught,
Such thoughts wil make you more in love with truth.
'Tis wisdom, and that high
For men to use their fortune reverently,
Even in youth.

This is no mere pindaric experiment. To whoever is addressed Jonson is giving extremely intimate personal advice, analysing a situation and a character instead of writing a conventional epithalamium, but his delicate movement and hesitating phrases, using the opportunities of the formal pattern, keep it free of all suggestion of patronage or importunity. There is great strength in the total effect of mature wisdom. Jonson is appealing to an ideal of human dignity and reasonable behaviour held in common with his reader which inspires frankness and at the same time sincere mutual respect. The ultimate basis is again the old idea of courtesy. This was a quality of the spirit which made it possible to consider serious moral matters in a social context without losing sight of their seriousness or doing anything in what would later be called "bad form." This ode by itself seems to me a refutation of Professor Herford's opinion that Jonson "for all his generous warmth lacked the finer graces of familiarity." It has both.

The wit of Jonson, like that of Donne, manifests itself in many ways. As an intellectual force it has a disciplinary and clarifying rather than a free-ranging and elaborating effect,[5] but the relationship between the two poets is shown in Jonson's admiration for Donne and in the common features of that group of elegies whose authorship has long been in dispute between them.[6] In discussing the more social aspect of Jonson's wit, the tone that he handed on to his "sons," usually in the form of an economy and polish of technique, I think that one can claim that these "finer graces" form one of Jonson's great qualities as a poet. "High-spirited friend . . ." and "Fair friend . . ." [7] that elegant, but closely reasoned and firmly phrased lyric, equally expressive of his distinctive classical urbanity, together give us the quintessence of Jonson's attitude towards his friends and fellow poets, his patrons and patronesses. It is not the formal decorum of a large polite world—such, in any case, did not yet exist—but one feels it to be, I think, the tone of small circles in which aristocratic and cultivated people knew each other intimately. One can back up these deductions by a short survey of Jonson's occasional and certain other verses and of imitations by his "sons." They have the kind of tone I have just noted, and they describe the life that contributed to produce that tone. Beside these poems much of the social verse, even of Pope, sounds brassy. One knows that life at Whitehall, particularly in the reign of James I, was often disorderly, not to say squalid, and that sports and pastimes on the best-ordered country estate were rough and cruel, but the refinement was also there, sometimes in the same people. In the poetry it is preserved for ever.

The epigram, *Inviting a Friend to Supper,* is admirable social verse, besides being a document of the Jonson world, an offering of scholarly conversation with simple but good food and wine—Virgil and Tacitus with canary. A long series of epigrams and complimentary verses sketch in the type of men with whom Jonson liked to associate and the qualities that for him made up a civilized life. *An Epistle, answering one that asked to be Sealed of the Tribe of BEN* is unfortunately little more than satire on smart London life and the masques of Inigo Jones. *An Epistle to a Friend, to persuade him to the Warres* with its finely realized opening:

> Wake, friend, from forth thy Lethargie: the Drum
> Beates brave and loude in Europe and bids come
> All that dare rowse . . .

is again mainly negative, a vigorous and racy denunciation of loose sexual morality and excessive drinking, but the ending sets up a heroic ideal of moral and physical valour, temperate, stoical and devout, the very reverse of the Renaissance braggart:

> Goe, quit 'hem all. And take along with thee
> Thy true friends wishes, *Colby*, which shall be
> That thine be just, and honest; that thy Deeds
> Not wound thy conscience, when thy body bleeds;
> That thou dost all things more for truth, then glory
> And never but for doing wrong be sory
> That by commanding first thyselfe, thou mak'st
> Thy person fit for any charge thou tak'st;
> That fortune never make thee to complaine,
> But what shee gives, thou dar'st give her againe;
> That whatsoever face thy fate puts on,
> Thou shrinke or start not, but be always one;
> That thou thinke nothing great, but what is good,
> And from that thought strive to be understood.
> So, 'live so dead, thou wilt preserve a fame
> Still pretious, with the odour of thy name.
> And last, blaspheme not, we did never heare
> Man thought the valianter, 'cause he durst sweare. . . .

The two poems to the brilliant young Earl of Newcastle, exalting his horsemanship and his fencing, show a kindred enthusiasm. As Professor Herford remarks, admiration for virility "gives eloquence to his verse." Vincent Corbet stands for graver and gentler virtues:

> His Mind was pure, and neatly kept,
> As were his Nourceries; and swept
> So of uncleannesse, or offence,
> That never came ill odour thence:
> And add his Actions unto these,
> They were as specious as his Trees.

'Tis true, he could not reprehend,
His very Manners taught to 'mend,
They were so even, grave, and holy;
No stubbornnesse so stiffe, nor folly
To licence ever was so light
As twice to trespasse in his sight,
His looks would so correct it, when
It chid the vice, yet not the Men.
Much from him I confesse I wonne,
And more, and more, I should have done,
But that I understood him scant.
Now I conceive him by my want. . . .

The poet's self-criticism emphasizes the respectfulness of his attitude and deserves particular notice in this essay. In addressing Selden his verse is less distinguished, but it must be quoted for the attitude to himself shown in:

Though I confesse (as every Muse hath err'd,
And mine not least) . . .

and for the conception of scholarship and the literary life described:

Stand forth my Object, then, you that have beene
Ever at home: yet, have all Countries seene;
And like a Compasse keeping one foot still
Upon your Center, doe your circle fill
Of generall knowledge; watch'd men, manners too,
Heard what times past have said, seene what ours doe:
Which Grace shall I make love to first? your skill,
Or faith in things? or is't your wealth and will
T'instruct and teach? or your unweary'd paine
Of Gathering? Bountie'in pouring out againe?
What fables have you vext! what truth redeem'd!
Antiquities search'd! Opinions dis-esteem'd!
Impostures branded! and Authorities urg'd! . . .

In writing to Drayton, Jonson notes that they have not followed the custom of exchanging verses and continues:

And, though I now begin, 'tis not to rub
Hanch against Hanch, or raise a rhyming *Club*
About the towne.

"Butter reviewers," said Mr. Nixon to the young Hugh Selwyn Mauberley.

This quotation rounds off my references to Jonson's verses on himself as a writer and his relation to the literary world. One does not take everything in seventeenth-century commendatory verses at its face value. Drayton was no Homer, but it is worth studying what Jonson says—and, more important, does not say—about the lesser figures whom he honours. The most interesting lines in the eulogy of Shakespeare are those calling upon the shades of the Greek tragedians. Jonson's critical acumen here breaks through all his own and the age's prejudices. Sir Henry Savile was somewhat above the Jonson circle and receives a formal epigram, but the ideals admired as embodied in him correspond to those of the epistle to Selden, literary skill joined to integrity of character [8]—a very solemn conception of the philosopher and the gentleman, to recall deliberately Addison's famous phrase:

> We need a man that knows the severall graces
>   Of historie, and how to apt their places;
> Where brevitie, where splendour, and where height,
>   Where sweetnesse is requir'd and where weight;
> We need a man, can speake of the intents,
>   The councells, actions, orders and events
> Of state, and censure them: we need his pen
>   Can write the things, the causes, and the men.
> But most we need his faith (and all have you)
>   That dares nor write things false, nor hide things true.

One sees in these poems the positive moral and intellectual values which are more usually merely implicit in the plays; young Wittipol in *The Devil is an Ass* emerges as a personality of some solidity and life, but the majestic Cicero is never an adequate dramatic foil to the political gangsters in *Catiline*. In the poems one can observe, described and felt in the texture of the poetry itself, the cultural ideals that gave Jonson his assurance and intellectual dignity and at the same time his feeling for civilized personal relationships. His tone only fails him when personal bitterness or excessive indignation causes him to lose his bearings and his sense of fellowship in the republic of letters.

Jonson was, however, conscious of a larger community than that meeting at the Devil Tavern with connections at the universities. Some of his finest verse celebrates this social scene and the characters who inhabited it and, in fact, led the nation. Courthope remarks that in this mode "Jonson is unequalled by any English poet, except perhaps

Pope at his best."[9] We know from the plays what he thought of the projectors and of other pioneers of nascent capitalism. He held older ideals of social justice and responsibility.[10] He saw the values he believed in embodied in certain noblemen and squires, and in statesmen and lawgivers such as Burleigh and Sir Edward Coke. The greatest document, and also the finest poem, in this connection is, of course, *To Penshurst:*

> Thou are not, PENSHURST, built for envious show,
> Of touch, or marble; nor canst boast a row
> Of polish'd pillars, or a roofe of gold:
> Thou hast no lantherne, whereof tales are told;
> Or stayre, or courts; but stand'st an ancient pile,
> And these grudg'd at, art reverenc'd the while.

It is a medieval house—it happens to have been built about the year of Chaucer's birth. For Jonson a new genius presides over it from:

> That taller tree, which of a nut was set,
> At his great birth, where all the *Muses* met.

It was now the seat of Sir Philip Sidney's brother, and Sidney appears several times in similar poems as the representative of civilization.[11] He brings the culture of *Il Cortegiano* to bear on the more active traditional idea of the gentleman expressed in, say, Langland's:

> Kings and knightes · sholde kepe it by resoun,
> Riden and rappe down · the reumes aboute,
> And taken transgressores · and tyen hem faste,
> Till treuthe had ytermyned · her trespas to ende,
> That is the profession appertly · that appendeth for knightes,
> And nought to fasten on Fryday · in fyvescore wynter,
> But holden with him and with her · that wolden al treuthe,
> And never leue hem for loue · ne for lacchyng of syluer.[12]

Penshurst is surrounded by all the beauty and wealth of nature, but it is much more than a house:

> And though thy walls be of the countrey stone,
> They'are rear'd with no mans ruine, no mans grone,
> There's none, that dwell about them, wish them downe. . . .
> Where comes no guest, but is allow'd to eate,
> Without his feare, and of thy lords own meate:

Where the same beere, and bread, and self-same wine,
That is his Lordships, shall be also mine.
And I not faine to sit (as some, this day,
At great mens tables) and yet dine away.

Jonson sees it is an active centre of a patriarchal community in which duties and responsibilities are as important as rights, and of a way of life in which all classes, including the poet—Jonson intimates that for him and for others such hospitality is becoming a thing of the past—yet live in close personal contact. *To Sir Robert Wroth* describes a very similar scene at Durance with rather more emphasis on the sporting life of the great estate—an aspect less likely to be forgotten:

Or if thou list the night in watch to breake,
A-bed canst heare the loud stag speake,
In spring, oft roused for thy masters sport,
Who, for it, makes thy house his court;
Or with thy friends the heart of all the yeare
Divid'st, upon the lesser Deere:
In Autumn, at the Patrich mak'st a flight,
And giv'st thy gladder guest the sight;
And, in the winter, hunt'st the flying hare,
More for thy exercise, than fare;
While all, that follow, their glad eares apply
To the full greatnesse of the cry:
Or hawking at the river, or the bush,
Or shooting at the greedie thrush,
Thou dost with some delight the day out-weare,
Although the coldest of the yeere!
The whilst, the severall seasons . . .
Thus PAN and SYLVANE having had their rites,
COMUS puts in, for new delights;
And fills thy open hall with mirth and cheere,
As if in SATURNES raigne it were;
APOLLO's harpe, and HERMES lyre resound,
Nor are the *Muses* strangers found.
The rout of rurall folk come thronging in,
(Their rudenesse then is thought no sinne)
Thy noblest spouse affords them welcome grace,
And the great *Heroes*, of her race,
Sit mixt with loss of state, or reverence.
Freedom doth with degree dispense.

The Golden Age is thus naturalized in the hall of an English mansion in a real agricultural setting, and we end with an almost Homeric scene of feasting, in which bounty and humanity have temporarily overthrown the whole social hierarchy. Other contemporary moralists and commentators lamented that this old-fashioned "house-keeping" was dying out. In Selden's *Table Talk* the account of the *Hall* is significantly in the past tense:

> The Hall was the Place where the great Lord used to eat, (wherefore else were Halls made so big?), where he saw all his Servants and Tenants about him. He eat not in private, except in time of sickness: when he became a thing cooped up, all his greatness was spilled. Nay, the King himself used to eat in the Hall, and his Lords sat with him, and then he understood Men.

Inigo's Jones's Double Cube Room at Wilton, say, would not have lent itself to such a life. It may sound cheap to say that Jonson made the most of two worlds; he certainly wrote at a time when a highly cultivated society still kept in close contact with the community which supported it and still preserved traditions which encouraged it to maintain this kind of give and take, social, economic and cultural.

Nevertheless, despite changing architecture and changing habits of life, the ideal persisted. Jonson initiated an extremely interesting line of what, borrowing a modern analogy, one may call documentary poetry. It deserves a brief exploration. The most obvious imitations of his poems are Carew's *To Saxham* and *To my Friend G. N., from Wrest*. No one is going to claim that Carew shared his master's powers of social observation. The first poem is a light and fanciful thing; the other, less well known, which gives a detailed picture of the scene and of the social organization represented there, illustrates a number of points already made:

> Such pure and uncompounded beauties blesse
> This Mansion with a usefull comelinesse,
> Devoide of art, for here the Architect
> Did not with curious skill a Pile erect
> Of carved Marble, Touch or Porphyry,
> But built a house for hospitalitie. . . .
> The Lord and Lady of this place delight
> Rather to be in act, than seeme in sight.
> Instead of Statues to adorne their wall,

They throng with living men their merry Hall,
Where, at large Tables fill'd with wholesome meates,
The servant, tenant, and kind neighbour eates.
Some of that ranke, spun of a finer thread,
Are with the Women, Steward, and Chaplaine fed
With daintier cates; Others of better note,
Whom wealth, parts, office, or the Heralds coate
Hath sever'd from the common, freely sit
At the Lords Table, whose spread sides admit
A large accesse of friends to fill those seates
Of his capacious circle. . . .
Nor crown'd with wheaten wreathes, doth *Ceres* stand
In stone, with a crook'd sickle in her hand;
Nor on a Marble Tun, his face besmear'd
With grapes, is curl'd uncizard *Bacchus* rear'd:
We offer not in Emblemes to the eyes,
But to the taste, those useful Deities,
We presse the juycie god and quaffe his blood,
And grind the Yeallow Goddesse into food.

The picture of the wine-press carries us away from the thoroughly English scene; it shows the Cavalier taking his eye off the object in order to classicize. But the mere fact that a man like Carew, derivative as he clearly is, recognized the existence—and the value—of such a scheme of things to the point of writing about it shows that the rather artificial culture of Charles I's court with its extravagant masques and its Italian pictures and Flemish painters had also not lost touch with its roots. Vandyck perhaps overdoes the elegance and refinement in his portrait of Carew and Killigrew, but when William Dobson paints Endymion Porter he shows us a florid country squire with beautiful laces and also dog and gun, leaning on a relief of muses and with a classical bust of a poet in the background; it is a superb and highly revealing work. Similarly Herrick in *The Hock-Cart* starts on the shores of the Mediterranean and then hurries home:

Come Sons of Summer, by whose toile,
We are the Lords of Wine and Oile:
By whose tough labours, and rough hands,
We rip up first, then reap our lands.
Crown'd with the eares of corne, now come,
And, to the Pipe, sing Harvest home. . . .
Well, on, brave boyes, to your Lords Hearth,

Glitt'ring with fire; where, for your mirth,
Ye shall see first the large and cheefe
Foundation of your Feast, Fat Beefe. . . .
With sev'rall dishes standing by,
As here a Custard, there a Pie,
And here all tempting Frumentie.
And for to make the merry cheere,
If smirking Wine be wanting here,
There's that, which drowns all care, stout Beere;
Which freely drink to your Lords health,
Then to the Plough, (the Common-wealth). . . .

As a whole it is, with its colloquial language, a vivid picture of a Devon harvest festival, and Herrick has suggested, in the reference to the plough, the deeper meaning. Lovelace shows us that he was something of a naturalist as well as a chivalrous Kentish squire in those fanciful and moralized descriptions of insects and in *The Falcon* for whom he laments:

Ah Victory, unhap'ly wonne!
Weeping and Red is set the Sun,
Whilst the whole Field floats in one tear,
And all the Air doth mourning wear:
Close-hooded all thy kindred come
To pay their Vows upon thy Tombe;
The *Hobby* and the *Musket* too,
Do march to take their last adieu.

The *Lanner* and the *Lanneret,*
Thy Colours bear as Banneret;
The *Goshawk* and her *Tercel,* rous'd
With Tears attend thee as new bows'd,
All these are in their dark array
Led by the various *Herald-Jay.*

But thy eternal name shall live
Whilst Quills from Ashes fame reprieve,
Whilst open stands Renown's wide dore,
And Wings are left on which to soar:
Doctor *Robbin,* the Prelate *Pye,*
And the poetick *Swan* shall dye,
Only to sing thy Elegie.

Whatever personal significance this may have had for Lovelace—it would seem to express a haunting regret for lost causes—its interest for us in the present context lies in his charming blend of the gentleman's knowledge of field sports and heraldry with poetic traditions—one thinks inevitably of the *Parlement of Foules.*[13] The idiom of these poems is, as Sir Herbert Grierson has put it, "that of an English gentleman of the best type, natural, simple, occasionally careless, but never diverging into vulgar colloquialism . . . or into conventional, tawdry splendour."[14] Several contributors to *Jonsonus Virbius* make plain the influence of Jonson in favour of "right and natural language." This is a stream of English poetry, the gentleman writing as a gentleman about his position and responsibilities, his interests and pleasures, which, if we omit Byron who is in any case often both vulgar and tawdry, now for better or worse dries up.

Early Stuart governments made several attempts to arrest the decay of the patriarchal household and the drift to London. Sir Richard Fanshawe wrote *An Ode, upon His Majesties Proclamation in the Year 1630. Commanding the Gentry to reside upon their Estates in the Countrey.* He sees what Jonson sees, and expresses the anxiety of those who realized how times were changing:

Nor let the Gentry grudge to go
Into those places whence they grew,
But think them blest they may do so
Who would pursue.

The smoky glory of the Town,
That may go till his native Earth,
And by the shining Fire sit down
Of his own hearth. . . .

The Countrey too ev'n chops for rain:
You that exhale it by your power,
Let the fat drops fall down again
In a full shower. . . .

One thus sees embodied in verse of considerable distinction a picture of a social order, its natural setting and its occupations, and a sense of some of the dangers threatening it. The fact that it was written by men of very varying distinction of character and intelligence shows how widely the ideals expressed were held. That they were not always lived up to one may take for granted, though the enthusiasm of the verse seems to be more than merely literary. And as regards cultural standards there must have been, for a small number of houses like Penshurst, Wrest, Wilton, Great Tew or Bolsover, a very large number like that of Mr. Henry Hastings [15] or of far less individuality and long forgotten. The scheme of knightly prowess, literary and musical interests and public spirit set forth by Peacham in *The Compleat Gentleman* was not universally followed; he bitterly reproaches those who waste their substance in London, "appearing but as Cuckoes in the Spring, one time in the yeare to the Countrey and their tenants, leaving the care of keeping good houses at Christmas, to the honest Yeomen of the Countrey." [16] However, one finds in this verse evidence of a climate of social opinion and, more important, feelings and habits which, with all their imperfections, were civilized in the narrower artistic sense, and also in the wider sense of having a foundation of social justice. This world provided Jonson with his larger *milieu,* or rather *milieux,* for its being made up of small groups is an important feature; he had lived in the house of Lord Aubigny and was a visitor at several others. One does not find this scene in English poetry after the Restoration. Though English noblemen never became, as Fanshawe feared they might, mere court sycophants or men about town, manners in the widest sense changed in the era of the coffee-house. Life became more formally decorous. Pope, in the *Epistle to Boyle,* presents an ideal vision comparable to Jonson's:

> His Father's Acres who enjoys in peace,
> Or makes his Neighbours glad if he increase:
> Whose chearful Tenants bless their yearly toil,
> Yet to their Lord owe more than to the soil;
> Whose ample Lawns are not asham'd to feed
> The milky heifer and deserving steed;
> Whose rising Forests, not for pride or show,
> But future Buildings, future Navies grow:
> Let his plantations stretch from down to down,
> First shade a Country, and then raise a Town.

But fine as it is, and central to Pope's work, it does not imply so intimate and personal a relationship between the classes as the earlier poetry. The whole domestic layout had altered as ideas changed, and the lord was benevolent from the portico or the church steps rather than from the dais in the hall. Nevertheless one finds the spirit still alive in the age of "Squire Allworthy," of Coke of Norfolk and of Dr. Johnson's Club, and it was the tradition of culture that died first.

It need hardly be said that Jonson used an independent tone towards his patrons—except when he was in extreme financial straits. He had opinions about his rightful place at table in an age when all knew their own degrees and had their rightful places by birth or merit; "my Lord," he says that he said to the Earl of Salisbury, evidently a more remote patron than Sir William Sidney, "you promised I should dine with you, but I do not."[17] *An Epistle to Sir Edward Sacvile, now Earl of Dorset* treats, after Seneca, of the question of patronage and gratitude:

> You cannot doubt, but I, who freely know
> This Good from you, as freely will it owe;
> And though my fortune humble me, to take
> The smallest courtesies with thankes, I make
> Yet choyce from whom I take them; and would shame
> To have such doe me good, I durst not name:
> They are the Noblest benefits, and sinke
> Deepest in Man, of which when he doth thinke,
> The memorie delights him more, from whom
> Then what he hath receiv'd. Gifts stinke from some,
> They are so long a coming, and so hard;
> Where any Deed is forc't, the Grace is mard.

He goes on to analyse the characters of niggardly and ungracious patrons and those who sponge upon them. Jonson thought he knew who deserved his respect and why. In *Timber* he defines his conception of manners by implication, in the act of defining Courtesy in its euphemistic sense:

> *Nothing* is a courtesie, unlesse it be meant us; and that friendly, and lovingly. Wee owe no thankes to *Rivers*, that they carry our boats. . . . It is true, some man may receive a Courtesie, and not know it; but never any man received it from him, that knew it not. . . . No: The doing of *Courtesies* aright, is the mixing of the respects for his owne sake, and for mine. He that doth them meerly for his owne sake, is like one that feeds his Cattell to sell them: he hath his Horse well drest for *Smithfield*.

Good manners for Jonson were something that, while adorning the upper tiers of the social hierarchy, should yet permeate through it. He expected the same kind of consideration from a patron as he showed towards his "high-spirited friend," and he admired similar qualities in his friends in every sense.

The grace of Jonson's manner comes out in his addresses to noble ladies, especially the Countesses of Rutland, Montgomery, and Bedford, and Lady Mary Wroth. A consideration of them will form a conclusion to this study, for, though he flatters splendidly, he does not cringe. There were certain fixed viewpoints in Jonson's outlook.

He praises his patronesses partly for their beauty and their taste, partly for deeper qualities. He writes to Lady Mary Wroth with full Renaissance exuberance:

> Madame, had all antiquitie beene lost,
> All historie seal'd up, and fables crost;
> That we had left us, nor by time, nor place,
> Least mention of a *Nymph*, a *Muse*, a *Grace*,
> But even their names were to be made a-new,
> Who could not but create them all, from you?
> He, that but saw you weare the wheaten hat,
> Would call you more than CERES, if not that:
> And, drest in shepherds tyre, who would not say:
> You were the bright OENONE, FLORA, or *May*?
> If dancing, all would cry th' *Idalian* Queene,
> Were leading forth the *Graces* on the greene:
> And, armed for the chase, so bare her brow
> DIANA' alone, so hit, and hunted so.

Lady Montgomery is a new Susanna, and in Lady Bedford he bows before qualities of character which belong peculiarly to his own vision:

> This morning, timely rapt with holy fire,
> I thought to forme unto my zealous *Muse*,
> What kind of creature I could most desire,
> To honor, serve, and love; as *Poets* use.
> I meant to make her faire, and free, and wise,
> Of greatest bloud, and yet more good then great;
> I meant the day-starre should not brighter rise,
> Nor lend like influence from his lucent seat.
> I meant she should be curteous, facile, sweet,
> Hating that solemne vice of greatnesse, pride;
> I meant each softest vertue, there should meet,
> Fit in that softer bosome to reside.
> Onely a learned, and a manly soule
> I purpos'd her; that should, with even powers,
> The rock, the spindle, and the sheeres controule
> Of destinie, and spin her owne free houres.

Such when I meant to faine, and wish'd to see,
My *Muse* bad, *Bedford* write, and that was shee.

This beautifully polished epigram is a suitable vehicle for the presentation of a vision of aristocratic elegance, charm, virtue and intelligence—one notices the emphatic and subtle rhythm of the third quatrain—and the poet's admiration for them. One is reminded of the undirected, and possibly therefore more perfect, *Elegie:*

Though Beautie be the Marke of Praise,
And yours of whom I sing be such
As not the World can praise too much,
Yet is't your vertue now I raise,

where the sense of the rarity and fragility of such qualities is delicately realized in the cadence of:

His falling Temples you have rear'd,
The withered Garlands tane away;
His Altars kept from the Decay,
That envie wish'd, and Nature fear'd.

The dangers and difficulties besetting his ideals of the lady are magnificently argued out in "Not to know vice at all . . ." and *To the World. A farewell for a Gentle-woman, vertuous and noble:*

No, I doe know, that I was borne
To age, misfortune, sicknesse, griefe:
But I will beare these, with that scorne,
As shall not need thy false reliefe.

This is the simple but dignified Stoicism which conditions of the age made both necessary and desirable. Jonson admired it in others and possessed it himself. This moral strength and perception, along with his erudition and conscious art, discoursed on in *Timber,* and an ever-present sense of the whole gamut of living, combine with the tone of the Jacobean noble household, "curteous, facile, sweet," where in season "freedome doth with degree dispense," to support the brilliance of the famous lyrics. Like his gentlewoman he could say,

Nor for my peace will I goe farre,
As wandrers doe, that still doe rome,

But make my strengths, such as they are,
Here in my bosome, and at home.

The end of it all is realized with unerring taste in such things as:

Would'st thou heare, what man can say
In a little? Reader, stay.
Under-neath this stone doth lye
As much beautie, as could dye:
Which in life did harbour give
To more vertue, then doth live.
If, at all, shee had a fault,
Leave it buryed in this vault.
One name was ELIZABETH,
Th' other let it sleepe with death:
Fitter, where it dyed, to tell,
Then that it liv'd at all. Farewell.

I am brought back to my starting-point, the *Elegie on the Lady Jane Pawlet,* through which the urbanity of Jonson links up directly with that of Pope. Jonson thought "couplets be the bravest sort of verses, especially when they are broken like hexameters," [18] and he has an important place in their development, but, as regards regularity, he broke them with a caesura in varied places, and the following lines from one of his livelier occasional poems are worth remembering:

To hit in angles, and to clash with time:
As all defence, or offence, were a chime!
I hate such measur'd, give me metall'd fire. . . .[19]

He liked a varied movement in poetry as well as fencing. The *Elegie,* like the other poems in couplets quoted, bears this out:

I doe obey you, Beautie! for in death
You seeme a faire one! O that you had breath,
To give your shade a name! Stay, stay, I feele
A horrour in mee! all my blood is steele!
Stiffe! starke! My joynts 'gainst one another knock!
Whose Daughter? ha? Great *Savage* of the Rock? . . .
Her Sweetnesse, Softnesse, her faire Courtesie,
Her wary guardes, her wise simplicitie,
Were like a ring of Vertues, 'bout her set,

And pietie the Center, where all met.
A reverend State she had, an awful Eye,
A dazling, yet inviting, Majestie:
What Nature, Fortune, Institution, Fact
Could summe to a perfection, was her Act!
How did she leave the world? with what contempt?
Just as she in it liv'd! and so exempt
From all affection! when they urg'd the Cure
Of her disease, how did her soule assure
Her suffrings, as the body had beene away!
And to the Torturers (her Doctors) say,
Stick on your Cupping-glasses, feare not, put
Your hottest Causticks to, burne, lance, or cut:
'Tis but a body which you can torment,
And I, into the world, all Soule, was sent!
Then comforted her Lord! and blest her Sonne!
Chear'd her faire Sisters in her race to runne!
With gladnesse temper'd her sad Parents teares!
Made her friends joyes to get above their feares!
And, in her last act, taught the Standers-by,
With admiration, and applause to die!
Let angels sing her glories, who can call
Her spirit home, to her originall! . . .

It combines a slightly naïve declamatory manner at the start with Jonson's characteristic blend of urbanity, shrewd observation and simplicity in the description of the Marchioness's personality and an anticipation of the more formal high decorum of the Augustans towards the end; but no Augustan would have written her words to the doctors, overflowing as they are with "enthusiasm." Here in a lady at the top of the social hierarchy one notes the hierarchy of virtues. They correspond fairly to the qualities of men we have already seen portrayed. Together Jonson's lords and ladies form a brilliant, dignified, benevolent and gracious society, "dazling, yet inviting." We can see from the poems, and other evidence corroborates, that there was no impassable gap between the world of the poet's vision and Jacobean and Caroline England. *Eupheme* on the Lady Venetia Digby is usually held up as an example of hyperbole; a passage in a quiet key on the character of the Lady, whether true to life in this particular case or not, shows, with a characteristic note of irony, a picture of deportment which would be appropriate to any of the scenes or characters discussed:

All Nobilitie,
(But pride, that schisme of incivilitie)
She had, and it became her! she was fit
T'have knowne no envy, but by suffring it!
She had a mind as calme, as she was faire;
Not tost or troubled with light Lady-aire;
But, kept an even gate, as some streight tree
Mov'd by the wind, so comely moved she.
And by the awfull manage of her Eye
She swaid all bus'nesse in the Familie!

Jonson himself, as we have seen at the start, was sometimes guilty of "that schisme of incivilitie." He probably needed the stimulus of good company to bring out the full refinement of his literary culture. But it is brought out over and over again, and was, and is, a model of its kind. It is imposible finally to separate the qualities presented in the poems from the poet's attitude towards them; social manner and manners are infectious and the one seems to have evoked the other. We should need more biographical information than we possess to take the matter further but I do not think it is base to attribute to Jonson what might be called poetic "party manners."

One cannot sum up an achievement such as Jonson's in a word. I have only touched in passing on his trenchancy and seriousness as a satirist and his strength and delicacy as a lyric poet. I wanted to deal at some length with his tone and accent because, in considering the meaning of wit, I believe that, though it changed from an intellectual to a social spirit as the century wore on, nevertheless a social spirit of a clear and peculiarly noble kind was present in poetry from the start and that this spirit is exemplified particularly in Ben Jonson. His poetry, even more than his plays, links seventeenth-century culture and the polite civilization of the Augustans to the better features of the medieval social order and to the half-religious ideal of Courtesy.

NOTES

[1] Dr. F. R. Leavis has analysed Pope's poem in *Revaluation,* Chap. III.

[2] See *Ben Jonson,* ed. Herford and Simpson, Vol. II, p. 340; and R. Walker, "Ben Jonson's Lyric Poetry," *The Criterion,* Vol. XIII, 1934.

[3] *Revaluation,* Chap. I.

[4] *Conversations,* 19.

[5] See the discussion of wit in Chap. I.

[6] Praise outweighs blame in the *Conversations,* and, if one takes these remarks along with the two epigrams to the poet and that to Lady Bedford

"with Mr. Donne's Satires," the whole forms a brief but apposite critical estimate.

With regard to the disputed authorship of the four elegies, I think that Mrs. Simpson gives good reasons for what should be a final division of responsibility, allotting *The Expostulation* to Donne and the others to Jonson (*Jonson and Donne, R.E.S.*, Vol. XV).

[7] Professor Herford and Mr. and Mrs. Simpson give this poem to Godolphin (*Ben Jonson,* Vol. VIII, p. 265). If it is his, it not only shows his distinction as a poet, but also the remarkable homogeneity of tone within the "Tribe."

[8] Courthope notes that in dedicating to Savile a translation of Cicero, *De Oratore,* Lib. II, 62–3, Jonson reverses the order of qualities, making moral strength more important than literary skill (*History of English Poetry,* Vol. III, p. 181); it is typical of him.

[9] Ibid., p. 179.

[10] For the background of what follows I am much indebted to Professor Trevelyan's *England under the Stuarts,* Chaps. I–II, and Professor L. C. Knights's *Drama and Society in the Age of Ben Jonson,* Chaps. I–IV.

[11] Cf. *To Sir Edward Sacvile, To the Countess of Rutland* and *To Lady Mary Wroth.*

[12] *Piers Plowman,* B., Passus I, 94–101. I am indebted to Mr. Dawson's *The Vision of Piers Plowman* in *Medieval Religion* for this quotation. I quote Langland as a representative spokesman. I do not wish to suggest that seventeenth-century noblemen made a habit of reading him; Peacham refers to "that bitter *Satyre of Piers Plowman*" (*Compleat Gentleman,* ed. Gordon, p. 95), but he may mean one of the imitations, as he attributes it to Lydgate.

In the matter of culture Peacham lays down a scheme of literary, musical and artistic studies for the gentleman and suggests a suitable blend of pride and condescension in manners; similarly Lord Herbert ends his educational recommendations: "I could say much more . . . and particularly concerning the discreet civility which is to be observed in communication either with friends or strangers . . . many precepts conducing there unto may be had in *Guazzo de la Civile Conversation,* and *Galateus de Moribus*" (*Life,* ed. Lee, p. 42).

[13] As regards Chaucer's position in the early seventeenth century, it is, I think, worth recalling that, though Jonson strongly discourages the uses of "Chaucerisms," Peacham encourages his gentleman to "account him among the best of [his] English books in [his] library. . . . He saw in those times without his spectacles" (*The Compleat Gentleman,* ed. Gordon, p. 94).

[14] *Metaphysical Poetry,* p. xxxi.

[15] See *Characters of the Seventeenth Century,* ed. Nichol Smith, p. 44.

[16] Op. cit., p. 220.

[17] *Conversations,* 13.

[18] *Conversations,* 1.

[19] *An Epigram. To William Earle of Newcastle.*

JOSEPH H. SUMMERS

The Poem as Hieroglyph

Too often Herbert is remembered as the man who possessed the fantastic idea that a poem should resemble its subject in typographical appearance, and who therefore invented the practice of writing poems in shapes such as wings and altars. Herbert, of course, no more invented the pattern poem than he invented "emblematic poetry" or the religious lyric: his originality lies in his achievement with traditional materials. "The Altar" and "Easter-wings," his two most famous pattern poems, are not exotic or frivolous oddities; they are the most obvious examples of Herbert's religious and poetic concern with what we may call the hieroglyph.

A hieroglyph is "a figure, device, or sign having some hidden meaning; a secret or enigmatical symbol; an emblem." [1] In the Renaissance "hieroglyph," "symbol," "device," and "figure" were often used interchangeably. Because of special meanings which have become associated with the other words, "hieroglyph" seems more useful than the others today, and even in the seventeenth century it was often considered the most inclusive term.[2] "Hieroglyphic," the older form of the noun, was derived from the Greek for "sacred carving," and the root usually retained something of its original religious connotation. Ralph Cudworth used it in its generally accepted meaning when he said in a sermon, "The Death of Christ . . . Hieroglyphically instructed us that we ought to take up our Cross likewise, and follow our crucified Lord and Saviour." [3] The hieroglyph presented its often manifold mean-

From *George Herbert, His Religion and Art* (London: Chatto & Windus, 1954; Cambridge: Harvard University Press), pp. 123–46. Reprinted by permission of the publishers.

ings in terms of symbolic relationships rather than through realistic representation. Francis Quarles's anatomy of the hieroglyphic significance of the rib is an extreme example of the general hieroglyphic state of mind:

> Since of a Rib first framed was a Wife,
> Let Ribs be Hi'rogliphicks of their life:
> Ribs coast the heart, and guard it round about,
> And like a trusty Watch keepe danger out;
> So tender Wiues should loyally impart
> Their watchfull care to fence their Spouses' heart:
> All members else from out their places roue
> But Ribs are firmely fixt, and seldom moue:
> Women (like Ribs) must keepe their wonted home,
> And not (like *Dinah* that was rauish't) rome:
> If Ribs be ouer-bent, or handled rough,
> They breake; If let alone, they bend enough:
> Women must (vnconstrain'd) be plyent still,
> And gently bending to their Husband's will.[4]

Quarles's poem suggests that wherever the poet found his hieroglyphs, their "meanings" tended to substantiate his own point of view. The central meanings for the serious religious poet were usually already established by the Bible and Christian tradition.

Aside from the metaphorical use of hieroglyphs common to almost all the poets of the time, the religious lyric poet could most obviously make his poem a meditation on one of the innumerable hieroglyphs in nature, art, or the Church, or he could use the hieroglyph as the central image in a meditation on some doctrine or experience. Quarles's poem and most of the poems written for the emblem books typify the first practice: the moral applications are drawn from the image point by point. Herbert never wrote a poem quite so crudely. "The Church-floore" is as close as he ever came, and that poem's departures from tradition are instructive. The first eighteen lines describe the hieroglyphic meanings of the "Church-floore":

> Mark you the floore? that square & speckled stone,
> Which looks so firm and strong,
> Is *Patience:*
>
> And th' other black and grave, wherewith each one
> Is checker'd all along,
> *Humilitie:*

The gentle rising, which on either hand
Leads to the Quire above,
Is *Confidence:*

But the sweet cement, which in one sure band
Ties the whole frame, is *Love*
And *Charitie.*

Hither sometimes Sinne steals, and stains
The marbles neat and curious veins:
But all is cleansed when the marble weeps.
Sometimes Death, puffing at the doore,
Blows all the dust about the floore:
But while he thinks to spoil the room, he sweeps.

An elaborate and promising hieroglyph is described, but in spite of many hints its meaning is both abstract and ambiguous. We are told that the elements which compose the floor are Patience, Humilitie, Confidence, and Charitie, and that Sinne and Death attempt (and fail) to deface it; but we are not told to what the floor is being compared. From the title of the poem the reader might assume that the floor is a hieroglyph of the Church's foundation, which is based on the theological virtues (Patience and Humilitie may be considered as defining Faith in action), and against which the "gates of Hell" (Sinne and Death) shall not prevail. Such an interpretation would be thoroughly conventional, and the first eighteen lines might almost serve as an unusually successful "explanation" of an emblem which made that point. But Herbert's characteristic final couplet changes that "explanation" and makes the poem:

Blest be the *Architect,* whose art
Could build so strong in a weak heart.

We discover with the last word of the poem that the principal referent of the hieroglyph is not the institution of the Church but the human heart. Patience, Humilitie, Confidence, and Charitie are the materials with which God builds the structure of salvation within the heart. God has built so that the "marble" heart will weep with repentance and cleanse Sinne's stains. Death's intended triumph in blowing "all the dust about the floore" only "sweeps" away the imperfections of that flesh which is dust. Herbert nearly always presents the institutional as a hieroglyph of the personal rather than *vice versa,* and the hieroglyph of "The Church-floore" has pictured primarily the marvellous art of God in decreeing the perseverance of the saints rather than His art in the construction of the Church. Yet those two arts are related; once raised, the image of the "Church-floore" as the foundation of Christ's Church is relevant. The final couplet is a dramatic reminder to the meditator that "the most high dwelleth not in temples made with hands" (Acts vii. 48), "that yee are the Temple of God, and that the Spirit of God dwelleth in you" (I Cor. iii. 16). But in relation to the subject of the meditation, the title of the poem, the couplet is also a reminder that the structure which God has built within the heart is truly the "floore" of both the Church Militant and the Church Triumphant; that the conviction within the "weak heart" that "Thou art the Christ, the sonne of the liuing God" is the "rocke" upon which Christ built His Church.[5] The artful "*Architect*" has built within the individual heart, equally indestructibly, the salvation of the individual and the foundation of His Church. The structure, moreover, is one. Such a complex unfolding of meanings is far removed from the practice of the emblematists, but it is characteristic of Herbert.

In "The Bunch of Grapes" Herbert used the hieroglyph in the second obvious fashion, as the central image in a meditation on a personal experience. The title of the poem indicates the hieroglyph, but the "cluster" is not mentioned until the end of the third stanza. The subject of meditation is the problem of the absence of joy from the Christian's life:

> Joy, I did lock thee up: but some bad man
> Hath let thee out again:
> And now, me thinks, I am where I began
> Sev'n yeares ago: one vogue and vein,
> One aire of thoughts usurps my brain.
> I did towards Canaan draw; but now I am
> Brought back to the Red sea, the sea of shame.

Joy, once possessed, has now escaped. Herbert prevents any misunderstanding of the traditional imagery of Canaan and the Red Sea by explaining in the next stanza Paul's teaching that every event during the wandering of the Children of Israel from Egypt to the Promised Land was a type of the Christian's experiences in his journey between the world of sin and heaven: [6] we may discover within the ancient history the heavenly evaluations and solutions for our problems. With the third stanza, Herbert enumerates some of the parallels:

Then have we too our guardian fires and clouds;
Our Scripture-dew drops fast:
We have our sands and serpents, tents and shrowds;
Alas! our murmurings come not last.
But where's the cluster? where's the taste
Of mine inheritance? Lord, if I must borrow,
Let me as well take up their joy, as sorrow.

Joy may not be fully achieved until we reach the Promised Land, but the Christian should at least experience a foretaste of it, such a rich proof of its existence as was the cluster of Eshcol to the Children of Israel. But the introduction of Eshcol provides the answer. That "branch with one cluster of grapes," which was so large that "they bore it betweene two vpon a staffe," had represented a joy which the Israelites refused. To them the bunch of grapes substantiated the report that it was "a land that eateth vp the inhabitants thereof, and all the people that we saw in it, are men of a great stature. And there we saw the giants, the sonnes of Anak, which come of the giants: and we were in our owne sight as grashoppers, and so wee were in their sight" (Num. xiii. 32–33). From fear they turned to the rebellion which caused God to decree the wandering of forty years. Of all the adults who saw the grapes, only Caleb and Joshua entered the Promised Land. The image of the bunch of grapes suggests, then, not only the foretastes of Canaan and heaven, but also the immeasurable differences between those foretastes under the Covenant of Works and the Covenant of Grace:

But can he want the grape, who hath the wine?
I have their fruit and more.
Blessed be God, who prosper'd *Noahs* vine,
And made it bring forth grapes good store.
But much more him I must adore,
Who of the Laws sowre juice sweet wine did make,
Ev'n God himself being pressed for my sake.

The bunch of grapes is a type of Christ and of the Christian's communion. "I have their fruit and more," for the grapes, of which the promise was conditional upon works, have been transformed into the wine of the New Covenant: "I" have both the foretaste and the assurance of its fulfilment. The prospering of "*Noahs* vine," like the cluster of Eshcol, was a sign of God's blessing. It was a partial fulfilment of "Bee fruitfull and multiply, and replenish the earth," and of God's covenant with all flesh: "neither shall there any more be a flood to destroy the earth" (Gen. ix. 1, 11). Yet, as at Eshcol, God's blessings under the Law could become man's occasion for the renewal of sin and the curse: Noah's misuse of the vine resulted in the curse on Ham. The bunch of grapes has furnished the image of the poet's lost joy, the image of blessings refused or perverted, and also the image of the Christian's source of joy, ever present if he will cease his murmurings. The Holy Communion is a constant reminder of Christ's sacrifice which established the joyful Covenant of Grace; it is the instrument of present grace; and it foretells the joy of heavenly communion. The examination of the Christian's lack of joy has resolved rather than explained the original problem. The blessing and adoration of the final lines indicate that joy is no longer lost.

Herbert frequently used a hieroglyph to crystallize, explain, or resolve the central conflict in a poem. "Josephs coat," a strange sonnet with an unrhymed first line, concerns the mixture of joy and sorrow in the Christian life, and Joseph is not mentioned in the text. The conclusion, "I live to shew his power, who once did bring My *joyes* to *weep*, and now my *griefs* to *sing*," is an acknowledgment of God's power, but without the title it might be construed as an acknowledgment of a powerful and inexplicable Fate. The title, a reference to a traditional Christian type, gives Herbert's interpretation of the experience of contradictory joys and sorrows. Joseph's "coat of many colours" was the sign of his father's particular love.[7] It was also the immediate occasion for his brothers' jealousy and hatred and for his slavery and suffering; but the presentation of the coat was, finally, the initial incident in the long chain of causes which led to the preservation of the Children of Israel in Egypt. After all the suffering, the sign of Jacob's love ended in beatitude. The extraordinary mixture of joy and sorrow in the Christian's life is a particular sign of God's love. Joy has been made "to *weep*" to forestall that self-sufficience which leads to wilful pride, and "*griefs*" have been made "to *sing*" to preserve the soul and body from despair and death. God's "Cross-Providences" also lead to beatitude. For Herbert, "Joyes coat," with which anguish has been "ticed" was evidenced by his ability to "sing," to compose lyrics even when the subject was grief.

At first reading "Church-monuments" appears to belong to the group of poems which are explanations of a hieroglyph. For once the modern reader could surmise the title from the contents, for the poem is a considered meditation on "Church-monuments" in which all their hieroglyphic applications are drawn.

While that my soul repairs to her devotion,
Here I intombe my flesh, that it betimes
May take acquaintance of this heap of dust;
To which the blast of deaths incessant motion,
Fed with the exhalation of our crimes,
Drives all at last. Therefore I gladly trust

My bodie to this school, that it may learn
To spell his elements, and finde his birth
Written in dustie heraldrie and lines;
Which dissolution sure doth best discern,
Comparing dust with dust, and earth with earth.
These laugh at Jeat and Marble put for signes,

To sever the good fellowship of dust,
And spoil the meeting. What shall point out them,
When they shall bow, and kneel, and fall down flat
To kisse those heaps, which now they have in trust?
Deare flesh, while I do pray, learn here thy stemme
And true descent; that when thou shalt grow fat,

And wanton in thy cravings, thou mayst know,
That flesh is but the glasse, which holds the dust
That measures all our time; which also shall
Be crumbled into dust. Mark here below
How tame these ashes are, how free from lust,
That thou mayst fit thy self against thy fall.

The first stanza states the purpose of the meditation, that "my flesh . . . betimes May take acquaintance of this heap of dust." Most obviously, the monuments form a hieroglyph worthy of the flesh's "acquaintance" because they contain the dust of formerly living flesh. Yet, with the identification of "heap of dust" as that "To which the blast of deaths incessant motion . . . Drives all at last," the meaning expands to include the dissolution of all earthly things. Through contemplating the monuments the "bodie" "may learn To spell his elements." The ambiguous "spell" (meaning both to "divine" the elements and to "spell out" the inscriptions) introduces as part of the hieroglyph the inscriptions on the monuments. Their "dustie" physical state (which makes them difficult to decipher) and their intended verbal meaning cause them to serve as intermediate symbols relating the flesh of man and the contents of the tomb. The "dustie heraldrie and lines" factually tell the genealogies of the deceased and include some conventional version of "for dust thou art, and vnto dust shalt thou returne." ("Lines," associated with "birth" and "heraldrie," seems to signify genealogical "lines" as well as the lines of engraving.) The monuments are an ironic commentary on mortality; their states and messages mock at their composition of "Jeat and Marble"—too obviously fleshly attempts to deny the dissolution of the bodies which they contain. Can there be monuments to monuments? Can monuments hope for a memorial "When they shall bow, and kneel" as the body of the meditator is doing, or "fall down flat" in dissolution, as his body will do and as the bodies within the monuments have already done? The flesh can learn its "stemme And true descent" both in its origin in dust and in its decline into dust.

The figure of the hour-glass summarizes what "thou mayst know" from the contemplation of the monuments and further enriches the meaning:

> That flesh is but the glasse, which holds the dust
> That measures all our time; which also shall
> Be crumbled into dust.

It is one of Herbert's most successful condensations, and it is difficult only if we have failed to follow the careful preparation for its introduction. The hour-glass defines the flesh in terms of what has been learned from the monuments. The monuments, like the traditional *memento mori,* have told of more than physical death. It is "the exhalation of our crimes" which "feeds" "the blast of deaths incessant motion"; and the monuments, like the "grasse" of the Psalmist and Isaiah and the New Testament,[8] have served to exemplify the vain dust of the sin and the "goodlinesse" and "glory" of living flesh as well as that flesh's final dissolution. The function of proud flesh and proud monument is the same: to hold "the dust That measures all our time," whether it is the figurative dust of our vain goodliness and glory and sinful wills or the actual dust of our bodies. Dust is the true measure of "all our time" (not our eternity): the vanity and endurance of our lives and of our ashes provide the sole significances to the flesh and the monument. Finally, the flesh and the monuments, the containers, "shall Be crumbled into dust," both symbolic of and undifferentiable from the dust contained. The closing address directs the flesh's attention to the "ashes" rather than to the monuments:

> Mark here below
> How tame these ashes are, how free from lust,
> That thou mayst fit thy self against thy fall.

The flesh can escape neither its measuring content nor its final goal. The knowledge it has gained may, however, serve as bridle to "tame" its lust. The flesh may "fit" itself "against" its "fall" in that, in preparation for its known dissolution, it may oppose its "fall" into pride and lust.[9]

Such an analysis indicates the manner in which Herbert explained the complex meanings of the hieroglyph, but it does not explain "Church-monuments." The movement of the words and the lines, of the clauses and the sentences, conveys even without analysis a "meaning" which makes us recognize the inadequacy of any such prose summary. Yvor Winters has called "Church-monuments" "the greatest poem by George Herbert": "George Herbert's *Church Monuments,* perhaps the most polished and urbane poem of the Metaphysical School and one of the half dozen most profound, is written in an iambic pentameter line so carefully modulated, and with its rhymes so carefully concealed at different and unexpected points in the syntax, that the poem suggests something of the quiet plainness of excellent prose without losing the organization and variety of verse." [10] The effect which Winters praised is achieved largely through the extraordinary use of enjambment and the looseness of the syntax. Only three lines of the poem come to a full stop, and nine of the twenty-four lines are followed by no punctuation. Many of the semi-cadences indicated by the punctuation, moreover, prove illusory: the syntax demands no pause, and the commas serve as fairly arbitrary directions for a slight voice rest, obscuring rather than clarifying the simple "prose" meaning. Winters seems to praise "Church-monuments" for practices which are found in no other poem in *The Temple.* Herbert characteristically considered his stanzas as inviolable architectural units. Each usually contained a complete thought, representing one unit in the logic of the "argument," and the great majority of his stanzas end with full stops.[11] In the form in which it was printed in 1633 "Church-monuments" provides the only example of complete enjambment between stanzas in *The Temple,* and two of the three examples of stanzas in which the final points are commas.[12] When Herbert departs so dramatically from his usual consistent practice, it is advisable to look for the reason. It cannot be found, I believe, in an intent to suggest "something of the quiet plainness of excellent prose without losing the organization and variety of verse." These straggling sentences fulfil the criteria for excellence by neither Ciceronian nor Senecan nor Baconian standards of prose. They possess neither the admired periodicity, nor trenchant point, nor ordinary clarity. The series of clauses and participial phrases, each relating to a word in some preceding clause or phrase, threaten to dissolve the sentence structure. The repetitions of "that" and "which" give the effect of unplanned prose, a prose which seems to function more by association than by logic.

The poem is a meditation upon a *memento mori*, the hieroglyph of the monuments. One reason for the slowness of the movement and the "concealed" rhymes might be that the tone of the meditation was intended to correspond to the seriousness of its object. The most important clue, however, is in the manuscripts: in neither the Williams nor the Bodleian MSS. is the poem divided into stanzas at all. As F. E. Hutchinson remarked, "the editor of 1633 recognized that the rhyme-scheme implies a six-line stanza,"[13] and subsequent editors followed the original edition and printed the poem in stanzas. But the manuscript arrangement was not the result of accident or carelessness. In the Williams MS., which Herbert corrected, the non-stanzaic form is emphasized by the indentation of line 17 to indicate a new paragraph.[14] The fact that Herbert established a six-line stanzaic rhyme scheme but did not create stanzas, either formally or typographically, is a minor but a convincing evidence that he intended the poem itself to *be* a *memento mori*, to function formally as a hieroglyph. The dissolution of the body and the monuments is paralleled by the dissolution of the sentences and the stanzas.

The movement and sound of the poem suggest the "falls" of the flesh and the monuments and the dust in the glass. The fall is not precipitous; it is as slow as the gradual fall of the monuments, as the crumbling of the glass, as the descent of the flesh from Adam into dust. Every cadence is a dying fall. Even the question of stanza 3 contains three commas and ends with the descriptive clause, "which now they have in trust," carrying no interrogation. Part of the effect is achieved by obvious "prose" means. "Dust" re-echoes seven times in the poem, and the crucial words and phrases describe or suggest the central subject: "intombe"; "blast of deaths incessant motion"; "dissolution"; "earth with earth"; "bow, and kneel, and fall down flat"; "descent"; "measures"; "crumbled";[15] "ashes"; "fall." Herbert has also used every means to slow the movement of the neutral words. With the clusters of consonants, it is impossible to read the poem rapidly.[16] The related rhymes, with their internal echoes and repetitions, both give phonetic continuity to the poem and suggest the process of dissolution: "devotion" and "motion" are mocked by "exhalation" and "dissolution"; "betimes" and "crimes" modulate to "lines" and "signes" as do "learn" and "discern" to "birth" and "earth." "Trust" and "lust" are echoed incessantly by "dust," and, internally, by "blast," and "last." Continual internal repetition deprives the end-rhymes of any chime of finality: "blast-last," "earth with earth," "bow-now," "they-pray," "that-that," "which-which" disguise and almost dissolve the iambic pentameter line. Three of the six sentences in the poem take up five and a half lines each, but, straggling as they are, each is exhausted before it reaches what should be the end of the stanza. Although the sentences are hardly independent (the many pronominal forms create a complex of interdependent meanings), the expiration of each sentence marks a break which requires a new beginning: after the opening of the poem, each new sentence begins with a long syllable which usually causes a break in the iambic rhythm. The sentences sift down through the rhyme-scheme skeleton of the stanzas like the sand through the glass; and the glass itself has already begun to crumble.

"Church-monuments" differs in kind as well as degree from such poems as "The Church-floore" and "The Bunch of Grapes." The natural or religious hieroglyph was an eminently pleasant and profitable subject for a poem, and it could be used either as the object which the poem explained or as the image which explained the poem. Yet Herbert seems to have believed that it was more pleasant and profitable to make the poem itself a hieroglyph. To construct the poem so that its form imaged the subject was to reinforce the message for those who could "spell"; for the others it would not distract from the statement—and if they read and meditated long enough, surely they would discover the mirroring of the meanings within the form of the poem!

There were fewer readers who could not "spell" in Herbert's day than in ours. The attempt to make formal structure an integral part of the meaning of a poem assumed a general consciousness of traditional formal conventions. The disturbances of the rhyme schemes in "Grief" and "Home," for example, depend for their effects on the reader's firm expectation of a conventional pattern. Such an expectation could be assumed in readers accustomed to Renaissance English poetry, whether the poetry of the Court or the hymns of the Church or the doggerel of the broadsides. In his hieroglyphs Herbert never attempted to abandon rational control for an "identity" with a natural object: the poems always embody or assume a firm pattern of logic, rhyme, and rhythm. The formal organization of the subject was imitated by the formal organization of the poem.

The poems in which Herbert's "imitations" are obvious are those which are likely to draw the fire of strict advocates either of that art which conceals art or of that upwelling inspiration which is oblivious of form. But Herbert often intended the form of a poem to be obvious. The opening stanzas of "Deniall," for example, picture the disorder which results when the individual feels that God denies his requests:

> When my devotions could not pierce
> Thy silent eares;
> Then was my heart broken, as was my verse:
> My breast was full of fears
> And disorder:
>
> My bent thoughts, like a brittle bow,
> Did flie asunder:
> Each took his way; some would to pleasures go,
> Some to the warres and thunder
> Of alarms.

The final stanza, with its establishment of the normal pattern of cadence and rhyme, is the symbol of reconstructed order, of the manner in which men (and the poem) function when God grants the request:

> O cheer and tune my heartlesse breast,
> Deferre no time;
> That so thy favours granting my request,
> They and my minde may chime,
> And mend my ryme.

The stanza which had been the symbol of the flying asunder of a "brittle bow" has become a symbol for the achievement of order. The form of the final prayer indicates that its request has already been answered. The individual and the poem have moved from fear through open rebellion and "unstrung" discontent. "Deniall" is overcome through renewal of prayer: the ordered prayer provides the evidence.

Of Herbert's many other formal hieroglyphs ("Sinnes round," "A Wreath," "Trinitie Sunday," etc.) "Aaron" is one of the most effective.

> Holinesse on the head,
> Light and perfections on the breast,
> Harmonious bells below, raising the dead
> To·leade them unto life and rest:
> Thus are true Aarons drest.

Profanenesse in my head,
Defects and darknesse in my breast,
A noise of passions ringing me for dead
Unto a place where is no rest:
Poore priest thus am I drest.

Onely another head
I have, another heart and breast,
Another musick, making live not dead,
Without whom I could have no rest:
In him I am well drest.

Christ is my onely head,
My alone onely heart and breast,
My onely musick, striking me ev'n dead;
That to the old man I may rest,
And be in him new drest.

So holy in my head,
Perfect and light in my deare breast,
My doctrine tun'd by Christ, (who is not dead,
But lives in me while I do rest)
Come people; Aaron's drest.

Herbert may have chosen the five stanzas of five lines each partially because of the five letters in "Aaron"; if so, the technical problem may have been of importance to the poet, but it does not matter particularly to the reader. Nor does it seem that Herbert primarily intended that each stanza should "suggest metrically the swelling and dying sound of a bell": [17] the "bells" and the "musick" occur only in the third line of each stanza, and the rhymes are hardly bell-like. The central meaning of those identical rhymes and those subtly transformed stanzas [18] is clearly stated in the poem. The profaneness in man's head, the defects and darkness in his heart, the cacophonous passions which destroy him and lead him to a hell of "repining restlessnesse" [19] *can* be transformed through the imputed righteousness of Christ into the ideal symbolized by Aaron's ceremonial garments.[20] The "clay" [21] (like the stanzas) retains its outward form, but inwardly all is changed in the divine consumption of the self. As the "Priest for euer after the order of Melchisedec" "dresses" the new Aaron with the inward reality for which the first Aaron's garments were but the hieroglyphs, the poem moves with a ritualistic gravity from opposition to a climactic synthesis.

When we have understood Herbert's use of form in these poems, or, say, his extraordinarily formal picture of anarchy in "The Collar" and his divine numerology in "Trinitie Sunday" we may see the poems which derive from the Elizabethan acrostics and anagrams in a different light. Aside from the courtiers to whom any exercise in ingenuity was welcome, this type of poem had its serious religious adherents in the seventeenth century. If biblical exegesis demanded the solution of anagrams,[22] and if the good man was truly "willing to spiritualize everything," the composition of such poetry was a logical result. With due appreciation of the wit involved, the good man was likely to treat such poetry seriously. The seriousness depended on a religious subject and on the assumption that the poet would draw "true" meanings from his word-play. Herbert abided by the rules, and he never repeated the various forms. In *The Temple* there is one true anagram (labelled as such), one echo poem, one "hidden acrostic," one poem based on the double interpretation of initials, one based on a syllabic pun, and "Paradise," which can only be described as a "pruning poem." For his unique example of each type, Herbert usually chose that Christian subject which was most clearly illuminated by the device.

In some of these poems typography becomes a formal element. In "Paradise," for example, the second and third rhymes of each stanza are formed by "paring" off the first consonant of the preceding rhyme:

> I blesse thee, Lord, because I GROW
> Among thy trees, which in a ROW
> To thee both fruit and order OW.
>
> What open force, or hidden CHARM
> Can blast my fruit, or bring me HARM
> While the inclosure is thine ARM?

The device is artificial in the extreme, and it requires some wrenching of orthography. As an abstract form it is hardly satisfactory. But Herbert never used forms abstractly, and we are left in no doubt as to the reason for the form of this particular poem:

> Inclose me still for fear I START.
> Be to me rather sharp and TART,
> Then let me want thy hand & ART.
>
> When thou dost greater judgements SPARE,
> And with thy knife but prune and PARE,
> Ev'n fruitfull trees more fruitfull ARE.

Such sharpnes shows the sweetest FREND:
Such cuttings rather heal then REND:
And such beginnings touch their END.

Except for the third stanza, the poem survives brilliantly the test of oral reading: its success does not depend upon the construction of the rhymes. Yet the "pruned" rhymes do compel the reader to "see" what the poem is saying concerning the positive function of suffering. The meaning is traditional, of course. The fate of the "unprofitable vineyard" was destruction rather than pruning. By changing the image from the vine to the English orchard, Herbert related the "pruning" more immediately to his readers' experience, but the point is the same: the surgical knife is necessary for the order which produces fruit. The final line of the poem is "naturally" ambiguous. For the religious man of the seventeenth century "end" nearly always implied purpose as well as finality. "And such beginnings touch their END" means that God's pruning causes the fruits of righteousness which are the end of man's creation. It also implies that the cutting away of the fruitless branches images the final "cutting away" of the body and the release of the soul at death.

In "The Altar" and "Easter-wings" Herbert extended the principle of the hieroglyph to a third level. If the natural or religious hieroglyph was valuable as content (used either as the object which the poem explained or as the image which crystallized the meaning of the poem), and if the poem could be constructed as a formal hieroglyph which mirrored the structural relationships between the natural hieroglyph, the poem, and the individual's life, it was but a further step to make the poem a visual hieroglyph, to create it in a shape which formed an immediately apparent image relevant both to content and structure.

Neither the conception of the pattern poem nor the two shapes which Herbert used were at all novel.[23] The Greek Anthology had included six pattern poems (including a pair of wings and two altars), and those patterns were widely imitated in the sixteenth century. Although Thomas Nashe, Gabriel Harvey, and Ben Jonson denounced such poems, the practice flourished.[24] After the appearance of *The Temple* patterns were published in profusion. Wither, Quarles,[25] Benlowes, Joseph Beaumont, Herrick, Christopher Harvey, and Traherne were among the practitioners. Both before and after 1633 the literary quality of most of these poems was notoriously low. The poets seemed usually to consider the shapes as a superficial or frivolous attraction for the reader. As the Renaissance poets and critics never tired of reiterating, pleasure *could* be made a bait for profit, but a superficial conception of the "bait" often resulted in very bad poems. Many of the patterns depended largely on wrenched typography, and it was a common practice to compose a poem in ordinary couplets, then chop the lines to fit the pattern.

Herbert's poems are another matter. From his knowledge of both the Greek originals and English practice,[26] Herbert chose the two patterns which could be most clearly related to the purposes of his Christian poetry. His patterns are visual hieroglyphs. The interpretation of them as naïve representations of "real" objects has resulted in the citation of "The Altar" as additional proof of Herbert's extreme Anglo-Catholicism. An examination of the poem in the light of its tradition and Herbert's formal practice shows it to be artistically complex and religiously "low."

A broken ALTAR, Lord, thy servant reares,
Made of a heart, and cemented with teares:
Whose parts are as thy hand did frame;
No workmans tool hath touch'd the same.
A HEART alone
Is such a stone,
As nothing but
Thy pow'r doth cut.
Wherefore each part
Of my hard heart
Meets in this frame,
To praise thy Name:
That, if I chance to hold my peace,
These stones to praise thee may not cease.
O let thy blessed[27] SACRIFICE be mine,
And sanctifie this ALTAR to be thine.

When one reads "The Altar" it is well to remember that the word "altar" was not applied to the Communion Table in the Book of Common Prayer, and that the canons of Herbert's time directed that the Table should be made of wood rather than stone. Throughout his English writings Herbert always used "altar" and "sacrifice" according to the "orthodox" Protestant tradition of his time: "altar" is never applied to the Communion Table nor is the Holy Communion ever called a "sacrifice."[28] Yet Herbert and his contemporaries cherished the conception of the altar and the sacrifice. The Mosaic sacrifices were considered types of the one true Sacrifice, in which Christ had shed blood for the remission of sins once for all time. To man were left the "sacrifices" of praise, good works, and "communication" (Heb. xiii, 15–16). The Hebrew altar which was built of unhewn stones was a type of the heart of man, hewn not by man's efforts but by God alone. The engraving on those stones with which "all the words of this Law" were written "very plainely" (Deut. xxvii. 8) was a type of the "Epistle of Christ," the message of salvation engraved on the Christian heart (2 Cor. iii. 3). Herbert's conceptions that the broken and purged heart is the proper basis for the sacrifice of praise and that even stones may participate in and continue that praise were firmly biblical. In his psalm of repentance (Ps. li.) David had stated that the true sacrifices of God are "a broken and a contrite heart"; Christ had promised that "the stones" would cry out to testify to Him (Luke xix. 40); and Paul had stated that "Ye also as liuely stones, are built vp a spirituall house . . . to offer vp spirituall sacrifice" (I Pet. ii. 5).

There is hardly a phrase in "The Altar" which does not derive from a specific biblical passage. Yet the effect of the poem is simple and fresh. In an important sense this, the first poem within "The Church" (the central section of *The Temple*), *is* the altar upon which the following poems (Herbert's "sacrifice of praise") are offered, and it is an explanation of the reason for their composition. God has commanded a continual sacrifice of praise and thanksgiving made from the broken and contrite heart. The condition of mortality as well as the inconstancy of the human heart requires that such a sacrifice be one of those works which "doe follow them" even when they "rest from their labours." For the craftsman and poet, construction of a work of art resulted in that continual sacrifice and introduced the concept of the altar: the poem is a construction upon which others may offer their sacrifices; it is a "speaking" altar which continually offers up its own sacrifice of praise. The shape of Herbert's poem was intended to hieroglyph the relevance of the old altar to the new Christian altar within the heart. It was fittingly, therefore, a modification of the traditional shape of a classic altar rather than of what Herbert knew as the Communion Table.[29] F. E. Hutchinson's description of the changes in the printing of the poem furnishes a miniature history of progressive misinterpretation.[30] From 1634 to 1667 the shape was outlined merely to draw the reader's attention to its significance. The change in religious temper and vocabulary by 1674 was indicated by "an engraving of a full-length Christian altar under a classical canopy, with the poem set under the canopy": the assumption was that Herbert had attempted to image a "Christian altar." The final liturgical representation of the poem did not, however, occur until the nineteenth century: "In 1809 there is Gothic panelling and canopy-work behind a modest altar with fringed cloth, fair linen cloth, and the sacred vessels." Herbert's attempt to use the shape of a classical altar as a hieroglyph of his beliefs concerning the relationships between the heart, the work of art, and the praise of God failed to communicate its meaning to a number of generations. While not one of Herbert's greatest poems, "The Altar" within its context in *The Temple* is still an effective poem if we take the pains to understand it.

"Easter-wings" has been subject to fewer misinterpretations than "The Altar." In the last twenty years particularly it has generally been considered a good poem, although there has been little agreement as to the meaning and effectiveness of its pattern. It is the final poem in the group concerning Holy Week, and to read it within its sequence helps to explain some of the difficulties for the modern reader.

Lord, who createdst man in wealth and store,
Though foolishly he lost the same,
Decaying more and more,
Till he became
Most poore:
With thee
O let me rise
As larks, harmoniously,
And sing this day thy victories:
Then shall the fall further the flight in me.

My tender age in sorrow did beginne:
And still with sicknesses and shame
Thou didst so punish sinne,
That I became
Most thinne.
With thee
Let me combine
And feel this day thy victorie:
For, if I imp my wing on thine,
Affliction shall advance the flight in me.

The pattern is successful not merely because we "see" the wings, but because we see how they are made: the process of impoverishment and enrichment, of "thinning" and expansion which makes "flight" possible. By that perception and by the rhythmical falling and rising which the shaped lines help to form, we are led to respond fully to the active image and to the poem. The first stanza is a celebration of the *felix culpa.* Man was created in "wealth and store," with the capacity for sinlessness. Through Adam's sin Paradise was lost, yet from one point of view the loss was not unhappy: "where sinne abounded, grace did much more abound" (Rom. v. 20). If man "rises" in celebration of Christ's victories, the fall will indeed further his flight to God. The second stanza concerns the reduction of the individual by God's punishment for sins. Again, if we "combine" with Christ "And feel this day thy victorie," affliction can prove an advance to flight, for it is through such affliction that souls are led to "waite vpon the Lord" and "renew their strength," and the promise is specific: "they shall mount vp with wings as Eagles, they shal runne and not be weary, and they shall walke, and not faint" (Isa. xl. 31). The New Testament had related the death and resurrection of the spirit and the body to the germinal cycle of nature, and the favourite English pun on "son-sun" seemed to acquire a supernatural sanction from Malachi iv. 2: "But vnto you that feare my Name, shall the Sunne of righteousnesse arise with healing in his wings." The "decaying" of the first stanza of Herbert's poem implies the fruitful image of the grain, and the conclusion of that stanza broadens to include the rise of the "Sun," the "harmonious" ascent both of the flight and the song of the larks.[31] The triumphant dichotomies are implied throughout the poem: sickness and health, decay and growth, poverty and wealth, foolishness and wisdom, punishment and reward, defeat and victory, the fall and rise of song and wings and spirit, sin and righteousness, burial and resurrection, death and life. These states are not in polar opposition. The poem and its pattern constantly insist that for man only through the fall is the flight possible; that the victory, resurrection, whether in this life or the next, can come only through the death of the old Adam.

The pattern poem is a dangerous form, and its successful practitioners before and after Herbert were few. The conception behind it, however, is neither so naïve nor so dated as some critics have assumed: writing with intentions differing greatly from Herbert's, E. E. Cummings and Dylan Thomas have created successful contemporary pattern poems.[32] For Herbert such poetry was a natural extension of his concern with the hieroglyph. Most of the other poets of his time, whether followers of Spenser, Jonson, or Donne, characteristically used hieroglyphs as the basis for their imagery in either short or extended passages. Herbert's distinction lies in his successful development of the conceptions that the entire poem could be organized around a hieroglyph and that the poem itself could be constructed as a formal hieroglyph.

The hieroglyph represented to Herbert a fusion of the spiritual and material, of the rational and sensuous, in the essential terms of formal relationships. It may have been that his delight in the power and beauty of the hieroglyphic symbol helped to keep his poems from becoming only rational exercises or pious teachings. Yet reason and piety were central, for to Herbert the hieroglyph did not exist as a total mystery or as isolated beauty, but as a beauty and mystery which were decipherable and related to all creation. The message was precise and clear even if complex and subtle. A differing conception of the religious hieroglyph led Crashaw to ecstatic adoration and worship. For Herbert, however, celebration could never be divorced from examination. The hieroglyphs, whether of God's or of man's creation, were to be "read" rather than adored, and they sent the reader back to God. The chief tool for such reading was the logical use of man's reason.

It was, moreover, delightful as well as edifying for the poet to imitate God in the construction of hieroglyphs. As Sir Philip Sidney had remarked long before, the way in which God had worked in the creation of nature was not so mysterious as marvellous; man could observe and could imitate:

> Neither let it be deemed too saucy a comparison, to balance the highest point of man's wit with the efficacy of nature; but rather give right honour to the heavenly Maker of that maker, who having made man to his own likeness, set him beyond and over all the works of that second nature; which in nothing he showeth so much as in poetry; when, with the force of a divine breath, he bringeth things forth surpassing her doings, with no small arguments to the incredulous of that first accursed fall of Adam; since our erected wit maketh us know what perfection is, and yet our infected will keepeth us from reaching unto it.[33]

NOTES

[1] *NED*, Sb. 2.

[2] In his *Hieroglyphicorum Collectanea, ex Veteribus et Neotericis Descripta* ("In hoc postrema editione recognita & expurgata"; Lvgdvni, 1626), p. 7, Giovanni Pierio Valeriano summarized the general usage: "Ad hieroglyphica accedunt emblemata, symbola, insignia, quaemuis nomine differant, reipsa multi modis conuenir videntur."

[3] Quoted in *NED*, "Hieroglyphically," 2, from "Sermon I" (1642) in *A Discourse Concerning the True Notion of the Lord's Supper* (London, 1670), p. 210.

[4] "Meditatio tertia," *Hadassa: or The History of Queene Ester* (1621), *The Complete Works*, ed. A. B. Grosart (Edinburgh, 1880–81), II, 50.

[5] Matt. xvi. 16–18. I give the Protestant interpretation of the passage.

[6] I Cor. x. The marginal reading for "ensamples," v.11, is "Or, Types."

[7] George Ryley, "The Temple explained and improved," pp. 315–16, summarizes the biblical allusions: "Joseph's Coat was of *many colours;* very beautifull; and it was a token of his father's peculiar affection. *Gen.* 37.3. . . . This poem speaks the language of the prophet, Is. 61. 10, *I will greatly rejoice in the Lord, &c. for he hath cloathed me with the garments of salvation,* and of the Apostle, 2 Cor. 6. 10, *As sorrowfull, yet always rejoicing.*"

[8] Ps. cii. 11; Isa. xl. 6; I Pet. i. 24.

[9] "Against" and "fall" are used ambiguously. "Against" means both "in preparation for" and "in opposition to," and "fall" means both physical collapse and "fall" into sin. These ambiguities are characteristic of Herbert's use of the device. Neither is at all recondite: "against" in the sense of "in preparation for" often carried something of the meaning of "in opposition to," and "the fall" of man and angels had traditionally equated physical and moral movement.

[10] *Primitivism and Decadence: A Study of American Experimental Poetry* (New York, 1937), pp. 10, 123.

[11] On the rare occasions when a stanza ends with a colon or semicolon, modern usage would often require a period.

[12] The third example is stanza 5 of "The Bag." Here the comma after line 30, "And straight he turn'd, and to his brethren cry'd," is strong, since it precedes the two stanzas of direct quotation.

[13] *Works*, p. 499.

[14] *Works*, p. 65. In *B* the line begins a new page.

[15] The only significant change which Herbert made after the version in W was to introduce "crumbled" in line 22 for the less effective "broken."

[16] In the twenty-four lines the sound of *t* occurs 59 times; *th* and th, 36; *s* and *z*, 51; *sh*, 16; *n*, 35; *d*, 27.

[17] Grierson, *Metaphysical Lyrics*, pp. 231–2.

[18] Douglas Bush has remarked that in the first stanza describing the "type," the consonants *l*, *m*, and *r* predominate; in the second concerning the "natural man," *p*, *st*, *t*, *z*, and *s;* and in the final stanza the two patterns of consonants are united.

[19] "The Pulley."

[20] Hutchinson, *Works*, p. 538, summarizes the relevant passages from Exod. xxviii.

[21] Cf. "The Priesthood."

[22] See Kenneth B. Murdock's discussion and quotations in *Handkerchiefs from Paul* (Cambridge, Mass., 1927), pp. liv–lvi.

[23] In the discussion which follows I am indebted to Miss Margaret Church's "The Pattern Poem" (Doctoral thesis, Radcliffe College, 1944), the most useful discussion of the history and development of the European pattern poem which I have found. Miss Church's Appendix C., pp. 240–427, "includes copies of all the pattern poems discussed in the text with the exception of several *carmina quadrata* by P. Optatianus Porfirius and Hraban Maur."

[24] Church, p. 161, cites the comments of Nashe, "Have with you . . . ," *The Works*, ed. R. B. McKerrow (London, 1900), III, 67; Harvey, *Letter-Book*, ed. E. J. L. Scott (Westminster, 1884), pp. 100–101; and Jonson, *The Works*, ed. F. Cunningham (London, 1816), III, 320, 470, 488.

[25] Except for one "lozenge," "On God's Law," in the *Divine Fancies* of 1632, all of Quarles's patterns, like his emblems, were published after 1633. If there was any influence, it was Herbert who influenced Quarles.

[26] See Church, pp. 297 ff. English composers of altars before Herbert included Richard Willis (1573), Andrew Willet, and William Browne of Tavistock (in *The Shepherd's Pipe*, 1614). Willet's shapes were printed at the beginning of Sylvester's *Bartas His Devine Weekes & Workes* (1605–8). It seems safe to assume that Herbert, rhetorician, classicist, and poet by profession, knew the poems of the "Greek Anthology" as well as current practice. Arthur Woodnoth's letter to Nicholas Ferrar shortly before Herbert's death, *Ferrar Papers*, pp. 268–9, makes doubtful the hypothesis that Italian poetry directly influenced Herbert: "Sauonorola in Latine he hath of the Simplicity of Chr: Religion and is of great esteme wth him. He sayth he doth Vnderstand Italian a lyttle." Hutchinson notes, *Works*, pp. 564–5, that Herbert's translation of Luigi Cornaro's *Treatise of Temperance and Sobrietie* was based not on the original (Padua, 1558) but on Lessius's Latin version (Antwerp, 1613, 1614, 1623). A "lyttle" understanding of Italian would have sufficed for the translations in *Outlandish Proverbs*. Unlike Ferrar, Crashaw, and Milton, Herbert never went to Italy.

[27] Hutchinson, *Works*, p. 26, notes that in *W* the word "onely" has been corrected to "blessed." The change is a poetic improvement, but the original word substantiates my interpretation of the poem.

[28] Cf. the references cited by Cameron Mann, *A Concordance to the English Poems of George Herbert* (Boston and New York, 1927). For "sacrifice," see "The Church-porch," ll. 6, 275; "The Sacrifice" throughout and especially l. 19; "Mattens," l. 3; "Providence," l. 14; "Love unknown," l. 30. For "altar" see "Love (I)," l. 21 and the first of the "Sonnets to his Mother," l. 6. At first reading Chapter vi, "The Parson Praying," of *A Priest to the Temple* (*Works*, pp. 231–2) seems to provide an exception to Herbert's customary use of "altar." After a description of the parson's actions "when he is to read divine services," Herbert adds, "This he doth, first, as being truly touched and amazed with the Majesty of God, before whom he then presents himself; yet not as himself alone, but as presenting with himself the whole Congregation, whose sins he

then beares, and brings with his own to the heavenly altar to be bathed, and washed in the sacred Laver of Christs blood." Despite the familiar imagery, there is no reference here to the Eucharist. The "altar" and "the sacred Laver of Christs blood" are truly *in* heaven. Reading "divine services" to Herbert did not imply administering the Holy Communion. In Chapter xxii (p. 259), Herbert notes that the Country Parson celebrates the Communion "if not duly once a month, yet at least five or six times in the year. . . . And this hee doth, not onely for the benefit of the work, but also for the discharge of the Church-wardens, who being to present all that receive not thrice a year; if there be but three Communions, neither can all the people so order their affairs as to receive just at those times, nor the Church-Wardens so well take notice who receive thrice, and who not."

[29] Herbert may have sacrificed accuracy to symmetry as part of his image of "A *broken* altar." The altars of both Dosiados and Richard Willis followed the pattern of two short lines, longer for four, much shorter for eight, and longer for five at the base (see Church, p. 46). The first two short lines which Herbert omits represent the slab (sometimes identified as the altar proper) on which the sacrifice takes place. The opening phrase of Herbert's poem makes attractive the conjecture that his pattern is intended to convey both the perfect ordering of the ideal spiritual altar and the fact that this altar is not constructed for the ancient blood-sacrifice. Such a significance is, however, perhaps too recondite for Herbert to have intended his audience to grasp it. And against such an interpretation is the fact that "an Altare and Sacrifice to Disdaine" in *A Poetical Rhapsody* had been symmetrical (four long lines, twelve short, four long) without iconographical significance. See *A Poetical Rhapsody* (*1602-1621*), ed. H. E. Rollins (Cambridge, Mass., 1931), I, sig. I_3^v.

[30] *Works*, p. 484.

[31] See Bennett, *Four Metaphysical Poets*, p. 66.

[32] As Lloyd Frankenberg has pointed out, *Pleasure Dome: on reading modern poetry* (Boston, 1949), pp. 172–9, Cummings continually writes such poems; the fact that his patterns are based on individual and spontaneous gestures or situations or personalities rather than on symmetrical and abstract forms has disguised the fact from some readers. John L. Sweeney, *The Selected Writings of Dylan Thomas* (New York, 1946), p. xxi, has suggested that the pattern of Thomas's "Vision and Prayer" may have been inspired by "Easter-wings." As Theodore Spencer once remarked, the formal effects of James Joyce's *Ulysses* are directly related to the tradition of George Herbert's poetry.

[33] *The Defence of Poesy, The Miscellaneous Works*, ed. William Gray (Boston, 1860), pp. 69–70.

MARGARET BOTTRALL

Herbert's Craftsmanship

The patterns of Herbert's thought and much of the imagery that he used were traditional; but this was no impediment to his originality. Provided that a poet does not simply acquiesce in a creed but grasps it imaginatively, it is a positive advantage to him to have at his command a store of symbols familiar to his contemporaries. He is so much the freer to concentrate upon the formal, structural, technical aspects of his problems. This is what we find with George Herbert. He forged for himself a style that was unmistakable and inimitable; and a poet, after all, is not obliged to invent anything else.

We have evidence in the Williams MS and in the divergences between earlier and later drafts of the same poem [1] that Herbert was a most careful craftsman. Even the slightest of the lyrics in *The Temple* is well-shaped, sinewy and apt. Herbert was a master of economy; where one word will do he does not use more. He seldom strikes off a phrase so brilliant that it lives in isolation, but his poems are wholes; single lines or stanzas suffer when detached from their context, and this is an indication of Herbert's architectonic skill. No poem in *The Temple* is so long that it cannot be rapidly read in its entirety and enjoyed as a well-proportioned structure.

Herbert's poems are full of intellectual vigour. His themes are always serious, sometimes weighty; but he handles them with such skilful grace that the reader follows the poetic logic without difficulty. In many of the "private ejaculations" the movement of the thought

From *George Herbert* (London: John Murray, 1954), pp. 99–116. Reprinted by permission of the publishers.

corresponds to the development of ideas in conversation or in an interior monologue, except that digressions do not occur. In poems of a more didactic type, the argument is presented lucidly, often symmetrically, so that the reader takes it in his stride, without having to pause (as so often with Donne's poems) to survey the obstacles in his path before being able to surmount them.

Mortification provides a good example of Herbert's more formal method of construction. He passes in review the ages of man, from infancy to senility, in order to show that each stage of existence has its *memento mori*. In every stanza he uses the rhyme-words "breath" and "death," which in themselves are the burden and core of his argument. In *Vanitie* he considers the futility of man's search for knowledge when all thought of God is neglected. He presents his case by citing the astronomer, the diver and the chemist as exemplars of man's desire to explore the universe. Three beautifully balanced stanzas are given to the activities of these searchers, and a fine sense of eagerness is conveyed by the abundant use of verbs that emphasize the different types of investigation:

> The fleet Astronomer can bore
> And thred the Spheres with his quick-piercing mind:

he runs, walks, surveys, sees and knows; while

> The subtil Chymist can devest
> And strip the creature naked, till he finde
> The callow principles . . . (p. 85).

The three stanzas, dryly ironic in tone, are capped by the final one in which the pregnant question is put:

> What hath not man sought out and found,
> But his deare God?

The texture of thought and imagery in Herbert's poems is as a rule closely woven, especially in his sonnets. There are fifteen of these in *The Temple*, not counting the two youthful sonnets, published in Walton's *Life*, which he sent to his mother at the outset of his Cambridge career. Herbert probably excluded them from his collected poems because of their slight tinge of priggishness; but as specimens of the sonnet, they are very creditable; the movement is lively, the word-order natural and the conceits apt. Herbert did not experiment with the sonnet form, using always the freest and least Italianate type, with seven rhymes; but he turned it to many uses. There are narrative sonnets, like *Redemption* and *Christmas;* compact arguments, like *The Sinner* or *Joseph's Coat; The Holdfast* is a colloquy, *Prayer* a reverie. The two sonnets entitled *Love* are clearly related to the rejected Cambridge sonnets, and their tone calls to mind Spenser, a poet with whom Herbert normally has little in common. Herbert excelled in packing the maximum of meaning into brief compass, and for that reason the sonnet suited him well.

Whatever stanza he chooses, he leaves no loose ends, but brings each poem to a fitting conclusion, sometimes to a brilliantly effective one. The dramatic force of the terse last line of *Redemption* is an example of this:

> At length I heard a ragged noise and mirth
> Of theeves and murderers: there I him espied
> Who straight, *Your suit is granted,* said, & died. (p. 40)

The fantastic catalogue of conceits that makes up the sonnet on prayer ends with the profoundly simple phrase, "something understood." *The Collar, Affliction i, Miserie, Thanksgiving,* are some of the poems which end with a sudden and most dramatic change of mood.

His openings are equally well contrived. The attention is immediately caught by such lines as

> Busie enquiring heart, what wouldst thou know?

or

> Meeting with Time, Slack thing, said I,

or

> Kill me not every day.

Sometimes the verses of a poem are made interdependent by the use of repetitive imagery. In *Ungratefulnesse,* for instance, cabinets and boxes figure in all but the last stanza; in *Obedience,* legal phrases are employed in all but two of the seven verses. Alternatively Herbert may use a refrain to bind his verses one to another; or he may restrict himself to a few repeated rhymes, as in *Aaron,* where the five words, head, breast, dead, rest, drest, are the rhyme-words in every one of the five stanzas, and their order is never varied; or as in *Clasping of Hands,* where a poem of twenty lines has only the four rhyming words, thine, mine, more, restore. It would be tedious to multiply examples of the devices which Herbert uses to make each poem a shapely and telling unit. No careful reader of *The Temple* can fail to be impressed by his good workmanship.

Herbert's conscious striving to achieve a style wholly free from affectation is expressed in the two *Jordan* poems, in *The Forerunners* and *A True Hymne*. It was not a merely literary pursuit, dictated by critical preference for a plain rather than an embellished style. It was an integral part of his moral struggle to achieve sincerity. His poetry, like his life, was dedicated to God, and for that reason it had to be disciplined and divested of "fictions . . . and false hair." There is plenty of evidence that elaboration attracted him. In *Dulnesse*, he openly envies the artifice of worldlier poets:

> The wanton lover in a curious strain
> Can praise his fairest fair;
> And with quaint metaphors her curled hair
> Curl o're again . . .
>
> Where are my lines, then? my approaches? views?
> Where are my window-songs? . . . (p. 115)

The sheer pleasure afforded by ingenuity accounts for poems like *A Wreath, Easter Wings* or *Paradise;* and Herbert was reluctant to give up this pleasure. Towards the end of his life, as ill-health wore him down, it would appear that his eloquence and verbal dexterity began at times to fail him; and he was grieved by this inability to express himself fluently. In *The Forerunners* he speaks of the white hairs that have appeared to warn him of approaching old age, and he laments that his mental powers too should be threatened with loss of brilliance. His brain no longer breeds "those sparkling notions," and he cries:

> Farewell, sweet phrases, lovely metaphors . . .
>
> Lovely, enchanting language, sugar-cane,
> Hony of roses, whither wilt thou flie? (p. 176)

This is the utterance of a man who indeed relished versing, and had a truly Elizabethan joy in the play and resources of the English language.

> I like our language, as our men and coast.
> Who cannot dresse it well, want wit, not words.
> (*The Sonne*, p. 167)

The Sidneian element in Herbert has been underestimated, because of the biographical link with Donne and the consequent critical assumption that he was strongly affected by the metaphysical fashion in poetry. We have only to compare George Herbert's poems with those of his eldest brother to see how independent he kept himself from any literary vogue. Lord Herbert's natural bent for metaphysics in the strict sense of the word naturally inclined him to outmatch Donne by loading his poems with a profusion of learned allusions and philosophical terms. George Herbert was familiar with the new line of wit, and sometimes he followed it; but an outstanding characteristic of his verse is its beautiful flexibility and singing quality. These are pre-eminently the merits of the Elizabethan song-writers. Campion and his fellows, writing for the voice, had evolved stanzas of extraordinary fluency which yet kept the natural rhythms of spoken English. Herbert's variety of stanza form is quite exceptional. So, in his period, is his frequent use of refrain and of various musician-like devices, common enough among lutenists from Wyatt onwards.

From Herbert's poetry we could deduce what Walton tells us, that music was, outside religion, his greatest joy. Not only are the allusions to music very numerous, but many of the poems are constructed with a sense of form that is in itself musicianly. Sometimes this is done almost too deliberately, as in *Sinnes Round.* Here the punning title gives a clue to the form. The concluding line of each stanza is repeated as the opening line of the next, and the last line of the poem is identical with the first, so that the sense comes full circle, and the movement is like that of a musical round. It is, however, highly appropriate to its subject, for the continual repetition of sin is the precise point that Herbert wants to make.

In *Home,* a lengthy poem of longing to be quit of "this world of wo," he produces exactly the effect of a modulation of key. The two concluding verses run:

> What have I left, that I should stay and grone?
>   The most of me to heav'n is fled:
> My thoughts and joyes are all packt up and gone,
>   And for their old acquaintance plead.
>   O show thyself to me,
>   Or take me up to thee!
>
> Come, dearest Lord, passe not this holy season,
>   My flesh and bones and joynts do pray:
> And ev'n my verse, when by the ryme and reason,

The word is *Stay*, says ever, *Come*.
O show thyself to me,
Or take me up to thee! (p. 109)

Not only does the substitution of "Come" for the rhyme-word "Stay" effect a key-change, it adds point to the title of the poem, in which the missing rhyme for "Come" is to be found. In *Deniall* the change of key at the end is brought about by the reverse process. Whereas the final rhyme of each stanza has been wanting, in the last stanza it is supplied, so that the minor modulates to the major. To quote the last two verses:

Therefore my soul lay out of sight,
Untun'd, unstrung:
My feeble spirit, unable to look right.
Like a nip't blossome, hung
Discontented.

O cheer and tune my heartlesse breast,
Defer no time;
That so thy favours granting my request,
They and my minde may chime,
And mend my ryme. (p. 80)

A number of poems in *The Temple* were clearly written to be sung. Some are suitable for singing in church and have in the course of time been included in hymn-books; others are intended for singing to the lute. *Easter*, for instance, is as well and as consciously adapted for a musical setting as any piece by Campion.

As regards the great variety of stanza-forms used by Herbert, his editor G. H. Palmer remarks that of the 169 poems in *The Temple*, 116 are written in metres that are not repeated; for Herbert "invents for each lyrical situation exactly the rhythmic setting that befits it." [2] Any number of examples can be adduced to prove this point. To match the headstrong mood of *The Collar*, we have an unparagraphed run of free (though rhyming) verse; for *Submission* a rather meek-sounding quatrain is chosen. The principle that the dominant emotion of each poem dictates its rhythmic form runs right through the book. It is perhaps worth remarking that Herbert makes no use of the octosyllabic couplet, so beautifully used by his contemporary Henry King, and later by Marvell and Milton; nor does he employ the lovely stanza that his brother Edward used several times with great success, which Tennyson adopted for *In Memoriam*.

Herbert may have learnt a good deal from Donne about the possibilities of varying stanza-forms, for Donne too is inventive in this respect; but whereas his verse struck some of his contemporaries as harsh and rhythmically unpleasant, Herbert's, though energetic, is never dissonant. His poems are all fashioned with a musician's attention to beauty of cadence.

Since he chose to cast so many of his poems in the form of colloquies, either with God or with his own heart, Herbert naturally employed with great freedom the phrases and rhythms of actual speech. The remarkable thing is that he managed to combine these colloquial rhythms with such elegant stanza-forms and rhyme-schemes. His verse is much more dramatic in effect than any of the Elizabethan song-writers' lyrics, for it is constantly enlivened with questions, exclamations and admonitions. Occasionally, as in *Love Unknown*, Herbert writes dialogue. This particular poem, with its many parentheses, its slowly developing narrative and the comments interjected by the second speaker, suggests that he could have turned his hand to dramatic verse if he had cared to do so. Often snatches of conversation are incorporated in the poems, as in *The Quip* or *Peace*. Herbert's favourite form, however, is the one-sided conversation. If he is addressing his conscience, or an unruly thought, or his recalcitrant heart, he will vary his tone, sometimes upbraiding, sometimes challenging. He makes his unsubstantial foes thoroughly human, investing them with bodies that can be seated or clad, even throats that can be choked:

> Now foolish thought go on,
> Spin out thy thread, and make thereof a coat
> To hide thy shame: for thou hast cast a bone
> Which bounds on thee, and will not down thy throat:
>
> (*Assurance*, p. 156)

or again:

> Content thee, greedie heart . . .
>
> To be in both worlds full
> Is more then God was, who was hungrie here.
> Wouldst thou his laws of fasting disanull?
> Enact good cheer?
> Lay out thy joy, yet hope to save it?
> Wouldst thou both eat thy cake, and have it? . . .

Wherefore sit down, good heart;
Grasp not at much, for fear thou losest all . . .
(*The Size*, p. 138)

The stanza quoted above is a good example of Herbert's fondness for proverbs and for a battery of questions. The first two verses of *Jordan i* are an unbroken series of questions. *Discharge* opens with two stanzas of questions, followed by four of admonition; then come three of general reflection, and the last two are again admonitory. Some twenty poems in *The Temple* begin with a question, and there are few in which Herbert does not use the interrogative. The opening of *The Glimpse* illustrates his skill in conveying the very cadences of the speaking voice; a reiteration of plaintive questions is followed by two reflective, half-humorous lines, as though he had added them in an undertone:

Whither away delight?
Thou cam'st but now; wilt thou so soon depart,
And give me up to night?
For many weeks of lingring pain and smart
But one half houre of comfort to my heart?

Me thinks delight should have
More skill in musick, and keep better time . . . (p. 154)

Though Herbert's language is normally colloquial, it can rise to occasional grandeur. We have only to compare his two very dissimilar treatments of the same image, one in *The Church-floore*, the other in *Church Monuments*, to perceive the variety of which he was capable. The first is characteristically domestic:

Sometimes Death, puffing at the doore,
Blows all the dust about the floore;
But while he thinks to spoil the room, he sweeps. (p. 67)

The second invests Death's outbreathings with solemn terror:

While that my soul repairs to her devotion,
Here I intombe my flesh, that it betimes
May take acquaintance of this heap of dust;
To which the blast of deaths incessant motion,
Fed with the exhalation of our crimes,
Drives all at last . . . (p. 64)

But Herbert very rarely writes with sustained magnificence, as he does throughout the entire poem from which these lines are taken. Coleridge's estimate of his diction is essentially perceptive and just: "nothing can be more pure, manly and unaffected."

His familiarity with country people as well as with those of the university and the court ensured that his language was free from preciousness. The proportion of rustic words in his vocabulary is not at all high, but when they do occur they take their place appropriately in phrases that are simple and energetic. Three successive verses from *Content* will serve to illustrate Herbert's style at its most countrified:

> The brags of life are but a nine days wonder;
> And after death the fumes that spring
> From private bodies make as big a thunder
> As those which rise from a huge King.
>
> Onely thy Chronicle is lost; and yet
> Better by worms be all once spent,
> Then to have hellish moths still gnaw and fret
> Thy name in books, which may not rent:
>
> When all they deeds, whose brunt thou feel'st alone,
> Are chaw'd by others pens and tongue;
> And as their wit is, their digestion,
> Thy nourisht fame is weak or strong. (p. 69)

Herbert's fondness for drawing his comparisons from episodes and objects of everyday life has been remarked by every critic, whether, as in the eighteenth century, in deprecation, or, as at present, in commendation. It scarcely needs illustration. Of anxiety, Herbert writes

> God chains the dog till night; wilt loose the chain
> And wake thy sorrow? . . .
> (*The Discharge*, p. 145)

God is compared to an angler:

> Thy double line
> And sev'rall baits in either kinde
> Furnish thy table to thy minde.
> (*Affliction v*, p. 97)

Of his misgivings, he observes

> My thoughts are all a case of knives. (*Affliction iv*, p. 90)

Many of his images and conceits, as Professor Tuve has amply illustrated, are not so far-fetched as they at first sight appear. A very large proportion are of biblical origin, and were not unfamiliar to people educated in the tradition of drawing parallels between scriptural incidents and church doctrines. Solomon's sea of brass, or Justice's balance of which

> The beam and scrape
> Did like some torturing engine show
> (*Justice ii*, p. 141)

were more easily comprehensible to Herbert's readers than to the average reader today.

The vitality of his conceits derives rather from the play of his lively, sensitive mind upon familiar and consecrated material than from brilliance of invention or daringness in juxtaposition. Sometimes his fancy leads him to embody a conceit in the title of his poem; there is no actual mention of a pulley or of a collar in the poems that go by these names. Often Herbert is content to indicate the analogy he wishes to make, and to leave it at that.

There are, however, poems in which he uses images in much the same way as did the compilers of Emblem Books. Miss Freeman makes some excellent points in her chapter on Herbert,[3] though she overstates her case when she maintains that "It cannot be too strongly emphasized that Herbert's images remain emblems and at no time encroach upon the wider province of the symbol. There is no necessary resemblance between the church floor and the human heart, between stained-glass windows and preachers, or between two cabinets containing treasure and the Trinity and the Incarnation. His method is always to create meanings by creating likenesses; the likenesses are rarely inherent in the imagery chosen, nor can they often be seen from the outset."[4] Although there are several poems in *The Temple* which perfectly illustrate "a readiness to see a relation between simple, concrete, visible things and moral ideas, and to establish that relation in as complete a way as possible without identifying the two or blurring the outline of either,"[5] there are many more that testify to the far rarer gift that Herbert possessed, of being able to discern the divine order in everyday experience, and to perceive, rather than establish, relations between the visible and the spiritual.

Surely Herbert's sustained use of imagery in *The Flower* shows an exquisite control of the symbolism of winter and desolation, spring and hope renewed, the garden and paradise. In *The Priesthood* he employs the image of the potter's clay in consecutive stanzas, varying its significance, but never in an arbitrary way. It is a valid symbol at once of man's creaturely inferiority and of his malleability in the hands of God. There is nothing "emblematic" in the use of the ancient symbols of rock and storm in this stanza from *Assurance:*

> Wherefore if thou canst fail,
> Then can thy truth and I: but while rocks stand,
> And rivers stirre, thou canst not shrink or quail:
> Yea, when both rocks and all things shall disband,
> Then shalt thou be my rock and tower,
> And make their ruine praise thy power. (p. 156)

Or again, to illustrate the rapidity with which Herbert sometimes shifts his imagery (not an "emblematic" trait), we may take the opening lines of *The Answer:*

> My comforts drop and melt away like snow:
> I shake my head, and all the thoughts and ends,
> Which my fierce youth did bandie, fall and flow
> Like leaves about me: or like summer friends,
> Flyes of estates and sunne-shine . . . (p. 169)

Miss Freeman also contends that "Herbert's poetry brings its pictures with it. It remains primarily visual, but the images presented have already been explored and when they enter the poem they enter it with their implications already worked out." [6] Well-defined his images certainly are; but not markedly pictorial. There are very few colours mentioned in Herbert's poems, although the symbolism of light is constantly used. Even when we might legitimately expect description, we do not get it. The first verse of *The Pilgrimage,* for instance, could scarcely be starker:

> I travell'd on, seeing the hill, where lay
> My expectation.
> A long it was and weary way.
> The gloomy cave of Desperation
> I left on th'one, and on the other side
> The rock of Pride. (p. 141)

If we imagine for a moment what Spenser would have made of this material, it seems scarcely just to describe Herbert as a visual poet. Similarly, when he personifies Obedience, only her attitude is conveyed, not her visible attributes:

> Humble Obedience neare the doore doth stand,
> Expecting a command:
> Then whom in waiting nothing seems more slow,
> Nothing more quick when she doth goe.
> (*The Familie*, p. 137)

Herbert makes his verbs work harder than his adjectives. This is one of the essential features of his energetic, masculine style, but it does not make for pictorial effects. Writing of afflictions, he uses an unexpected simile, the force of which depends chiefly upon the succession of words expressing action:

> We are the earth; and they
> Like moles within us, heave, and cast about,
> And till they foot and clutch their prey,
> They never cool, much lesse give out.
> (*Confession*, p. 126)

But if Herbert's visual sensibility was not remarkable, we may deduce from his imagery that his sense of smell and taste was very acute, for his customary way of expressing moods of ecstasy is by reference to perfumes and delicious sweetness. *The Odour* and *The Banquet* are obvious examples, but there are plenty of others scattered throughout *The Temple:*

> I felt a sugred strange delight,
> Passing all cordials made by any art,
> Bedew, embalme, and overrunne my heart . . .
> (*The Glance*, p. 171)

> What though some have a fraught
> Of cloves and nutmegs, and in cinamon sail;
> If thou hast wherewithall to spice a draught,
> When griefs prevail;
> And for the future time art heir
> To th' Isle of spices, is't not fair?
> (*The Size*, p. 137)

Lovely enchanting language, sugar-cane,
Hony of roses, whither wilt thou flie?
(*The Forerunners*, p. 176)

These, and similar passages, testify to Herbert's protest, "My stuffe is flesh, not brasse; my senses live." Of all his sense-allusions, perhaps the simplest and most sensitive of all is the line from *The Flower*

I once more smell the dew and rain,

where these few words convey the essence of the joy that accompanies the cessation of spiritual aridity.

Musical analogies, as we should expect, are very numerous in Herbert's verse, and so, not surprisingly, are sick-room metaphors. A great many images are derived from the domestic background of house and garden. To illustrate these would be wearisome; they leap to the eye of even the cursory reader.

Herbert's sheer enjoyment of metaphor comes out in the first two stanzas of *Dotage*, where the pleasures and sorrows of life are summed up and contrasted in a long series of juxtaposed images. The same thing can be seen even more vividly in *Prayer i*, a poem that contains not a single direct statement, but consists entirely of brief analogies that combine to throw light on the mystery that is the poet's theme.

Usually Herbert's imagery is unobtrusive. He seldom labours his points; indeed, his jests are sometimes so quiet that they almost escape notice, as in the lines

Who sweeps a room as for thy laws
Makes that and th' action fine.
(*The Elixir*, p. 184)

He can occasionally be grotesque:

Death, thou wast once an uncouth, hideous thing,
Nothing but bones,
The sad effect of sadder grones;
Thy mouth was open, but thou couldst not sing.
(*Death*, p. 185)

Very rarely does he let his fancy play around an abstract notion, though he does so in *Sinne ii*, which is the amplification of a scholastic quibble. It is in every sense of the word a metaphysical poem, and not a distinguished one. It would not have disgraced Edward Herbert, but it is quite untypical of his brother.

As a rule George Herbert's conceits blend into the general texture of his verse. The whole mattered to him more than the parts, and his desire to co-ordinate generally prevented him from embroidering any one conceit so elaborately that it would draw attention to itself and away from the gist of the poem as a whole. A sense of proportion and balance characterized his thinking and also his poetic workmanship.

We might almost deduce from his writings, if we did not know it from the record of his life, that Herbert was an accomplished speaker. He manages his rhythms and diction as though he were actually expending his breath. There are no strident forcings of the voice, no lapses into colourless undertone. He knows the range of the instrument at his command and uses all its resources with discrimination and skill. Practitioners of verse can learn much from a study of *The Temple.*

NOTES

[1] The revisions made in *The Elixir,* for example, can be profitably studied in F. E. Hutchinson's edition of Herbert's *Works.*

[2] *English Works of George Herbert,* 3 vols., 2nd ed. 1915, Houghton Mifflin. Vol., I, p. 135.

[3] *English Emblem Books* (Chatto & Windus, 1948).

[4] Op. cit., p. 163.

[5] Op. cit., p. 155.

[6] Op. cit., p. 155.

AUSTIN WARREN

Symbolism in Crashaw

The poet's birthright, his imagery, is that part of him which is least controllable by effort and discipline. His sensuous aridity or fertility; the relative predominance of eye over ear or of both over the nostrils; his sensitivity to tint and shade or his bold reduction to line drawing or charcoal sketch; the precision of his observation or his subjective diminutions and hyperboles; the domains from which he elicits his tropes—whether moor and mountain, or cathedral and drawing room, from natural history or unnatural: these aesthetic characters reveal his breed. Doubtless the poet as self-critic can prune the luxuriance of the imagery, make austere sacrifice of those clusters growing in contiguity too close; but the kind of grapes he rears owes dependence to soil and climate. So far, that is, as imagery is not pastiche and imitation, it lays bare the temperamental self and can change its character only as, and so far as, the poet is susceptible of personal conversion.

In his life alone does Nature live. Even among the romantic poets, one notes their unconscious selection from what they have experienced. The spirit of Childe Harold finds representative embodiment in the vast and horrendous, in altitude and solitude—the ocean, the mountain, the storm; Shelley, the aerial, in the cloud, the skylark, the west wind; Wordsworth in the quietly pastoral, the landscape domesticated by man or indwelt and tempered by the World Spirit.

From *Richard Crashaw: A Study in Baroque Sensibility* (Louisiana State University Press, 1939; reissued by The University of Michigan Press, and by Faber & Faber, 1957), pp. 176–93. Reprinted by permission of the publishers.

All imagery is double in its reference, a composite of perception and conception. Of these ingredients, the proportions vary. The metaphorist can collate image with image, or image with concept, or concept with image, or concept with concept. He can compare love to a rose, or a rose to love, or a pine grove to a cathedral, or religious ecstasy to intoxication. Then, too, the metaphorists differ widely in the degree of visualization for which they project their images. The epic simile of Homer and of Spenser is fully pictorial; the intent, relative to the poet's architecture, is decorative. On the other hand, the "sunken" and the "radical" types of imagery [1]—the conceits of Donne and the "symbols" of Hart Crane—expect scant realization by the senses.

Symbolism may be defined as imagery understood to imply a conceptual meaning: such definition is latitudinarian enough to admit the poetry of Mallarmé as well as the ceremonial of the Church. The concept may be a mere overtone, a darkly descried vista, or it may be a category susceptible of prose statement. Some symbolisms are private, founded upon the poet's childhood associations of thing and sentiment; without biographical aid, the reader is likely to find them mere imagism or a congeries of oddly juxtaposed perceptions. Others —like the Christian emblems of dove, lamb, shepherd, cross—are communal. Others must be well-nigh universal, even to men topographically untraveled: the plain, the mountain, the valley, the ocean, the storm, darkness and light, are broadly human.

Parable and allegory may be defined as symbolic narratives in which a conceptual sequence runs parallel to—or, rather, is incarnate in—an imaginative sequence; they are, too, the most explicit forms. Christ parabolically identifies himself with the Good Shepherd; the Word, with the seed; the fig tree, with the unproductive life. Spenser and Bunyan label their persons and places: the Giant Despair, Fidessa, Orgolio, Mr. Worldly Wiseman, Faithful; the Bower of Bliss, the House of Holiness, Doubting Castle, the Delectable Mountains.

The proportion of strength between the image and the concept ranges widely. In eighteenth-century personification, the picture frequently evaporated till but a capital remained; in Mallarmé, the imagery only is presented, though, by its lack of naturalistic congruence, its disjunction, it disturbs the consciousness till the latter evokes some coherent psychological pattern for which all the images are relevant.

Crashaw, sensuous of temperament, wrote a poetry mellifluously musical, lavishly imagistic. At first acquaintance it seems the song of the nightingale hovering over her skill, "bathing in streams of liquid melody"; later, it seems the passage work, the cadenzas, the glissandi of an endowed and much-schooled virtuoso. Yet his life shows him to have been an ascetic, denying his senses all save their homage to God. In turning to religion and religious poetry, he "changed his object not his passion," as St. Augustine said of the Magdalen: [2] the images of his secular poetry recur in his sacred. He loves his God as he might have loved his "supposed mistress."

Not a preacher or prophet, Crashaw had no "message" to announce. He had suffered and exulted, and exulted in suffering; but his experiences did not tempt him to philosophy or other prose formulation. His was to be a poetry in which the rhythms and images would tell their own tale.

To his symbolism he supplied no chart of prose equivalents. Yet no reader has long studied his poems without feeling that their imagery is more than pageant; that, rather, it is a vocabulary of recurrent motifs.[3]

Nor is this symbolism really undecipherable. In the main it follows traditional Christian lines, drawing on the Bible, ecclesiastical lore, and the books of such mystics as St. Bernard and St. Teresa. Even when it is "private"—as, in some measure, every poet's will be—it yields to persistent and correlating study. Not widely ranging, Crashaw's images reappear in similar contexts, one event elucidating another. No casual reader of his poems, for example, but has been arrested by the recurrence of "nest," usually in rhyming union with "breast"; and, surely, no constant reader has long doubted its psychological import, its equivalence to shelter, refuge, succor.

It need not be maintained—it is, indeed, incredible—that Crashaw constructed a systematic symbolism. It is unlikely, even, that he knew why certain images possessed, for him, particular potence. Obviously much concerned with his technique, given to revision, a lover of the arts, he seems, as a man, ingenuous, free from self-consciousness, imaginatively uncensored.

In his steady movement from secular poetry to an exclusive preoccupation with sacred, from Latin to the vernacular, he relinquished —deliberately, it would seem—the Renaissance decoration of classical mythology. As a schoolboy he had written hymns to Venus, poems on Pygmalion, Arion, Apollo and Daphne, Aeneas and Anchises; and in his Latin epigrams, and in "Music's Duel," there occur classical embellishments. From the English sacred poems, however, such apparatus is conspicuously absent. Giles Fletcher, of his English predecessors closest to him in temper and idiom, had compared the ascending Christ to Ganymede, snatched up from earth to attend upon Jupiter; but no such bold correlation of pagan and Christian finds place in

Crashaw's poetry. Donne and Herbert, also erudites, had made a similar surrender of their classicism; [4] and to Herbert's example in particular he may have been indebted.

Otherwise, Crashaw makes no attempt to differentiate his sacred from his secular imagery; many characteristic figures and metaphors, "delights of the Muses," are reënlisted in the service of Urania. For example, the familiar paradox of the Incarnation, whereby Jesus is at once the son and the father of the Blessed Virgin, is anticipated in the apostrophe to Aeneas carrying Anchises: "Felix! *parentis* qui *pater* diceris esse tui!" [5] The persistent motif of the mystical poems first appears in "Wishes":

> A well tam'd heart
> For whose more noble smart
> Love may bee long chusing a Dart.

Unlike Herbert, Crashaw rarely recollects homely images of market place and fireside; and allusions to the polities and economies of the Stuart world come but seldom. Christ, dying, is called "his own legacy." With the Blessed Virgin, Crashaw, who, too, has set "so deep a share" in Christ's wounds, would draw some "dividend." To these financial metaphors, one may add what at first view seems Herbertian —the angels with their bottles, and the breakfast of the brisk cherub.[6] Yet, though "breakfast" Herbert would surely not have disdained, such intimacy with the habits of cherubs is peculiarly alien to the Anglican spirit of *The Temple*. It is Mary's tears which, having wept upwards, become, at the top of the milky river, the cream upon which the infant angel is fed, adding "sweetnesse to his sweetest lips"; and this context, by its extravagant lusciousness, reduces the blunt word to but a passing grotesquerie.

Some feeling for Nature, especially the dawn and flowers, the young Crashaw undoubtedly had; but even the early poems evince no botanical niceness, no precision of scrutiny. The first of the Herrys poems develops a single metaphor, that of a tree whose blossoms, ravished by a mad wind, never deliver their promised fruit; but unlike Herbert's "orange tree," this is a tree of no specific genus.[7] Crashaw's habitual blossoms are the conventional lily and rose.

These flowers, which appear briefly, in his earliest poems, as outward and visible creatures, do not disappear from his later verse; but they soon turn into a ceremonial and symbolical pair, a liturgical formula, expressive of white and red, tears and blood, purity and love. Already in the panegyric on the Duke of York, lines which begin with a delicate naturalism, end with a reduction to liturgical red and white, in a prefigurement of Crashaw's final style.

> So have I seene (to dresse their Mistresse *May*)
> Two silken sister flowers consult, and lay
> Their bashfull cheekes together, newly they
> Peep't from their buds, shew'd like the Gardens eyes
> Scarce wakt: like was the Crimson of their joyes,
> Like were the Pearles they wept. . . .[8]

In the "Bulla," or "Bubble," the flowers have become antithetic colors in shifting transmutations.[9]

If Crashaw's *flora* soon turn symbols, his *fauna* have never owed genuine allegiance to the world of Nature. The worm; the wolf, the lamb; the fly, the bee; the dove, the eagle, the "self-wounding pelican," and the phoenix: all derive their traits and their significance from bestiary or Christian tradition, not from observation; and their symbolism is palpable. In their baseness men are "all idolizing worms"; in their earthly transience and fickleness and vanity, foolish wanton flies. The bee, a paragon of industry, is still more a creator, preserver, or purveyor of mystic sweetness. The Holy Name of Jesus is adored by angels that throng

> Like diligent Bees, And swarm about it.
> O they are wise;
> And know what *Sweetes* are suck't from out it.
> It is the Hive,
> By which they thrive,
> Where all their Hoard of Hony lyes.

The dove and lamb, of frequent appearance, betoken innocence and purity; they are also meet for votive offering. Sometimes the doves emblemize elect souls, whose eyes should be "Those of turtles, chaste, and true"; sometimes, the Holy Ghost. The *Agnus Dei,* the white lamb slain before the foundation of the world, was Crashaw's favorite symbol for Christ and for him, among all symbols, one of the most affecting.

"By all the Eagle in thee, all the dove": so Crashaw invokes the chaste Teresa, the mystic whose wings carried her high, whose spiritual vision was unflinching and acute.

> Sharpe-sighted as the Eagles eye, that can
> Out-stare the broad-beam'd Dayes Meridian.

Meditating her books, the responsive reader finds his heart "hatcht" into a nest "Of little Eagles, and young loves." [10]

To the phoenix, Crashaw devoted a Latin poem, a "Genethliacon et Epicedion," in which the paradox of a fecund death shows its expected fascination for him. The fragrant, unique, and deathless bird reappears in the Latin epigrams, and in the English poems, both secular and sacred. It occurs twice in the sequence of Herrys elegies; it is belabored at length in the panegyric to Henrietta Maria, "Upon her Numerous Progenie," where it becomes a symbol of supreme worth. In the sacred poems, it assumes its traditional Christian office as sign of the God-man, virgin-born, only-begotten, and immortal.

With most artists, the pleasures of sight are pre-eminent; with Crashaw, in spite of his interest in pictures and emblems, the fuller-bodied and less sharply defined senses would appear to have afforded richer, more characteristic delight.

His colors are elementary, chiefly conventional, readily symbolic. In his religious poetry, but three occur: red (or purple = *purpureus*), with its traditional relation, through fire and the "Flaming Heart" to love; black; and white. Black is, for him, the sign not of mourning or penitence but of sin and, still more, of finiteness, of mortality: "Dust thou art, and to dust thou shalt return." In his translation of Catullus, men are "dark Sons of Sorrow." Augmented, the phrase reappears in "The Name of Jesus" as "dark Sons of Dust and Sorrow." Elsewhere in the religious poems, man is "Disdainful dust and ashes" or "Darke, dusty Man."

White, perhaps as the synthesis of all colors, perhaps as the symbol of luminous purity, is the most exalting adjective in Crashaw's vocabulary. It occurs in his secular verse, especially in his panegyrics upon the royal family. But it is more frequent in his *carmina sacra,* used customarily of the Blessed Virgin or Christ, and most strikingly of Christ as the Lamb.

> Vain loves, avaunt! bold hands forbear!
> The Lamb hath dipp't his white foot here.[11]

The absence from the religious poetry of green, the color of nature, and blue—in the tradition of Christian art, the color of truth and of the Blessed Virgin—is conspicuous; so is the absence of chiaroscuro. By other means, he produces a sensuous luxuriance; but, in respect to the palette, he turns, like the Gospels, to bold antithesis of black and white.

For evidence that Crashaw was a lover of music, one need not appeal to "Music's Duel." "On the Name of Jesus," among his four or five masterpieces, calls to celebration all sweet sounds of instrument—

> Be they such
> As sigh with supple wind
> Or answer Artfull Touch. . . .

These flutes, lutes, and harps are the "Soul's most certain wings," Heaven on Earth; indeed, in a moment of quasi-Platonic identification of reality with highest value he equates "All things that Are" with all that are musical. Assuredly, Crashaw intended his own poetry to be—what by virtue of his mastery of vowel and consonant sequences and alliteration it habitually is—sweet to the ear, Lydian. But, for him, it is also true, human music was an initiation into an archetypal music, the harmonious concert of the spheres "which dull mortality more feels than hears." The ears are "tumultous shops of noise" compared with those inner sensibilities which, properly disciplined, may hear, as from afar, the inexpressive nuptial hymn.[12]

Crashaw's favorite adjectives, "sweet" and "delicious," mingle fragrance and taste. His holy odors are chiefly traditional—those of flowers and of spices. "Let my prayer be set forth in Thy sight as the incense," said the Psalmist; but the simile finds its analogy in the ascent of both. The fragrance of spices pervades that manual of the mystics, the *Song of Songs*. To the Infant Jesus, the magi brought frankincense and myrrh. The Magdalen dies as "perfumes expire." The Holy Name is invoked as a "cloud of condensed sweets," bidden to break upon us in balmy and "sense-filling" showers. In his ode on Prayer, the most mystical of his poems, Crashaw bids the lover of God, the virgin soul, to seize the Bridegroom

> All fresh and fragrant as he rises
> Dropping with a baulmy Showr
> A delicious dew of spices. . . .

Sometimes Crashaw's gustatory delights, like those of the

> sweet-lipp'd Angell-Imps, that swill their throats
> In creame of Morning *Helicon* . . .[13]

remain innocently physical. But customarily the pleasure of the palate, too, becomes symbolic, as it is when the Psalmist bids us "taste . . .

how good the Lord is." The angels who swarm about the Holy Name are wise because they "know what Sweetes are suck't from out of it." This palatal imagery might be expected to culminate in apostrophes to the Blessed Sacrament; but not so. For Protestants, the Holy Communion is a symbolic as well as commemorative eating and drinking; to Crashaw, who believed in Transubstantiation, the miraculous feast seemed rather the denial of the senses than their symbolic employment. His expansive paraphrases of St. Thomas' Eucharistic hymns are notably sparse in sensuous imagery. It is not the Blood of Christ on the altar but the redeeming blood on the cross which prompts him to spiritual inebriation.

Crashaw's liquids are water (tears, penitence); milk (maternal succor, nutrition); blood (martyrdom on the part of the shedder, transference of vitality to the recipient); wine (religious inebriation, ecstasy). Fluid, they are constantly mixing in ways paradoxical or miraculous. In one of his earliest poems, a metrical version of Psalm 137, blood turns into water. In one of the latest, "Sancta Maria," "Her eyes bleed Teares, his wounds weep Blood." From the side of Christ, crucified, flowed an "amorous flood of Water wedding Blood." The angels, preparing for a feast, come with crystal phials to draw from the eyes of the Magdalen "their master's Water: their own Wine." Milk and blood may mingle, as when maternal love induces self-sacrifice; water turns to wine when tears of penitence become the happy token of acceptance and union; wine is transubstantiated into blood in the Sacrament; blood becomes wine when, "drunk of the dear wounds," the apprehender of Christ's redeeming sacrifice loses control of his faculties in an intoxication of gratitude and love.

The last of the senses is at once the most sensuous and the least localized. To it belong the thermal sensations of heat and chill. Fire, the cause of heat, is, by traditional use, the symbol of love; its opposites are ordinarily lovelessness and—what is the same—death. The "flaming Heart" of Christ or of the Blessed Virgin is the heart afire with love. St. Teresa's ardor renders her insensitive to love's antonym and opposite, the chill of the grave. Crashaw is likely to unite the opposites. Since she is both Virgin and Mother, Mary's kisses may either heat or cool. Lying between her chaste breasts, the Infant Jesus sleeps in snow, yet warmly.[14]

The supremities of touch, for Crashaw's imagination, are experienced in the mystical "wound of love," in martyrdom, and in nuptial union. In the former states, torment and pleasure mix: the pains are delicious; the joys, intolerable. In his mystical poems, Crashaw makes free use of figures drawn from courtship and marriage. Christ is the "Noble

Bridegroom, the Spouse of Virgins." Worthy souls are those who bestow upon His hand their "heaped up, consecrated Kisses," who store up for Him their "wise embraces." The soul has its flirtations, its "amorous languishments," its "dear and divine annihilations." St. Teresa, love's victim, is sealed as Christ's bride by the "full Kingdom of that final Kiss"; and her mystic marriage has made her the mother of many disciples, many "virgin-births."

In the spirit of St. Ignatius' *Exercitia Spiritualia,* Crashaw performs an "Application of the Senses" upon all the sacred themes of his meditation. God transcends our images as He transcends our reason; but, argues the Counter-Reformation, transcension does not imply abrogation. Puritanism opposes the senses and the imagination to truth and holiness; for Catholicism, the former may be ministering angels. "How daring it is to picture the incorporeal," wrote Nilus Scholasticus in the *Greek Anthology;* "but yet the image leads us up to spiritual recollection of celestial beings." [15] Not *iconoclasts,* some censors would grant that visual imagery, emanating from the "highest" of the senses, may point from the seen to the unseen; there they would halt. Crashaw, like one persistent school of mystics, would boldly appropriate the whole range of sensuous experience as symbolic of the inner life.

Studied case by case, Crashaw's striking imagery will yield its symbolic intent. But its most characteristic feature emerges only when image is collated with image. Poetic symbolism may constantly devise new alliances of sense and concept; indeed, the poet Emerson objected to Swedenborg's "Correspondences" on the precise ground of their fixed and systematic character. With Crashaw, though rigidity is never reached, his metaphors yet form a series of loosely defined analogies and antitheses and cross references, a system of motifs symbolically expressive of themes and emotions persistently his.

Associated images recur like ceremonial formulas. In the secular poems, the lily and the rose have appeared, singly and together. The association continues into the religious poems, but the metaphorical character of the flowers has become explicit. In the epigram on the Holy Innocents, the mother's milk and the children's blood turn, for Crashaw's pious fancy, into lilies and roses. A characteristic later juxtaposition, in the "Hymn for the Circumcision," gives the metamorphosis: "this modest Maiden Lilly, our sinnes have sham'd into a Rose."

A similar ritual coupling is that of the pearl and the ruby. Sometimes these symbols appear singly, sometimes together. In the same "Hymn for the Circumcision" Crashaw sees Christ's drops of blood as rubies. The tears of the Magdalen are Sorrow's "richest Pearles." They are united in the eighteenth stanza of "Wishes." Still united, they reappear in the religious poetry: When men weep over the bloody wounds of Christ,

> The debt is paid in *Ruby*-teares,
> Which thou in Pearles did'st lend.[16]

Another frequent union—and this not of contrasts but of contradictories—couples fire and water, an oxymoron of images. Already, in an early poem, the sun is represented as paying back to the sea in tears what, as fire, it borrowed. When the Magdalen washes Christ's feet with tears, wiping them with her hair,

> Her eyes flood lickes his feets faire staine,
> Her haires flame lickes up that againe.
> This flame thus quench't hath brighter beames:
> This flood thus stained fairer streames.[17]

The Blessed Virgin is the "noblest nest Both of love's fires and floods." The tears of contrition or of sorrow, so far from extinguishing the fire of love, make it burn more ardently.

But one cannot thus far have surveyed Crashaw's imagery without perceiving how the whole forms a vaguely defined but persistently felt series of inter-relations. There are things red—fire, blood, rubies, roses, wine—and things white—tears, lilies, pearls, diamonds: symbols of love and passion; symbols of contrition, purity, innocence.

On its sensuous surface, his imagination sparkles with constant metamorphosis: tears turn into soft and fluid things like milk, cream, wine, dew; into hard things like stars, pearls, and diamonds. Beneath, the same experiences engage poet and poem.

All things flow. Crashaw's imagery runs in streams; the streams run together; image turns into image. His metaphors are sometimes so rapidly juxtaposed as to mix—they occur, that is, in a succession so swift as to prevent the reader from focusing separately upon each. The effect is often that of phantasmagoria. For Crashaw, the world of the senses was evidently enticing; yet it was a world of appearances only—shifting, restless appearances. By temperament and conviction, he was a believer in the miraculous; and his aesthetic method may be interpreted as a genuine equivalent of his belief, as its translation into a rhetoric of metamorphosis. If, in the Gospels, water changes to wine and wine to blood, Crashaw was but imaginatively extending this principle when he turned tears into pearls, pearls into lilies, lilies into pure Innocents.

Style must incarnate spirit. Oxymoron, paradox, and hyperbole are figures necessary to the articulation of the Catholic faith. Crashaw's *concetti,* by their infidelity to nature, claim allegiance to the supernatural; his baroque imagery, engaging the senses, intimates a world which transcends them.

NOTES

[1] These terms come from H. W. Wells' admirable analysis of *Poetic Imagery.*

[2] "I believe without any levity of conceipt, that hearts wrought into a tendernesse by the lighter flame of nature, are like mettals already running, easilier cast into Devotion then others of a hard and lesse impressive temper, for Saint *Austin* said, *The holy Magdalen changed her object only, not her passion* . . ." (Walter Montagu, *Miscellanea Spiritualia* . . . , 32).

[3] Cf. intimations in Osmond, *Mystical Poets,* 118, and Watkin, *The English Way,* 287.

Discussing "Conceits," Kathleen Lea wrote: "In his frequent use of the word 'nest' I do not believe that the image of a bird's nest presented itself to him. . . . For Crashaw we have an even longer list of words, such as 'womb,' 'tomb,' 'grave,' 'day,' 'death,' and 'fount,' which he used as it were ritualistically and in a colourless sense of his own. While it is proof of his greatness that he had this peculiar idiom of speech, it is also significant of his weakness that this idiom must be re-learned and explained." (*Modern Language Review,* XX [1925], 405.) This was a penetrating insight into the nature of Crashaw's poetic method; and it is the central merit of Miss Wallerstein's *Crashaw* that in some brilliant pages (especially 126–8) it develops and extends this thesis.

[4] Cf. Warren, "George Herbert," *American Review,* VII, 258 ff.

[5] "Fortunate man, you who may be said to be the father of your parent" (Martin, 222–3).

[6] Ibid., 286 (stanza 9); cf. "Charitas Nimia," ibid., 280, and ibid., 309 ("The Weeper," stanza 5).

[7] Ibid., 167; Herbert, "Employment."

[8] Ibid., 178.

[9] Ibid., 218

> Flagrant sobria lilia.
> Vicinis adeo rosis
> Vicinae invigilant nives,
> Ut sint et nivae rosae
> Ut sint et rosae nives. . . .

[10] On the lore of the eagle, cf. Phipson, *Animal-Lore,* 232–3.

[11] Cf. "Hymn to St. Teresa":

> Thou with the LAMB, thy Lord, shalt goe;
> And whereso'ere he setts his white
> Stepps, walk with HIM those wayes of light . . .

and the "To the Queen's Majesty":

A Golden harvest of crown'd heads, that meet
And crowd for kisses from the LAMB'S white feet.

[12] In my discussion of sensuous correspondences I am indebted to Miss M. A. Ewer's important *Survey of Mystical Symbolism.*

[13] "Music's Duel."

[14] "A Hymne of the Nativity" (Martin, 107):

With many a rarely-temper'd kisse,
That breathes at once both Maid and Mother,
Warmes in the one, cooles in the other.

[15] *Greek Anthology,* Bk. I, epigram 33. Cf. also epigram 34 (from Agathias Scholasticus): "Greatly daring was the wax that formed the image of the invisible Prince of the Angels, incorporeal in the essence of his form. But yet . . . a man looking at the image directs his mind to a higher contemplation. No longer has he a confused veneration, but imprinting the image in himself, he fears him as if he were present. The eyes stir up the depths of the spirit, and Art can convey by colours the prayers of the soul."

[16] "On the Wounds of our Crucified Lord" (Martin, 99).

[17] English epigram (Martin, 97).

ROBERT MARTIN ADAMS

Taste and Bad Taste in Metaphysical Poetry: Richard Crashaw and Dylan Thomas

I will start with three axioms about metaphysical poetry, none altogether self-evident, but all distinct enough, I think, to be worth testing against a metaphysical poet of the seventeenth century and one of the twentieth. The distinctive effects of metaphysical poetry are built upon conflict, opposition, tension; metaphysical poets often exploit a "dissociation of sensibility" (even though they disapprove of it), to achieve the effect of tension; one effect of this exploitation may be the disruption of those harmonies which one sometimes supposes necessary to a unified esthetic effect.

What adjustment do these considerations require in the standards by which one judges the esthetic achievement of a metaphysical poem? Mr. Merritt Hughes, in the course of his eloquent protest against the kidnapping of Donne by modern critics, took a number of grounds against making the wit of Donne a touchstone for the judgment of all poetry—among others, the interesting one that Donne's wit led him into certain faults of taste. While glancing back to Dr. Johnson and John Dryden, Mr. Hughes made primary reference to Professor Grierson's 1912 deprecation of the epicedes and obsequies, and to his tentative critique of the coarser and more cynical of the

From *The Hudson Review,* VIII (1955), pp. 60–77. Reprinted by permission from *The Hudson Review,* Vol. VIII, No. 1, Spring 1955.

love poems. "There is bad taste in some of Donne's work" [1]—no doubt. But how much, where, relative to what standard of good taste, and is the wit responsible for it? To develop a few misgivings about the generalization, one need look no further than Grierson's Introduction or Johnson's *Life of Cowley*. Professor Grierson quotes as a model of subtle, pure, and lovely verse a poem by the then laureate, which simply has not stood the test of forty years. It is an atrocious piece of mawk, even by laureate standards. Does this poem represent the standard by which Donne was condemned? Pure its diction may be, though the idea of "unrisen lustres" slaking the "o'ertaken moon" is a queer one indeed; but subtle and lovely it is not; and if it is a deficiency in Donne not to have written in this way, we may be well on the way to confusing Ella Wheeler Wilcox with William Shakespeare. As for Dr. Johnson, though much of his critical attack concerns Cowley and some genuinely unfortunate mortuary poems by Donne, his blame also falls unerringly on the one image of Donne's which recent critics have most generally praised. Of the compass-image at the end of *A Valediction Forbidding Mourning* he can only say that he does not know whether ingenuity or absurdity predominates. This thundering dictum leaves us pretty much at a stand; when we start looking for "bad taste" in metaphysical poetry, where shall we stop, where draw the line? Where indeed shall we begin?

To start with Dr. Johnson, who is a good, explicit point of departure, it is true, as he says, that the faults of metaphysical poetry can often be laid to a striving for effect. But several subdivisions of the crime may be distinguished. The poet perhaps aims at an effect perfectly proper, even sublime, in itself, but of which he falls lamentably short; or he perhaps strives to dazzle the reader with pyrotechnics either irrelevant to the form or improper to the nature of poetry; or else, perhaps, he undertakes to render a discord which is grotesque in character or proportions. Johnson seems to have followed Dryden in having the second variety of sin chiefly in mind. "Donne affects the metaphysics," says Dryden in the *Discourse Concerning Satire*, "not only in his satires, but in his amorous verses, where nature only should reign; and perplexes the minds of the fair sex with nice speculations of philosophy, when he should ingage their hearts, and entertain them with the softnesses of love." The point is simply that Donne pursued effects inappropriate to the genre or the situation. There is an imputation, even, that metaphysics would be all right in satire, or in poems which had the overall intent of making the reader think. But Johnson goes a step further by declaring "that whatever is improper or vicious [among the metaphysicals] is produced by a voluntary deviation from nature in pursuit of something new and strange; and that the writers fail to give delight, by their desire of exciting admiration." [2] They are, in other words, pursuing an objective which is poetically wrong in general. Johnson grants that "where scholastic speculation can be properly admitted, their copiousness and acuteness may justly be admired"; but this area does not seem to coincide, in any degree, with that of poetry. For nature (which, though it includes feelings as well as thoughts, is general nature, and therefore neither new nor strange) is in Johnson's final opinion the only topic proper for a poet, and delight rather than admiration is the proper end of all poetry.

I do not think critics of any persuasion can have much quarrel with Johnson's condemnation of a flamboyant striving after effect, at least in poetry. Though we like or expect our poets' learning to be displayed where it can be admired, we are suspicious of rhetoric in the grand manner and the large, direct, peremptory style. Like Coleridge, we suppose that "the poetic power . . . subordinates art to nature; the manner to the matter; and our admiration of the poet to our sympathy with the poetry"; with Keats, we are disposed to "hate poetry that has a palpable design upon us, and, if we do not agree, seems to put its hand in its breeches pocket." [3] *Ars celare artem* has an ancient prescription, and one (it may be suspected) deeply imbedded in the psychological character of an art which depends (like poetry) on evocation. On the other hand, contemporary taste does not attribute much of this striving after effect to Donne because we are likely to take a broader definition of propriety than Johnson or Dryden; we are more disposed to grant that a metaphysical mind can look at almost anything in a metaphysical way. We are perhaps likely to insist upon some evidence of the metaphysical temperament; the cold raptures of Cowley often seem, in the terms of Donne's most melancholy metaphor, like "embroidered works" left upon "the slimy beach" by the tide of fashion. But granted the metaphysical excitement (one aspect of which is the much-discussed "metaphysical shudder"), we tolerate a great deal of elaboration as true to the poet's mind and temperament, which Johnson rejected as false to the social fact. Metaphysics have proved themselves no less successful in attracting "the fair" than nature itself, and quite as intriguing to readers; though it is perhaps significant that the relatively small volume of Donne's sacred verse has been more widely influential—perhaps because it has seemed less contrived—than the artifices of the love-poetry, the elegies or satires. At all events, whether because our comprehension is broader or our critical standards lower, we suffer the suspicion of theatricality more gladly; perhaps also because we are not sure where the accusation of theatricality will lead us. (If Donne is theatrical, therefore bad, what of Byron, Poe, Baudelaire, Rilke, Rimbaud, Yeats?—the list is endless.)

Hence, conscious exhibitionism is not very often attributed to Donne any more; and though there is no doubt it enters into his poetry, it would have to be much more potent and explicit than it is to disturb our appreciation of, say, the *Valediction Forbidding Mourning.* As for the first charge, that of bathos, it has not very often been explicitly levelled at Donne, but there seems no reason to doubt that his poetry is occasionally bathetic. For random examples one might refer to the teeming fish-roes in the *Elegy on Mris Boulstred,* or the commercial metaphor of the *Elegie on the Lord Chamberlain:*

> no familie
> Ere rigg'd a soule for heavens discoverie
> With whom more Venturers more boldly dare
> Venture their states. . . . (I, 287)

But the fault of bathos is not peculiarly metaphysical; any poet aiming at an elevated style may collapse into the bathetic, Milton and Wordsworth no less than Cowley and Donne; and there is nothing much to be observed about the collapse when it has occurred. It is really the third variety of false or wrong effect which is of special metaphysical concern. Crashaw is the most troubling poet, and the problem is, supposing the taste to be bad, in what context is it bad? Is a grotesque metaphor bad because of the kind of thing attempted or because of the way it is performed? When we object to some of Crashaw's erotic-devotional verse, are we really objecting to the poet's technique or to his subject?

Most discussions of the literary artist's rights and responsibilities with regard to his subject take as the extreme examples themes of unqualified nastiness. As a painter, we say, may choose to represent a pile of garbage and yet represent it beautifully, so a poet may describe filthy and depraved experiences, wretchedness and horror, and yet derive from them beauty. Henry James has said many cogent and pertinent things about the folly of quarreling with a literary artist's *donnée;* and so long as we presume the subject to be such as may produce one single effect, one harmonious impression, the notion does not seem open to serious challenge. But whether or not there are subjects essentially incongruous, there certainly are combinations of subjects which invite if they do not necessarily involve incongruity. One of Donne's frequent themes, and Crashaw's primary topic, the yearning for a physical union with the deity, seems almost to defy the possibility of a unified emotional reaction. Its inherent tensions, if pushed very far, must either explode into a joke or balloon into a grotesque. With Donne the topic seems to have remained essentially a metaphor, a bit of conscious hyperbole; when he speaks of God ravishing him, or of his amorous soul courting Christ's mild dove, he is using language which he knows (and sometimes explicitly tells us, as in *Holy Sonnet XIII*) is exaggerated and "poetic." This is merely an inversion of the sort of semi-blasphemous joke that occurs in *The Relique*, where he glances at a comparison between himself and Jesus Christ; if it were anything more than a joke, it would quickly become intolerable. But in Crashaw's verse, Donne's "puzzled and humorous shuffling of the pieces" becomes a fusion. That is, it becomes a poetic unity; the poet unites feelings and thoughts about things which have, indeed, some points of genuine similarity, but between which common sense maintains a degree of antipathy. And the special quality of his fusion is that he does not try to gloss over the latent antipathy, for to sense it is to sense the depth of the feelings that override it. The poet loves God as a baby loves its mother's breast and as a martyr loves the final spear-thrust, he loves God as a gaping wound and a voluptuous mouth, in sophisticated paradox and childish innocence—until all his imagery becomes, as Mr. Warren has finely said, "a phantasmagoria . . . of shifting, restless appearances."[4] The unity of opposites, of pain with pleasure, life with death, fruition with denial, assertion with surrender, is his favorite theme. It always involves a degree of incongruity, often of incongruity unresolved, a sense of strain and grotesquerie. It is precisely because he succeeds so well in unifying into one assertion, over the most intense opposition, his "highest" thoughts and "lowest" feelings, his most physical sensations and his most spiritual aspirations, that contemporary taste is sometimes revolted and sometimes amused by Crashaw.

One aspect of Crashaw's "bad taste" is the deliberate injection of a homely word or circumstance amid lofty spiritual reflections. His "financial" metaphors are one example; he likes to speak of shares and dividends, investments and profit-sharing by man in Christ and vice-versa. More striking even than this is the conceit in *The Weeper*, whereby the Magdalen's tears are imagined as rising, like cream, to the top of a cosmic bottle:

IV

Upwards thou dost weep.
Heavn's bosome drinks the gentle stream.

Where the milky rivers creep,
Thine floats above; & is the cream.
Waters above th' Heavns, what they be
We'are taught best by thy TEARES & thee.

V

Every morn from hence
A brisk Cherub something sippes
Whose sacred influence
Addes sweetnes to his sweetest Lippes.
Then to his musick. And his song
Tasts of this Breakfast all day long. (259–260)

The transformation of salt tears to milk is queer; raising the butterfat content to make it cream is odder yet. The delicacy of "sippes" gives us a slight respite; but the domestic word "Breakfast" in congruence with the idea of aftertaste (the whole image being underlain by notions of cud-chewing, angelic saliva, and a delicate series of cosmic belches) would seem to be in the worst possible taste. Actually, Crashaw seems to be trying to convey the idea of intimacy in the most intimate terms available to earthly creatures. The underlying metaphor is perhaps that which calls tears the milk of human kindness; the edible aspects of the image are extended from its center, not imposed from without. The fact that there is something slightly nauseating about the terms of this extension is not wholly apart from Crashaw's intent; for it is precisely *human* kindness he is describing, hence incommensurate with the divine nature. The swooning, erotic ecstasy which Crashaw delights to describe is one ultimate expression of a human malaise, but like all others it is inadequate. There is a sort of God (he is Crashaw's) in whose eyes a human being is always a joke in slightly bad taste, particularly when most "heroically" aware of his own human limitations. One doesn't, under these circumstances, know quite where the critical imputation of "bad taste" can meaningfully lie.

Another interesting vulgarity of the same order is that in the epigram *On Our Crucified Lord, Naked and Bloody:*

They'have left thee naked, LORD, O that they had!
This Garment too, I would they had deny'd.
Thee with thy selfe they have too richly clad,
Opening the purple wardrobe in thy side:
O never could there be garment too good
For thee to weare, but this of thine own blood. (85)

Blood is a royal garment as it is precious, purple, and confers a crown; yet it clothes many souls otherwise naked, hence the wound from which it proceeds is a clothes-closet. Nothing, from one point of view, could be more digusting and grotesque. Yet how else to convey the combination of sacred, spiritual preciousness with the vulgar, social utility which is most oddly betrayed by our expression "*Good* Friday"? One may, presumably, feel that it is silly to think about Christ's blood in two such different ways at once; given the objective, it's not clear how one could hit off such a thought more neatly than in a phrase like "purple wardrobe"—though (*because*) in the process decorums wonderfully collide.

Aside from the grating and dynamic plebeianism, Crashaw also has a sometimes disturbing way of dealing with orifices, which he likes to dwell upon. The little poem *On the Wounds of Our Crucified Lord* has an almost surrealist way with a wound:

> O these wakeful wounds of thine!
> Are they Mouthes? or are they eyes?
> Be they mouthes, or be they eyne,
> Each bleeding part some one supplies.
>
> Lo, a mouth! whose full bloom'd lips
> At too deare a rate are roses:
> Lo, a blood-shot eye! that weeps,
> And many a cruell teare discloses.
>
> O thou that on this foot hast laid
> Many a kisse, and many a teare,
> Now thou shalt have all repaid
> What soe're thy charges were.
>
> This foot hath got a mouth and lips
> To pay the sweet summe of thy kisses,
> To pay thy teares, an eye that weeps,
> Instead of teares, such gems as this is.
>
> The difference only this appeares,
> (Nor can the change offend)
> The debt is paid in Ruby-teares
> Which thou in Pearles did lend. (85)

The vulgarity of the bargain ("too deare a rate" and "whatsoe're thy charges were" are touches worthy of Cowley) counterpoints the extravagant wound-imagery; the wounds which become mouths to kiss and eyes to weep have distinctly traumatic overtones, and the sensual cherishing of wounds plays off very finely against the counting-out of a money debt. If we resist the poet's imaginative unification of his feelings about Christ on the grounds that kissing wounds is unlovely and perverse, and counting out change is vulgar, we may seem to quarrel with the poet's central point, that love of Christ includes all extremes and reconciles all contraries. The white tear of innocence is repaid by the red blood of anguish; "nor can the change offend"—or, for that matter, the combination. Under the circumstances, "bad taste" seems an irrelevant notion, and the door is open to any sort of violent incongruity which can be yoked (preferably in the name of religion but really in the interests of any strong feeling) to a higher unity. The difficulty of drawing incongruities together thus becomes a measure of the loftiness of the impulses which unite them; bad taste has become a form of good taste.

Crashaw himself never carried the revolting aspects of his imagery farther than in the epigram on Luke 11, "Blessed be the Paps which thou hast sucked":

> Suppose he had been tabled at thy Teates,
> Thy hunger feels not what he eates:
> Hee'l have his Teat e're long, a bloody one,
> The mother then must suck the son. (80)

The poet here comes close to a direct statement that the Incarnation was a revolting joke on Jesus and Mary; incest, perversion, cannibalism, and the extra incongruity of "tabled at thy Teates" make the quatrain a little gem of encrusted grotesquerie. Most striking of all is the neat, swift, rather pleased tone of the antithesis; in notions not only lovely but familiar, it seems, horrid possibilities may lurk. Certainly in this poem Crashaw can hardly have intended anything but a nasty twist to the spiritual-carnal relation.

Equally outrageous to the conventional sense of decorum, but comic in its startling release of inappropriate connotations is the famous stanza XIX of *The Weeper:*

> And now where're he strayes
> Among the Galilean mountaines,
> Or more unwellcome wayes,
> He's follow'd by two faithfull fountaines;
> Two walking baths; two weeping motions;
> Portable, & compendious oceans. (262)

This deservedly famous stanza reminds one of nothing so much as a landscape by Dali. The Magdalen's grief is grotesque, it distorts her out of all resemblance to humanity. The human features as they distort and break down into tears have usually been accounted ugly; her tears, as they transcend ordinary grief, transcend ordinary ugliness and absurdity. It is not, as grief, even specially acceptable to Christ. The "more unwellcome wayes" are of course those leading to his crucifixion, but in conjunction with the cumulative absurdities at the end of the stanza, they may also be taken to suggest an attitude. Her grief is helpless, uncontrollable, pathetic, yet portable and abridged because of her absurd humanity. One laughs at the images, but one squirms under them too; and this effect can, if Crashaw's art is art and not accident, be taken as meaningful. The whole technique of loosely, floridly extended metaphor seems to culminate in this stanza, which is ridiculous, of course, as an operatic duet between a pair of duellists is ridiculous; the art is developed beyond and in defiance of nature. But its absurdity can be seen as true to a sort of feeling; and if the feeling doesn't assert itself irresistibly over the difficulties imposed by flesh, blood, and a sense of humor, irresistible triumph is not, as I take it, what is intended. The feeling is to be colored by a radical sense of absurdity—even to be derived, by a queer kind of negative emphasis, from the absurdity, as if the absurdity were somehow a guarantee of the point of view from which alone a grief so ghastly could seem absurd. A Christian poet, at least, can scarcely be blamed for assuming, and asking his readers to assume for the moment, a definition of reality which includes more than the humanly demonstrable; and how to suggest such a reality if not through the feelings imagined as appropriate to it?

Severe judges with nineteenth-century tastes used to cite passages from *The Weeper* and similar poems as evidence of Crashaw's complete inability to criticize his own work; Miss Wallerstein, intent on rehabilitating Crashaw, undertook to minimize them as youthful follies, soon outgrown. But Mr. Austin Warren, picking up the old-fashioned view with a difference, was the first to suggest that they are the product of a different sort of taste than conventional "good" taste; not failures to resemble Marvell's *Garden*, but poems formed on a different model altogether.[5] Miss Wallerstein's compromise is charitable, but scarcely seems compatible with the personal chronology of Richard Crashaw; after all, the 1648 version of *The Weeper* added the stanzas on "walking baths," and as Crashaw died early in 1649, one can scarcely dismiss the stanza as immature work. The "purple wardrobe" epigram was first published in *Steps to the Temple* (1646) only three years before his death, and reprinted in 1652, along with the "financial" *Caritas Nimia* and a specially visceral and sanguinary song, *Upon the Bleeding Crucifix*. Crashaw's taste, it appears, developed neither toward nor away from the grotesque metaphor which we consider in "bad taste"; it simply included an area of "very bad taste" within a larger area of "inoffensive taste," and rose occasionally to something we can call "impeccable taste," always provided our standards of taste are purely conventional. In less colored words, Crashaw's images sometimes contain much of the grotesque (plebeian or visceral), sometimes little, sometimes none at all. What they contain they subordinate to a purer harmony sometimes easily, sometimes with difficulty, sometimes only by violent imputation.

That metaphysical devotional poetry of this order involves two radically different sorts of taste rather than two stages in an individual's poetic development may be seen by turning to an example of modern devotional baroque. It is perhaps too early to tell if the so-called *Religious Sonnets* of Dylan Thomas will survive or on what terms, whether because or in spite of their taste, supported by more conventional poems or under impulse of their own buoyancy. But it is clear that enjoyment of poems which describe Christ as a "hang-nail cracked from Adam," the angel Gabriel as a cowboy, and God the Father as an "old cock from nowheres," depends on a taste which is not only metaphysical but includes a tolerance for the baroque and the grotesque.

There is a great deal about Thomas's sonnets that is interesting, aside from their taste. Technically, they are a rare treat—driving, energetic, complex, and lawless. They sometimes accept offrhyme, or assonance as the equivalent of rhyme, and feminine endings as the equivalent of assonance; sometimes they forget recognizable rhymes altogether. Their basic rhyme-pattern is set by the first sonnet of the ten, if my ear serves me, as abcbacdedefgfg, but the c-c rhyme, originally as weak as Adam-scream, soon fades altogether, and some of the other rhymes are forgotten when convenient. The punctuation of particular sonnets is odd; a semicolon, particularly, seems to belong one line down in I,2 and II,6; and a question mark in IV,6 cries out to be made a comma. The grammar as written often defies parsing, the reference of pronouns is chaotic (I's, you's, he's, and we's being used without either distinct or consistent points of reference); and the imagery, always violent and often grotesque, is based in turn on castration, Homer, Apocalypse, Egyptology, pastoral, Wild West, and playing cards.

So dark is the imagery, indeed, that there lingers about even the central theme a whole series of difficulties, the explanations of which have blurred the poetry quite as much as have the difficulties themselves. Mr. Elder Olson, for instance, in an ingenious and persuasive, but (I fear) essentially wrong-headed volume, has recently argued that, among the six levels of symbolism in the sonnets, are included "a level based on ancient myth, principally Greek, representing the fortunes of the sun in terms of the adventurers of the sun-hero Hercules; and a level based on relations of the *constellation* Hercules to other constellations and astronomical phenomena" (*Poetry of Dylan Thomas,* Chicago, 1954, p. 64). Now most of Mr. Olson's levels make good sense without wholesale importations of symbolic material; and so they should do. But Hercules and astronomy must be imposed on the poem by main force. In the first sonnet, for example, Hercules is said to be the "hang-nail cracked from Adam" because he is mortal; but he simply does not fit here for a number of reasons including the facts that (1) he wasn't strictly mortal, (2) he didn't derive from Adam but from Jove and Alcmena, and (3) he isn't properly referred to as a "hang-nail" under any circumstances. Christ on the other hand is subject to none of these disabilities. Considering the poem as a jigsaw puzzle for the moment, Hercules simply does not fit. In the same sonnet, Mr. Olson identifies Hercules with "the gentleman of wounds" because of the shirt of Nessus and because the atlas-eater (Cerberus-death) has bitten out his mandrake. But the shirt of Nessus is pure extrapolation here; no shirt is mentioned, no Nessus or centaur, no Deianira, no treacherous gift, no fire or poison; while the wounds of the atlas-eater might as well be inflicted on Achilles, King David, or the Church Militant as on Hercules.

By the time he has explicated his Herculean way through the first three sonnets, Mr. Olson may well claim a breather—"the Hercules narrative is interrupted"; and when it resumes, so much of the emphasis has shifted to Christ as the central figure in the poem, that one is puzzled to know what Hercules was doing in the first sonnets. It is significant that almost all the references to Hercules and his accompanying cast of characters have to be offset by Mr. Olson through at least one intermediate symbol and sometimes more. Thomas speaks of the gentleman lying graveward "with his furies"; he means to say, apparently, that Hercules is declining to the West followed by Scorpio, Draco, and Serpens Caput. In Sonnet III the tree-tailed worm is "Horned down with skullfoot and the skull of toes"; and this means that Hydra is put down by rising Aries and Cameleopardus, and Cameleopardus who should suggest to us a giraffe is recognized here because (it seems) he does not resemble a giraffe at all, but a sea-nettle and therefore a cephalopod and therefore a skullfoot. The ingenuity of this multiple transposition surpasseth understanding; but bewildering ingenuity is necessary only because Mr. Olson has tried to rebuild the whole poem around one of its very minor and peripheral overtones. There is enough complexity in the sonnets as Thomas wrote them, without adventitious confusions imported from astrology. We shall come closer to appreciating Thomas's verse if we assume that the central theme is just what it appears to be, crucifixion and resurrection; that the "levels of symbolism" are somewhat fewer than half a dozen; and that the point of view is explicitly that at which Crashaw only hinted, that Incarnation represents a vicious joke played by a malicious God on Christ, Mary, and mankind.

The appropriateness of this topic to the metaphysical style is apparent; indeed, the style is inherently sympathetic to the theme, for its essence is the mingling under stress of an over-riding emotion of two disparate spheres amid deliberate overtones of esthetic as well as ethical anguish. But the blinding closeness of Thomas's contrasts has not many parallels in literature; for intensity seems to be the chief value of his style, and the effect is brilliantly achieved by a close, compact grinding together of images under the impulse of a steady, rhythmic pulse and a taut, heavily end-stopped line. The fact that this poetry is "hard reading," as it undoubtedly is, appears to have bulked large enough in many readers' minds to obscure the question, what sort of effect is being aimed at. Thomas evidently intends, like Crashaw, a chaotic mingling of many different sorts of anguish, a phantasmagoria of pain and grief. To achieve this end, he uses language percussively, like a pianist playing with his forearms, creating a furious, barbaric, dissonant clangor, which has all sorts of intensity but not a great deal of structure. Thus, though he has imposed several sorts of uniformity on his material, there is almost nothing about it which could be described as unity. Images are repeated, varied, punned upon, transformed, and trodden down by other images; but there is no one logical or emotional development which exercises control over all others.

In this respect, Thomas's sonnets contrast strikingly with Donne's, or even with Crashaw's poetic style. The searching, darting movement of Donne's thought is proverbial; though the motivating and directing force is generally temperament, the shape it assumes is logical, and it rarely defies logical possibilities, certainly never exaggerates that defiance without qualification or ultimate resolution in a larger logical unity. So with Crashaw; though the movement of images is more emotional than logical, and so the texture of the verse is looser, the images cluster and exalt themselves in a clear pattern of responses to the intensity of the poet's feeling. But when, for example, Thomas in *Sonnet IV* undertakes a series of paradoxical questions in the manner of "Go and catch a falling star," they neither come from anywhere nor lead to anything. The one assertion which seems to derive is the poet's vision of the Resurrection after the Entombment:

> Corset the boneyard for a crooked lad,
> Button your bodice on a hump of splinters,
> My camel's eyes will needle through the shroud.

Of any other poet, it would be ridiculous to say, he has nothing to lead up to but the Resurrection. But here we are faced with a Resurrection which occurs (*Sonnet IV*) before the Crucifixion (*VIII*), and which is not built into an event of any stature anyhow. When his camel's eyes have needled through the shroud, Thomas does not see anything in particular. He goes on to discuss with an orphic absence of verbs, the process of seeing, but says nothing of the central actor or incident:

> Love's reflection of the mushroom features,
> Stills snapped by night in the bread-sided field,
> Once close-up smiling in the wall of pictures,
> Arc-lamped thrown back upon the cutting flood.

Whether one looks at *Sonnet IV* by itself or as one of a sequence, it trails off without either conclusion or attachment; and the accumulated absurdities of the first seven lines lead to no such resolution as their rising energy seems to be preparing for.

The fact is that the sonnets are fragmentary in much the same way as *The Weeper*, but more radically; they lack not only overall form but defined relations between parts. One mark of this lack is a vagueness about the attempts at explication; most of them suffer from a hesitant, either-or tone which seems to contrast with Mr. Olson's energetic imposition of the Hercules-pattern, but is really just another consequence of the fact that the relations between elements—between, say, the bagpipe-breasted sirens and the crucifixion, or the white bear quoting Virgil and two-gunned Gabriel—has been defined by the critic, not the poet. "Maybe Thomas means this or perhaps that." The implication is that it doesn't matter very much which alternative one chooses; and since, in a sense, Thomas himself hasn't made any definite choice, it isn't really up to the reader to choose either . . . All this is well and good; while the rich six-fold complexity invoked by Mr. Olson is no doubt extravagant, there is on the other hand no need to impoverish the poem by forcing it into any flat pattern of unity. Better a fragile fretwork of casually related or unrelated imagery than a schematic allegory torturing unrelated details into artificial unity. But then if the whole structural unity of the poems is resolved into a single drumming, extravagant antithesis, along with all hope for variety of effect, the greater part of our notion of decorum must go by the board.

No one, I take it, is so naive as to suppose there is any decorum about the sonnet as a form to which the value of Thomas's poems can be in any way related. In addition, it appears there is no particular decorum of the subject, which, so long as each individual section is built of sufficiently violent and intensive contrasts, can require of the poet no structure of mood, tone, imagery, temporal order or grammatical assertion. Mr. Hughes might well find the set of puns on Jacob's ladder (*Sonnet II*) in execrable taste. (I should make clear that I write without benefit of Mr. Hughes' actual opinion on Thomas's sonnets; but the specific reference is for example's sake only.) Yet he could scarcely deny that they contribute powerfully to the tangled, intense, contradictory impressions which the poet has undertaken to convey. Will he now argue that these particular impressions, as a given subject matter, are in "bad taste"? Or else withdraw his notions of "bad taste" as irrelevant to this sort of poem? Or perhaps seek some form of compromise in allowing the effects undertaken but condemning the means used to achieve them? The only obstacle to this last procedure is that it would be hard to find an element of "bad taste" in the sonnets which does not contribute directly to the effect chosen by the poet. Hence one concludes that it is folly to apply the ideas of "good" and "bad taste" in any other way than wholesale. If the central meaning of a poem is not subject to the imputation of bad taste, no meaning can attach to a condemnation of ornaments which may be perfectly appropriate to, and expressive of, the central theme. Thus the real complaint against metaphysical poetry is not that it assumes one sort of taste as a touchstone in opposition to all others, but that it casts a doubt on the general relevance of *any* single standard of taste.

Poems may, in fact, be written either for men under tension or for men at rest (there are other categories, but for metaphysical poets this is crucial). Abraham sacrificing Isaac is not possessed of the same taste as Abraham among his flocks and herds and silver and gold and menservants and maidservants and camels and asses. Metaphysical poems are properly written by and for Abrahams on the mountain; they assume a state of tension as primary, and if one sometimes suspects that slitting Isaac's weasand isn't altogether unwelcome to the poets, nothing could make clearer the essential decorous character of the anguish which they find obligatory. Abraham's taste in his anguish is neither better nor worse than his taste at rest; it is simply different, radically different. It is no longer esthetic, or at least purely esthetic; it proclaims itself ethical, and in the very act of repudiating esthetic standards, at its paradoxical best, it fulfills them.

The only decorum which metaphysical poetry retains seems to be that dramatic one which relates to the mind and condition of man. How much of a decorum this actually is may very well be questioned; it is certainly far less strict than decorums based either on form or on subject. In fact, one can scarcely conceive a state of mind so remote from the conventionally placid, smoothly functioning "norm" as not to imply a valid decorum of its own, however primitive. From the point of view of critical values, this leaves matters in a good deal of a mess. One would like to be able to say that certain minds are too commonplace and unstrained, while others are too remote and tormented, to be proper theaters of poetic drama. So, in a sense, one can say—so long as one makes clear that the judgment is purely social, not literary. It is a fair bet that readers of the future will expect rather more play of sentiment over facts than is found, say, in *The Loves of the Plants,* and rather less than one finds in *The Four Zoas*. But the one poem is as decorous to the mind and condition of the writer as the other, or as any intermediate work; our prediction is based merely on a vague, middle-of-the-road notion of human nature, not on a literary principle.

Thus critics cannot place one decorum above another without exalting one subject-matter above another, so that all systems of critical value rest ultimately on systems of general value which are only remotely comparable, if at all. This is a discouraging observation for critics. But writers are not apt to be so seriously disturbed by an all-but-universal relativism. Unprincipled creatures at best, they can rest content with a merest fragment of that value-hierarchy at which the critics' Babel is constantly building. Thomas quite properly welcomed the chance to judge for himself how close poetry can come to the psychopathic and still survive. He drew the line closer than poets since Blake have generally drawn it; there are plenty of reasons for thinking *Angst* so permanent and general a condition of thinking mankind as to more than justify his choice.

Yet our final note should be uneasy. The audience for poetry is always fickle and a treacherous element on which to wager; the more special his commitment, the bolder the venture on which a metaphysical poet embarks. Perhaps a slender pastoral like *Fern Hill* puts down a broader and more tenacious root than the *Religious Sonnets;* though one always hesitates to take an artist at his less strenuous valuation, still it is not unknown that a man's diversions should outlast his more solemnly conceived undertakings. The single contrast to which the metaphysical poet sacrifices so much may repay him poorly. What man, especially poetry-reading man, will be like fifty years from now seems utterly unpredictable; and in this matter particularly the 17th-century parallel falls down completely. For the 17th-century revolution was quick and in its own way relatively thorough; by creating new areas of agreement, new classes of readers and writers, and new vulgar standards of taste, it promptly paved the way for an enlightened literature of which the first great exponent was Dryden. Simplified and standardized, rendered systematic or sentimental, the plain, rational style of Dryden easily became the common possession of all 18th-century Englishmen save fantastics and madmen like Smart and Blake. So splendid an act of uniformity seems unlikely at present. Unless it be sought among the colonial semi-classicals like Roy Campbell and John Manifold, or among those queer old-fashioned hybrids which are peddled under the label of "socialist realism," nothing on the current horizon seems to correspond to the enlightened literature which after the civil wars succeeded the metaphysical age in England. We have Cowleys aplenty but no visible Drydens. The metaphysical style is decaying, sure enough, but no area of agreement, no common definition of reality, appears ready to support the plain, rational style which should take its place.

NOTES

[1] M. Y. Hughes, "Kidnapping Donne," *California Essays in Criticism,* second series, IV, 63. The following editions of the poets were used in this essay: Donne, *Complete Poems,* ed. Grierson; Crashaw, *Poems,* ed. A. R. Waller; Thomas, *Collected Poems.* Page references immediately following quoted passages are to these editions.

[2] Dryden, "Discourse Concerning Satire," *Works* (Cambridge ed.) p. 283; Johnson, *Lives of the English Poets* (Everyman), I, 23.

[3] Coleridge, *Biographia Literaria,* Chap. XIV; Keats, Letter to J. H. Reynolds, 3 Feb. 1818.

[4] James, *The Art of Fiction, passim;* Austin Warren, *Richard Crashaw,* p. 192.

[5] George Saintsbury, *History of Elizabethan Literature,* p. 369; Ruth Wallerstein, *Richard Crashaw, passim;* Warren, op. cit., Chap. III.

DON CAMERON ALLEN

Richard Lovelace: "The Grasse-Hopper"

This poem was written and sent by Lovelace to his fellow poet and royalist, Charles Cotton, sometime after the collapse of the great cause and the execution of King Charles. It is not unlikely that it was written by Lovelace in a moment of dejection after his own imprisonment and impoverishment. The story of the summer grasshopper that makes no provision for winter, that plays its violin while the ants are busy at harvest, obviously supplies the pre-text of the poem. The cavaliers were grasshoppers, and when this poem was written they were learning the lesson of the insect. Any reader can find all of this in "The Grasse-Hopper," and it is not surprising that the poem has been usually described as a simple cavalier lyric, a powerful overflow of alcoholic feelings recollected in adversity. But the poem is richer than it seems on first reading, and an examination of the tradition, of the metaphoric history of the insect that is the subject, will suggest that the theme has emotional possibilities that have not been understood.

> Oh thou that swing'st upon the waving haire
> Of some well-filled Oaten Beard,
> Drunke ev'ry night with a Delicious teare
> Dropt thee from Heav'n, where now th'art reard.
>
> The Joyes of Earth and Ayre are thine intire,
> That with thy feet and wings dost hop and flye;

From *Image and Meaning: Metaphoric Traditions in Renaissance Poetry* (Baltimore: The Johns Hopkins Press, 1960), pp. 80–92. Reprinted by permission of the publishers.

And when thy Poppy workes thou dost retire
  To thy Carv'd Acron-bed to lye.

Up with the Day, the Sun thou welcomst then,
  Sportst in the guilt-plats of his Beames,
And all these merry dayes mak'st merry men,
  Thy selfe, and Melancholy streames.

But ah the Sickle! Golden Eares are Cropt;
  Ceres and *Bacchus* bid good night;
Sharpe frosty fingers all your Flowr's have topt,
  And what sithes spar'd, Winds shave off quite.

Poore verdant foole! and now green Ice! thy Joys
  Large and as lasting, as thy Peirch of Grasse,
Bid us lay in 'gainst Winter, Raine, and poize
  Their flouds, with an o'reflowing glasse.

Thou best of *Men* and *Friends!* we will create
  A Genuine Summer in each others breast;
And spite of this cold Time and frosen Fate
  Thaw us a warme seate to our rest.

Our sacred harthes shall burne eternally
  As Vestall Flames, the North-Wind, he
Shall strike his frost-stretch'd Winges, dissolve and flye
  This *Aetna* in Epitome.

Dropping *December* shall come weeping in,
  Bewayle th' usurping of his Raigne;
But when in show'rs of old Greeke we beginne,
  Shall crie, he hath his Crowne againe!

Night as cleare *Hesper* shall our Tapers whip
  From the light Casements where we play,
And the darke Hagge from her black mantle strip,
  And sticke there everlasting Day.

Thus richer than untempted Kings are we,
  That asking nothing, nothing need:
Though Lord of all what Seas imbrace; yet he
  That wants himselfe, is poore indeed.

At first reading, the poem separates rather naturally into two parts. Stanzas I-V set a familiar measure by recalling in a submerged but subpersonified fashion the literary ancestry of the insect that is the subject. We recognize the subtune at once; it is Anacreon, whose poem on the grasshopper had been earlier translated by Belleau and Cowley. But Lovelace's poem is no forthright rendering; it is a more complicated chorus of voices. With the sixth stanza the imaginative rhythm begins to alter, and not only is Horace heard, but there is also an immediate contrast between the past and the present, between the symbolic history of the grasshopper and the immediate history of the poet and his friends. The prudent morality of stanzas IV and V is rejected and, after a series of variations, replaced by a Horatian act of will. In this artistic voluntary there are both Christian and pagan tones. The remedy for the moment is provided by the doctrine of Horace, although the inner conviction of an infinite present, once satisfaction is procured, is totally Christian. This rough summation, however, must be annotated in terms of Lovelace's gift from his predecessors.

Almost at the beginning of the history of poetic transformations, Anacreon of Teos heard the grasshopper in the fields of summer and put him into song. He took delight in the insect because it could be as drunk as a happy king on dew, because it owned all that it saw about it and took tribute from the seasons. It is beloved of the Muses for its singing, he tells us, and blessed by Phoebus; and if this is not merit enough, the unsuffering song-lover is as ethereal as a god.

Ἀπαθὴς δ', ἀναιμόσαρκος
Σχεδὸν εἶ θεοῖς ὅμοιος.[1]

This in substance is what Anacreon wrote, and the first twelve lines of Lovelace's poem [2] reproduce these themes against a now universal landscape. But in these stanzas there is obviously more than a pleasant rewarming of Anacreon's poem, and we do well to turn the hands of the poetic clock backward for a better understanding.

Hesiod had also known the "blue-winged" grasshopper that perched on green boughs, singing in the heat of the dog days when the beard grew on the oats; [3] the grasshopper that made sonorous odes in the luxuriant months when goats were fattest, wine best, women amorous, and men languid.[4] It is, however, Homer who creates a symbolic prejudice, when he compares the song of the grasshopper to the "lily-like voices" of the old Trojan aristocrats, who chattered on the wall as Queen Helen walked through the wide-way to the Skaian Gate.[5] From poems of this nature, the champions of Charles might imagine that the grasshopper, the βασιλεύς of Anacreon, had aristocratic pretensions; if they did not heed the whisper of these texts, there were those that flatly stated the case. "It is only recently," Thucydides writes of the Athenians, "that their rich old men left off . . . fastening their hair with a tie of golden grasshoppers." [6] The so-called Suidas states that the grasshopper was the insignia of the Athenian nobles because not only was the insect a musician, but like Erechtheus, founder of the city, it was also born of the earth.[7] So the insect that sings throughout the rich and prosperous seasons of the year, the insect of warmth and light, is given the colors of wisdom possessed among the Greeks by the noblemen of Athens.

If for the Greeks the grasshopper is a symbol of the gay months and their magic, if he is also the representative in nature of the ἄριστοι, he is most triumphantly the analogue of the poet-singer, whose verses he so delicately graced throughout antiquity.[8] For this reason Meleager is securely in the tradition when he invokes the grasshopper as the "Muse of the cornlands" (ἀρουραίη Μοῦσα), the song writer of the dryads, the challenger in voice and verse of the great Pan.[9] In one ancient myth, a singing grasshopper, by alighting on the peg from which the lyre string had broken, helped Eunomos of Locris win the prize at the Pythian games by supplying the wanting notes.[10] Another legend, probably invented by Plato, may be used to fortify this one.

Once, when Socrates and Phaedrus were talking, the old philosopher heard the grasshoppers singing and said that they had received gifts from the gods which, in turn, they imparted to men. When the exquisite Phaedrus inquired about the nature of these gifts, Socrates related the following story:

> A lover of the Muses should surely not be ignorant of this. It is said that once these grasshoppers were a race of men that lived before the Muses existed. When the Muses were born and song appeared, they were so moved by pleasure that as they sang, they forgot to eat and death caught them unawares. They live now in the grasshoppers, having that boon from their birth until their death. When they die, they inform the Muses in Heaven who worships them here below. Terpsichore, they tell of those who have honored her in the dance, and thus make them dearer to her; Erato, they tell of her lovers and to each sister they report according to her honorers. But to Calliope, the eldest, and to Urania, the second of the nine, they bear tidings of those who pass their lives in philosophic study and the observance of their spe-

cial music; for these are the Muses, who having Heaven for their particular sphere and words both human and divine, speak most gladly.[11]

So with Plato, whose own musical voice was likened by Timon[12] to the "lily-songs" of the Hecademian grasshoppers, the insects become the apotheoses of human singers who have lost their lives through their love of art. "Dropt thee from Heav'n, where now th'art reard." The insect—Plato's myth and Anacreon's poem intermarry—is now a poet, and the evidence of its transformation, with a further qualification, is found in the writings of Flavius Philostratus.

Among the letters of the author of *Apollonius* and the *Imagines*, books popular with men of the Renaissance, is one commending the poet Celsus to a wealthy patron. This poet, Philostratus writes, has, "as do the good grasshoppers [οἱ χρηστοὶ τέττιγες], devoted his life to song; you will see to it that he is fed on more substantial food than dew."[13] At the touch of metaphor the poet is made a grasshopper; but in the *Apollonius,* Philostratus associates the grasshopper with the plight of men who have lost out. The philosopher Demetrius, exiled to Dicæarchia by the Roman despot, cries out in envy of the singing insects and says to Apollonius that they, at least, are never in danger of persecution and are above human calumny, for they have been set aloft by the Muses so that they "might be the blissful poets of that felicity which is theirs."[14] This comparison of Demetrius is close to the central tone of "The Grasse-Hopper."

By following the tradition through antiquity, we come on imaginative identifications that help us read this seventeenth-century poem. We know that the grasshopper was beloved of the Muses; that it had once been a human artist and continued to accompany and instruct human artists; that it was a king, an aristocrat, a badge of royalty, a poet; and that it was identified with men in political disfavor. This multiple suggestiveness may explain why Cowley translated Anacreon's poem and why Lovelace sought to remake it into something at once familiar yet novel. When we read the first three stanzas of Lovelace's poem, all that we have learned from the Greeks is born again. The grasshopper is drunk on dew, now a "Delicious teare"; he swings from the oaten beard on which Hesiod had placed him, but like the song-obsessed Platonic grasshoppers, he has been "reard" to Heaven. We see at once behind the literal front, for we know that the grasshopper is an aristocrat, a King. We have been reading a poem about a King and a cause that are dead on earth but living in Heaven. The poem has nothing to do with grasshoppers.

Choosing what in many respects was an optimistic symbol, Lovelace annotated it with melancholia. According to the bright Attic tradition, as represented by the poem of Meleager, the grasshopper's music was the anodyne of sorrow, and Lovelace remembers this in the latter lines of the third stanza. But the living grasshopper of the Greek solar months is made a poetic prelude to the inexperienced innocent, "poore verdant foole," who is in Heaven. In this interplay of life and death, tersely suggested by stanzas IV and V, we pass from what is light and warm into the cold darkness of inescapable defeat and death.

> But ah the Sickle! Golden Eares are Cropt;
> *Ceres* and *Bacchus* bid good night;
> Sharpe frosty fingers all your Flowr's have topt,
> And what sithes spar'd, Winds shave off quite.
>
> Poore verdant foole! and now green Ice! thy Joys
> Large and as lasting, as thy Peirch of Grasse,
> Bid us lay in 'gainst Winter, Raine, and poize
> Their flouds, with an o'reflowing glasse.

The quiet warning of the first stanza, which had been further muted by the bright Anacreontic quatrains, is now made into a torrent of trumpets. Behind the allegory of nature and the classical figments, the emotional current of the decade in which the poem was written comes plain. The grasshopper King, who symbolically loved the sun, has been harvested with the harvest. The flowers of his realm are topped by the "sithes" or, spared by these, shaved by the cruel winds. The merry men, faced by winter, look to the lesson of the summer singer. At this point, too, the poet makes his own self-identifications, for all that antiquity had attributed to the grasshopper—the sign of the aristocrat, the symbol of the poet-singer, and the man in political ill favor—suit him. The emphasis is solemn enough and with it Lovelace remembers many things. He recalls, perhaps, the legend of the impotent Tithonus, but he expresses the tragedy of the summer-happy insect with that prudent variant of the Aesopica.[15] He leaves the myrtles and laurels of the Greek sea islands to inhabit for a while the north of cold and sunlessness.

In the gathering shadows of the world of death we hear for a moment an ancient funeral chant. The crops are harvested. Ceres and Bacchus have departed to a deeper sleep than that enjoyed by the sunlight grasshopper when its "Poppy workes." Winter has frozen even Fate. The North Wind strikes with "his frost-stretch'd Winges."

December comes in tears far different from those that "Dropt thee from Heav'n." Sullenly, the "darke Hagge" hangs about "light Casements." Anacreon's season is over. Nature is now sternly present, thinly veiling with her realities the parallel actualities of the poet's life. We leave the dark external world to enter the poet's heart. In this black moment of cold, the Christian tone begins, for Lovelace remembers the once bright celebration of the wintered year.

> Dropping *December* shall come weeping in,
> Bewayle th' usurping of his Raigne;
> But when in show'rs of old Greeke we beginne,
> Shall crie, he hath his Crowne againe!

Pathos and hope, together with December memories of the Roman Saturnalia, are joined in this somberly happy stanza, but to increase its emotion we must remember the Christmas prince, who wore his crown during the festivities of the Christmas week as proudly as Charles had worn his.[16] But the royalty of Christmas, shared by all who kept the feast, had been despoiled, as the royalists were despoiled, by the new masters of the state. For a number of years John Evelyn recorded the dismal fall of the Christmas king. One of his entries reads: "Christmasday, no sermon any where, no church being permitted to be open, so observed it at home." [17]

Lovelace's solution, like Evelyn's, is based on privacy and withdrawal. The aristocratic poets may be the victims of a frosty fortune, but they can "create / A Genuine Summer in each others breast," a summer that inwardly is more real than the winters of Nature and Fate. So when December comes lamenting the usurping of "his Raigne," the "his" means both the King of England and the King of Christmas. To emend this tragic state, Lovelace and Cotton can make bowers in each other's breasts where the two rejected kings may dwell with them. By this act of the imagination, Christian in its import (for "the Kingdom of Heaven is within you"), they will privately establish a reality greater than the facts allow. To the winter rains, which are December's tears as opposed to those that banished Ceres wept for the crops, the poets will offer a counterblast, "show'rs of old Greeke," wine and, perhaps, the Greek point of view. Both they and the mourning month can then say of the two dead kings, "he hath his Crowne againe."

It could be said that "The Grasse-Hopper," in spite of these more subtle undertones, is simply a cavalier drinking song, not unlike Cotton's "Chanson à Boire" or "Clepsydra." Alcohol had always been a cavalier cure, and Alexander Brome can advise his friends to seek refuge in wine, "in big-bellied bowls," "true philosophy lies in the bottle." Some of this drunken logic certainly seeps into Lovelace's poem; in fact, it is the ostensible mode. We must not forget that the poem, though it began in death, passed into warmth and light, that though we are now in the night and the cold, we shall emerge into an eternal beatitude that will cancel temporal despair. A consciousness of eternity is present in this poem even when the metaphors of death and despair are paraded in stanzas IV and V; it comes resolutely forward in "Our sacred harthes shall burne eternally / As Vestall Flames." Opposed to the North Wind, the savage symbol of death and evil, are the virginal fires of the ever burning hearth within the human heart. This is the kingdom of the heart—this "Aetna in Epitome"; but it is also something that cannot be lost because it is something "we will create." The general state has perished and Lovelace proposes to replace it with another state, one that is inner, private.

The kingdom of the heart that Lovelace would restore is not one of retreat and withdrawal, the resolution in isolation that charmed so many of his fellow sufferers; [18] it is rather a revision of his own cosmogony. The hovering emblem of the winged North Wind, against which Lovelace directs the symbolic fires of the "sacred harthes," makes firm this revision; for Lovelace must have seen in Aquilo, as Milton did, the bony face of death. The wind that the ancients called "horrisonus," "saevus," "ferus," "horrifer," and "crudelis" was a bitter symbol for this generation. Evil was North, from whence streamed the gonfalon of death, a banner that men said blew significantly "ab sinistro." [19] The vestal fires that blast with their heart heat the North and the cold, the "show'rs of old Greeke" that dry up tears and rain, are augmented in their symbolic services by the display of lights that whip the "darke Hagge" of Night from "the light Casements." Within themselves, the frozen poets will remake the lost summer of the grasshopper. It is more than a lost summer; it is a shore of light as Vaughan would have understood it. This will be done, Lovelace informs Cotton, by means of candles as potent as the planet Venus, the "cleare *Hesper*." They are candles in the way that the fire is a fire; in one sense they are wax, in another, they are an inward light. By them Night is stripped forever of her dark cloak, for they will "sticke there everlasting Day." The warmth and brightness of the grasshopper's year, realized literally and, consequently, finitely in the early part of the poem, are thus made eternal. The poet puts down Gothic horror; the grasshopper is made immortal; antique fearlessness is restored.

With the last stanza, the king, who has until now been hidden from us by a series of artistic translucencies, is revealed in his clear title. He is more than king of the summer fields or of Britain, for in governing the world of his creative imagination, he is untempted by the world. The poet and his friend, who may also be the "himselfe" of the last line, have created a kingdom privately. This kingdom cannot go down because it is invincible to outward attack. With this last stanza, the Horatian music that we have heard steadily since the dreary center of stanza V seems to achieve symphonic fullness. We have the impression of the Horatian tone because we know it has to be here. Horace, who fought on the wrong side at Philippi, must have appeared to Lovelace and Cotton as a Roman cavalier who, when all was lost, found the good way. His metaphors repeat themselves once more. The tempest comes with the rain and the North Wind, but one forgets them before a heaped fire and a full cup.

> Horrida tempesta caelum contraxit, et imbres
> Nivesque deducunt Iovem; nunc mare, nunc silvae
> Threicio Aquilone sonant. Rapiamus, amici,
> Occasionem de die, dumque virent genua
> Et decet, obducta solvatur fronte senectus.
> Tu vina Torquato move consule pressa meo.
> Cetera mitte loqui: deus haec fortasse benigna
> Reducet in sedem vice.[20]

In Horace's poetic promises there is little eternity; this illusion is shunned. The fire on the Sabine hearth is as real as the wind and the rain. It is Lovelace who creates the illusion for which he lives. In another sense "himselfe" may not be Cotton at all, but the private world of the poet's heart, where all is warm and light and the grasshopper lives in a kingdom made eternal by his song.

NOTES

[1] XXXIV. 17–18. The Greeks do not distinguish clearly between the various singing insects, and it is not always clear what they mean when they use τεττιξ, καλαμαια, μάντις and ἀκρίς. The translators have done little better, for Anacreon's poem is probably about the cicada.

[2] I have used the text of C. H. Wilkinson (Oxford, 1930). The two last lines of the third stanza may be paraphrased as "days make men merry, yourself merry, and melancholy streams away" or "make melancholy streams (rivers) also merry."

[3] "Shield of Achilles," *Opera*, ed. Flach (Leipzig, 1878), pp. 393–400.

[4] *Theogony* 581–6.

[5] *Iliad* III. 151–3.
[6] *History* I. 6.
[7] *Historica* (Basel, 1564), col. 959.
[8] It is everywhere part of rural decoration; see Theocritus XVI. 94–6; Vergil *Eclogues*. II, 12–13; *Georgics* III, 328; "Culex" 151; *Copa* 27–8. The *Greek Anthology* is filled with poems to the grasshopper; see VII. 189–94, 197–8, 201; IX. 92.
[9] *Greek Anthology* VII. 195–6.
[10] Strabo *Geography* VI. 1, 9. Paulus Silentiarius (G.A., VI, 54) puts this myth into elegant verse.
[11] *Phaedrus* 259. I cannot find this legend in any text prior to Plato's; Photius mentions it as if it were common knowledge (*Bibliotheca* [*PG*, CIII, 1354]).
[12] Diogenes Laertius *Lives* III. 7.
[13] *Opera*, ed. Kayser (Leipzig, 1870), p. 364.
[14] Ibid., p. 261.
[15] The fable of the industrious ant and the careless grasshopper was popularized in the Middle Ages by Alexander Neckham (*Novus Aesopus* XXIX). It also appears in various French redactions; see J. Bastin, *Recueil Général des Isopets* (Paris, 1929), and Marie de France, *Poésies*, ed. De Roquefort (Paris, 1832), II, 123–5. Seneca suggests the legend in *Epistolae Morales* LXXXVII. 19–20. The early Fathers think of the insect in the metaphoric manner of the poets (Ambrose, *Hexameron* [*PL*, XIV. 251–2]), or commend it for some Christian quality (Gregory, *Oratio* [*PG*, XXXVI, 59]; and Jerome, *Epistulae* XXII. 18).
[16] The career of such a prince, who had in his titles the distinction of "high Regent of the Hall" (probably Gloucester Hall, Lovelace's college) has come down to us in an eyewitness account; see G. Higgs, *An Account of the Christmas Prince, as it was exhibited in the University of Oxford in the year 1607* (London, 1816).
[17] See the *Diary* (de Beer edition) for December 25 in 1652, 1654, 1655. The parliamentary order of December 19, 1644, abolished the observance of Christmas.
[18] On the cavaliers' praise of solitude as an escape from the evils of the Commonwealth, see H. G. Wright, "The Theme of Solitude and Retirement in Seventeenth Century Literature," *Études Anglaises*, VII (1954), 22–35.
[19] For some associations, see St. Augustine, *In Iobam*, ed. Zycha (Vienna, 1895), p. 608, and his *Epistulae*, ed. Goldbacher (Vienna, 1904), p. 201; see also Eucherius, *Liber Formularum* (*PL*, L, 740–41).
[20] *Epodes* XIII. 1–8; *Carmina* I. 9, 5–8, 13–14; 17; 18; II. 7, 11.

FRANK KERMODE

The Argument of Marvell's "Garden"

I

"The Garden" is an *étude d'exécution transcendante* which has been interpreted by so many virtuosi in the past few years that a stiff-fingered academic rendering is unlikely to be very entertaining. However, since it appears that the brilliant executants have been making rather too many mistakes, there may be some value in going slowly over the whole piece.

It may be useful to point out in advance that these mistakes are of three kinds. The first is historical, as when Mr. Milton Klonsky, writing in the *Sewanee Review* (LVIII, 16–35), seizes on a passage in Plotinus as the sole key to the poem. He is wrong, not because there is no connection at all between Plotinus and Marvell's lyric, but because he has misunderstood the relationship and consequently exaggerated its importance. He fails to observe that Marvell, like other poets of the period, uses philosophical concepts, including those of Neo-Platonism, in a special way, with reference not to the body of formal doctrine in which those concepts are originally announced, but to genres of poetry which habitually and conventionally make use of them. The process is familiar enough; for example, the nature of the relationship between pastoral poetry and philosophic material such as the debates on Action and Contemplation, Art and Nature, is tolerably well understood. It is not customary to find the only key to the works of Guarini or Fletcher in some Greek philosopher; but these poets have

From *Essays in Criticism*, II (1952), pp. 225–41. Reprinted by permission of the publishers.

not, like Donne and Marvell, been distorted by the solemn enthusiasm of modern exegetes. In a sense all philosophical propositions in Marvell are what Professor Richards used to call "pseudo-statements," and his is a "physical" rather than a "platonic" poetry. However, rather than risk myself in these deep waters, I shall support myself on a raft of Mr. Wellek's construction: "The work of art . . . appears as an object *sui generis* . . . a system of norms of ideal concepts which are intersubjective. . . ." Above all, it is possible "to proceed to a classification of works of art according to the norms they employ" and thus "we may finally arrive at theories of genres."[1] The point is that we must not treat these "norms" as propositions, for if we do we shall fall into the toils of Mr. Klonsky. Miss Ruth Wallerstein, who has worked so hard and so sanely to liberate seventeenth-century poetry from modern error, is none the less guilty of Mr. Klonsky's fault, in her *Studies in Seventeenth Century Poetic* (1950). Not only the indolent cry out against the suggestion that "The Garden" needs to be explicated in terms of Hugo of St. Victor and Bonaventura. Doubtless there is, for the historian of ideas, a real connection between the poem and the Victorine and Neo-Platonic systems of symbolic thought; for there is a connection between Plato and "Trees." However interesting this may be, it has nothing to do with what most of us call criticism. If we read "The Garden" as historians of poetry, and not as historians of ideas, we shall resist all such temptation to treat the "norms" as ideas, even if it proceeds from Diotima herself, to whom Professor Richards succumbed in a recent lecture on the poem.

The second kind of mistake is one which, particularly when it assumes its more subtle shape, we are all liable to yield to, though it appears to be seductive even in its usual grossness. Sufficient, however, to say that "The Garden" must not be read as autobiography. "What was Marvell's state of mind as he wandered in Fairfax's Yorkshire garden?" is a very bad question to ask, but it is obviously one which comes readily to the minds of learned and subtle interpreters; both Marvell and Donne have suffered greatly from this form of misapplied scholarship, and it is comforting to reflect that the date of "The Garden," is quite unknown, so that it cannot be positively stated to be the direct record of some personal experience at Nun Appleton. It could conceivably have been written much later. The pseudo-biographical critic is wasteful and deceptive; he diverts attention from the genre just as certainly as Mr. Klonsky does when he presents a picture of the poet torturing himself with Chinese boxes of Forms, or Mr. Empson when he invites us to reflect upon the Buddhist enlightenment (*Some Versions of Pastoral*, pp. 119–20).

The third kind of critical failure is clearly, in this case, the most important, for the others would not have occurred had there not been this cardinal error. It is the failure to appreciate the genre (the system of "norms" shared by other poems) to which "The Garden" belongs. Despite the labours of Miss Bradbrook, Miss Lloyd Thomas,[2] and Miss Wallerstein, poets like Théophile, Saint-Amant, Randolph, Lovelace, Fane and Stanley have simply not been put to proper use in the criticism of Marvell. This is the central difficulty, and the one which this paper is intended to diminish. The first necessity is to distinguish between the genre and the history of the ideas to which the genre is related.

II

"We cannot erre in following Nature": thus Montaigne, "very rawly and simply," with this addition: "I have not (as *Socrates*) by the power and vertue of reason, corrected my natural complexions, nor by Art hindered mine inclination." [3] This is a useful guide to that aspect of "naturalism" in the thought of the late Renaissance which here concerns us. The like consideration governs all the speculations of the older Montaigne; Nature is to be distinguished from Custom; the natural inclinations are good, and sensual gratifications are not the dangerous suggestions that other and more orthodox psychologies hold them to be. Sense and instinct seek and find their own temperance without the interference of reason. It is good to satisfy a natural appetite, and it is also, of course, innocent. Thus men behaved, says Montaigne, in the Golden World, and thus they still behave in the Indies.

The question how far Montaigne believed in his own "primitivism" seems to me a difficult one, but it scarcely concerns us at the moment. It is legitimate to use him as spokesman for naturalism; and before we leave him it will be prudent to glance at some of his references to Plato, in order to have at hand some record of the naturalist reaction to the Platonic theory of love. In short, as the foregoing quotation implies, Platonic love is rejected. No longer "an appetite of generation by the mediation of beauty," love is in fact "nothing else but an insatiate thirst of enjoying a greedily desired subject" (III, 105). "My Page makes love, and understands it feelingly; Read *Leon Hebraeus* or *Ficinus* unto him; you speake of him, of his thoughts and of his actions, yet undersands he nothing what you meane . . ." (III, 102). Much more sympathetic are "the ample and lively descriptions in *Plato,* of the loves practised in his dayes" (III, 82). If one is not overcareful—if, for instance, one fails to discriminate between the orations of Socrates and those who precede him, one may without much difficulty extract from the *Symposium* itself very different theories of love from those developed by Ficino or Milton. In Marvell's own youth antithetical versions of Platonism flourished contemporaneously at Cambridge and at Whitehall.

So far we have concerned ourselves, very briefly, with the informal naturalism of Montaigne, and hinted at a naturalistic version of Plato. What of the poetry which concerns itself with similar issues? One thinks at once of Tasso, and specifically of that chorus in his *Aminta, O bella età de l'oro,* which was so often imitated and debated in the poetry of the age. In the happy Golden Age lovers concerned themselves with their own love and innocence, and not with honour, that tyrant bred of custom and opinion, that enemy of nature. In the garden of the unfallen just, whatever pleases is lawful. The paradise of these fortunate innocents is abundant in its appeal to the senses; law and appetite are the same, and no resolved soul interferes with the banquet of sense offered by created pleasure. Thus an ancient pastoral tradition accommodates new poetic motives, and poetry, though affirming nothing, strengthens its association with the freer thought of its time. The formal opposition to Tasso's statement is properly made in poetry which belongs to the same genre; and it may be found in the Chorus in Act IV of Guarini's *Il Pastor Fido*. Parallel debates could go on in the great world, and in the little world of poetry; the debate about naturalism was a serious one, since it involved theological censures. The poetical debate is of a different quality. The proper answer to Tasso is Guarini's. A genre of poetry developed which assumed the right to describe the sensuality of a natural Eden, and a specialized kind concentrated on sexual gratifications as innocent, and the subject of unreasonable interference from Honour. The proper reply is, again, in terms of the "norms" of the genre, and there is evidence that the very poets who stated the extreme naturalist case were quite capable of refuting it. One might call the "norms" of the refutation an anti-genre. "The Garden" is a poem of the anti-genre of the naturalist paradise.

Marvell therefore rejects the naturalist account of love, and with it that Platonism which was associated with the delights of the senses. The poets of the Renaissance were profitably aware of the possible antitheses in Platonic theories of love, just as they were aware of Plato's argument against their status as vessels of the truth.[4] Spenser makes comfortable bedfellows of two Platonisms in his *Hymns;* the two Aphrodites easily change into each other in poem and emblem. Nothing is more characteristic of Renaissance poetry than the synthesis of spiritual and erotic in poetic genre and image. It was encouraged by centuries of comment on the *Canticum Canticorum* and the eclecticism of mystics as well as by the doctrinaire efforts of Bruno to spiritualize the erotic Petrarchan conceits. Much more evidence could be brought, if it were necessary, to establish the existence of genre and anti-genre in Platonic love-poetry. They not only co-exist, but suggest each other. Marvell could pass with ease from the libertine garden to the garden of the Platonic *solitaire,* soliciting the primary *furor* of spiritual ascent. (The ease of such transitions was partly responsible for the development of another genre—that of the palinode.)

"The Garden" stands in relation to the poetry of the gardens of sense as the *Hymn of Heavenly Beauty* stands in relation to the *Hymn of Beauty*. It is poetry written in the language of, or using the "norms" of, a genre in a formal refutation of the genre. In fact, this was a method Marvell habitually used, sometimes almost with an affectation of pedantry, as I have elsewhere shown of "The Mower Against Gardens." [5]

III

The garden is a rich emblem, and this is not the place to explore it in any detail; indeed I shall say nothing of the symbolic gardens of the Middle Ages which were still alive in the consciousness of the seventeenth century. The gardens to which Marvell most directly alludes in his poem are the Garden of Eden, the Earthly Paradise, and that garden to which both Stoic and Epicurean, as well as Platonist, retire for solace or meditation. The first two are in many respects one and the same; the third is the garden of Montaigne, of Lipsius, and of Cowley. I shall not refer to the *Hortus conclusus,* though at one point in my explication of Marvell's poem I allude to a Catholic emblem-writer. Doubtless the notion of Nature as God's book affects the poetic tradition; it certainly occurs in poems about solitude at this period. But I think it is misleading to dwell on the history of the idea.

Of the complexity of the Earthly Paradise, with all its associated images and ideas, it is not necessary to say much: it is of course a staple of pastoral poetry and drama, and the quality of Marvell's allusions to it will emerge in my explication. But a word is needed about the garden of the solitary thinker, which Marvell uses in his argument against the libertine garden of innocent sexuality.

It is to be remembered that we are not dealing with the innocence of Tasso's Golden Age, where there is a perfect concord between appetite and reason, or with the garden of innocent love that Spenser sketches in *Faerie Queene*, IV, x, where "thousand payres of louers walkt, Praysing their god, and yeelding him great thankes," and "did sport Their spotlesse pleasures, and sweet loues content." The libertines use the argument of the innocence of sense to exalt sensuality and to propose the abolition of the tyrant Honour, meaning merely female chastity. This is the situation of the *Jouissance* poetry which was fashionable in France, and of which Saint-Amant's well-known example, excellently translated by Stanley, is typical. It is equally the situation of Randolph's "Upon Love Fondly Refused" and his "Pastoral Courtship," Carew's "Rapture" and Lovelace's "Love Made in the first Age." In Randolph's Paradise there is no serpent—"Nothing that wears a sting, but I" [6]—and in Lovelace's

> No Serpent kiss poyson'd the Tast
> Each touch was naturally Chast,
> And their mere Sense a Miracle.[7]

And so it is throughout the libertine versions of sensual innocence. The garden, the place of unfallen innocence, is identified with a naturalist glorification of sensuality. The garden which is formally opposed to this one by Marvell is the garden where sense is controlled by reason and the intellect can contemplate not beauty but heavenly beauty.

It was Montaigne, this time in his Stoic role, who gave wide currency to the pleasures of *solitary* seclusion. The relevant ideas and attitudes were developed into a poetic genre. Many poets certainly known to Marvell practised this genre, among them Fane and Fairfax and the French poets, notably Saint-Amant, whose *Solitude* demonstrates how easily he moved in this, the antithesis of the *Jouissance* mode. This famous poem was translated by Fairfax and by Katharine Phillips. This is the poetry of the meditative garden, whether the meditation be pseudo-Dionysian, or Ciceronian, or merely pleasantly Epicurean, like Cowley's. There is, of course, a play of the senses in which woman has no necessary part, though the equation of all appetite with the sexual appetite in the libertines tends to ignore it; this unamorous sensuality is firmly castigated by Lipsius in his treatment of gardens. If the garden is treated merely as a resort of pleasure, for the "inward tickling and delight of the senses" it becomes "a verie sepulchre of slothfulnes." The true end of the garden is "quietnes, withdrawing from the world, meditation," the subjection of the distressed mind to right reason.[8] The true ecstasy is in being rapt by intellect, not by sex.

Retirement; the study of right reason; the denial of the sovereignty of sense; the proper use of created nature: these are the themes of Marvell's poem laboriously and misleadingly translated into prose. As poetry the work can only be studied in relation to its genre, though that genre may be related to ethical debates. To the naturalist *Jouissance* Marvell opposes the meditative *Solitude*. The fact that both these opposed conceptions are treated in the work of one poet, Saint-Amant, and a little less explicitly in Théophile and Randolph also, should warn against the mistaking of seriousness for directness of reference to ethical propositions. "The Garden" uses and revalues the "norms" of the genre: it is not a contribution to philosophy, and not the direct account of a contemplative act.

IV

Henry Hawkins, the author of the emblem-book *Partheneia Sacra*, adopts a plan which enables him, in treating the emblematic qualities of a garden, to direct the attention of the pious reader away from the delights of the sense offered by the plants to a consideration of their higher significance. As in Marvell, sensual pleasure has to give way to meditation.[9] We now proceed to the explication of Marvell's poem, with a glance at Hawkins's wise disclaimer: "I will not take upon me to tel al; for so of a Garden of flowers, should I make a Labyrinth of discourse, and should never be able to get forth" (p. 8).

The poem begins by establishing that of all the possible gardens it is dealing with that of retirement, with the garden of the contemplative man who shuns action. The retired life is preferred to the active life in a witty simplification: if the two ways of life are appraised in terms of the vegetable solace they provide it will be seen that the retired life is quantitatively superior. The joke is in the substitution of the emblem of victory for its substance. If you then appraise action in terms of plants you get single plants, whereas retirement offers you the solace of not one but *all* plants. This is a typical "metaphysical" use of the figure called by Pluttenham the Disabler. The first stanza, then, is a witty dispraise of the active life, though it has nothing to distinguish it sharply from other kinds of garden-poetry such as libertine or Epicurean—except possibly the hint of a secondary meaning "celibate" in the word *single* and a parallel sexual pun on *close,*[10] which go very well with the leading idea that woman has no place in this garden.

The Innocence of the second stanza cannot itself divide the poem from other garden-poems; for Innocence of a sort is a feature of the libertine paradise, as well as of the Epicurean garden of Cowley and indeed most gardens.

> Your sacred Plants, if here below,
> Only among the Plants will grow—

lines which are certainly a much more complicated statement than that of *Hortus*—seem to have stimulated Mr. Klonsky to astonishing feats. But the idea is not as difficult as all that. Compare "Upon Appleton House"—

> For he did, with his utmost Skill,
> *Ambition* weed, but *Conscience* till,
> *Conscience,* that Heaven-nursed Plant,
> Which most our Earthly Gardens want. (XLV)

Your sacred plants, he says, addressing Quiet and Innocence, are unlike the palm, the oak and the bays in that if you find them anywhere on earth it will be among the plants of the garden. The others you can find "in busie Companies." The joke here is to give Quiet and her sister plant emblems like those of the active life, and to clash the emblematic and the vegetable plants together. The inference is that Innocence may be found only in the green shade (*concolor Umbra* occurs at this point in the Latin version). Society (with its ordinary connotations of "polish" and "company") is in fact all but rude (unpolished) by comparison with Solitude, which at first appears to be lacking in the virtues Society possesses, but which possesses them, if the truth were known, in greater measure (the Ciceronian-Stoic "never less alone than when alone" became so trite that Cowley, in his essay "Of Solitude," apologized for referring to it).

We are now ready for a clearer rejection of libertine innocence. Female beauty is reduced to its emblematic colours, red and white (a commonplace, but incidentally one found in the libertine poets) and unfavourably compared with the green of the garden as a dispenser of sensual delight. This is to reject Saint-Amant's "crime innocent, à quoi la Nature consent." [11] A foolish failure to understand the superiority of green causes lovers to insult trees (themselves the worthier objects of love) by carving on them the names of women. (This happens in Saint-Amant's *Jouissance.*) Since it is the green garden, and not women that the poet chooses to regard as amorous, it would be farcically logical for him to carve on the trees their own names. The garden is not to have women or their names or their love in it. It is natural (green) and amorous (green—a "norm" of the poem) in quite a different way from the libertine garden.

Love enters this garden, but only when the pursuit of the white and red is done, and we are without appetite. (Love is here indiscriminately the pursued and the pursuer. Weary with the race and exertion (*heat*) it "makes a retreat" in the garden; hard-pressed by pursuers it carries out a military retreat.) The place of retreat has therefore Love, but not women: they are metamorphosed into trees. The gods, who might be expected to know, have been misunderstood; they pursued women not as women but as potential trees, for the green and not for the red and white. Marvell, in this witty version of the metamorphoses, continues to "disable" the idea of sexual love. Here one needs quite firmly to delimit the reference, because it is confusing to think of *laurel* and *reed* as having symbolic significations. It is interesting that this comic metamorphosis (which has affinities with the fashionable mock-heroic) was practised for their own ends by the libertine poets; for example, in Saint-Amant's "La Metamorphose de Lyrian et de Sylvie," in Stanley's Marinesque "Apollo and Daphne," in Carew's "Rapture," where Lucrece and other types of chastity become sensualists in the libertine paradise, and very notably in Lovelace. Thus, in "Against the Love of Great Ones":

> *Ixion* willingly doth feele
> The Gyre of his eternal wheele,
> Nor would he now exchange his paine
> For Cloudes and Goddesses againe. (*Poems*, p. 75)

The sensuous appeal of this garden is, then, not sexual, as it is in the libertines. It has, none the less, all the enchantment of the Earthly Paradise, and all its innocence: this is the topic of the fifth stanza. The trees and plants press their fruit upon him, and their gifts are in strong contrast to those of the libertine garden,

> Love then unstinted, Love did sip,
> And Cherries pluck'd fresh from the Lip,
> On Cheeks and Roses free he fed;
> Lasses like *Autumne* Plums did drop,
> And Lads, indifferently did crop
> A Flower, and a Maiden-head. (*Poems*, p. 146)

The fruits of green, not of red and white, are offered in primeval abundance, as they are in the Fortunate Islands or in any paradise.

Everything is by nature lush and fertile; the difference between this and a paradise containing a woman is that here a Fall is of light consequence, and without tragic significance. ("Insnar'd with *flowers, I* fall on grass.") In the same way, Marvell had in "Upon Appleton House" (LXXVII) bound himself with the entanglements not of wanton limbs, in the libertine manner of Carew, Randolph and Stanley, but of woodbine, briar and bramble. The same imagery is still in use for amorous purposes in the poetry of Leigh.

In this garden both man and nature are unfallen; it is therefore, for all its richness, not a trap for virtue but a paradise of perfect innocence. Even the fall is innocent; the sensuous allurements of the trees are harmless, and there is no need to "fence The Batteries of alluring Sense." It is evident that Empson and King were quite right to find here a direct allusion to the Fall.

Modern commentators all agree that the sixth stanza, central to the poem, is a witty Platonism, and of course this is so. The danger is that the Platonism can be made to appear doctrinal and even recherché, when in fact it is reasonably modest, and directly related to genre treatments of love in gardens. There is, however, a famous ambiguity in the first two lines: how are we to take "from pleasure less"? It can mean simply (1) reduced by pleasure, or (2) that the mind retires because it experiences less pleasure than the senses, or (3) that it retires from the lesser pleasure to the greater. The first of these might be related to the doctrine of the creation in *Paradise Lost,* VII, 168f.—"I am who fill Infinitude, nor vacuous the space. Though I uncircumscrib'd myself retire, And put not forth my goodness. . . ." This would be consistent with the analogy later drawn between the human and the divine minds. But the second is more likely to be the dominant meaning, with a proper distinction between mind and sense which is obviously relevant to the theme ("None can chain a mind Whom this sweet Chordage cannot bind"). The third meaning is easily associated with this interpretation. The mind withdraws from the sensual gratification offered in order to enjoy a happiness of the imagination. In terms of the genre, it rejects the *Jouissance* for the *Solitude*—indeed, Saint-Amant, in a poem which prefers the contemplative garden, writes of it thus:

> Tantost, faisant agir mes sens
> Sur des sujets *de moindre estofe,*
> De marche en autre je descens
> Dans les termes du philosophe;
> Nature n'a point de secret

Que d'un soin libre, mais discret,
Ma curiosité ne sonde;
Et, dans ma recherche profonde,
Je loge en moy tout l'univers.
Là, songeant au flus et reflus,
Je m'abisme dans cette idée;
Son mouvement me rend perclus,
Et mon âme en est obsedée. (I, 32; my Italics)

To put it another way, one prefers a different kind of ecstasy from that of the libertine, described by the same poet in his *Jouissance,* which Stanley translated. Saint-Amant represents his solitary as acquiring from nature knowledge of the forms, and the next two lines of Marvell's stanza seem to do likewise. The metaphor is not unfamiliar—"Some have affirm'd that what on earth we find The sea can parallel for shape and kind"—and the idea is that the forms exist in the mind of man as they do in the mind of God. By virtue of the imagination the mind can create worlds and seas too which have nothing to do with the world which is reported by the senses. This is the passage which seems to have caused such trouble to commentators, who look to learned originals like Plotinus and Ficino for the explanation: but in fact the Platonism here is dilute and current.

It is commonplace of Renaissance poetic that God is a poet, and that the poet has the honour of this comparison only because of the creative force of fancy or imagination. Nor is the power exclusive to poets. The mind, which "all effects into their causes brings,"[12] can through the imagination alone devise new and rare things: as Puttenham says, "the phantasticall part of man (if it be not disordered) is a representer of the best, most comely and bewtifull images or apparences of thinges to the soule and according to their very truth" (p. 19). Puttenham shuns "disordered phantasies . . . monstruous imaginations or conceits" as being alien to the truth of imagination, but it is conceivable that Marvell, in his suggestion of the mind's ability to create, refers to a more modern psychology and poetic, with its roots in the Renaissance, but with a new emphasis. Thus Cowley in his Pindaric "The Muse" says that the coach of poetry can go anywhere:

And all's an *open Road* to *thee.*
Whatever *God* did say,
Is all thy plain and smooth, uninterrupted *Way.*
Nay, ev'n beyond his *Works* thy *Voyages* are known,
Thou hast a thousand *Worlds* too of thine *own.*

> Thou speak'st, great *Queen*, in the same *Stile* as *he*,
> And *a new World* leaps forth, when *thou* say'st, *Let it be*.

And in a note he obligingly explains this:

> The meaning is, that *Poetry* treats not only of all Things that are, or can be, but makes *Creatures* of her own, as *Centaurs, Satyrs, Fairies*, &c., makes *Persons* and *Actions* of her own . . . makes *Beasts, Trees, Waters*, and other irrational and insensible Things to act above the Possibility of their Natures as to *understand* and *speak;* nay makes what *Gods* it pleases too without *Idolatry*, and varies all these into innumerable *Systems*, or *Worlds* of Invention.

These other worlds are thoughts in the mind of man as the world is a thought in the mind of God. Empson is probably right in his guess that *streight* means "packed together" as well as "at once." The whole idea is illuminated by a passage of extraordinary interest in Leigh (who was imbued with that passion for optics which later became common among poets) in which the reduced images of the eye are contrasted with the illimitable visions of the mind. The mind contains everything undiminished by the deficiencies of sense.[13] The mental activity which Marvell is describing is clear; it is the working of the imagination, which, psychologically, follows sense and precedes intellection, and is therefore the means of rejecting the voluptuous suggestions of sense; and which "performs its function when the sensible object is rejected or even removed."[14] The mind's newly created worlds are, in the strict sense, phantasms, and without substance: and since they have the same mental status as the created world, it is fair to say that "all that's made" is being annihilated, reduced to a thought.

But a green thought? This is a great bogey; but surely the thought is green because the solitude is green, which means that it is also the antithesis of voluptuousness? Here the normative signification of green in the poem is in accord with what is after all a common enough notion —green for innocence, Thus, in "Aramantha" Lovelace asks:

> Can trees be green, and to the Ay'r
> Thus prostitute their flowing Hayr? (*Poems*, p. 112)

But I cannot think the green has any more extensive symbolic intention. Green is still opposed to red and white; all this is possible only when women are absent and the senses innocently engaged.

The stanza thus alludes to the favourable conditions which enable the mind to apply itself to contemplation. The process is wittily described, and the psychology requires no explanation in terms of any doctrinaire Platonism, whether pseudo-Dionysian, Plotinian, or Florentine.

The seventh stanza is also subject to much ingenious comment. The poet allows his mind to contemplate the ideas, and his soul begins a Platonic ascent. Here there are obvious parallels in the English mystics, in Plotinus, in medieval and Florentine Platonism; but we must see this stanza as we see the rest of the poem, in relation to the genre. Failing to do this we shall be involved in an endless strife between rival symbolisms, as we are if we try to find an external significance for *green.* As it is, there is no need to be over-curious about the fountain; its obvious symbolic quality may have an interesting history, but it is primarily an easily accessible emblem of purity As for the use of the bird as an emblem of the soul, that is an image popularized by Castiglione,[15] and used by Spenser of the early stages of the ascent:

> Beginning then below, with th'easie vew
> Of this base world, subject to fleshly eye,
> From thence to mount aloft by order dew,
> To contemplation of th'immortall sky,
> Of that soare faulcon so I learne to fly,
> That flags awhile her fluttering wings beneath,
> Till she her selfe for stronger flight can breath.
> (*Hymne of Heavenly Beauty,* pp. 22–8)

Spenser has just passed from the consideration of woman's love and beauty to the heavenly love and beauty. The bird which prepares its wings for flight is evidently a symbol with as settled a meaning as the dew, which Marvell also shared with many other poets.

The hungry soul, deceived with false beauties, may have "after vain deceiptfull shadowes sought"—but at last it looks "up to that soveraine light, From whose pure beams al perfect beauty springs" (*H.H.B.,* 291, 295). Marvell's bird "Waves in its Plumes the various Light." Once more we might spring to Ebreo or Plotinus or even Haydocke, but we shall do better to note how this same image is used in literature more closely related to Marvell.

> Les oyseaux, d'un joyeux ramage,
> En chantant semblent adorer
> La lumière qui vient dorer
> Leur cabinet et leur plumage—

thus Théophile, in his Ode, "Le Matin."[16] In *Partheneia Sacra* Hawkins uses the dove as other poets use the dew or the rainbow—

> Being of what coulour soever, her neck being opposed to the Sun wil diversify into a thousand coulours, more various then the Iris it-self, or that Bird of *Juno* in al her pride; as scarlet, cerulean, flame-coulour, and yealding a flash like the Carbuncle, with vermilion, ash-coulour, and manie others besides. . . . (p. 202)

Marvell's use of the Platonic light-symbolism is therefore not technical, as it might be in Chapman, but generalized, as in Quarles or Vaughan, and affected by imagery associated with the garden genres. We are thus reminded that the point about the ascent towards the pure source of light is not that it can be achieved, but that it can be a product of *Solitude* rather than of *Jouissance* and that it is an alternative to libertine behaviour in gardens. It is the ecstasy not of beauty but of heavenly beauty.

The eighth stanza at last makes this theme explicit. This is a special solitude, which can only exist in the absence of women, the agents of the most powerful voluptuous temptation. This has been implied throughout, but it is now wittily stated in the first clear reference to Eden. The notion that Adam would have been happy without a mate is not, of course, novel; St. Ambrose believed it. Here it is another way of putting the case that woman offers the wrong beauty, the wrong love, the red and white instead of the green. Eve deprived Adam of solitude, and gave him instead an inferior joy. Indeed she was his punishment for being mortal (rather than pure Intelligence?). Her absence would be equivalent to the gift of a paradise (since her presence means the loss of the only one there is). This is easy enough, and a good example of how naturally we read references to the more familiar conceptions of theology and philosophy as part of the play of wit within the limited range of a genre.

In the last stanza the temperate quiet of the garden is once more asserted, by way of conclusion. (The Earthly Paradise is always in the temperate zone.) The time, for us as for the bee (a pun on "thyme") is sweet and rewarding; hours of innocence are told by a dial of pure herbs and flowers. The sun is "milder" because in this zodiac of flowers fragrance is substituted for heat; Miss Bradbrook and Miss Lloyd Thomas have some good observations here. The time computed is likewise spent in fragrant rather than hot pursuits. This is the *Solitude*, not the *Jouissance;* the garden of the *solitaire* whose soul rises towards divine beauty, not that of the voluptuary who voluntarily surrenders to the delights of the senses.

This ends the attempt to read "The Garden" as a poem of a definite historical kind and to explore its delicate allusions to a genre of which the "norms" are within limits ascertainable. Although it is very improbable that such an attempt can avoid errors of both sophistication and simplification, one may reasonably claim for it that in substituting poetry for metaphysics it does no violence to the richness and subtlety of its subject.

NOTES

[1] "The Mode of Existence of a Literary Work of Art," *Critiques and Essays in Criticism, 1920–1948*, ed. R. W. Stallman, 1949, pp. 210–23.

[2] M. C. Bradbrook, "Marvell and the Poetry of Rural Solitude," *RES*, XVII (1941), 37–46; M. C. Bradbrook and M. G. Lloyd Thomas, *Andrew Marvell* (Cambridge, 1940).

[3] Montaigne, *Essayes*, trans. by John Florio, Everyman Edition, III, 316.

[4] See F. A. Yates, *The French Academies of the Sixteenth Century*, 1947, pp. 128 ff. From Plato (*Symposium* 202A, *Republic* 477, et seq.) through the Pléiade to Sidney there ran the argument that poets were not competent to make philosophical statements; they affirm nothing.

[5] *Notes and Queries*, March 29th, 1952, pp. 136–8.

[6] *Poems*, ed. G. Thorn-Drury, 1929, p. 110.

[7] *Poems*, ed. C. H. Wilkinson, 1930, p. 147.

[8] *De Constantia, Of Constancie*, trans. by Sir J. Stradling, ed. R. Kirk and C. M. Hall, 1939, pp. 132 ff.

[9] *Partheneia Sacra*, ed. Iain Fletcher, 1950 (reprint of 1633), p. 2.

[10] Proposed by A. H. King, *English Studies*, XX (1938), 118–21.

[11] *Œuvres Complètes*, ed. Ch.-L. Livet, 1855, I, 119.

[12] Sir John Davies, *Nosce Teipsum* ("The Intellectual Powers of the Soul," stanza 5).

[13] *Poems*, ed. Hugh Macdonald, 1947, pp. 36 ff.

[14] Gianfrancesco Pico della Mirandola, *De Imaginatione*, ed. and trans. H. Caplan, 1930, p. 29.

[15] *The Book of the Courtier*, translated by Thomas Hoby, Everyman Edition, p. 338.

[16] *Œuvres Complètes*, ed. M. Alleaume, 1856, I, 174–5.

LEO SPITZER

Marvell's "Nymph Complaining for the Death of Her Faun": Sources versus Meaning

In the considerable literature in which attempts have been recently made to define the meaning of Marvell's poem there may be distinguished three schools of thought: one that takes literally the love of the nymph for her fawn (Legouis in his book on Marvell published thirty years ago; T. S. Eliot in his essay on Marvell; LeComte [1]); a second that proposes an allegorical explanation (the fawn is Christ [Bradbrook and Thomas] or the stricken Anglican church [Douglas Bush, E. H. Emerson]); a third that attempts to reconcile these two views by admitting "religious overtones" without claiming that the "ground bass" is religious (Karina Williamson and, it seems to me, Legouis in his latest utterance: "la perte de son faon par une jeune âme *religieuse*"; italics mine).

In this discussion critics have analyzed mainly the vocabulary and the imagery of the poem according to its historic or stylistic provenance, with the blind faith that the origin of the images or motifs must decide implicitly the meaning of the poem. If LeComte is able to prove the pagan origin of expressions such as "nymph," "Diana's shrine," or of the central motif of the grief for a pet that has been killed (in Ovid, Virgil,[2] etc.), he believes that no religious meaning is implied in the poem. If, on the contrary, Miss Williamson has located the origin of the motifs "fawn" or "feeding among lilies" in the Song of

From *Modern Language Quarterly*, XIX (1958), pp. 231–43. Reprinted by permission of the publishers and Anna Granville Hatcher.

Songs,[3] she is convinced that the meaning of the poem includes religious overtones.

It has been for a long time my conviction that what I would call "imagistic positivism" (the exaggerated reliance of contemporary critics on imagery to the detriment of other elements of poetry) is likely to preclude the understanding of a poem such as Marvell's in which structure, thought, psychology, must play parts at least equal to imagery. In the case of our poem, it strikes me as strange that none of the critics has analyzed this from beginning to end as a structured whole whose parts correspond to the phases of the psychological development of the Nymph. This is the more indicated since T. S. Eliot has remarked that "the suggestiveness of the poem" is "the aura around a bright clear center" (Marvell takes a "slight affair, the feeling of a girl for her pet,"[4] and gives it a connection with that "inexhaustible and terrible nebula of emotion which surrounds all our exact and practical passions"), which remark is echoed by Miss Williamson: "The experience manifested in the poem is felt to belong to the total of human experience."

But none of these critics tells us what exactly and actually the "nebula of emotion" or the "total experience" of the Nymph who has lost her fawn is, although that nebula of total experience seems to me clearly, if discreetly, indicated in the poem. Whenever the critics think that a "slight affair" is treated with enormous seriousness of tone, either the poem cannot be good (but all critics are agreed as to the excellence of our poem), or there must be a flaw in their understanding. In a good poem form cannot go its own way, apart from content. Obviously, then, the poem is not about a "slight affair"—how could it possibly be if the end of the Nymph is that of Niobe?[5]

The protagonist of our poem is, indeed, not the fawn, but the Nymph, who dies together with the fawn, and it is quite incomprehensible why the critics have shown no curiosity as to the reason why a young girl whose pet has died should herself have chosen death. To explain this reason, my analysis will consist in simply repeating elements expressed in the poem as well as in pointing out some elements that are only slightly, but clearly, suggested in it. The delicate art of the poet has so willed it that, in the inner monologue of the Nymph that is the poem, the description of her pet reflects on her own character in indirect characterization, the increasing idealization of the fawn allowing inferences about the maiden who so idealizes it. It is the task of the commentator—a commentator who should be less a "professional" of literary criticism than a simple reader who asks relevant human questions[6]—to bring out clearly the deep tragedy of the Nymph. We are, indeed, given an indirect description of her feelings while the animal is dying (lines 1–92), after its death (93–110), and before the death of the Nymph, when she is planning the consecration by a monument to her own as well as to the fawn's memory (111–22).

The poem starts with the address of the Nymph to the fatally wounded fawn in which she reveals her, as it were, modern attitude of revulsion against the wanton slaying of a harmless animal. That this is a passage significant for the history of ideas (or feelings) has been duly noted by Legouis who devotes one and one-half pages to the rise and growth of this feeling as expressed in English literature. But I would point out two other, more personal, attitudes of the Nymph that are expressed in the first verse paragraph (1–24), both indicative of a feeling that her life has come to an end with the death of the fawn: that of evangelical forgiveness for the murderers of the pet—she does not "wish them ill," but prays for them, weeping (6–12)—and that of readiness to offer her own life as a sacrifice to the God of revenge (17–24). That this is indeed the meaning of these lines may perhaps be contested. Legouis translates (italics mine):

> Quand bien même ils laveraient leurs mains criminelles
> *dans ce sang chaud qui se sépare*
> *de ton cœur et dont la vue perce le mien,*
> ils ne pourraient se purifier: leur souillure
> est empreinte sur eux d'une pourpre trop éclatante.
> Il n'y a pas au monde *un autre animal*
> semblable qu'ils puissent offrir pour racheter leur péché.

But if "this warm life-blood" were that of the fawn "which doth part / From thine" (understood as "thy heart," with "heart" taken from the following "wound me to the heart"), this anticipative ellipsis would seem rather difficult. More important, however, how should we understand that the criminals who killed the fawn would think, in order to become guiltless, of washing their bloody hands in the blood of their victim (would Lady Macbeth wash off her guilt in King Duncan's blood)? And how would the lines 23–24 which obviously allude to a sacrificial offering (a *deodand*) connect with the preceding lines, especially if "such another" meant an animal, as Legouis has it: in the preceding lines there was to be found only an allusion to criminals who wish to wash off their guilt.

Thus I am led to believe that in "this warm life-blood" the pronoun *this* represents the first person ("my") and means the warm blood of the Nymph who would wish to redeem (a new Iphigenia, as LeComte has seen) the spilt blood of the fawn, though to no avail for its murderers whose "stain" is irremovable.[7] With this explanation the lines "There is not such another in / The World to offer for their Sin" connect excellently with the thought of the preceding passage: "no other *being* (including me) could atone for that unique fawn." What strikes us here is that at the moment of the fawn's death the Nymph is already considering her own death, a death of expiation which she, however, seems to reject at this time because of her unworthiness. Thus this first part of the poem must be interpreted not only in the light of the history of ideas, but as a story of an extraordinary human being, the Nymph.

What this story has been we learn from the second paragraph (lines 25–36): it is the story of her love for Sylvio who betrayed her. We notice that between Sylvio and the troopers there exists a certain analogy (the vocatives *inconstant Sylvio–ungentle men,* underline this parallelism): both acted wantonly, cruelly, regardless of the "smart" of the girl; both killed, the one her young loving heart, the others the young object of her later love. Sylvio's frivolity appears in the words with which he accompanies his gifts, the fawn and the silver chain: "look how your Huntsman here / Hath taught a Faun to hunt his *Dear*"—words that made a deep impression on her at the time, but which gained an even stronger significance after Sylvio's breach of faith, as is indicated by the elaborate manner in which she reports these words:

> One morning (I remember well)
> . . . nay and I know
> What he said then; I'me sure I do.
> Said He. . . .

These simple words and this simple syntax carry a sense of convincingness and sincerity. What is more, the repetitious phrasing seems to imply that the maiden, even now, must make an effort not to wince at the hurting quality which those words still contain. She realizes, of course, in retrospect, that Sylvio spoke as a "huntsman" who saw the fawn in the light of his huntsmanship (as an animal trained to "hunt his *Dear,*" to pursue her, frolic around her) and that she herself was for Sylvio the huntsman nothing but a quarry or a plaything.

Thus in his words, she now realizes, fate had spoken. What should we think of the puns in this passage (*dear–deer, heart–hart*)? They seem practically superfluous, but they are probably intended to characterize the ambiguous atmosphere of "huntsman's frivolity" which is proper to Sylvio's adventures.[8] The sober significance of lines 25–36 is that the early experience of the Nymph who suffered from her lover's faithlessness must be seen together with the love which will develop between her and the fawn: the one conditions the other. There is also an indication of a parallelism in the Nymph's and the animal's fate: both fall prey to wanton, cruel men. Although the Nymph's feelings for Sylvio are worded in a simple, untragic manner ("smart" is the only word that allows us to measure her grief), we may assume that a deep wound has existed in her since the time of Sylvio's betrayal.

There apparently followed upon the adventure with Sylvio, as the third paragraph suggests (37–46), a respite from grief, respite from deep feeling, in which the playful animal helped the Nymph to forget. The fawn meant to her first relaxation, a "content" in "idleness": the sportive nimbleness of the fawn invited her to the "game" of racing, of "hunting." But with the lines "it seem'd to bless / Its self in me" a new note is sounded. The happiness enjoyed by the animal in her company, within her atmosphere, could not be depicted more graphically than by the surprising reflexive use of the English verb "to bless" that I may translate by the Italian *bearsi* (which has a relation to *beato, beatitudine,* similar to that of *to bless oneself* to *bliss*). The fawn "called itself blessed," "found its delight, happiness, bliss in her."

Strangely enough, Miss Williamson has failed to list this extraordinary use of the verb "to bless" among the expressions with "religious overtones." It is first attested in 1611 in the biblical passage (Jeremiah 4:2): *the nations shall bless themselves in him* [sc. God]. The pivotal line "it seem'd to bless / Its self in me" with its solemn (as if religious) ring marks the first sign of true love[9] that came to the Nymph and asked from her the response of love. The wording of the next lines, again very simple and truly convincing, "How could I less / Than love it? / O I cannot be / Unkind," sounds apologetic: the Nymph herself feels the momentum of the totally unexpected, sudden inner development. The Nymph who had experienced inconstancy and frivolity in love has now received a new revelation, that of pure, unsolicited, gratuitously, unselfishly offered, abiding love that developed imperceptibly, gradually, out of gaiety and playfulness (the even flow of the lines in question mirrors this development).

But, as the next paragraph (47–54) shows, the Nymph, even at the moment of the fawn's death, is still not quite prepared to believe that the revelation of true love that was imparted to her was final: "Had it liv'd long" might the fawn not have developed into another

Sylvio? (We infer from the lingering comparison and from the lingering doubt even at this moment how deeply wounded by her first experience the Nymph still is.) But no, she is now assured that the fawn's love "was far more than the love of false and cruel men" ("cruel" being a word used by her now when she is able to compare Sylvio and the fawn).

The next three paragraphs (55–92), the last of which ends with the line "Had it liv'd long" that gives the answer to the question voiced there, are inspired by an ever-growing sureness about the significance of her love. In these paragraphs Sylvio is finally forgotten, yet some of the Nymph's statements suggest to the reader the contrast between then and now:

> It is a wond'rous thing, how fleet
> 'Twas on those little silver feet.
> With what a pretty skipping grace,
> It oft would challenge me the Race:
> And when 't had left me far away,
> 'Twould stay, and run again, and stay.
> For it was nimbler much than Hindes;
> And trod, as on the four Winds.

We may contrast the fawn's "silver feet" with the "silver chain" given by Sylvio: now there is no need for a chain, since the fawn, more faithful than Sylvio, though it leaves the maiden temporarily, always returns to her, leaves her playfully to return faithfully.

The commentators who point out that lines 67–69 may be inspired by Pliny and the expression "trod, as on the four Winds" by the Psalmist, have missed the main point: the contrast between the nimbleness given to the animal by nature and its unfailing conscientious returnings to its mistress (note the repeated *stay* in Marvell's wording and the repeated *fuga* in Pliny: with the latter, the stag runs—stays—runs; with the former it stays—runs—stays). When we read lines such as "It oft would challenge me the Race," we realize—and perhaps the Nymph realized it too at that point of her "Complaint" —that the fickle hunter's definition of the fawn has unexpectedly come true, only in another sense than was meant by him: the fawn has been trained to "hunt Sylvio's *Dear*," to hunt her "constantly."

The reader will note the lavish use of metaphysical wit in these paragraphs which are intended to extol the fawn's virtues and its beauty, qualities that become more and more of a supernatural kind as they transcend the Nymph's own virtues and beauty. The description proceeds by comparison (or identification) of these virtues and beauties with those of other objects and beings in which they are traditionally embodied in undefiled purity. The fawn was nourished with milk and sugar by the fingers of the maiden—it became more white and sweet than this food (it acquires, in addition, sweet fragrance [10]) and its feet more soft and white than her (or any lady's) hand; it lies in a bed of lilies and feeds on roses (so that its mouth will seem to bleed)—had it lived longer, it could have become "Lillies without, Roses within."

This sequence of images which climaxes in this last "witty" identification may have its origin in the Song of Songs, but its function here is the metamorphosis of the animal into a paragon of virtues that are not found combined even in a human being: the coolness of virginal chastity and the flame of ardent love (the rose being the symbol of the latter—witness the fawn's rose-kiss that seems to come from a bleeding heart). Wit, which here, as always with Marvell, has a functional role, suggests the possibility of a miracle: the possibility of moral or spiritual qualities becoming sensuously perceptible as though they were objects in outward nature in a καλοκἀγαθία of their own. A miracle is after all nothing but the substantiation of the supernatural.[11]

Here I may permit myself a digression about metaphysical wit in general. In T. S. Eliot's statements on this subject (espoused by Miss Williamson) one feels a certain embarrassment, as though he, who appreciates so highly seventeenth-century wit, had not reached a description quite satisfactory to himself, when, after having set wit (but not entirely) apart from "erudition" and "cynicism," he writes the final sentence: "It involves, probably [!], a recognition, implicit in the expression of every experience, of the other experiences which are possible" (and this is basically the same idea as that, quoted above, on the "slight affair," supposedly treated in our poem, to which the poet would have added that "inexhaustible and terrible nebula of emotion" that surrounds all our "exact and practical passions").

But such a description of wit seems to me far too general: would the metaphysical poet add any other experience to the one he is treating? [12] Marvell envisages a metamorphosis of the fawn into lilies and roses, a very precise change related to its way of living, not some vague connection with, or nebula of, "other experiences." His metamorphosis seems to me based on a public belief in miracles whereby a supernatural development may not only become physically perceptible in beautiful forms, but may live a physical life of its own according to a precise pattern of psychological analogy. The fawn who lies in a bed of lilies and feeds on roses (that is, is pure as the lily and embodies, like the rose, the flame of love) may become lilies and roses because organic beings may, in a sort of mythological metabolism, become what they eat.

This is, of course, a miracle of the poet's making, but one that goes back historically [13] to medieval religious beliefs, according to which the spirituality of saints and martyrs acted in similar analogy on the physical world. Metaphysical wit has here simply laicized, and preserved in poetry, the substantiation of the supernatural current in hagiographic legend. To give but one example, borrowed from Curtius' *European Literature and the Latin Middle Ages* (appendix on "comic spirit in hagiography"): St. Lawrence, when grilled over the flames, is reported by St. Ambrose to have said to his torturers: *assum est, versa et manduca* "my body is cooked, turn it to the other side and eat it"—the underlying idea being that the saint's supernatural fortitude was able to triumph over physical pain to the point that he could accept, in its most extreme form, the transformation of his flesh into meat to which, then, all the normal culinary procedures (the mechanics of cooking) and pleasures (the eating—which here becomes anthropophagy) may be applied, while his mind remains miraculously intact (able to formulate the physical miracle).

The comic spirit in hagiography is probably at the bottom of metaphysical wit. Just as, according to Bergson, all comic effect is a result of mechanization of the organic, in the process of living flesh becoming meat we are faced with a mechanization of a spiritual force—whose comic effect is, of course, different from other comic writing, surrounded as it is, at least for the believer, with awe. Some of this quasi-religious comic spirit or awesome wit (poetry being, as is so often the case, the reënactment in secularized form of ancestral beliefs) is also present in Marvell's suggestion that the animal lying among lilies and feeding on roses may become all lilies and roses. Here the poetic miracle has inherited from the truly religious miracle its paradoxical logic, its psycho-physical analogy, and the mechanization of the spiritual (there is no "cynicism" involved in such a transfer).

The extension of the orinigally religious wit to secular subject matter [14] may have been encouraged by certain genres of pagan poetry that were revived in modern poetry, for instance, by the Ovidian metamorphosis: for the change of the fawn into lilies and roses is nothing but an Ovidian imagination. With Ovid such a metamorphosis would fancifully explain, according to a mythical, that is prescientific, science of analogy, the birth of an object or being in nature by means of a legendary event that once befell a human being (the cypress was originally the youth Cyparissus, the laurel was originally the nymph Daphne), the underlying idea being one of pantheism which "sees a nymph behind every tree." Certain analogies obtain between the form of the object in nature and the human situation that gave birth to it. With Ovid the change of forms is from the human to the non-human, the latter being anthropomorphosized. When the Christian spirit moves the medieval and the Renaissance poets, their metamorphosis will emphasize the superhuman that is present in the physical: we will remember the medieval tradition (not lost in the Renaissance) of *Ovide moralisé* which will give to the pagan metamorphosis Christian religious or moral overtones (cf. the *Roman de la Dame à la Lycorne* mentioned below in note 15).

Thus Marvell's wit in our poem is located at the point of confluence of two powerful literary currents, Ovidian and Christian—no wonder that modern classifications of our poem, now as pagan, now as Christian, do violence to one-half of its inspiration since it participates in both currents. We shall find, in harmony with that Protean quality, inherited from Ovid, of poetry of wit, or its "omnivorousness," as Father Ong calls its ability "to attract into its orbit experiences on most various levels provided that they are brought together with a higher meaning"—we shall find in our poem several other examples of wit, of psycho-physical analogy and change of forms particularly in the scenes of the death and the afterlife of the fawn.

The death of the fawn (93–100) is surrounded by an atmosphere of beauty and virtue combined in a miracle. It is the death of a "saint" who, in spite of his "calm," is accessible to human emotions to the point of shedding tears, tears of farewell to love (as it appears from the comparison with the tears of the "brotherless *Heliades*"). And the tears will become beautiful substances: wit will compare them, in their fragrance and visual beauty, with "gumme," "frankincense," and "amber" (the last of which, suggested by Ovid's metamorphosis of the sisters of Phaëthon, has probably given the impulse to the series of analogies).[15] It is the acme of metaphysical wit that the liquid substances into which the tears of the fawn have been changed can themselves be presented anthropomorphically: "So weeps the wounded Balsome." In the world of poetic identification of opposites the road between human being and thing may be traveled in both directions. The final identification of the flowing tears with solid amber suggested to the poet a further "substantification" of the tears of the animal, their congealing into "two crystals" (each representing one eye of the fawn), a jewel, as it were, a thing of beauty that will forever preserve the essence of the transient moment of the fawn's death, a pagan relic to be offered in a golden vial (which should also contain the Nymph's tears, that are less "crystallized" and "overflow" its brim) to Diana's shrine. It is only at this moment and by this gesture that our realization that the destiny of the fawn and of its mistress is one and the same becomes final. Both being too sublime for this world of wantonness and cruelty, both victims of their own purity, they belong together forever like their tears that will be preserved in the shrine of chastity.

In the whole description of her relationship with the living animal the Nymph has kept herself in the background, minimizing the depth of her feeling and indeed comparing herself disadvantageously with the animal (she "blushed" at its whiteness). Even in death the white fawn will transcend her: for while her own final destiny is not mentioned, she is assured that he will dwell in Elysium with the other white animals that embody purity. The animal that has "stayed" with her (faithfully) is asked not "to run too fast" toward Elysium (109)—a graceful conceit: even in death the deer will preserve its natural fleetness. And even in the monument to be erected after her death the figure of the fawn will be of "alabaster" that never can be "as white as thee," but whiter than the "marble" that will perpetuate her own figure. While the relationship between mistress and animal will be expressed by the position of the fawn's image at her feet (just as on medieval tombstones traditionally faithful dogs lie at the feet of their masters), the mistress will remain forever the human mourner rather than the traditional owner. The Nymph will become a Niobe,[16] endowed, if not with the boastfulness, with the disconsolate feelings of that "unhappy" mother. Her evolution which began with simple delight and enjoyment of a graceful young being, after having reached the depth of true love, ends in the grief of a bereaved mother. Her tears (that overflow all boundaries) will petrify into the statue that weeps, that is "engraved" by her tears: the two aspects of grief, the feeling of numbness and of dissolution, are brought together in the image of the stone-that-weeps.[17]

This tragic story could be called in modern (Freudian) terms one of frustration overcome by sublimation [18]—and as such it would verge on comedy, replacement of love for a person by love for an animal (the stock situation in which old spinsters are involved) coming dangerously close to the grim caricature of Flaubert's *Un cœur simple.* But Marvell has placed this story of disillusionment within a baroque setting of sad beauty,[19] a metamorphosis of ancient tradition being overlaid by the feeling for the transiency of things earthly. The *lacrimae rerum* are made to crystallize into things of beauty that commemorate tragedy (the statue, the crystals in the golden vial), just as in another, typically baroque and conceptual, poem of Marvell's, disillusionment becomes beauty, tears become jewels:

> What in the world most fair appears,
> Yea, even Laughter, turns to tears;
> And all the Jewels which we prize
> Melt in these pendants of the Eyes.

We understand now the particular tone of our "Complaint" in which the protagonist tells her story in an "inner monologue" of rather simple, direct words which contrast with the sophisticated examples of metaphysical wit.[20] This stylistic contrast reflects the inner contrast between sadness and beauty: the sadness of disillusionment is reflected convincingly by the simple speech, not unknown to Marvell, while the miraculous metamorphosis into sensuous beauty finds its expression in the mirages of wit.[21]

NOTES

[1] The bibliography of this discussion may be found in the two articles by LeComte and Miss Williamson in *MP*, L (1952) and LI (1954), to which there must be added the article by E. H. Emerson and Legouis's rejoinder in *Études Anglaises,* VIII (1955), 107–12.

Needless to say, I share the outspokenly "French" horror of Legouis ("un esprit français . . . n'arrive pas à se débarrasser d'un excès de logique quand il étudie la poésie anglaise") when faced with the lack of logic implied by the assumption of allegorical explanations that explain only parts of the literary work—a procedure, now current in America, obviously based on the gratuitous belief that an allegorical explanation is in itself of higher quality than a non-allegorical one (whereas the true touchstone of any explanation is whether or not it actually "explains" convincingly and completely), a belief that in turn may represent an excessive reaction of overcompensation for traditional American qualities which have come to be felt in certain quarters as too pedestrian: good sense, matter-of-factness, realism. As for Marvell, the various ambiguities which Emerson, enthusiastically followed by some American critics, found in our poet can generally be discarded, after a close analysis, in favor of one explanation that alone fits the context. In other words, Marvell, like Góngora for whom Dámaso Alonso has found the key of understanding, is "difficult, but clear." Those poets ask from the reader the effort to make his way through the maze of ambiguities toward the unique true explanation. The critic who stops at pointing out several possible meanings has stopped halfway on the road that Marvell expected him to travel. To superimpose contemporary anarchy of meanings on Marvell's poetry is a blatant anachronism.

[2] But why does he not mention also the ancient and Renaissance tradition of epitaphs for pets (Catullus, Martial, Navagero, Du Bellay, Ronsard, etc.)?

[3] It may be noted, however, that the comparison in the Song of Songs of the beloved with a roe or hart is not identical with Marvell's presentation of a deer as a lover: in the first case a human being is represented with the freshness, unpurposiveness, and mystery of nature; in the second, an animal in nature with the potentialities of feeling of human beings. Surely the first is a more sensuous, the second a more spiritual approach—and the second is the procedure of our metaphysical poet who is following, as we shall see later, a medieval tradition.

[4] How does this assertion fit another, to be found later on in the article on Marvell, emphasizing the "precise taste" of Marvell's which finds for him the proper degree of seriousness for every subject which he treats?

[5] The presence of this ancient motif has been mentioned only in passing by LeComte. Indeed, at the end of his article, when he comes to formulate pointedly the role of Marvell's Nymph, he says that if she should be given a name, it should be "Silvia rather than Pietà"—he should rather have contrasted with the Pietà the ancient equivalent of a mourning mother.

[6] We have indeed come to the point where the quiet de-humanized professional of literary criticism considers it his duty to deal with "imagery" and similar specialized, technical, or philological questions, to the exclusion of the human element which is at the bottom of all poetry and consequently should inform philology, the humanistic science.

[7] "This warm life-blood, which doth part / From thine" must then mean "which now departs [must depart] from thy life-blood"; "and wound me to the Heart" belongs rather together with "Though they should wash their guilty hands" (if they should wash . . . and wound me . . . , that is, kill me).

[8] The puns may be considered within the framework of the other examples of metaphysical wit to be found in our poem and also within the framework of other puns to be found in the poetry of Marvell and Marvell's contemporaries. But, believing as I do that any stylistic device is an empty form which may be filled by most divers contents, I should prefer to treat each manifestation of wit, puns, etc., *in situ,* in the precise situation in which it appears. It is the juncture of a particular *significandum* and *significatum* that gives precise meaning to any stylistic device (as well as to any linguistic utterance). Consequently, I feel entitled to treat the puns of the passage just mentioned separately from the other examples of wit which we shall find in our poem.

[9] It must be noted that in the episode which, according to LeComte, constitutes the model of our poem, Virgil's *Aeneid* VII, 475 (Sylvio's stag wounded by Ascanius; cf. also the story of Cyparissus in Ovid's *Metamorphoses* X, 106, which is an imitation of the Virgilian passage), we

find as the only active person the mistress who tames her stag and takes loving care of him ("soror omni Silvia cura / mollibus intexens ornabat cornua sertis / pectebatque ferum puroque in fonte lavabat"; cf. in Ovid: "tu [Cyparissus] pabula cervum / ad nova, tu liquidi ducebas fontis ad undam, / tu nodo texebas varios per cornua flores . . ."). With Marvell it is the fawn who has the active part: it is he, already trained by Sylvio, who by his loving behavior makes his mistress love him. And, of course, there can be no question in Virgil or Ovid of the animal becoming superior to its mistress.

[10] For Miss Williamson this is an echo of the Song of Songs: "his lips like sweet lilies, dropping sweet myrrh . . . his mouth is most sweet." But I find in the epitaph of the French Renaissance poet Du Bellay on the dog Peloton (in *Divers jeux rustiques*) the lines:

> Peloton ne mangeoit pas
> de la chair à son repas:
> ses viandes plus prisees,
> c'estoient miettes brisees,
> que celui qui le paissait
> de ses doights ammollissait:
> *aussi sa bouche estoit pleine*
> *toujours d'une douce haleine.*

[11] On the contrary "poetic miracles" performed by a Marino have, it seems to me, no supernatural connotations: with him the transformation is from one sensuous object to another, more perfect in its sensuous beauty. To choose an example, parallel to Marvell, in which a comparison between animal and human body is involved:

> Mentre Lidia premea
> dentro rustica coppa
> a la lanuta la feconda poppa,
> i' stava a rimirar doppio candore,
> di natura e d'amore;
> nè distinguer sapea
> il bianco umor da le sue mani intatte,
> ch'altro non discernea che latte in latte.

Thanks to the alchemy of *amore,* the white hand of the beloved becomes milk (milk that encompasses milk)—an entirely sensuous miracle.

[12] Probably Eliot's description was prompted by the lines of Cowley on wit which he quotes:

> In a true piece of Wit all things must be
> Yet all things there agree . . .

Or as the primitive forms of all
(If we compare great things with small)
Which, without discord or confusion, lie
In that strange mirror of the Deity.

It seems to me that Father Ong was better inspired when, quoting the same lines of Cowley, he considered as a secondary result of a poetry that moves on higher and lower planes at the same time, what he calls the "omnivorousness" which enables wit poetry "to devour all sorts of experience in one gulp," "to digest all experience, raw if necessary, and make something of it."

[13] This historical succession has been proved by Father W. J. Ong, S.J., in his classical article, "Wit and Mystery: A Revaluation in Medieval Latin Hymnody" (*Speculum*, XXII [1947], 310 ff.), who attests wit (including puns, paradoxes, etc.) in the hymns of Prudentius, Thomas Aquinas, Adam of St. Victor, used as a device to express certain paradoxical mysteries inherent in the Christian dogma (for example, the Tri-une Godhead). One facet of the same procedure is what I am treating here: wit expressing miracles, the miracle being different from the mystery in that the former constitutes a temporary interruption of the so-called laws of nature while the religious mystery is above those laws or underlying them.

The historical fact, stated by Eliot, that poetry of wit is absent from eighteenth- and nineteenth-century poetry may be explained in the same manner as the disappearance of allegory in those same centuries. At that time belief in the concrete reality of abstract qualities of perfection had become lost while previous centuries had retained from earlier medieval thought the capacity of thinking, at least poetically, of shapes into which perfection is able to materialize. In allegorical poetry abstractions assume a body; in poetry of wit abstract qualities concretize themselves in objects. With a renascence in the twentieth century of abstract thought, as a reaction against the overcrowding material world; poetry of wit has been reinstated.

[14] What is called in English "metaphysical wit" is called in French *préciosité,* although the realization of this identity has not yet found its way into orthodox French literary history. The usual definition given for *précieux* passages: "une métaphore poussée jusqu'au bout" (*il en rougit, le traître,* said of a dagger; *brûlé de plus de feux que je n'en allumai,* said of a lover) would seem to suggest a futile automatic game, while in reality the "metaphor pushed to its extreme" originates in France as elsewhere in religious poetry (La Cépède, D'Aubigné, etc.) and has, even in its better known secular variety, inherited something of that "miraculous psycho-physical parallelism" that is characteristic of the belief in the efficacy of spiritual forces. In that poetic world there exists a blushing of shame that may become indistinguishable from blood, a love whose flame is more consuming than actual fires multiplied.

[15] The coupling of Christian with pagan elements, which I mentioned above

as characteristic of our poem, is reflected by the outspoken reference to a metamorphosis of Ovid (the Heliades) following immediately after the expression "holy frankincense" which points to Christian church service.

The lack of nuances in the poetic sensibility of those critics who decide for an "either-or" in our poem may be explained in part by their unfamiliarity with medieval lay poetry that combines the worldly and the unworldly to a degree unbelievable for us moderns; for instance, in the fourteenth-century French *Roman de la Dame à la Lycorne et du Chevalier au Lyon,* we find the story of the love of a noble lady, who is a paragon of virtue and grace, for a courageous and virtuous knight. This story is replete with romantic adventures à la Chrétien de Troyes of one of whose heroes the knight riding on a lion is reminiscent—while the *dame à la lycorne* rides the unicorn which equals her in virtue (ed. Gennrich, lines 183 ff.):

> . . . par ce qu'est [la dame] de tout bien affinee
> *Jhesu Christ* volt, que li fust destinee
> *Une merveille,* que chi vus conterai:
> C'est d'une bieste, que *Diex* donna l'otrai,
> Et tel franchise e si tres grant purté
> Il li donna, qu'ele avoit en vilté
> Tous vilains visces . . .
> Pource donna a la dame tel don
> *Li Diex d'Amours,* que tous temps avoit non:
> "La dame blanche qui la Lycorne garde,"
> Qui onc nul temps de mal faire ne tarde.

Here then, in a medieval secular, if moralizing, love story, it is Christ and Amor who give to the perfect lady the animal that, in bestiaries and tapestries alike, was thought to embody Christ. The evidently present "religious overtones" do not guarantee the presence of a religious poem.

[16] Niobe was killed by the arrows of the two children of Leto whom she had offended, Apollo and Diana—we may surmise that it was Diana who killed Marvell's Nymph out of pity for her fate.

[17] We witness here the paradoxical coupling of two opposite attitudes as before when "cold virginity" and "ardent love" were found combined in the fawn. Already in Ovid, *Metamorphoses* VI, 303 ff., we find:

> Deriguitque malis . . .
> . . . intra quoque viscera saxum est:
> Flet tamen . . .
> . . . et lacrimis etiam nunc marmora manant.

But the "witty" idea of the statue being "sculptured" by the Nymph's tears belongs, of course, to Marvell.

[18] In Gottfried of Strassburg's medieval romance *Tristan und Isold* we have

perhaps a story reminiscent of that of Marvell, though leading to a quite different conclusion. With Gottfried, the absent Tristram, thinking faithfully of Isold and reflecting how he could relieve her loneliness, sends her the graceful dog, Petitcreü, a dog possessed of miraculous qualities, about whose neck is hung on a chain a bell with a tone so sweet that all who hear it forget their grief. But Isold, unwilling to forget her grief while Tristram is unable to forget his own, finally decides to tear the marvelous bell from the chain of the dog—which thereby loses immediately its miraculous power. By parallel wording the poet emphasizes the exemplary behavior of these two faithful lovers who refuse consolation: Tristram "who has given up his joy and his life to grief . . ."—Isold "the faithful, constant one who has given up her life to longing and to Tristram."

[19] Another baroque combination of sadness and beauty consists in presentation of the beauty of the world as undermined by transiency (the motif of *sic transit gloria mundi*).

[20] To that rather modern technique belong those temporal elements in the spoken complaint that mark the passing of time ("The wanton Troopers . . . *Have shot* my Faun"; "Oh help! o help! *I see* it faint"; "Now my Sweet Faun *is vanish'd"; "*for *I Will* but *bespeak* thy Grave"). It may very well be that the second passage just quoted reflects the *auxilium vocat* of Silvia in the *Aeneid,* but Marvell has fitted it into the, as it were, temporal economy of the "Complaint."

[21] After having handed in this article to the *MLQ,* I read a study of our poem by D. C. Allen, published in *ELH,* XXIII (June, 1956). I am pleased to note that he considers the fawn a *surrogatus amoris,* but he fails to follow through in detail the development of the motif in the poem and rather concentrates on the history of the *topoi* that went into its composition (without mentioning, however, the—for me essential—parallel of Niobe).

CLEANTH BROOKS

Marvell's "Horatian Ode"

The easiest error into which we may fall in defining the relationship between historical and critical studies is illustrated by the preface of Maurice Kelley's interesting book on Milton, *This Great Argument*. For Kelley, the problem of exegesis is almost amusingly simple: we will read Milton's *Christian Doctrine* to find out what Milton's ideas are, and then we shall be able to understand his *Paradise Lost*, explaining the tangled and difficult poetic document by means of the explicit prose statement. But Kelley's argument rests not only upon the assumption that the Milton who wrote the *Christian Doctrine* was precisely and at all points the same man who composed *Paradise Lost* —a matter which, for all practical purposes, may well be true; it rests upon the further and much more dangerous assumption that Milton was able to *say* in *Paradise Lost* exactly what he intended to say; and that what he supposed he had put into that poem is actually to be found there. In short, Mr. Kelley tends to make the assumption about poetry which most of us constantly make; namely, that a poem is essentially a decorated and beautified piece of prose.

But I propose to deal here with a more modest example than Milton's epic. I propose to illustrate from Marvell's "Horatian Ode." If we follow the orthodox procedure, the obvious way to understand the "Ode" is to ascertain by historical evidence—by letters and documents of all kinds—what Marvell really thought of Cromwell, or, since Marvell apparently thought different things of Cromwell at different

From *English Institute Essays, 1946* (New York: Columbia University Press, 1947), pp. 127–58. Reprinted by permission of the publishers and the author.

times, to ascertain the date of the "Ode," and then neatly fit it into the particular stage of Marvell's developing opinion of Cromwell. But this is at best a relatively coarse method which can hope to give no more than a rough approximation of the poem; and there lurk in it some positive perils. For to ascertain what Marvell the man thought of Cromwell, and even to ascertain what Marvell as poet consciously intended to say in his poem, will not prove that the poem actually says this, or all this, or merely this. This last remark, in my opinion, does not imply too metaphysical a notion of the structure of a poem. There is surely a sense in which any one must agree that a poem has a life of its own, and a sense in which it provides in itself the only criterion by which what it says can be judged. It is a commonplace that the poet sometimes writes better than he knows, and, alas, on occasion, writes worse than he knows. The history of English literature will furnish plenty of examples of both cases.

As a matter of fact, Marvell's "Ode" is not a shockingly special case. Indeed, I have chosen it for my example, not because it is special—not because I hope to reveal triumphantly that what it really says is something quite opposed to what we have supposed it to be saying—but because it seems to me a good instance of the normal state of affairs. Yet, even so, the "Ode" will provide us with problems enough. To the scholar who relies upon the conventional approach, the problems become rather distressingly complicated.

Let us review the situation briefly. Hard upon his composition of the "Ode" in 1650, Marvell had published in 1649 a poem "To his Noble Friend, Mr. Richard Lovelace," and a poem "Upon the Death of the Lord Hastings." Both Margoliouth and Legouis find these poems rather pro-Royalist in sentiment and certainly it is difficult to read them otherwise. If we add to these poems the "Elegy upon the Death of My Lord Francis Villiers," a Cavalier who was killed fighting for the King in 1649, the Royalist bias becomes perfectly explicit. As Margoliouth puts it: "If [the elegy on Villiers] is Marvell's, it is his one unequivocal royalist utterance; it throws into strong relief the transitional character of *An Horatian Ode* where royalist principles and admiration for Cromwell the Great Man exist side by side. . . ."

A transition in views there must have been, but the transition certainly cannot be graphed as a steadily rising curve when we take into account Marvell's next poem, "Tom May's Death." May died in November, 1650. Thus we have the "Horatian Ode," which was almost certainly written in the summer of 1650, preceding by only a few months a poem in which Marvell seems to slur at the Commander of the Parliamentary armies—either Essex or Fairfax—as "Spartacus," and to reprehend May himself as a renegade poet who has prostituted the mystery of the true poets. The curve of Marvell's political development shows still another surprising quirk when we recall that only a few months after his attack on May, Marvell was to be living under Spartacus Fairfax's roof, acting as tutor to his little daughter Mary.

Let me interrupt this summary to say that I am not forcing the evidence so as to crowd the historian into the narrowest and most uncomfortable corner possible. On the contrary, whatever forcing of the evidence has been done has been done by the editors and the historians. If we limit ourselves to historical evidence, it is possible to suppose that "Tom May's Death" was actually written on the Hill at Billborrow; and Margoliouth chooses early 1651 as the probable date for Marvell's arrival at Appleton House only because, as he says, " 'Tom May's Death' is not the sort of poem Marvell would have written under Fairfax's roof."

There is no need, in view of our purposes, to extend the review of Marvell's political development through the late 1650's with their Cromwellian poems or through the Restoration period with its vexed problems concerning which of the anti-court satires are truly, and which are falsely, ascribed to Marvell. The problem of Marvell's attitude through the years 1649–51 will provide sufficient scope for this examination of some of the relations and interrelations of the historical approach and the critical approach. For there is still another complication, which has received less attention than it deserves. It is the curious fact that the "Horatian Ode" in which Marvell seems to affirm the ancient rights of the monarchy—

> Though Justice against Fate complain,
> And plead the antient Rights in vain—

is full of echoes of the poetry of Tom May, the poet whom Marvell was, a few months later, to denounce for having failed poetry in the hour of crisis:

> When the Sword glitters ore the Judges head,
> And fear the Coward Churchmen silenced,
> Then is the Poets time, 'tis then he drawes,
> And single fights forsaken Vertues cause.
> He, when the wheel of Empire, whirleth back,
> And though the World's disjointed Axel crack,
> Sings still of *antient Rights* and better Times,
> Seeks wretched good, arraigns successful Crimes.

The echoes of May's poetry, of course, may well have been unconscious: to me it is significant that they are from May's translation of Lucan's poem on the Roman civil wars. (The relevant passage from Margoliouth's notes will be found on pp. 339–40.) I must say that I find the parallels quite convincing and that I am a little surprised at Margoliouth's restraint in not pushing his commentary further. For one is tempted to suppose that in the year or so that followed the execution of Charles, Marvell was obsessed with the problem of the poet's function in such a crisis; that the poet May was frequently in his mind through a double connection—through the parallels between the English and the Roman civil war, Lucan's poem on which May had translated, and through May's conduct as a partisan of the Commonwealth; and that the "Horatian Ode" and "Tom May's Death," though so different in tone, are closely related and come out of the same general state of mind. But to hazard all this is to guess at the circumstances of Marvell's composition of these poems. It can be only a guess, and, in any case, it takes us into a consideration of what must finally be a distinct problem: how the poem came to be; whereas our elected problem is rather: what the poem is. I am, by the way, in entire sympathy with the essay "The Intentional Fallacy," by W. K. Wimsatt and M. C. Beardsley, recently published in *The Sewanee Review*. We had best not try to telescope the separate problems of "the psychology of composition" and that of "objective evaluation." I have no intention of trying to collapse them here.

Well, what is "said" in the "Horatian Ode"? What is the speaker's attitude toward Cromwell and toward Charles? M. Legouis sees in the "Ode" a complete impartiality, an impartiality which is the product of Marvell's nonparticipation in the wars. Legouis can even speak of the poem as "ce monument d'indifférence en matière de régime politique." But the "Ode," though it may be a monument of impartiality, is not a monument of indifference. To read it in this fashion is to miss what seems to me to be a passionate interest in the issues, an interest which is manifested everywhere in the poem. It is true that we have no evidence that Marvell ever served in the civil war, but we had better not leap to conclusions of his indifference from that. My own guess is that some young Cavaliers who shed their blood for the King thought and felt less deeply about the issues than does the speaker of this poem. The tone is not that of a "plague o' both your houses" nor is it that of "the conflict provided glory enough to be shared by both sides."

Mr. Margoliouth comes much closer to the point. He sums up as follows: "The ode is the utterance of a constitutional monarchist, whose sympathies have been with the King, but who yet believes more in men than in parties or principles, and whose hopes are fixed now on Cromwell, seeing in him both the civic ideal of a ruler without personal ambition, and the man of destiny moved by and yet himself driving a power which is above justice." This statement is plausible, and for its purposes, perhaps just. But does it take us very far—even on the level of understanding Marvell the man? What sort of constitutional monarchist is it who "believes more in men than in . . . principles"? Or who can accept a "power which is above justice"? I do not say that such a monarchist cannot exist. My point is that Margoliouth's statement raises more problems than it solves. Furthermore, in what sense are the speaker's hopes "fixed . . . on Cromwell"? And how confident is he that Cromwell is "without personal ambition"? I have quoted earlier Margoliouth's characterization of the "Ode" as a poem "where royalist principles and admiration for Cromwell the Great Man exist side by side." I think that they do exist side by side, but if so, how are they related? Do they exist in separate layers, or are they somehow unified? Unified, in some sense, they must be if the "Ode" is a poem and not a heap of fragments.

I hope that my last statement indicates the kind of question which we finally have to face and answer. It is a problem of poetic organization. As such, it addresses itself properly to the critic. The historical scholars have not answered it, for it is a question which cannot be answered in terms of historical evidence. (This is not to say, of course, that the same man may not be both historical scholar and critic.) Moreover, I have already taken some pains to indicate how heavily the critic, on his part, may need to lean upon the historian. To put the matter into its simplest terms: the critic obviously must know what the words of the poem mean, something which immediately puts him in debt to the linguist; and since many of the words in this poem are proper nouns, in debt to the historian as well. I am not concerned to exalt the critic at the expense of specialists in other disciplines: on the contrary, I am only concerned to show that he has a significant function, and to indicate what the nature of that function is.

But I am not so presumptuous as to promise a solution to the problem. Instead, the reader will have to be content with suggestions—as to what the "Ode" is not saying, as to what the "Ode" may be saying—in short, with explorations of further problems. Many critical problems, of course, I shall have to pass over and some important ones I shall only touch upon. To illustrate: there is the general Roman cast given to the "Ode." Marvell has taken care to make no specifically Christian references in the poem. Charles is Caesar; Cromwell is a Hannibal; on the scaffold, Charles refuses to call with "vulgar spight," not on God, but on "the Gods," and so on. Or to point to another problem, metaphors drawn from hunting pervade the poem. Charles chases himself to Carisbrooke; Cromwell is like the falcon; Cromwell will soon put his dogs in "near/The *Caledonian* Deer." Or, to take up the general organization of the poem: Marvell seems to have used the celebrated stanzas on Charles's execution to divide the poem into two rather distinct parts: first, Cromwell's rise to power; and second, Cromwell's wielding of the supreme power. This scheme of division, by the way, I intend to make use of in the discussion that follows. But I shall try, in general, to limit it to the specific problem of the speaker's attitude toward Cromwell, subordinating other critical problems to this one, which is, I maintain, essentially a critical problem too.

From historical evidence alone we would suppose that the attitude toward Cromwell in this poem would have to be a complex one. And this complexity is reflected in the ambiguity of the compliments paid to him. The ambiguity reveals itself as early as the second word of the poem. It is the "forward" youth whose attention the speaker directs to the example of Cromwell. "Forward" may mean no more than "high-spirited," "ardent," "properly ambitious"; but the *New English Dictionary* sanctions the possibility that there lurks in the word the sense of "presumptuous," "pushing." The forward youth can no longer now

> in the Shadows sing
> His Numbers languishing.

In the light of Cromwell's career, he must forsake the shadows and his "Muses dear" and become the man of action.

The speaker, one observes, does not identify Cromwell himself as the "forward youth," or say directly that Cromwell's career has been motivated by a striving for fame. But the implications of the first two stanzas do carry over to him. There is, for example, the important word "so" to relate Cromwell to these stanzas:

> So restless *Cromwel* could not cease. . . .

And "restless" is as ambiguous in its meanings as "forward," and in its darker connotations even more damning. For, though "restless" can mean "scorning indolence," "willing to forego ease," it can also suggest the man with a maggot in the brain. "To cease," used intransitively, is "to take rest, to be or remain at rest," and the *New English Dictionary* gives instances as late as 1701. Cromwell's "courage high" will not allow him to rest "in the inglorious Arts of Peace." And this thirst for glory, merely hinted at here by negatives, is developed further in the ninth stanza:

> Could by industrious Valour climbe
> To ruine the great Work of Time.

"Climb" certainly connotes a kind of aggressiveness. In saying this we need not be afraid that we are reading into the word some smack of such modern phrases as "social climber." Marvell's translation of the second chorus of Seneca's *Thyestes* sufficiently attests that the word could have such associations for him:

> Climb at *Court* for me that will
> Tottering favors Pinacle;
> All I seek is to lye still.

Cromwell, on the other hand, does not seek to lie still—has sought something quite other than this. His valor is called—strange collocation—an "industrious valour," and his courage is too high to brook a rival:

> For 'tis all one to Courage high
> The Emulous or Enemy;
> And with such to inclose,
> Is more then to oppose.

The implied metaphor is that of some explosive which does more violence to that which encloses it, the powder to its magazine, for instance, than to some wall which merely opposes it—against which the charge is fired.

But the speaker has been careful to indicate that Cromwell's motivation has to be conceived of as more complex than any mere thirst for glory. He has even pointed this up. The forward youth is referred to as one who "would appear"—that is, as one who wills to leave the shadows of obscurity. But restless Cromwell "could not cease"—for Cromwell it is not a question of will at all, but of a deeper compulsion. Restless Cromwell could not cease, if he would.

Indeed, the lines that follow extend the suggestion that Cromwell is like an elemental force—with as little will as the lightning bolt, and with as little conscience:

> And, like the three-fork'd Lightning, first
> Breaking the Clouds where it was nurst,

> Did thorough his own Side
> His fiery way divide.

We are told that the last two lines refer to Cromwell's struggle after Marston Moor with the leaders of the Parliamentary party. Doubtless they do, and the point is important for our knowledge of the poem. But what is more important is that we be fully alive to the force of the metaphor. The clouds have bred the lightning bolt, but the bolt tears its way through the clouds, and goes on to blast the head of Caesar himself. As Margoliouth puts it: "The lightning is conceived as tearing through the side of his own body the cloud." In terms of the metaphor, then, Cromwell has not spared his own body: there is no reason therefore to be surprised that he has not spared the body of Charles.

I do not believe that I overemphasized the speaker's implication that Cromwell is a natural force. A few lines later the point is reinforced with another naturalistic figure, an analogy taken from physics:

> Nature that hateth emptiness,
> Allows of penetration less:
> And therefore must make room
> Where greater Spirits come . . .

The question of right, the imagery insists, is beside the point. If nature will not tolerate a power vacuum, no more will it allow two bodies to occupy the same space. (It is amusing, by the way, that Marvell has boldly introduced into his analogy borrowed from physics the nonphysical term "Spirits"; yet I do not think that the clash destroys the figure. Since twenty thousand angels can dance on the point of a needle, two spirits, even though one of them is a greater spirit, ought to be able to occupy the same room. But two spirits, as Marvell conceives of spirits here, will jostle one another, and one must give way. True, the greater spirit is immaterial, but he is no pale abstraction—he is all air and fire, the "force of angry Heavens flame." The metaphor ought to give less trouble to the reader of our day than it conceivably gave to readers bred up on Newtonian physics.)

What are the implications for Charles? Does the poet mean to imply that Charles has angered heaven—that he has merited his destruction? There is no suggestion that Cromwell is a thunderbolt hurled by an angry Jehovah—or even by an angry Jove. The general emphasis on Cromwell as an elemental force is thoroughly relevant here to counter this possible misreading. Certainly, in the lines that follow there is nothing to suggest that Charles has angered heaven, or that the Justice which complains against his fate is anything less than justice.

I began this examination of the imagery with the question, "What is the speaker's attitude toward Cromwell?" We have seen that the speaker more than once hints at his thirst for glory:

> So restless *Cromwel* could not cease . . .
> Could by industrious Valour climbe . . .

But we have also seen that the imagery tends to view Cromwell as a natural phenomenon, the bolt bred in the cloud. Is there a contradiction? I think not. Cromwell's is no vulgar ambition. If his valor is an "industrious Valour," it contains plain valor too of a kind perfectly capable of being recognized by any Cavalier:

> What Field of all the Civil Wars,
> Where his were not the deepest Scars?

If the driving force has been a desire for glory, it is a glory of that kind which allows a man to become dedicated and, in a sense, even selfless in his pursuit of it. Moreover, the desire for such glory can become so much a compulsive force that the man does not appear to act by an exercise of his personal will but seems to become the very will of something else. There is in the poem, it seems to me, at least one specific suggestion of this sort:

> But through adventrous War
> Urged his active Star. . . .

Cromwell is the marked man, the man of destiny, but he is not merely the man governed by his star. Active though it be, he cannot remain passive, even in relation to it: he is not merely urged by it, but himself urges it on.

Yet, if thus far Cromwell has been treated as naked force, something almost too awesome to be considered as a man, the poet does not forget that after all he is a man too—that "the force of angry Heavens flame" is embodied in a human being:

> And, if we would speak true,
> Much to the Man is due.

The stanzas that follow proceed to define and praise that manliness—the strength, the industrious valor, the cunning. (You will notice that I reject the interpretation which would paraphrase "Much to the Man is due" as "After all, Cromwell has accomplished much that is good." Such an interpretation could sort well enough with Legouis's picture of Marvell as the cold and detached honest broker between the factions: unfortunately it will not survive a close scrutiny of the grammar and the general context in which the passage is placed.)

One notices that among the virtues comprising Cromwell's manliness, the speaker mentions his possession of the "wiser art":

> Where, twining subtile fears with hope,
> He wove a Net of such a scope,
> That *Charles* himselfe might chase
> To *Caresbrooks* narrow case.

On this point Cromwell has been cleared by all the modern historians (except perhaps Mr. Hilaire Belloc). Charles's flight to Carisbrooke Castle, as it turned out, aided Cromwell, but Cromwell could have hardly known that it would; and there is no evidence that he cunningly induced the King to flee to Carisbrooke. Royalist pamphleteers, of course, believed that Cromwell did, and used the item in their general bill of damnation against Cromwell. How does the speaker use it here—to damn or to praise? We tend to answer, "To praise." But then it behooves us to notice what is being praised. The things praised are Cromwell's talents as such—the tremendous disciplined powers which Cromwell brought to bear against the King.

For the end served by those powers, the speaker has no praise at all. Rather he has gone out of his way to insist that Cromwell was deaf to the complaint of Justice and its pleading of the "antient Rights." The power achieved by Cromwell is a "forced Pow'r"—a usurped power. On this point the speaker is unequivocal. I must question therefore Margoliouth's statement that Marvell sees in Cromwell "the man of destiny moved by . . . a power that is above justice." Above justice, yes, in the sense that power is power and justice is not power. The one does not insure the presence of the other. Charles has no way to vindicate his "helpless Right," but it is no less Right because it is helpless. But the speaker, though he is not a cynic, is a realist. A kingdom cannot be held by mere pleading of the "antient Rights":

> But those do hold or break
> As Men are strong or weak.

In short, the more closely we look at the "Ode," the more clearly apparent it becomes that the speaker has chosen to emphasize Cromwell's virtues as a man, and likewise, those of Charles as a man. The poem does not debate which of the two was right, for that issue is not even in question. In his treatment of Charles, then, the speaker no more than Charles himself attempts to vindicate his "helpless Right." Instead, he emphasizes his dignity, his fortitude, and what has finally to be called his consummate good taste. The portraits of the two men beautifully supplement each other. Cromwell is—to use Aristotle's distinction—the man of character, the man of action, who "does both act and know." Charles, on the other hand, is the man of passion, the man who is acted upon, the man who knows how to suffer. The contrast is pointed up in half a dozen different ways.

Cromwell, acted upon by his star, is not passive but actually urges his star. Charles in "acting"—in chasing away to Carisbrooke—actually is passive—performs the part assigned to him by Cromwell. True, we can read "chase" as an intransitive verb (the *New English Dictionary* sanctions this use for the period): "that Charles himself might hurry to Carisbrooke." But the primary meaning asserts itself in the context: "that Charles might chase himself to Carisbrooke's narrow case." For this hunter, now preparing to lay his dogs in "near/The *Caledonian* Deer," the royal quarry has dutifully chased itself.

Even in the celebrated stanzas on the execution, there is ironic realism as well as admiration. In this fullest presentation of Charles as king, he is the player king, the king acting in a play. He is the "Royal Actor" who knows his assigned part and performs it with dignity. He truly adorned the "Tragick Scaffold"

> While round the armed Bands
> Did clap their bloody hands.

The generally received account is that the soldiers clapped their hands so as to make it impossible for Charles's speech to be heard. But in the context this reference to hand-clapping supports the stage metaphor. What is being applauded? Cromwell's resolution in bringing the King to a deserved death? Or Charles's resolution on the scaffold as he suffered that death? Marvell was too good a poet to resolve the ambiguity. It is enough that he makes the armed bands applaud.

It has not been pointed out, I believe, that Robert Wild, in his poem on "The Death of Mr. Christopher Love," has echoed a pair of Marvell's finest lines. Love was beheaded by Cromwell on August 22, 1651. In Wild's poem, Marvell's lines

But with his keener Eye
The Axes edge did try

become: "His keener words did their sharp Ax exceed." The point is of no especial importance except that it indicates, since Wild's poem was evidently written shortly after Love's execution, that in 1651 the "Horatian Ode" was being handed about among the Royalists. For Wild was that strange combination, an English Presbyterian Royalist.

I have pointed out earlier that the second half of the poem begins here with the reference to

that memorable Hour
Which first assur'd the forced Pow'r.

Cromwell is now the *de facto* head of the state, and the speaker, as a realist, recognizes that fact. Cromwell is seen henceforth, not primarily in his character as the destroyer of the monarchy, but as the agent of the new state that has been erected upon the dead body of the King. The thunderbolt simile, of the first part of the poem, gives way here to the falcon simile in this second part of the poem. The latter figure revises and qualifies the former: it repeats the suggestion of ruthless energy and power, but Cromwell falls from the sky now, not as the thunderbolt, but as the hunting hawk. The trained falcon is not a wanton destroyer, nor an irresponsible one. It knows its master: it is perfectly disciplined:

She, having kill'd, no more does search,
But on the next green Bow to pearch . . .

The speaker's admiration for Cromwell the man culminates, it seems to me, here. Cromwell might make the Fame his own; he *need* not present kingdoms to the state. He might assume the crown rather than crowning each year. Yet he forbears:

Nor yet grown stiffer with Command,
But still in the *Republick's* hand . . .

Does the emphasis on "still" mean that the speaker is surprised that Cromwell has continued to pay homage to the republic? Does he imply that Cromwell may not always do so? Perhaps not: the emphasis is upon the fact that he need not obey and yet does. Yet the compliment derives its full force from the fact that the homage is not forced, but voluntary and even somewhat unexpected. And a recognition of this point implies the recognition of the possibility that Cromwell will not always so defer to the commonwealth.

And now what of the republic which Cromwell so ruthlessly and efficiently serves? What is the speaker's attitude toward it? To begin with, the speaker recognizes that its foundations rest upon the bleeding head of Charles. The speaker is aware, it is true, of the Roman analogy, and the English state is allowed the benefit of that analogy. But it is well to notice that the speaker does not commit himself to the opinion that the bleeding head is a happy augury:

> And yet in that the *State*
> Foresaw it's happy Fate.

The Roman state was able to take it as a favorable omen, and was justified by the event. With regard to the speaker himself, it seems to me more to the point to notice what prophecy he is willing to commit himself to. He does not prophesy peace. He is willing to predict that England, under Cromwell's leadership, will be powerful in war, and will strike fear into the surrounding states:

> What may not then our *Isle* presume
> While Victory his Crest does plume!
> What may not others fear
> If thus he crown each year!

Specifically, he predicts a smashing victory over the Scots.

But what of the compliments to Cromwell on his ruthlessly effective campaign against the Irish? Does not the speaker succumb, for once, to a bitter and biased patriotism, and does this not constitute a blemish upon the poem?

> And now the *Irish* are asham'd
> To see themselves in one Year tam'd:
> So much one Man can do,
> That does both act and know.
> They can affirm his Praises best,
> And have, though overcome, confest
> How good he is, how just. . . .

Margoliouth glosses the word "confessed" as follows: "Irish testimony in favor of Cromwell at this moment is highly improbable. Possibly there is a reference to the voluntary submission of part of Munster with its English colony." But surely Margoliouth indulges in understatement. The most intense partisan of Cromwell would have had some difficulty in taking the lines without some inflection of grim irony. The final appeal in this matter, however, is not to what Marvell the Englishman must have thought, or even to what Marvell the author must have intended, but rather to the full context of the poem itself. In that context, the lines in question can be read ironically, and the earlier stanzas sanction that reading. Cromwell's energy, activity, bravery, resolution—even what may be called his efficiency—are the qualities that have come in for praise, not his gentleness or his mercy. The Irish, indeed, are best able to affirm such praise as has been accorded to Cromwell; and they know from experience "how good he is, how just," for they have been blasted by the force of angry Heaven's flame, even as Charles has been. But I do not mean to turn the passage into sarcasm. The third quality which the speaker couples with goodness and justice is fitness "for highest Trust," and the goodness and justice of Cromwell culminate in this fitness. But the recommendation to trust has reference not to the Irish, but to the English state. The Irish are quite proper authorities on Cromwell's trustworthiness in this regard, for they have come to know him as the completely dedicated instrument of that state whose devotion to the purpose in hand is unrelenting and unswerving.

To say all this is not to suggest that Marvell shed any unnecessary tears over the plight of the Irish, or even to imply that he was not happy, as one assumes most Englishmen were, to have the Irish rebellion crushed promptly and efficiently. It is to say that the passage fits into the poem—a poem which reveals itself to be no panegyric on Cromwell but an unflinching analysis of the Cromwellian character.

The wild Irish have been tamed, and now the Pict will no longer be able to shelter under his particolored mind. It is the hour of decision, and the particolored mind affords no protection against the man who "does both act and know." In Cromwell's mind there are no conflicts, no teasing mixture of judgments. Cromwell's is not only an "industrious valour," but a "sad valour." Margoliouth glosses "sad" as "steadfast," and no doubt he is right. But sad can mean "sober" also, and I suspect that in this context, with its implied references to Scottish plaids, it means also drab of hue. It is also possible that the poet here glances at one of Virgil's transferred epithets, *maestum timorem,* sad fear, the fear that made the Trojans sad. Cromwell's valor is *sad* in that the Scots will have occasion to rue it.

Thus far the speaker has been content to view Cromwell from a distance, as it were, against the background of recent history. He has referred to him consistently in the third person. But in the last two stanzas, he addresses Cromwell directly. He salutes him as "the Wars and Fortunes Son." It is a great compliment: Cromwell is the son of the wars in that he is the master of battle, and he seems fortune's own son in the success that has constantly waited upon him. But we do not wrench the lines if we take them to say also that Cromwell is the creature of the wars and the product of fortune. The imagery of the early stanzas which treats Cromwell as a natural phenomenon certainly lends support to this reading. Cromwell can claim no sanction for his power in "antient Rights." His power has come out of the wars and the troubled times. I call attention to the fact that we do not have to choose between readings: the readings do not mutually exclude each other: they support each other, and this double interpretation has the whole poem behind it.

Cromwell is urged to march "indefatigably on." The advice is good advice; but it is good advice because any other course of action is positively unthinkable. Indeed, to call it advice at all is perhaps to distort it: though addressed to Cromwell, it partakes of quiet commentary as much as of exhortation. After all, it is restless Cromwell who is being addressed. If he could not cease "in the inglorious Arts of Peace" when his "highest plot" was "to plant the Bergamot," one cannot conceive of his ceasing now in the hour of danger.

> And for the last effect
> Still keep thy Sword erect.

Once more the advice (or commentary) is seriously intended, but it carries with it as much of warning as it does of approval. Those who take up the sword shall perish by the sword: those who have achieved their power on contravention of ancient rights by the sword can only expect to maintain their power by the sword.

What kind of sword is it that is able to "fright the spirits of the shady night"? Margoliouth writes: "The cross hilt of the sword would avert the spirits. . . ." But the speaker makes it quite plain that it is not merely the spirits of the shady night that Cromwell will have to fight as he marches indefatigably on. It will not be enough to hold the sword aloft as a ritual sword, an emblematic sword. The naked steel will still have to be used against bodies less diaphanous than spirits. If there is any doubt as to this last point, Marvell's concluding lines put it as powerfully and explicitly as it can be put:

> The same *Arts* that did *gain*
> A *Pow'r* must it *maintain*.

But, I can imagine someone asking, What is the final attitude toward Cromwell? Is it ultimately one of approval or disapproval? Does admiration overbalance condemnation? Or, is the "Ode," after all, merely a varied Scottish plaid, the reflection of Marvell's own particolored mind—a mind which had not been finally "made up" with regard to Cromwell? I think that enough has been said to make it plain that there is no easy, pat answer to such questions. There is a unified total attitude, it seems to me; but it is so complex that we may oversimplify and distort its complexity by the way in which we put the question. The request for some kind of summing up is a natural one, and I have no wish to try to evade it. For a really full answer, of course, one must refer the questioner to the poem itself; but one can at least try to suggest some aspects of the total attitude.

I would begin by reemphasizing the dramatic character of the poem. It is not a statement—an essay on "Why I cannot support Cromwell" or on "Why I am now ready to support Cromwell." It is a poem essentially dramatic in its presentation, which means that it is diagnostic rather than remedial, and eventuates, not in a course of action, but in contemplation. Perhaps the best way therefore in which to approach it is to conceive of it as, say, one conceives of a Shakespearean tragedy. Cromwell is the usurper who demands and commands admiration. What, for example, is our attitude toward Macbeth? We assume his guilt, but there are qualities which emerge from his guilt which properly excite admiration. I do not mean that the qualities palliate his guilt or that they compensate for his guilt. They actually come into being through his guilt, but they force us to exalt him even as we condemn him. I have chosen an extreme example. I certainly do not mean to imply that in writing the "Ode" Marvell had Shakespeare's tragedy in mind. What I am trying to point to is this: that the kind of honesty and insight and whole-mindedness which we associate with tragedy is to be found to some degree in all great poetry and is to be found in this poem.

R. P. Warren once remarked to me that Marvell has constantly behind him in his poetry the achievement of Elizabethan drama with its treatment of the human will as seen in the perspective of history. He had in mind some of the lyrics, but the remark certainly applies fully to the "Ode." The poet is thoroughly conscious of the drama, and consciously makes use of dramatic perspective. Charles, as we have seen, becomes the "Royal Actor," playing his part on the "Tragick Scaffold." But the tragedy of Charles is merely glanced at. The poem is Cromwell's—Cromwell's tragedy, the first three acts of it, as it were, which is not a tragedy of failure but of success.

Cromwell is the truly kingly man who is *not* king—whose very virtues conduce to kingly power and almost force kingly power upon him. It is not any fumbling on the poet's part which causes him to call Cromwell "a Caesar" before the poem ends, even though he has earlier appropriated that name to Charles. *Both* men are Caesar, Charles the wearer of the purple, and Cromwell, the invincible general, the inveterate campaigner, the man "that does both act and know." Cromwell is the Caesar who must refuse the crown—whose glory it is that he is willing to refuse the crown—but who cannot enjoy the reward and the security that a crown affords. The tension between the speaker's admiration for the kingliness which has won Cromwell the power and his awareness that the power can be maintained only by a continual exertion of these talents for kingship—this tension is never relaxed. Cromwell is not of royal blood—he boasts a higher and a baser pedigree: he is the "Wars and Fortunes Son." He cannot rest because he is restless Cromwell. He must march indefatigably on, for he cannot afford to become fatigued. These implications enrich and qualify an insight into Cromwell which is as heavily freighted with admiration as it is with a great condemnation. But the admiration and the condemnation do not cancel each other. They define each other; and because there is responsible definition, they reinforce each other.

Was this, then, the attitude of Andrew Marvell, born 1621, sometime student at Cambridge, returned traveler and prospective tutor, toward Oliver Cromwell in the summer of 1650? The honest answer must be: I do not know. I have tried to read the poem, the "Horatian Ode," not Andrew Marvell's mind. That seems sensible to me in view of the fact that we have the poem, whereas the attitude held by Marvell at any particular time must be a matter of inference—even though I grant that the poem may be put in as part of the evidence from which we draw inferences. True, we do know that Marvell was capable of composing the "Ode" and I must concede that that fact may tell us a great deal about Marvell's attitude toward Cromwell. I think it probably does. I am not sure, for reasons given earlier in this paper, that it tells us everything: there is the problem of the role of the unconscious in the process of composition, there is the possibility of the poet's having written better than he knew, there is even the matter of the happy accident. I do not mean to overemphasize these matters. I do think, however, that it is wise to maintain the distinction between what total attitude is manifested in the poem and the attitude of the author as citizen.

Yet, though I wish to maintain this distinction, I do not mean to hide behind it. The total attitude realized in the "Ode" does not seem to me monstrously inhuman in its complexity. It could be held by human beings, in my opinion. Something very like it apparently was. Listen, for example, to the Earl of Clarendon's judgment on Cromwell:

> He was one of those men, quos vitupare ne inimici quidem possunt, nisi ut simul laudent [whom not even their enemies can inveigh against without at the same time praising them], for he could never have done halfe that mischieve, without great partes of courage and industry and judgement, and he must have had a wonderful understandinge in the nature and humours of men, and as greate a dexterity in the applyinge them, who from a private and obscure birth (though of a good family), without interest of estate, allyance or frenshippes, could rayse himselfe to such a height, and compounde and kneade such opposite and contradictory humours and interests, into a consistence, that contributed to his designes and to ther owne distruction, whilst himselfe grew insensibly powerful enough, to cutt off those by whom he had climed, in the instant, that they projected to demolish ther owne buildinge. . . .
>
> He was not a man of bloode, and totally declined Machiavells methode . . . it was more then once proposed, that ther might be a generall massacre of all the royall party, as the only expedient to secure the government, but Crumwell would never consent to it, it may be out of to much contempt of his enimyes; In a worde, as he had all the wikednesses against which damnation is denounced and for which Hell fyre is praepared, so he had some virtues, which have caused the memory of some men in all ages to be celebrated, and he will be looked upon by posterity, as a brave, badd man.

The resemblance between Clarendon's judgment and that reflected in the "Ode" is at some points so remarkable that one wonders whether Clarendon had not seen and been impressed by some now lost manuscript of the "Ode": "Who from a private and obscure birth"—"Who, from his private Gardens, where/He liv'd reserved and austere"—"could rayse himself to such a height . . . by whome he had climed"—"Could by industrious Valour climbe," and so on and so forth. But I do not want to press the suggestion of influence of Marvell on Clarendon. Indeed, it makes for my general point to discount the possibility. For what I am anxious to emphasize is that the attitude of the "Ode" is not inhuman in its Olympian detachment, that something like it could be held by a human being, and by a human being of pronounced Royalist sympathies.

I have argued that the critic needs the help of the historian—all the help that he can get—but I have insisted that the poem has to be read as a poem—that what it "says" is a question for the critic to answer, and that no amount of historical evidence as such can finally determine what the poem says. But if we do read the poem successfully, the critic may on occasion be able to make a return on his debt to the historian. If we have read the "Ode" successfully—*if*, I say, for I am far from confident—it may be easier for us to understand how the man capable of writing the "Ode" was also able to write "Tom May's Death" and "On Appleton House" and indeed, years later, after the Restoration, the statement: "Men ought to have trusted God; they ought and might have trusted the King."

Since completing this essay, I have come upon a further (see p. 332) item which would suggest that the "Horatian Ode" was circulating among Royalists—not Puritans—in the early 1650's. The stanza form of the "Horatian Ode" was used only once by Marvell (in this poem) and does not seem to occur in English poetry prior to Marvell. Margoliouth and Legouis think it probable that this stanza was Marvell's own invention. Perhaps it was. But in Sir Richard Fanshawe's translation of Horace's Odes (*Selected Parts of Horace . . . Now newly put into English*, London, 1652) the "Horatian Ode" stanza is used several times. If Marvell invented the stanza in the summer of 1650, he must have been in close association with Fanshawe for Fanshawe to have borrowed and made use of the stanza so frequently in poems which were to be in print two years later. I suspect that Marvell borrowed the stanza from Fanshawe. Fanshawe had begun to publish translations of Horace (though none in this stanza pattern) as early as 1648 in the volume which contained his translation of *Il Pastor Fido*. But in either case a Royalist connection for Marvell is implied, for Fanshawe (1608–66) was a fervent and active Royalist throughout the war, and after the Restoration was a trusted servant of Charles II.

The following notes appear in H. M. Margoliouth's edition of *The Poems and Letters of Andrew Marvell* (Oxford: Clarendon Press, 1927), I, 237–38:

> A correspondent in *The Times Literary Supplement* (29 January 1920) compares with ll. 9–16 of this Ode Lucan, *Pharsalia*, i. 144 *et seq*. . . .
>
> Marvell perhaps had in mind both the Latin (cf. successus

urgere suos and "Urg'd his active Star") and Tom May's translation, which here reads as follows (2nd edition, 1631):

But restlesse valour, and in warre a shame
Not to be Conquerour; fierce, not curb'd at all,
Ready to fight, where hope, or anger call,
His forward Sword; confident of successe,
And bold the favour of the gods to presse:
Orethrowing all that his ambition stay,
And loves that ruine should enforce his way;
As lightning by the wind forc'd from a cloude
Breakes through the wounded aire with thunder loud,
Disturbes the Day, the people terrifyes,
And by a light oblique dazels our eyes,
Not *Joves* owne Temple spares it; when no force,
No barre can hinder his prevailing course,
Great waste, as foorth it sallyes and retires,
It makes and gathers his dispersed fires.

Note the verbal resemblances, "restlesse valour" and "industrious Valour," "forward Sword" and "The forward Youth," "lightning . . . from a cloude Breakes" and "Lightning . . . Breaking the Clouds." Further I suggest with diffidence that the striking phrase "active Star" owes something to the chance neighbourhood of the two words in another passage in the same book of May's translation (*Pharsalia*, i. 229–32):

. . . the active Generall
Swifter than Parthian back-shot shaft, or stone
From Balearick Slinger, marches on
T' invade Ariminum; when every star
Fled from th' approaching Sunne but Lucifer . . .

Caesar is up betimes, marching when only the morning star is in the sky: Cromwell urges *his* "active star."

Sir Edward Ridley, carrying on the correspondence in *The Times Literary Supplement* (5 February 1920), points out further a likeness between Marvell's account of the death of Charles I and *Pharsalia*, viii. 613–17 (the death of Pompey):

ut vidit comminus ensem
involvit vultus atque indignatus apertum
fortunae praestare caput, tunc lumina pressit
continuitque animam, ne quas effundere voces
posset et aeternam fletu corrumpere famam . . .

DOUGLAS BUSH

Marvell's "Horatian Ode"

The "Horatian Ode" is commonly regarded not only as one of Marvell's finest poems but as an embodiment of two usually distinct poetic modes, the classical and the "metaphysical." For all its metaphysical texture and originality, it is the nearest approach in English to the form and the *gravitas* of Horace's patriotic odes. There is the further fact that the poem is not a conventional eulogy but a subtle portrait of its subject, warts and all. At a time when Cromwell aroused violently conflicting passions among Englishmen (as indeed he has ever since), Marvell was able to contemplate both him and King Charles with a mixture of warm admiration and cool, analytical detachment. To read the poem as poetry is also to read it as an historical document, for we must ask what Marvell is saying, in and between the lines, about Cromwell.

In *English Institute Essays 1946*, Professor Cleanth Brooks, attacking "the specific problem of the speaker's attitude toward Cromwell," gives an elaborate and acute analysis of the ode which is intended to illustrate, in contrast to the "coarse" method of historical criticism, the critic's obligation to interpret the poem as it stands, to bring out all the conscious and unconscious hints and complexities that it contains, and thereby to define Marvell's view of Cromwell from the inside. One might stop to quarrel with such an arbitrary doctrine of criticism, since the critic's obligation is surely to use all helpful evidence of any kind (and Mr. Brooks himself, when he wishes, goes outside the poem), but in this case one may be quite willing to suspend disbelief

From *Sewanee Review*, LX (1952), pp. 363–76. Reprinted by permission of the publishers and the author.

and consider the ode on Mr. Brooks's terms. Accepting the judgment of Marvell's editor, Mr. Margoliouth, that "royalist principles and admiration for Cromwell the Great Man exist side by side," Mr. Brooks holds that the problem is a subtle one of poetic organization and therefore addresses itself properly to the critic.

But the moment we enter upon Mr. Brooks's exegesis we see that, far from making a disinterested inquiry into the evidence provided by the poem, he is forcing the evidence to fit an unspoken assumption —namely, that a sensitive, penetrating, and well-balanced mind like Marvell could not really have admired a crude, single-minded, and ruthless man of action like Cromwell. This is a prejudice natural enough in a good modern liberal, who is bound to see Cromwell, even the Cromwell of 1650, as a sort of Puritan Stalin, but it is a prejudice; and it leads, as I have said, to frequent straining or distortion of what Marvell says and to the supplying of things he does not say. Indeed, if people in 1681 would have read the poem with Mr. Brooks's eyes, as in the main a condemnation of Cromwell, there would not have been much reason for the poem's being cut out of the first edition of Marvell, since such a view of Cromwell would have been welcome enough to the Restoration. But that is irrelevant historical speculation, and we must look at the poem.

Mr. Brooks's special pleading begins with his gloss on the first lines:

> The forward Youth that would appear
> Must now forsake his Muses dear,
>   Nor in the Shadows sing
>   His Numbers languishing.
> 'Tis time to leave the Books in dust,
> And oyl th' unused Armours rust:
>   Removing from the Wall
>   The Corslet of the Hall.

To the unprejudiced reader, the lines say that, in these troubled times, the young man of spirit must leave bookish and poetical pursuits for military action. Says Mr. Brooks (pp. 135–6): "'Forward' may mean no more than 'high-spirited,' 'ardent,' 'properly ambitious'; but the *New English Dictionary* sanctions the possibility that there lurks in the word the sense of 'presumptuous,' 'pushing,'" and "It is the 'forward' youth whose attention the speaker directs to the example of Cromwell." Thus the critic has already made up his mind about the poet's view of Cromwell, and, instead of taking "forward" in its common and natural sense, must grasp at a pejorative possibility (the meaning "presumptuous," to judge from the *New English Dictionary*, has been commoner in modern times than it was in Marvell's).

After the prelude, Marvell shifts to Cromwell, stressing his tremendous, superhuman energy, with the aid of a violent and elaborate simile:

> So restless Cromwel could not cease
> In the inglorious Arts of Peace,
> But through adventrous War
> Urged his active Star.
> And, like the three-fork'd Lightning, first
> Breaking the Clouds where it was nurst,
> Did thorough his own Side
> His fiery way divide.
> For 'tis all one to Courage high
> The Emulous or Enemy;
> And with such to inclose
> Is more than to oppose.
> Then burning through the Air he went,
> And Pallaces and Temples rent:
> And Caesars head at last
> Did through his Laurels blast.

Here, as before, Mr. Brooks makes a pejorative choice among "ambiguous" possibilities. "'Restless' is as ambiguous in its meanings as 'forward,' and in its darker connotations even more damning" (p. 136). The critic finds Cromwell's thirst for glory hinted at in many phrases—"*could* not cease," "the inglorious Arts of Peace," in the fact that, instead of being led by his star, Cromwell "Urged" his (pp. 140, 143). Mr. Brooks may, theoretically, or ultimately, be correct, but has Marvell, so far, given warrant for these "darker connotations"? At any rate Mr. Brooks is consistent in always loading the dice against Cromwell.

The simile, says Mr. Brooks (p. 138), makes Cromwell "like an elemental force—with as little will as the lightning bolt, and with as little conscience." Cromwell manifestly is likened to an elemental force, but, again, has Marvell given any warrant for the interpretative phrases, or are they a prejudiced addition? Does a lightning bolt have "Courage high"? But comment on the full meaning of the simile must wait for a moment. The nature of Mr. Brooks's special pleading becomes conspicuous in his treatment of the next two lines, which are, for his problem, perhaps the most significant lines in the whole poem:

'Tis Madness to resist or blame
The force of angry Heavens flame.

Mr. Brooks writes (p. 139):

> Does the poet mean to imply that Charles has angered heaven—that he has merited his destruction? There is no suggestion that Cromwell is a thunderbolt hurled by an angry Jehovah—or even by an angry Jove. The general emphasis on Cromwell as an elemental force is thoroughly relevant here to counter this possible misreading. Certainly, in the lines that follow there is nothing to suggest that Charles has angered heaven, or that the Justice which complains against his fate is anything less than justice.

I do not know what to make of such a statement as "There is no suggestion that Cromwell is a thunderbolt hurled by an angry Jehovah—or even by an angry Jove," since that is what Marvell unmistakably says. In keeping with the pagan tone of a Horatian ode, of course, he nowhere permits a Christian allusion, but the poem is not a period piece of artificial classicism and the reader makes an obvious transfer from pagan Rome to Christian England. Even if Cromwell be conceived only as a traditional "Scourge of God," he is the agent of the Providence whose will, in the common view of history, has worked in human affairs. Mr. Brooks seems to be merely rejecting evidence that is signally inconvenient for his reading of the poem.

Since, as we observed, Mr. Brooks himself, in spite of his premise, goes outside the poem for desired data, one may venture to do likewise—although the poem itself is sufficiently clear and emphatic in presenting Cromwell as the agent of angry heaven. We need not assume that Marvell's view of men and events remained quite unaltered up to the time, between four and five years later, when he wrote so wholly eulogistic a poem as "The First Anniversary of the Government under O. C.," but it is altogether unlikely either that he had made a *volte-face* or that he had become a mere time-server. We might take a few bits from the later poem as glosses on "angry Heavens flame" which—however inferior the poetry—are not less reliable than a modern critic's inferences:

While indefatigable Cromwell hyes,
And cuts his way still nearer to the Skyes,
Learning a Musique in the Region clear,
To tune this lower to that higher Sphere. (Ll. 45–48)

Hence oft I think, if in some happy Hour
High Grace should meet in one with highest Pow'r,
And then a seasonable People still
Should bend to his, as he to Heavens will,
What we might hope, what wonderful Effect
From such a wish'd Conjuncture might reflect. (131-36)

What since he did, an higher Force him push'd
Still from behind, and it before him rush'd,
Though undiscern'd among the tumult blind,
Who think those high Decrees by Man design'd.
'Twas Heav'n would not that his Pow'r should cease,
But walk still middle betwixt War and Peace;
Choosing each Stone, and poysing every weight,
Trying the Measures of the Bredth and Height;
Here pulling down, and there erecting New,
Founding a firm State by Proportions true. (239-48)

And, especially for the sake of one phrase, we might add a couplet from the opening of Marvell's "Poem upon the Death of O. C.":

And he whom Nature all for Peace had made,
But angry Heaven unto War had sway'd. . . .

In these later poems Cromwell is unquestionably the instrument of God, and if in the earlier one the lines about "angry Heavens flame" do not say the same thing, one does not know what they do say. The modern liberal—who normally reacts against Toynbee and Butterfield—can seldom fully understand the providential conception of history which was traditional in Marvell's age (witness Ralegh's *History of the World*) and which was indeed a necessary part of Christian belief; and Marvell, however liberal and emancipated from common prejudices, was a Christian. All this is not to say that he takes, here or elsewhere, a simple, one-sided view of either Cromwell or Charles, but one must emphasize the central importance of Cromwell's being a divine agent and hence endowed with the power of a force of nature.

In the next few lines Cromwell is associated with peaceful rural nature:

And, if we would speak true,
Much to the Man is due.

> Who, from his private Gardens, where
> He liv'd reserved and austere,
> As if his highest plot
> To plant the Bergamot. . . .

The first two lines are something more than a transition. "Much to the Man is due," in focusing on the actual person in himself, helps to define the previous conception of the being who was an instrument of Providence. The next quatrain is clearly intended to link Cromwell the man with the simple, frugal heroes of Roman tradition, like Cincinnatus, called from the plough to rule the state. In what they say, and in the affinity they imply, the lines are a quiet refutation of some of Mr. Brooks's darker inferences.

Then we come to a passage where the warts may seem to protrude. The man who lived as if only to plant the bergamot

> Could by industrious Valour climbe
> To ruine the great Work of Time,
> And cast the Kingdome old
> Into another Mold.
> Though Justice against Fate complain,
> And plead the antient Rights in vain:
> But those do hold or break
> As Men are strong or weak.
> Nature that hateth emptiness
> Allows of penetration less:
> And therefore must make room
> Where greater Spirits come.
> What Field of all the Civil Wars
> Where his were not the deepest Scars? . . .

Mr. Brooks thinks that "climbe" "certainly connotes a kind of aggressiveness" and a thirst for glory, and that, in the lines on "Nature," "The question of right, the imagery insists, is beside the point," since the question of power alone is being weighed (pp. 136, 138–9). He admits that Marvell recognizes Cromwell's martial valor, even a dedicated rather than a merely selfish sense of glory, and the role of a man of destiny; and he points out, following Margoliouth and Firth, that there is no ground for the contemporary charge, which Marvell repeats, that Cromwell had engineered Charles's flight to Carisbrooke Castle. But the critic maintains nevertheless that Cromwell has "thus far . . . been treated as naked force" (p. 140); he has been praised for "the tremendous disciplined powers" he has brought to bear against the king. However, Mr. Brooks proceeds,

> For the end served by those powers, the speaker has no praise at all. Rather he has gone out of his way to insist that Cromwell was deaf to the complaint of Justice and its pleading of the "antient Rights." The power achieved by Cromwell is a "forced Pow'r"—a usurped power. On this point the speaker is unequivocal. I must question therefore Margoliouth's statement that Marvell sees in Cromwell "the man of destiny moved by . . . a power that is above justice." Above justice, yes, in the sense that power is power and justice is not power. The one does not insure the presence of the other. Charles has no way to vindicate his "helpless Right," but it is no less Right because it is helpless. But the speaker, though he is not a cynic, is a realist. A kingdom cannot be held by mere pleading of the "antient Rights":
>
> But those do hold or break
> As Men are strong or weak.
>
> In short, the more closely we look at the "Ode," the more clearly apparent it becomes that the speaker has chosen to emphasize Cromwell's virtues as a man, and likewise, those of Charles as a man. The poem does not debate which of the two was right, for that issue is not even in question. (p. 142)

This may be the right, or a tenable, view of the central passage we have arrived at, and of the whole poem, yet it seems open to query. In the first place, if the issue of "right" is not even in question, how can anyone be concerned, as Mr. Brooks is all along, with distinguishing right from power, with sifting moral praise and blame, and, in short, making the strongest possible case for the prosecution? In the second place, although elsewhere he is on the watch for sinister ambiguities, even in words that appear innocent, here words of at least equal ambiguity have become moral absolutes that condemn Cromwell. The word "right" ("the antient Rights," "his helpless Right") may mean not only abstract rightness but traditional claims which may or may not be wholly right. "Justice" may be absolute justice, or it may be the limited vision of human law that must give way before the divine will ("Fate," in Roman terms). The "great Work of Time" that

Cromwell has ruined is not necessarily or wholly the good work of time; a great nation may have nourished wrongs that must, at whatever cost, be righted. Marvell was assuredly not of "Machiavellian" outlook, but in his view of Cromwell he may—with some inportant differences—have somewhat resembled Machiavelli: while Machiavelli's ideal was the old Roman republic, a republic could not bring order out of chaos, and the strong man who could must be welcomed. Though Marvell does not go into the causes of the civil war but concentrates on Cromwell and his royal opponent, he indicates that he sees "the Kingdome old" as undergoing the pangs of both death and rebirth, and, with all his admiration for the royal actor, he bows to the man of action who can, however violently, establish order. And, as we have seen, he bows not only to the heroic individual but to the Providence who has raised him up.

After the account of Charles's execution—which for too many readers disturbs the center of gravity of the poem—the poet turns, as Mr. Brooks says, from Cromwell the destroyer of the monarchy to "the agent of the new state that has been erected upon the dead body of the King" (p. 144). The execution was "that memorable Hour Which first assur'd the forced Pow'r." But while Cromwell has been an illegal regicide, the effect of "forced Pow'r" is partly countered by what follows, the incident from Roman history in which "the State Foresaw it's happy Fate." If the execution was evil, it can bring forth good. As Mr. Brooks sees it, Marvell "does not commit himself to the opinion that the bleeding head is a happy augury," but makes this the popular opinion. I doubt if Marvell—whatever he privately felt—is here consciously disassociating himself from "the State." If he were, would he go so far elsewhere in the poem in celebrating Cromwell with his own voice?

There follows at once a passage that is probably more embarrassing than any other part of the ode to anyone intent upon proving that Marvell's main attitude toward Cromwell is hostility or at most unwilling respect for unscrupulous strength and courage:

> And now the Irish are asham'd
> To see themselves in one Year tam'd:
> So much one Man can do,
> That does both act and know.
> They can affirm his Praises best,
> And have, though overcome, confest
> How good he is, how just,
> And fit for highest Trust.

Mr. Margoliouth remarks that "Irish testimony in favour of Cromwell at this moment is highly improbable" (though he sees a possible reference to the voluntary submission of part of Munster), and we may, with Mr. Brooks, take the remark as an understatement. For Mr. Brooks the appeal "is not to what Marvell the Englishman must have thought, or even to what Marvell the author must have intended, but rather to the full context of the poem itself" (p. 147). One may not quite understand these several possibilities, since the poem did not get itself written by some agency outside of Marvell. However, Mr. Brooks is driven to what may be thought the desperate solution of finding the lines ironical, a view he thinks sanctioned by the earlier stanzas because the Irish have learned of the qualities in Cromwell that Marvell had praised, energy, activity, and the like. "The Irish, indeed, are best able to affirm such praise as has been accorded to Cromwell; and they know from experience 'how good he is, how just,' for they have been blasted by the force of angry Heaven's flame, even as Charles has been" (p. 147).

Since I cannot follow much of Mr. Brooks's reading of the earlier stanzas, I cannot follow such an explanation. Nothing in the wording seems to me to carry the faintest trace of irony; it is as straightforward a statement as we could have, however little we like it. Nor do I see how irony could pass at once into what Mr. Brooks accepts as eulogy without the slightest hint of a change of tone. Although, as he says, the recommendation of trust has reference to the English state, it is the Irish who have "confest" it, and I see nothing in the text to support Mr. Brooks's oblique interpretation of Marvell's account of Irish feelings: "The Irish are quite proper authorities on Cromwell's trustworthiness in this regard, for they have come to know him as the completely dedicated instrument of that state whose devotion to the purpose in hand is unrelenting and unswerving" (p. 148). But, instead of twisting Marvell's plain words into irony, and thereby molding him into the likeness of a modern liberal, we really must accept the unpalatable fact that he wrote as an Englishman of 1650; and, in regard to what seems to us a strange assertion, we must say that he is indulging in some wishful thinking—Cromwell is so great a conqueror that even the Irish must share English sentiment and accept the course of history. In the poem on Cromwell's death, it may be added, Marvell glanced at his Irish campaign with nothing but admiration for his religious zeal and martial prowess (ll. 179 ff.). It may be added further that Milton was far closer to Marvell than any modern reader can be (and Milton was bold enough, a few years later when Cromwell was at the height of his power, to rebuke him for turning a republic into a dictatorship), and we have only to look at Milton's *Observations on the Articles of Peace* (1649) to see what the English attitude was. That is not to say that Marvell thought just as Milton thought; it is to say that the text of Marvell's poem means what it says, and that the suggestion of irony raises a much more difficult problem, within the poem, than the one it seeks to explain.

Early in his essay Mr. Brooks observed that "the critic obviously must know what the words of the poem mean, something which immediately puts him in debt to the linguist" (p. 134), but he neglects this sound precept in his comment on the next lines:

> Nor yet grown stiffer with Command,
> But still in the Republick's hand.

Says Mr. Brooks:

> Does the emphasis on "still" mean that the speaker is surprised that Cromwell has continued to pay homage to the republic? Does he imply that Cromwell may not always do so? Perhaps not: the emphasis is upon the fact that he need not obey and yet does. Yet the compliment derives its full force from the fact that the homage is not forced but voluntary and even somewhat unexpected. And a recognition of this point implies the recognition of the possibility that Cromwell will not always so defer to the commonwealth. (p. 145)

But such "darker connotations" are quite gratuitous. "Still" here—as later in "Still keep thy Sword erect"—has its normal seventeenth-century meaning, "always," and Marvell's words afford no ground for an ominous hint of a possible change of heart in Cromwell.

We need not concern ourselves with the rest of the ode, in which Marvell sees Cromwell as the obedient servant of Parliament, the prospective conqueror of the Scots, and a leader to be feared by Europe. But we may notice the last lines, where Mr. Brooks again finds sinister implications:

> But thou the Wars and Fortunes Son
> March indefatigably on;
> And for the last effect
> Still keep thy Sword erect:
> Besides the force it has to fright

The Spirits of the shady Night,
The same Arts that did gain
A Pow'r must it maintain.

The salutation in the first line means, as Mr. Brooks says (p. 149), that "Cromwell is the son of the wars in that he is the master of battle, and he seems fortune's own son in the success that has constantly waited upon him." But he goes on to say that "we do not wrench the lines if we take them to say also that Cromwell is the creature of the wars and the product of fortune." I think this is a very decided wrenching of the lines; we must remember that Marvell has seen Cromwell as the agent of heaven. And there is some further wrenching in Mr. Brooks's comment on "Still keep thy Sword erect": "Those who take up the sword shall perish by the sword: those who have achieved their power on contravention of ancient rights by the sword can only expect to maintain their power by the sword" (p. 150). Does Marvell give any hint toward such an interpretation?

Mr. Brooks always offers general and particular insights that sharpen our perceptions, and this essay, like his others, is precise and provocative. His readers, if they came to it with the notion that Marvell's ode is a simple poem, could never again be misled in that way. But they could be misled into finding a greater degree of complexity than the text warrants. There is surely a line between legitimate and illegitimate ambiguity, a line to be respected by both poet and critic, and Mr. Brooks seems continually to overstep that line. He sees the poem as expressing a "unified total attitude," though a very complex one, yet it would be hard to merge his findings into any total unity unless Marvell is more or less lifted out of his age into ours. As we have seen, the result, if not the aim, of Mr. Brooks's inquiry is, in large measure, to turn a seventeenth-century liberal into a modern one. That is one reason why historical conditioning has a corrective as well as a positive value, although in this case we do not need to go outside the poem to recognize fallacies and distortions in what purports to be a purely critical and unprejudiced analysis.

CLEANTH BROOKS

A Note on the Limits of "History" and the Limits of "Criticism"

I have been asked by the editor to comment upon Mr. Douglas Bush's discussion of my reading of Marvell's "Horatian Ode." Mr. Bush writes that "the poem is not a conventional eulogy but a subtle portrait of its subject, warts and all. At a time when Cromwell aroused violently conflicting passions among Englishmen . . . , Marvell was able to contemplate both him and King Charles with a mixture of warm admiration and cool, analytical detachment." Now with this statement I am in complete agreement. In my essay I attempted to show just how subtle the portrait was, how the warts had their place in the poem, and how the total attitude as reflected *in the text of the poem* would allow room for warm admiration and cool analytical detachment. But when I try to show how the detachment reflects itself in the poem, Mr. Bush is troubled by my reading sinister and darker meanings into Marvell's terms. For example, when I suggest that the line "But still in the Republick's hand" implies a recognition of the possibility that Cromwell may not always so defer to the commonwealth, Mr. Bush tells us that "Still" has "its normal seventeenth-century meaning 'always,' and Marvell's words afford no ground for an ominous hint of a possible change of heart in Cromwell." Mr. Bush may be right: "Still" may mean nothing more than "always," and I was careful to put the possibility only as a question. I wrote: "Does he imply that Cromwell may not always do so? Perhaps not: the emphasis is upon the fact that he need not obey and yet does." But what, by the way, would Mr.

From *Sewanee Review,* LXI (1953), pp. 129–35. Reprinted by permission of the publishers and the author.

Bush do with the line immediately preceding: "Nor yet grown stiffer with Command"? Surely this line implies the possibility that men in whom so much power is vested may grow stiffer; and I find it amusing that in this same passage of Mr. Bush's essay he points out that a few years later Milton was to rebuke Cromwell for turning a republic into a dictatorship. Is it out of the question that Marvell might have envisaged as a possibility what other men of like training and background were indeed soon to see come to pass?

So with my interpretations of words like "forward," "restless," "climb," etc. Mr. Bush finds me choosing each time the more sinister implication and avoiding the normal and obvious meanings of the words—as if I were suggesting that the more sinister implication were the sole or dominant element rather than a qualifying element. But Mr. Bush himself cannot always accept the "common and normal sense" of certain words. For example, "Though Justice against Fate complain/And plead the ancient Rights in vain" would, if we want to take the common and natural sense of the words *justice* and *rights,* make Cromwell guilty of an attack on justice and an infringement of Charles's rights. And in the same way, the statement that it was the execution of Charles "Which first assur'd the forced Pow'r" would seem a plain statement that Cromwell had acted as a usurper.

But nothing is more boring to the reader than such a point-by-point refutation. I hope that the interested reader will go back over my essay in the light of Mr. Bush's observations. I hope most of all that Mr. Bush will go back over that essay on the assumption that through a fault of my writing or his reading, he has misunderstood my interpretation of Marvell's poem. I can assure him that I find in the "Ode" genuine admiration of Cromwell. I wrote: "Cromwell is the truly kingly man who is not king—whose very virtues conduce to kingly power and almost force kingly power upon him . . . Cromwell is the Caesar who must refuse the crown—whose glory it is that he is willing to refuse the crown—but who cannot enjoy the reward and the security that a crown affords." I suspect that Mr. Bush and I are much more nearly in agreement about the genuineness of the speaker's admiration for Cromwell than his reading of my essay has led him to believe.

But Mr. Bush is stalking bigger game. He has not written his reply merely to argue over a few niceties of interpretation of a poem—important as that poem is. Mr. Bush means to vindicate the biographer and the historian against the mere critic and to show that "historical conditioning has a corrective as well as a positive value." On these points our differences are considerable and will require more detailed discussion.

In the first place, there is the matter of my own place in history with its accompanying bias. Mr. Bush accounts for my interpretation of the poem by assuming that I am a "good modern liberal." (He refers to the bias of a *modern liberal* four times in his essay, and concludes by writing "the result, if not the aim, of Mr. Brooks's inquiry is, in large measure, to turn a seventeenth century liberal into a modern one.") But the title *liberal,* alas, is one that I am scarcely entitled to claim: I am more often called a reactionary, and I have been called a proto-fascist. For instance, Mr. Robert Gorham Davis, in order to account for a bias which he thought he discerned, once read my history rather differently: I had taught at a university closely related to the late Huey Long—? perhaps I had been brought there as window-dressing?—but in any case my close-up view of a modern dictatorship had qualified and complicated my attitudes toward dictatorship and political power. This ingenious theory—I could demonstrate it is merely that—might yield particularly interesting results if applied to my account of the "Horatian Ode." But would it account for the bias that Mr. Bush wants to account for?

The historical method has its own temptations: among them, to explore, with insufficient "history," the biases of one's opponent. At any rate, I find it amusing that my attitudes turn out to be quite different from those which Mr. Bush infers that I hold, including my sympathy for Toynbee and my acceptance of an orthodox Christian position. This is not to claim, of course, that I am necessarily consistent in my beliefs or that my beliefs guarantee my being right about the "Horatian Ode"; but Mr. Bush's guesses as to the biases which make me, in his opinion, "wrench" the meaning of Marvell's poem, just happen to be wrong.

In the second place, what do the relevant historical facts tell us about Marvell's attitude? I am surprised that Mr. Bush has chosen this of all poems to vindicate his general thesis, for the evidence from history points several ways, but in so far as it supports either interpretation, seems to support mine. Mr. Bush cites Marvell's poem on "The First Anniversary of the Government under O[liver] C[romwell]," 1655, and his "Poem on the Death of O.C.," 1658. But what of Marvell's poems written within a year of the "Horatian Ode?" I can do no better here than to repeat my summary of the situation:

> Hard upon his composition of the "Ode" in 1650, Marvell had published in 1649 a poem "To his Noble Friend, Mr. Richard Lovelace," and a poem "Upon the Death of the Lord Hastings." Both Margoliouth and Legouis find these

> poems rather pro-Royalist in sentiment, and certainly it is difficult to read them otherwise. If we add to these poems the "Elegy upon the Death of My Lord Francis Villiers," a Cavalier who was killed fighting for the King in 1649, the Royalist bias becomes perfectly explicit. As Margoliouth puts it: "If the 'Elegy on Villiers' is Marvell's, it is his one unequivocal royalist utterance; it throws into strong relief the transitional character of *An Horatian Ode* where royalist principles and admiration for Cromwell the Great Man exist side by side. . . ."
>
> A transition in views there must have been, but the transition certainly cannot be graphed as a steadily rising curve when we take into account Marvell's next poem, "Tom May's Death." May died in November 1650. Thus we have the "Horatian Ode," which was almost certainly written in the summer of 1650, preceding by only a few months a poem in which Marvell seems to slur at the Commander of the Parliamentary armies—either Essex or Fairfax—as "Spartacus," and to reprehend May himself as a renegade poet who has prostituted the mystery of the true poets.

I might add that the two new bits of evidence that I brought forward in my essay both point to Royalist associations for Marvell. I recur to them here, not because I think that they "prove" very much, but because I want to emphasize the fact that my position involves no disparagement of history. The purpose of my essay was conciliatory. I had hoped that the act of finding and bringing forward new evidence—however meager it turned out to be—might be the best way of indicating my concern for history and its claims.

I reiterate that concern and I say again that the literary historian and the critic need to work together and that the ideal case is that in which both functions are united in one and the same man. But historical evidence does not solve critical problems. In the first place, it is often inadequate or problematical. In the second place, the objective facts that can be pegged down and verified do not in themselves yield a judgment: the "historian" finds himself working with probabilities and subjective evaluations almost as much as the "critic." If the critic does well to remind himself how heavily he leans upon history, the historian does well to remind himself how often he is making a critical evaluation. The basic difference between Mr. Bush and me lies in this area of critical theory.

It is evident that my conception of what a poem is is rather different from Mr. Bush's. For example, I have not been content to see Marvell pay some fine compliments to Cromwell and then adjust the balance by paying some compliments to King Charles, but have asked for a meaningful and responsible relation between the elements which he finds praiseworthy in both men. Mr. Bush writes: "Mr. Brooks sees the poem as expressing a 'unified total attitude,' though a very complex one, yet it would be hard to merge his findings into any total unity unless Marvell is more or less lifted out of his age into ours." I am not concerned to lift Marvell out of his age into ours; I am concerned with what transcends his age. I am concerned with what is universal in the poem, and that means that I am concerned with more than seeing the "Horatian Ode" as merely a document of its age. If we unify the poem as document merely by saying that it reflects the uncertainties and contradictions of a man who was uncertain and self-contradictory and sometimes foolish, as the men of any age are, then we may have a useful historical document, but I am not at all sure that we have a poem. That is why I have attempted something that may well be desperate: namely, to try to find a justification in terms of the poem for the two stanzas beginning "And now the Irish are ashamed." The stanzas apparently do not trouble Mr. Bush, who writes "We really must accept the unpalatable fact that [Marvell] wrote as an Englishman of 1650." Perhaps we must, and I have tried to allow for that fact by saying that the appeal here "is not to what Marvell the Englishman must have thought, or even to what Marvell the author must have intended, but rather to the full context of the poem itself." Certainly I should agree with Mr. Bush that the poem "did not get itself written by some agency outside of Marvell." But I had hoped that Marvell here had written perhaps better than he knew and that the praise accorded to Cromwell in the poem as a whole was one which would allow in the perspective of the entire poem for a sardonic reading of the lines which made them something other than merely a statement, probably even in 1650 rather silly, and in any case wishful thinking. That defense may or may not be convincing, but I think that the fact that I feel it necessary to make such a defense (or else to concede that the passage is a blemish in an otherwise fine poem) and that Professor Bush sees no reason to make a defense is a sufficient indication of how different our aims are.

In this connection I should like to allude briefly to Leslie Fiedler's "Archetype and Signature" (Spring, 1952) and to the Editorial in the Autumn (1952) number of this review. In his able statement of policy, the Editor wrote: "The point has been made, the lesson learned, and we have plenty of critics able to do good formal analysis. We need now, in addition, a consciously impure criticism which . . . will interpret literature in relation to the rest of man's concerns. . . ." With this call to a wider series of applications, I am in hearty agreement, just as I am in agreement with Mr. Fiedler's concern for a means of binding together our "fractured world." But I do not think that the lesson has been learned—not, for instance, if Mr. Fiedler really thinks that a basic contention of formalist criticism is that a poem is "*nothing but* 'words,'" and not if Mr. Bush can write "One may not quite understand these several possibilities, since the poem did not get itself written by some agency outside of Marvell." Mr. Bush's and Mr. Fiedler's reasons for defending a biographical interest are amusingly at loggerheads, and I can imagine Mr. Bush's feeling that Mr. Fiedler conceives of the poem as a kind of handy pincushion into which an engaging ambiguity can be thrust; and on the other hand, I can imagine that Mr. Fiedler might feel that Mr. Bush's indifference to the dark side of the poet's mind and to the depth psychologists, Jung and Freud, represents a hopelessly truncated view of the poet's personality.

Mr. Fiedler provides a neat, almost jaunty survey of recent literary history. If I may fill in some names, Mr. Fiedler might presumably see Mr. Bush as the thesis (the old fashioned historical scholarship), me as the antithesis (the doctrinaire antibiographer), and himself as the triumphant synthesis. And perhaps he is right. But, at the least, his "generations" are positions in a dialectic and not really flesh-and-blood generations.

I should like to view the formalist critics in a somewhat different perspective. In their concern for the break-up of the modern world, Mr. Bush, Mr. Fiedler and a host of other scholars and critics are anxious to see literature put to work to save the situation. The insistence upon definitions—warnings against the intentional fallacy, attempts to distinguish between poem and historical document—all seem petty and niggling in view of a culture threatened with collapse, and so the temptation is to find in literature a support for religion or perhaps a surrogate for religion. Mr. Bush's recent MLA address took the one course; Mr. Fiedler, in his article, takes the other. As he puts it, "We cannot get back into the primal Garden of the unfallen archetypes, but we can yield ourselves to the dreams and images that mean paradise regained." We can still, through anthropology and depth psychology, have the value of the myths even though as modern men we see through them.

I suggest that the shadow of Matthew Arnold still rests heavily upon our era, and that it is the formalist critics who make the fullest rejection of Arnold. They do so because they are aware of the implications. Mr. Fiedler, on the other hand, can see the future of criticism as immense for the same reason that Arnold saw the future of poetry as immense.

I cannot speak for the other formalist critics—I cannot even claim to know certainly who they are—but I shall hazard one or two concluding observations. In the first place, though poetry has a very important role in any culture, to ask that poetry save us is to impose a burden upon poetry that it cannot sustain. The danger is that we shall merely get an ersatz religion and an ersatz poetry. In the second place, I think it no accident that so many of the formalist critics either hold, or are sympathetic to, an orthodox Christian faith. In the third place, I think it significant that those critics who hold such a position have been precisely those critics who have been anxious to distinguish between aesthetic judgment and ethical judgment, and who have tried to find a role for poetry which would make it more than a handmaiden for religion or a substitute for religion.

It is precisely because I agree with the editor that "all our problems, from literature to politics, are ultimately religious" that I think that we should distinguish literature from religion: otherwise "the intellectual lion and the clerical lamb"—or is it the clerical lion and the intellectual lamb?—will lie down, not together, but perhaps with one inside the other.

VIVIAN DE S. PINTO

John Wilmot, Earl of Rochester, and the Right Veine of Satire

I

For more than two centuries judgements of the Court poets of the reign of Charles II have been coloured by the legends which have clustered round their lives and personalities. The "Whig view of history" (shared by many who were by no means Whigs in politics) regarded them simply as the debauched and worthless companions of Charles II who wrote sophisticated love songs and bawdy lampoons. Macaulay in the second chapter of his *History of England* (1849) speaks in horrified tones of "the open profligacy of the Court and the Cavaliers" and the "outrageous profaneness and licentiousness of the Buckinghams and the Sedleys." "The Restoration Muse," writes Beljame about thirty years later, "did not . . . aim very high, it sought neither lofty ideas nor style: its ideal was a slight, delicate thought in simple and harmonious form." Leigh Hunt in his review of Keats's *Poems* of 1817 in the *Examiner* declared that "the school which existed till lately since the restoration of Charles the 2d, was rather a school of wit and ethics in verse than anything else; nor was the verse, with the exception of Dryden's, of a very high order."

Here we can see the origins of the stereotyped view of the Restoration literary scene presented by nearly all the literary historians: a frivolous, licentious Court, where a number of profligate, dilettante

From *Essays and Studies 1953* (London: John Murray, 1953), pp. 56–70. Reprinted by permission of The English Association and the author.

courtiers write rather worthless verses, and one great poet who panders to their taste and half ruins his genius by his servility:

> Dryden in immortal strain
> Had raised the Table Round again,
> But that a ribald King and Court
> Bade him toil to make them sport;
> Demanded for their niggard pay,
> Fit for their souls, a looser lay,
> Licentious satire, song and play;
> The world defrauded of the high design
> Profaned the God-given strength and marred
> the mighty line.

Scott was no Whig but this view of the literary history of the Restoration harmonized well with the conception of the Glorious Revolution of 1688 as the turning point in English history, when the wicked, papistical Stuarts were expelled and the foundations of the sober Protestant individualistic England of the Victorian age were securely laid.

II

The work of twentieth-century scholars and critics has done much to clear the reputation of the Restoration Court Wits. Charles Whibley's chapter on them in *The Cambridge History of English Literature* was a pioneer work of rehabilitation by a clear-sighted critic who refused to allow his judgement to be warped by traditional views. More recently an American scholar Professor J. H. Wilson in his admirable book *The Court Wits of the Restoration* has shown that a great part of the commonly accepted mass of anecdotes concerning these writers is apocryphal. For instance there is no evidence for the story that the Countess of Shrewsbury held the Duke of Buckingham's horse while he fought his duel with her husband or the still more lurid sequel that he slept with her in his bloodstained shirt after the duel. The commonly repeated tale about the exploits of Rochester and Buckingham, when they are said to have set up as innkeepers on the Newmarket Road, appears to be synthetic romance concocted by some eighteenth-century hack writer. Finally there seems to be no real historical basis for the allegation which has done most harm to Rochester's reputation. John Dryden was certainly cudgelled by ruffians in Rose Alley, Covent Garden, on a December night in 1679, but it seems very unlikely that

Rochester had any connection with this outrage, which was probably instigated by the Duchess of Portsmouth and perhaps perpetrated by her homicidal brother-in-law, the Earl of Pembroke.

III

The group of Restoration Wits (Andrew Marvell's "Merry Gang") consisted of men who were living between two worlds, one of which was dying, the other struggling into existence. One was the old world of medieval and renaissance culture with its conception of an integrated theocentric universe and on earth of a sovereign at the apex of an ordered society with a Court consisting of his trusted servants, who were representative of the accepted moral, aesthetic and religious ideals of the nation. Shakespeare and others saw that this world was in danger even in the sixteenth century:

> Take but degree away, untune that string,
> And hark what discord follows!

It was the world that Clarendon tried (and failed) to restore in 1660 after the collapse of the Puritan régime. Then there was the new world of what in the language of Spengler can be called "civilization" as opposed to "culture," the world of the great modern city, of international trade and finance, political parties and newspapers with its atomized society of "free" individuals and its Copernican universe of infinite space governed not by the laws of God but by mathematical laws which the scientists were busy discovering. In such a world the Court would cease to be the real centre of national life and become merely a fashionable club for idle irresponsible young people. Spenser in his *Mother Hubberds Tale* had already noted the beginning of the process when he contrasted the "rightfull courtier" with the "young lustie gallants" who spent their time playing "thriftless games" and ruined themselves with "courtezans and costly riotize." An anonymous ballad writer of the reign of James I contrasted the Old Courtier of the Queen with the King's New Courtier:

> A new flourishing gallant, new come to his land,
> Who kept a brace of new painted creatures to his command,
> And could take up a thousand readily upon his new bond,
> And be drunk at a new Tavern till be not able to go or stand.

The development suggested by these extracts was enormously accelerated by the Civil War and the exile of the Court. Dr. F. R.

Leavis has commented acutely on the change in the courtly background which took place after the Restoration.

"Charles II was a highly intelligent man of liberal interests, and his mob of gentlemen cultivated conversation and the Muses. But that the fine order, what was referred to above as the 'Court culture,' did not survive the period of disruption, exile and 'travels' is apparent even in the best things of Etherege, Sedley, Rochester and the rest: the finest specimens of the tenderly or cynically gallant and polite lack the positive fineness, the implicit subtlety, examined above in Carew. The cheaper things remind us forcibly that to indicate the background of Restoration poetry we must couple with the court, not as earlier the country house, but the coffee-house, and that the coffee-house is on intimate terms with the Green Room." [1]

Dr. Leavis is speaking here particularly of the lyric which was the characteristic poetic form of the old "Court culture." Many good lyrics were written in the Restoration period, but the tradition of the courtly lyric that began with Wyatt was dying with that integrated courtly culture of which it was the fine flower. The need for a new kind of English poetry was as manifest in the sixteen-seventies as it was in the seventeen-nineties and the nineteen-twenties.

IV

Two ways were open to the courtier poet in the reign of Charles II. He could accept what might be called the new orthodoxy based on the illusion of the approach of an "Augustan" age, a world of good sense and good taste combining rationalism with dignity and grace. It was the new city described by Dryden at the end of *Annus Mirabilis:*

> Methinks already from this chymic flame,
> I see a city of more precious mould;
> Rich as the town that gives the Indies name
> With silver pav'd and all divine with gold.
>
> . . . .
>
> More great than human now and more august,
> Now deified she from her fires does rise:
> Her widening streets on new foundations trust,
> And, opening, into larger parts she flies.

This vision was exciting in 1666. It was to lead to the smugness of Addison, the complacency of Thomson's *Liberty* and Dr. Pangloss's "best of all possible worlds." In such a world politics, trade and science would be the serious occupations of men of sense; poetry would be an ornament and a recreation. The poets would strive to be "smooth" and "correct" and Waller had provided them with suitable models. The traditional escape from everyday banality was the golden arcadia of the pastoral tradition. This became the correct "poetical" subject (as romantic medievalism was in the Victorian age). In *Lycidas* the theme had been charged with imaginative grandeur for the last time. In the hands of court poets like Sedley and Sheffield it became dainty, graceful and suitable for the "tenderly or cynically gallant or polite." The Restoration song-writers (*pace* Dr. Leavis) still had some of the grace and charm of the old Court culture but they were the progenitors of Johnson's poets who used "descriptions copied from descriptions, imitations copied from imitations . . . traditional imagery and traditional similes" and to Crabbe's "sleepy bards";

> On Mincio's banks in Caesar's bounteous reign
> If Tityrus found the Golden Age again,
> Must sleepy bards the flattering dream prolong,
> Mechanic echoes of the Mantuan song?

There was, however, another way open to the courtier poet in the reign of Charles II; it was more difficult and less likely to gain applause. This was the way of realistic satire which was to be the most vital kind of English poetry for nearly a hundred years. Such a poetry would ignore the tradition of the "poetic" subject and would concentrate on the contradictions and the ironies of a society which professed to be "rational," "elegant" and "polite" but was actually greedy, heartless and cynical, a world in which it was only a step from Whitehall to Mother Bennet's brothel, and which fully justified the description of Defoe:

> Wealth (howsoever got) in England makes
> Lords, of mechanics! Gentlemen, of rakes!
> Antiquity and Birth are needless here.
> 'Tis Impudence and Money makes a Peer.

One of the mistresses of Louis XIV is reported to have said that beneath his magnificent exterior that monarch "puait comme une charogne." One possible function of the poet in the new world that was coming into existence at the Restoration was to make poetry out of the contrasts between the highflown professions and ornamental façade of the English aristocracy and the "stinking carcass" that lay behind them. Such satire could only be successfully written by poets who had thoroughly absorbed the culture of that aristocracy and understood its excellencies as well as its weaknesses. Such was the satire of the great Augustan poets, Dryden, Pope, Swift and Johnson. The pioneer was not, however, as all the text-books tell us, John Dryden, but the youngest and most gifted of the Restoration courtier poets, John Wilmot, Earl of Rochester, whom Andrew Marvell, no mean judge, declared to be "the best English satyrist" and to have "the right veine."

V

The most surprising quality of Rochester's genius was the rapid development of his mind. He started as a wholehearted disciple of Thomas Hobbes, that eloquent and persuasive materialist. On his death-bed, he declared that the "absurd and foolish Philosophy, which the world so much admired, propagated by Mr. Hobbs and others, had undone him, and many more, of the best parts in the Nation." [2] From the beginning Rochester's utterances have that quality of "terrifying honesty" which Mr. T. S. Eliot has ascribed to Blake. The logical outcome of Hobbes's thoroughgoing materialism and sensationalism was the complete rejection of the Petrarchan convention which had dominated courtly love poetry since the days of Wyatt. In a lyric probably written very early in his career Rochester defiantly reverses the sentiments expressed in Lovelace's famous poem:

> I could not love thee, Dear, so much,
> Loved I not honour more.

For the young disciple of Hobbes "love" (of this sort) and "honour" were simply examples of what their master called "the frequence of insignificant speech":

> How perfect Cloris, & how free
> Would these enjoyments prouve,
> But you with formall jealousie
> Are still tormenting Love.
>
> Lett us (since witt instructs us how)
> Raise pleasure to the topp,

> If Rivall bottle you'l allow
> I'le suffer rivall fopp
>
> . . . .
>
> All this you freely may confess
> Yet wee'll not disagree
> For did you lòve your pleasures less
> You were not fitt for mee.

This hedonism leads inevitably to the naked self-worship proclaimed in his Epistle to Mulgrave, a poem probably written about 1669:

> But from a Rule I have (upon long Trial)
> T'avoid with Care all sort of Self-denial,
> Which way soe'er Desire and Fancy lead,
> (Contemning Fame) that Path I boldly tread.

This, of course, was the principle governing the lives of most of the men of Rochester's class in the reign of Charles II, but he was the only one who had the courage to proclaim it openly. One suspects that it was statements of this kind quite as much as any of his licentious exploits which injured Rochester's reputation. Like Shaw's Andrew Undershaft, he not only did wrong things, "he said them and thought them: that was what was so dreadful." The Rochester who wrote these lines was the perfect "wild gallant" of the period, portrayed by his friend Etherege in his famous play as Dorimant, the prototype of a long line of attractive rakes in English comedy from Congreve's Mirabel to Wilde's Lord Goring. He was the embodiment of the type which Mr. W. H. Auden has called the Aesthetic Hero, the man who lives entirely for pleasure only and whose life bears no relation to truth. Eleven years after he wrote the Epistle to Mulgrave, when he was lying on his death-bed at Woodstock, he had reached a position diametrically opposed to that of Dorimant. His ideal now was the Religious Hero, the completely selfless character portrayed by the Second Isaiah, whose description of the Suffering Servant of Jahweh he paraphrased in the following words:

"The meanness of his appearance and Person has made vain and foolish people disparage Him because he was not dressed in such a Fools-coat as they delight in." [3] The dying poet has now discovered that only in the contemplation of a figure embodying Absolute Truth could he find that "felicity and glory" which he mentions in one of his letters to his wife. His position could now be summed up in the words of Oscar Wilde reported by André Gide: "Above all, not happiness. Pleasure! We must always want the most tragic." [4]

VI

Rochester's mind was essentially dialectical. He was always aware of the voice of the opponent. Robert Parsons in his Funeral Sermon reports an illuminating story which Rochester told him in the last days of his life.

"One day at an Atheistical Meeting, at a person of Qualitie's, I undertook to manage the Cause, and was the principal Disputant against God and Piety, and for my performances received the applause of the whole company; upon which my mind was terribly struck, and I immediately reply'd thus to my self. Good God! that a Man, that walks upright, that sees the wonderful works of God, and has the uses of his senses and reason, should use them to the defying of his Creator." [5] Rochester was always "replying to himself." His celebrated "conversion" was no *volte-face*. It was the end of a dialectical process which had been going on for years. His satiric poems are of two kinds. Some, like his attacks on Mulgrave and Sir Car Scroope are simply lampoons in the fashion of the day and only distinguished from the numerous other examples of this kind of writing, the work of the authors whom Dryden called "our common libellers," by their greater literary force and pungency. He wrote other poems, however, which are what Wordsworth called in the Preface to his Poems of 1815 "philosophic satire." They must be read as stages in that exploration of reality that led from the gentlemanly dissipation of Dorimant to the rapt contemplation of the figure of the Suffering Servant.

VII

Mr. Ian Jack in his recent study of *Augustan Satire,* in which strangely enough Rochester is hardly mentioned, rightly stresses the elements of "imitation" and parody (in the old sense of the word) in this kind of writing. The Augustan satirists were the products of a classical education, but this education instead of leaving behind it, as it usually does in the modern world, simply some vague memories of ancient masterpieces and a few tags, still at this time provided a living culture. In a man of genius this culture could become creative. Rochester was the first author who used his cultural background creatively in the manner afterwards developed by Dryden, Pope and

Johnson.[6] Not only his brilliant adaptation of the tenth satire of the First Book of Horace, but each of his major satiric poems is both a criticism of contemporary life and also the result of a creative use of his reading. As Burnet writes: "Sometimes other mens thoughts mixed with his Composures, but that flowed rather from the Impressions they made on him when he read them, by which they came to return upon him as his own thoughts; than that he servilely copied from any." [7] Two satiric poems which perhaps mark an early stage in his exploration of contemporary realities are both "parodies" of the heroic manner and "imitations" shot through with memories of ancient and modern literature. The famous lines *Upon Nothing* are really a kind of ironic inversion of Cowley's *Hymn to Light* and at the same time the poet makes use of the conception of Nothing as an active force, found in the Latin poems of Wouwerus and Passerat quoted by Johnson in his account of Rochester in *The Lives of the Poets.* Behind the whole poem also lie still more august antecedents, the Book of Genesis, the first verses of the Fourth Gospel and the Aristotelian doctrine of Form and Matter. In the last stanzas the irony is transferred from metaphysics to contemporary society:

> *Nothing*, who dwell'st with Fools in grave Disguise,
> For whom they reverend Shapes and Forms devise,
> Lawn Sleeves, and Furs, and Gowns, when they like thee
> look Wise.
>
> . . . .
>
> The Great Man's Gratitude to his best Friend,
> King's Promises, Whore's Vows, tow'rds thee they bend,
> Flow swiftly into thee, and in thee ever end.

The emptiness that lies behind the outward shows of humanity is visualized here as a positive force with special reference to the contemporary scene. Swift's doctrine of man as a "micro-coat" is clearly foreshadowed. Pope must have studied this poem carefully for he wrote a clever "imitation" of it in his youth and the Triumph of Dullness at the end of the *Dunciad* probably owes a good deal to Rochester's Triumph of Nothing.

The Maimed Debauchee, that "masterpiece of heroic irony" as Charles Whibley called it, recalls Davenant as *Upon Nothing* recalls Cowley. The stately metre and diction of *Gondibert* are used to exhibit the old age of a gentlemanly rake who is ironically equated to a superannuated admiral watching a naval battle. Like all Rochester's best satiric work this poem is not a statement but a vision. We are made to see the absurdly fierce old sailor:

> From his fierce Eyes Flashes of Rage he throws,
> As from black Clouds when Lightning breaks away,
> Transported thinks himself amidst his Foes,
> And absent, yet enjoys the bloody Day.

The image is, as it were, superimposed on that of the old roué urging on his young friends to the life of pleasure:

> My Pains at last some Respite shall afford,
> When I behold the Battels you maintain:
> When Fleets of Glasses sail around the Board,
> From whose Broad-sides Volleys of Wit shall rain.

Are we looking at a riotous banquet or a sea-fight? It is impossible to say: the two images are fused into a single whole. Again there are layers of allusion here. Not only Gondibert, but the sea-fights in Dryden's *Annus Mirabilis* are suggested, and the poem is also certainly a kind of ironic "parody" of Horace's *Vixi puellis nuper idoneus*.

VIII

An important phase of Rochester's development is to be seen in his satiric treatment of the relations between the sexes. In the old courtly world of "degree" and subordination, women were either regarded as wives and daughters owing obedience to the authority of husbands and fathers or as the idealized object of courtly love, Petrarchan "mistresses" worshipped by adoring "servants." These traditional relationships were breaking down in the middle of the seventeenth century and indeed Donne's *Songs and Sonets* show that the process had begun much earlier. If, as Hobbes taught, goodness and badness were to be equated with pleasure and pain, pleasure was obviously to be chosen, and Rochester, following the example of his king and his fellow courtiers took his pleasure with many women. The dialectical bent of his mind, however, made him see the matter from the woman's standpoint and in two of his most interesting satiric poems it is a woman who speaks. These are, I believe, the only Augustan satires where the woman's point of view is expressed with real sympathy and understanding. Rochester saw that the relationship between the sexes, in his own class at any rate, at that time was more in the nature of war than of "love." In a fragment that survives in his autograph in the Portland collection he puts into the mouth of a cultivated woman an indignant protest against the condition of women in contemporary society:

> What vaine unnecessary things are men
> How well we doe without 'em, tell me then
> Whence comes that meane submissiveness wee finde
> This ill bred age has wrought on woman kinde . . .

The speaker of those lines shows the gallants of Whitehall, not as the Strephons and Damons of the pastoral convention, but as cynical sensualists choosing and buying their mistresses like horses at a fair:

> To the Pell Mell, Playhous nay the drawing roome
> Their Woemen Fayres, these Woemen Coursers come
> To chaffer, chuse, & ride their bargains home,
> Att the appearance of an unknown face
> Up steps the Arrogant pretending Ass
> Pulling by th' elbow his companion Huff
> Cryes looke, de God that wench is well enough . . .

In Rochester's most finished social satire, *A Letter from Artemisa in the Town to Cloe in the Country,* again the voice of a cultivated and intelligent woman is heard. Artemisa is made to lament the decay of "love" between the sexes and its transformation into a commercialized game:

> *Love,* the most gen'rous Passion of the Mind;
> The softest Refuge Innocence can find:
> The safe Director of unguided Youth:
> Fraught with kind Wishes, and secur'd by Truth:
> That Cordial-drop Heav'n in our Cup has thrown,
> To make the nauseous Draught of Life go down:
> On which one only Blessing God might raise,
> In Lands of Atheists, Subsidies of Praise:
> For none did e'er so dull and stupid prove,
> But felt a God, and bless'd his Pow'r in Love:
> This only Joy, for which poor we are made,
> Is grown, like Play, to be an arrant Trade.

It is true that Rochester is not speaking here in his own person but the rhythm and imagery of this passage show that this is a view of sex which he could understand and appreciate. It is Artemisa's friend the eccentric country lady who tells the story of Corinna, a picture of a Restoration prostitute etched with the vigour, the vitality and the unsentimental indignation of Hogarth:

> Now scorn'd of all, forsaken and opprest,
> She's a *Memento Mori* to the rest:
> Diseas'd, decay'd, to take up half a Crown
> Must Mortgage her long Scarf, and Manto Gown;
> Poor Creature, who unheard of, as a Fly,
> In some dark Hole must all the Winter lye: . . .

Johnson may well have had this passage in mind when he wrote the story of Misella (*Rambler*, nos. 170–72).

IX

The culminating point in Rochester's spiritual odyssey is reached in his famous *Satyr against Mankind.* It is to be noted that this poem in some form was apparently circulating as early as the spring of 1675–76 and therefore antedates all Dryden's satiric poetry. It was formerly regarded chiefly as an "imitation" of the Eighth Satire of Boileau. S. F. Crocker in his valuable study of the background of the poem [8] has shown that it owes a much greater debt to Rochester's study of Montaigne and especially of the *Apologie de Raimond de Sébond,* and that it also contains echoes of the *Maximes* of La Rochefoucauld and other French works. Nevertheless it is a profoundly original work, for Rochester, like Pope, is never so original as when he is making full use of his reading. He never wrote anything more moving than the image of the fruitless quest of mankind misled by the *ignis fatuus* of reason at the beginning of the poem. It was the passage which Goethe quoted (without acknowledgement) in his *Dichtung und Wahrheit* and which Tennyson is reported by Lecky to have been in the habit of declaiming "with almost terrible force."

> Then old Age and Experience, Hand in Hand,
> Lead him to Death, and make him understand,
> After a Search so painful, and so long,
> That all his Life he has been in the wrong.

Rochester never saw "old Age" but he lived through more "Experience" in his thirty-three years than most men in three score and ten.

These lines undoubtedly sum up his own realization that "the life of reason" as conceived by his class and generation was an illusion. They make us feel what it was like, after the intoxication of youth had passed to face the fact that you were living in the soulless "universe of death" of the new "scientific" philosophy:

> Hudled in Dirt, this reas'ning Engine lyes,
> Who was so proud, so witty, and so wise . . .

The application of the term "reas'ning Engine" to man is highly significant. It is probably an allusion to a phrase of Robert Boyle who called men "engines endowed with wills"[9] and it is a bitterly ironic commentary on the mechanistic conception of humanity which was the logical outcome of the new science.

The dialogue on reason with the "formal Band and Beard" which follows ends with a denunciation of the fashionable intellectualism of the period in terms that recall D. H. Lawrence's insistence on the claims of "blood" as opposed to those of intellect. Rochester's "right Reason" is a reason that admits the claims of the body as well as those of the mind:

> Thus whil'st against false Reas'ning I inveigh,
> I own right Reason, which I would obey;
> That Reason, which distinguishes by Sense,
> And gives us Rules of Good and Ill from thence;
> That bounds Desires with a reforming Will,
> To keep them more in Vigour, not to kill:

From Reason he passes to Man, contemporary "civilized" Man, whom he compares with the beasts:

> Be Judge your self, I'll bring it to the Test,
> Which is the basest Creature, Man, or Beast:
> Birds feed on Birds, Beasts on each other Prey;
> But Savage Man alone, does Man betray.
> Press'd by Necessity, *They* kill for Food;
> Man undoes Man, to do himself no good.
> With Teeth and Claws by Nature arm'd, *They* hunt
> Nature's Allowance, to supply their Want:
> But Man, with Smiles, Embraces, Friendships, Praise,
> Inhumanly, his Fellow's Life betrays:
> With voluntary Pains works his Distress;

Not through Necessity, but Wantonness.
For Hunger, or for Love, *They* bite or tear,
Whilst wretched Man is still in Arms for Fear:
For Fear he arms and is of Arms afraid;
From Fear to Fear successively betray'd.
Base Fear, the source whence his best Passions came,
His boasted Honour, and his dear-bought Fame.
The lust of Pow'r, to which he's such a Slave,
And for the which alone he dares be brave . . .

This passage, as Crocker has shown, owes much to Montaigne, but its application and satiric force are Rochester's own. Here he is piercing the defences of his own class, the governing class of Europe, and showing what really lies behind phrases like "honour" and "fame." Again this is a passage that communicates forward to Swift. It contains the essence of *Gulliver's Travels:* the King of Brobdingnag's denunciation of the Europeans as portrayed by Gulliver and the superiority of those wise and humane quadrupeds, the Houyhnhnms, to the filthy, cowardly Yahoos.

X

The nihilism of the *Satyr against Mankind* is slightly mitigated in a curious epilogue or "postscript" added, apparently, after the rest of the poem had been printed, possibly as a rejoinder to the "Answer" ascribed to "the Reverend Mr. Griffith," which appeared in the summer of 1679 shortly after the publication of the broadside containing the first printed version of Rochester's poem. In this epilogue Rochester agrees to "recant" his "Paradox" if he can find one truly good man:

a meek humble Man of modest Sense,
Who preaching Peace does practise Continence;
Whose pious Life's a Proof he does believe
Mysterious Truths which no Man can conceive.

These rather uninspired lines seem to show Rochester trying to force himself to believe that a merely ethical hero could now satisfy him. He found "felicity and glory," however, not in an abstract ideal of this kind, but in the very different vision that came to him like a thunderbolt when he was listening to Robert Parsons reading the Second Isaiah's description of the Suffering Servant on 19th June, 1680. Parsons in his Funeral Sermon tells us that Rochester's "vow and purpose" in his last sickness was to produce "an Idea of Divine Poetry, under the Gospel, useful to the teaching of virtue . . . as his profane Verses have been to destroy it." He also tells that in the nine weeks that elapsed between his "conversion" and his death "he was so much master of his reason, and had so clear an understanding (saving thirty hours, about the middle of it when he was delirious) that he never dictated or spoke more composed in his life."[10] It is clear from these passages that Rochester dictated something (unfortunately Parsons gives no details) in the last weeks of his life and also that he planned to write "Divine Poetry." Two poems first published in Thorncome's edition of 1685 may well have been dictated by him on his death-bed. They are called *Consideratus Considerandus* and *Plain Dealings Downfall,* and both seem to be connected with the vision of the Suffering Servant. Both present images of virtue as despised and rejected like the Man of Sorrows in the Second Isaiah. *Plain Dealings Downfall* has a terseness and homely realism that recall the manner of George Herbert:

> Long time Plain Dealing in the Hauty Town,
> Wand'ring about, though in a thread-bare Gown,
> At last unanimously was cry'd down.
>
> When almost starv'd she to the Country fled
> In hopes though meanly, she shou'd there be fed,
> And tumble nightly on a Pea-straw Bed.
>
> But Knav'ry knowing her intent, took post,
> And Rumour'd her approach through every Coast,
> Vowing his Ruin that shou'd be her host.
>
> Frighted at this, each *Rustick* shut his door,
> Bid her begone, and trouble him no more,
> For he that entertain'd her must be poor.
>
> At this grief seiz'd her, grief too great to tell,
> When weeping, sighing, fainting, down she fell,
> Whil's Knavery Laughing, Rung her passing Bell.

In this powerful little poem, as in the concluding lines of *The Vanity of Human Wishes,* we seem to see the transition from satire to religious poetry. The emphasis is not so much on "the Hauty Town" (as it was in the story of Corinna) or upon the almost medieval image of "knavery," but upon the sorrow of the betrayed country girl, who becomes a tragic figure putting a mean and heartless world to shame. Rochester was not the greatest of the Augustan satirists, but he was the boldest spiritual adventurer among them. Strange as the collocation of the two names may seem to many readers, he seems to have reached at the end of his life a position not unlike that of the poet who was to write *The Ruined Cottage* and *Peter Bell* a little more than a hundred years after his death.

NOTES

[1] *Revaluation*, p. 34 [above, p. 48].

[2] Robert Parsons, *A Sermon. Preached at the Funeral of the Rt. Honourable John Earl of Rochester* (Oxford, 1680), p. 26.

[3] Gilbert Burnet, *Some Passages of the Life and Death of the Right Honourable John Earl of Rochester* (London, 1680), p. 142.

[4] André Gide, *Oscar Wilde* (London, 1951), p. 28.

[5] Robert Parsons, op. cit., p. 23.

[6] Dryden's earliest satire, *MacFlecknoe*, was probably written in 1678. Rochester's chief satiric poems seem to have been in circulation about 1675–76 though it is possible that some of them were written at an earlier date.

[7] Gilbert Burnet, op. cit., p. 14.

[8] *West Virginia University Studies* III, *Philological Papers*, Vol. 2, May 1937.

[9] Quoted by E. A. Burtt in *The Metaphysical Foundations of Modern Science*, p. 176.

[10] Robert Parsons, op. cit., pp. 7, 33.

REUBEN A. BROWER

An Allusion to Europe: Dryden and Tradition [1]

It is perhaps easier to bury Dryden than to praise him: so much depends on the tradition we choose to place him in and on the standards by which we measure poetic success. If we follow Dr. Johnson and set Dryden in the succession of Waller and Denham, we arrive at a pious tribute to the "reformer of our numbers." If we follow Dr. Leavis and trace "the line of wit," we bring out Dryden's undeniable limitations as compared with Donne or Marvell. (Dr. Leavis's strategy was justified in relation to his aims and results: he has made us aware that "serious wit" did not end with the Metaphysicals.) But if we are to make a positive estimate of Dryden's achievement, we should include in his ancestry English poets of the earlier and later Renaissance and their ancient predecessors, and we need to maintain a keen sense of what Dryden accomplished for his contemporaries. So viewed, Dryden marks the re-affirmation of "Europe" in English poetry and culture after an experiment in insularity and at a time of artificial essays in continental "Classicism."

Again, it would be easy to arrive at a rather tepid estimate of Dryden's career—true enough, but hardly of much concern to readers with a live interest in either history or poetry. Dryden's re-affirmation matters—aesthetically and historically—because it is a poet's affirmation, realized in the shaping of new modes of expression and in the writing of poetry which is imaginatively various and unified. His direct

From *ELH: A Journal of English Literary History*, XIX (1952), pp. 38–48. Reprinted by permission of the publishers.

critical propaganda for French and Latin literary standards counts for relatively little in the continuing life of the Renaissance tradition. A more adaptable Arnold, like Pope

> He won his way by yielding to the tide.

By "indirection," by creating his unique satirical mode, Dryden reaffirmed important European values, while engaging the most lively concerns of his readers. It is to this poetic feat that I want to draw attention.

Dryden's accomplishment is more remarkable in view of the situation in which he wrote. Charles had been "restored," and with him an audience that was alien to the most vigorous of the surviving older poets. Milton withdrew; Cowley retired without producing much of the "wit" he prescribed. Marvell dived as a Metaphysical and came up as a satirist; but as a poet he belonged to another world. Although Dryden talked sentimentally of "retiring," he was unequivocally the "first" man of this

> Laughing, quaffing, and unthinking time.

His success lay in his ability to draw on a wide range of English and European literary traditions while "speaking home" to this audience of Court and City. A glance at his development as a dramatist will suggest how he attained a style which had this two-fold effectiveness.

In the period between *Astraea Redux* and *Absalom and Achitophel*, while Dryden was mightily pleasing his auditors in the theatre, he struck out two more or less distinct styles which were blended in the successes of his maturity: one, the "heroic"; and the other, the style of public address which he somewhat scornfully regarded as Horatian. Whatever we call them, both styles bear traces of their mixed European and English origin. In the process of making his outrageous experiments in drama, the Heroic Plays, Dryden invented a style that gave an impression of ancient epic grandeur; at times, in narratives of quite incredible exploits, the impression became almost convincing, thanks to the skill with which Dryden combined Virgilian allusions with rather obvious echoes of Virgilian rhythm.

In the last and best of these plays, *Aureng-Zebe*, we first hear distinctly what Professor Van Doren calls Dryden's "grouping" of couplets, an enlargement of rhythm which comes when he had been reading Shakespeare, and, more significantly, soon after his re-working of *Paradise Lost.* Milton's example, along with Sylvester's and Cowley's, helped fix the Old Testament-ecclesiastical strain in Dryden's mature heroic style, as it finally emerged in *Absalom and Achitophel.* In tone the style is unmistakably a "translation out of the original tongues."

While Dryden was cultivating a manner that had almost no appropriateness to his auditors—except by a law of literary contraries—he was learning to speak to them with directness and ease in his prologues and epilogues. Here he acquired his mastery of more varied tones; and here "the great reform" of language and rhythm was most happily realized. The language is "such words as men did use" (in an age less polished than our own); and the molding of speech idiom to the patterns of the couplet is admirable. After the tepid velleities of Waller—the "crooner" of the couplet—Dryden's prologues mark a partial recovery of the toughness and "juice" of Jonsonian English. But though they are highly original, they are linked via Jonson with an earlier tradition. The prologue, as used by Jonson to give instruction in literary taste, is a theatrical form of the Roman epistle. Dryden's later blend of the prologue-satirical style with the heroic is anticipated in the insolent debates of the plays and in the prologues themselves. Given a very slight excuse, Dryden will sound off with an ancient literary parallel, or a debased parody of one. Part of the game of amusing his listeners consisted in deliberately talking over their heads.

The "huddled notions" of Dryden's satiric mode lay in readiness when the Monmouth "conspiracy" offered the occasion his genius had been waiting for. He could now compose heroic narrative and dialogue while talking to his familiar audience. What is remarkable is that in scoring a journalistic and political success he produced poetry of a high order. Here is a representative passage, the commemoration of Titus Oates, the Presbyterian "weaver's issue" who testified that the Jesuits were plotting to murder Charles II.

> Yet, *Corah,* thou shalt from Oblivion pass;
> Erect thy self thou Monumental Brass:
> High as the Serpent of thy Metal made,
> While Nations stand secure beneath thy shade.
> What though his Birth were base, yet Comets rise
> From Earthy Vapours, e'r they shine in Skies.
> Prodigious Actions may as well be done

By Weaver's issue as by Prince's son.
This Arch-Attestor for the Publick Good
By that one Deed enobles all his Bloud.
Who ever ask'd the Witnesses high race
Whose Oath with Martyrdom did *Stephen* grace?
Ours was a *Levite*, and as times went then,
His tribe were God-almighties Gentlemen.
Sunk were his Eyes, his Voice was harsh and loud,
Sure signs he neither Cholerick was, nor Proud:
His long Chin prov'd his Wit; his Saint-like Grace
A Church Vermilion, and a *Moses's* Face.
His Memory, miraculously great,
Coud Plots, exceeding mans belief, repeat;
Which, therefore cannot be accounted Lies,
For humane Wit coud never such devise.
Some future Truths are mingled in his Book;
But where the Witness fail'd, the Prophet spoke:
Some things like Visionary flights appear:
The Spirit caught him up, the Lord knows where:
And gave him his *Rabinical* degree,
Unknown to Foreign University.

To see the imaginative unity of these lines is to see the blending of Dryden's earlier styles and to feel the active pressure of older literary traditions. As in most satirical verse, the lines are held together in part by the broad illogic of irony: Dryden makes a series of triumphant assertions every one of them the opposite of the truth from the Court point of view. But it is Dryden's "intonation" that sets his mark on the lines and gives them life and singleness of effect. His note is clearly heard in "arch-attestor," with its upper level of churchly associations, and in "prodigious," which nicely combines Latin solemnity with the literal Latin meaning of "monstrous." Dryden has anticipated the high level of this commemoration by suggesting that it belongs to a Homeric catalogue; he then addresses Oates in a line so nobly reminiscent of Virgil that it is hardly recognizable as parody:

Yet, *Corah*, thou shalt from Oblivion pass . . .

The occasionally Latin flavor of the diction is also vaguely suggestive of Virgilian epic, while at many points the language is more or less

Biblical, ranging from near-quotation to expressions with religious or churchly associations. Working within a fairly narrow range of allusion Dryden maintains a declamatory tone that is both Biblical-ecclesiastical and Roman-heroic. But the "venom" of the address depends on the contrast of another tone which is unmistakably the voice of the prologues, insolently vulgar and knowingly unliterary:

> Ours was a *Levite*, and as times went then,
> His tribe were God-almighties Gentlemen.

The blend of manners is most subtle in the lines of greatest imaginative variety:

> Yet, *Corah*, thou shalt from Oblivion pass;
> Erect thy self thou Monumental Brass:
> High as the Serpent of thy Metal made,
> While Nations stand secure beneath thy shade.

The focus of the ironies is also the focus of opposing styles and of the widest range of literary and religious associations, the ironies arising mainly from the double references of "monumental" and "brass." Taking "monumental" on its high Latinate side, in a Virgilian address, we feel that this beneficent hero is "monumental" in greatness. Or we may read the whole line as a preposterous parody of Horace's

> Exegi monumentum aere perennius. . . .

But Biblical and ecclesiastical connotations of "brass" and "monuments" suggest that our hero is worthy of a "monumental brass" in an English church, the rude command implying that this monument, contrary to decent custom and the laws of gravity will rise of its own power. Finally, "brass" in its vulgar sense reminds us that such effrontery is otherwise "monumental."

In these lines Dryden's satirical mode appears at its characteristic best. There are the black-and-white oppositions of irony with rhetorical and metrical emphasis striking in unison. There is the smack of life and vulgarity in a word from "Jonsonian" London, the word which imparts the ironic intention and gives force to Dryden's thrust. But the irony is most concentrated in a word of classical origin which is rich in literary and historical connotations and which suggests the Roman oratorical tone.

These features appear in close combination in many of the best lines in Dryden's satirical verse:

> A fiery Soul, which working out its way,
> Fretted the Pigmy Body to decay:
> And o'r informed the Tenement of Clay.

(The reminiscences of Aristotle and Plato, Bishop Fuller and Carew have often been pointed out.) Or

> Besides, his goodly Fabrick fills the eye
> And seems design'd for thoughtless Majesty:
> Thoughtless as Monarch Oakes that shade the plain,
> And, spread in solemn state, supinely reign.
> *Heywood* and *Shirley* were but Types of thee,
> Thou last great Prophet of Tautology:

or

> But gentle *Simkin* just reception finds
> Amidst this Monument of vanisht minds;

or

> Thou leaps't o'r all eternall truths in thy
> *Pindarique* way!

Finally, a delicious blend of neo-Platonic fancy and shrewd analysis in these lines on the Church of England:

> If as our dreaming Platonists report,
> There could be spirits of a middle sort,
> Too black for heav'n, and yet too white for hell,
> Who just dropt half way down, nor lower fell;
> So pois'd, so gently she descends from high,
> It seems a soft dismission from the skie.

From these examples and from our analysis, it is clear that "allusive irony" is a more adequate term than "mock-heroic" for Dryden's satirical mode, whether in *Absalom and Achitophel* and *Mac Flecknoe* or in passages of incidental satire in his argumentative verse. His mode is allusive in a wide variety of ways: in close imitation or parody of other writers, in less exact references to language, styles, and conventions of other literatures—Classical, Biblical, and French—in drawing on the large materials of philosophy and theology, in playing on popular parallels between contemporary religious and political situations and those of ancient history, sacred and secular. Through this mode Dryden makes his "affirmation of Europe."

A solemn claim and a preposterous one, if we think of the mode as devices for heightening style. The difference between allusive irony and the heroic trimmings added to the *Annus Mirabilis* lies in the imaginative union of tones and levels of meaning that I have been describing: "thou Monumental Brass"! The vulgar thrust is inseparable from the reference to high literary styles and to heroic behavior and ecclesiastical splendor.

That the union of styles was more than an academic trick is further shown by the success of the poem with contemporary readers. As compared with Restoration plays or lampoons and gazettes, *Absalom and Achitophel* spoke to more of the interests of the reading public in 1681, and, as Beljame observed, to *more* of the public. Although the Classical heroic was especially flattering to the aristocrats' view of themselves, Latin culture was the common possession of educated men, whatever their political and religious allegiances might be. Dryden, Milton, and Marvell have at least this in common. The Old Testament flavor, satirically amusing to the Court, was richly meaningful and insidiously attractive to Nonconformists. And the colloquial idiom brought the high talk down to the level where Court and City lived. By responding so naturally to the double claims of both his audience and his development as a poet, Dryden "made himself heard" and created a fresh form of art in English poetry.

By this fact alone, he affirmed an important European value to his audience: that poetic craft matters. Dryden's admiration for what Boileau had done for French satire is a sign of his belief that he had performed a similar service for English satire. Boileau would have recognized as art of a high order the poise and finish of Dryden's mode:

> At his right hand our young *Ascanius* sate,
> *Rome's* other hope and Pillar of the State.
> His Brows thick fogs, instead of glories, grace,
> And lambent dullness plaid around his face.

The poise is evident in the balance between crude burlesque in "thick fogs" and the subtle gravity of "lambent dullness"; the finish is felt in the melodious and resilient verse. But the smoothness is not merely fashionable: it functions poetically in the strategy of civilized irony. The reader is momentarily beguiled into taking the lines as an exquisite compliment. Dryden had a right to claim that like Boileau he was bringing into modern satire a Virgilian refinement of "raillery." In the fine Latin wit of "*lambent* dullness" or "spread in solemn state, *supinely* reign," Dryden is "alluding" to a culture and the fineness of response which it fostered.

It is no great compliment to describe Dryden's achievement as a triumph of neo-classicism, if we mean by neo-classicism mechanical use of conventions borrowed from Boileau or Rapin. Dryden's achievement is not one of "meeting requirements"; the conventions "at work," as in the lines just quoted, are expressive of larger aesthetic and cultural values. In writing verse which combined the normality and vigor of good talk with a musical pattern that was the apt accompaniment of ironic wit and in using language which was equally alive in its reference to immediate interests and to literary tradition, Dryden expressed a community in attitude and standards of art with European poets and critics. Some of these attitudes and standards—the detachment, the refinement of ironic censure, the insistence on design and precise mastery of language—were particularly salutary for readers too well pleased with *Hudibras* and for writers who mistook ease for art. But Dryden did not sacrifice the vigor of Butler to "correctness." The Augustan reform, as initiated by Dryden, unlike that of Addison, kept close contact with a masculine audience. Dryden's allusive mode shows a positive strength in neo-classicism which the odious term and its theories completely conceal.

Let us consider more particularly how this mode worked, how and why epic allusions offered Dryden a way of expressing important values. In ironic contexts, the more or less close imitations of epic introduced a standard of manners and actions by which the exploits of politicians and poetasters might be measured. Fomenters of Popish plots and rash rebellions and slipshod writers were exposed to ancient and Biblical ideals of prince and prophet, and their operations were socially and intellectually "placed." In contexts less purely ironic, as in parts of the Shaftesbury and Monmouth "characters," the allusions to Classical and Biblical heroic had another effect. The magnificence imparted by the Miltonic flavor was not merely literary. For Shaftesbury had great abilities as a judge and diplomat; Monmouth had noble looks and manners, and Dryden himself confessed a "respect" for "his heroic virtues." By granting their loftiness some degree of pride the satirist, too, attained a largeness of temper: "Preposterous plottings, but rather splendid persons!" Nevertheless, as Dr. Johnson observed, there are limits in heroic allegory: "Charles could not run continually parallel with David." But though the David-Aeneas incarnation cannot be taken seriously, the tone adopted in addressing Charles and attributed to him and his courtiers, did have a certain validity. The parallel between state manners and Roman aristocratic manners was justified, even in Restoration England. In public discourse, the English aristocracy, like the Roman, had a hereditary right to high oratory. And heroic poetry had been by a long tradition an aristocratic possession.

The grand yet lively eloquence that characterizes and satirizes Shaftesbury and Buckingham is thus quite different from the inflated and dully insistent rant of the heroic plays, for Dryden had found the one kind of situation in which a Restoration poet might adopt the heroic style. As spokesman for aristocracy, Established Church, and monarchy, he could rightly assume the Roman dignity of Renaissance epic. As the critic of the King's enemies, he could parody his own heroic style and so express still another true relationship between contemporary events and the heroic ideal. The discovery of relationships which were true for Dryden both as poet and citizen made it possible for him to use his accumulated literary skills with a new freedom. His satirical poetry exhibits a fluidity and force and a concentrated range of reference which his earlier verse had rarely shown.

Why may we reasonably describe this success as "European"? Not simply because Dryden's satiric mode was widely and often precisely allusive to European writers and styles and to English writers who were most consciously European in their styles and critical standards. Nor simply because he satisfied a continental standard of literary craft, although this is significant. But rather because he brought the larger light of European literature and a European past into verse of local public debate. He invited his readers, including Nonconformists, to take a less parochial attitude toward the persons and events of contemporary history. We have only to compare *Absalom and Achitophel* or *The Medal* with Marvell's satires to appreciate the imaginative value of linking these smaller and greater worlds. The Marvell of the *Ode* on Cromwell had brought to political history a similar largeness of scene and a poise of values much finer than Dryden's. But breadth of vision and sureness of rhythm are missing in *Last Instructions to a Painter,* although the poem has some of the obvious earmarks of epic satire. The spectacle is rather painful: the earlier Marvell could not address this world without sacrificing many of his virtues as a poet. Dryden could; with losses, too, if his poetry is measured by the standard of the Cromwellian *Ode;* but he managed to translate to his audience something of the larger historic vision, the noble manner, and the justness of style of the Renaissance tradition in which the younger Marvell wrote. He was a vigorous civilizer among the sons of Belial.

Dryden did something else for his generation that Marvell and Milton, much less Cowley, could not do: he reaffirmed the public role of the poet, the Graeco-Roman conception of the poet as the voice of a society. It is true that Dryden succeeded only too well in fixing the public tone as the Augustan norm; but the voice we hear is not solely that of the party or class or church. Thanks to Dryden the tone of Augustan poetry is less parochial than it might have been: it is resonant with echoes of other literary worlds, of larger manners and events. Minor Augustan poetry is dead for modern readers not because it was too "general," but because it was too local.

In praising Dryden for reaffirming the European tradition in his satirical mode, it is well to recall the conditions of our praise. The eighteenth century is littered with epics, odes, and philosophical poems that are traditional in the academic sense; the "forms" and the "diction" are too often reminiscent of the best writers of Greece and Rome. Dr. Johnson's remark on Gray's *Odes* is the appropriate comment on such products: "They are forced plants raised in a hot-bed; and they are poor plants; they are but cucumbers after all." Dryden's achievement matters because the verse through which he draws on the European tradition satisfies us as other poetry does by offering concentrated and surprising richness of relationship: we feel that language is being "worked" for all it is worth. (The allusive mode is for Dryden what the symbolic metaphor was for the Metaphysicals.) But Dryden's use of tradition satisfies also a condition of another sort. In the act of writing poetry that was far from provincial in implication, Dryden engaged the most active political and intellectual interests of his immediate audience. The particular issues are of little concern for us at present; but we can recognize their importance in the late seventeenth century, and see that the general issues involved are of a sort that is central in any conçeivable society. There are local successes in literature that are instructive to later generations: Dryden's is one of them.

NOTE

[1] This paper was one of a series on English writers and tradition that was read at the 1950 meeting of the Modern Language Association in New York. The analysis of *Absalom and Achitophel*, lines 632–659, is taken with some changes from the author's book, *The Fields of Light*, copyright by the Oxford University Press, Inc., 1951, and is reprinted here with the publisher's permission.

MARK VAN DOREN

John Dryden: The Lyric Poet

Dryden owes his excellence as a lyric poet to his abounding metrical energy. The impetuous mind and the scrupulous ear which Wordsworth admired nourished a singing voice that always was powerful and sometimes was mellow or sweet. The songs, the operas, and the odes of Dryden are remarkable first of all for their musical excitement.

The seventeenth century was an age of song. Composers like John Dowland, Thomas Campion, William and Henry Lawes, Nicholas Laniere, John Wilson, Charles Coleman, William Webb, John Gamble, and the Purcells, together with publishers like John and Henry Playford, to mingle great with small, maintained a long and beautiful tradition of "ayres"; miscellanies and "drolleries," with their fondness for tavern tunes, urged on a swelling stream of popular melody; while poets, from Ben Jonson to Tom D'Urfey, never left off trifling with measured catches high or low. But there were changes from generation to generation. The poets of the Restoration sang in a different key from that of the Jacobeans; and it was generally believed that there had been a falling off.

"Soft words, with nothing in them, make a song,"

wrote Waller to Creech. It was charged that France had corrupted English song with her Damons and Strephons, her "Chlorisses and

From *John Dryden: A Study of His Poetry* (New York: Holt, 1946; reissued by The University of Indiana Press, 1960), pp. 174–206.

Phyllisses," and that the dances with which she was supposed to have vulgarized the drama and the opera had introduced notes of triviality and irresponsibility into all lyric poetry. Dryden for one was fond of dances, and ran them into his plays whenever there was an excuse. In *Marriage à la Mode* Melantha and Palamede quote two pieces from Molière's ballet in *Le Bourgeois Gentilhomme*. Voiture's airy nothings also had their day in England. The second song in Dryden's *Sir Martin Mar-All*, beginning,

> Blind love, to this hour,
> Had never, like me, a slave under his power.
> Then blest be the dart
> That he threw at my heart,
> For nothing can prove
> A joy so great as to be wounded with love,

was adapted from Voiture:

> L'Amour sous sa loy
> N'a jamais eu d'amant plus heureux que moy;
> Benit soit son flambeau,
> Son carquois, son bandeau,
> Je suis amoreux,
> Et le ciel ne voit point d'amant plus heureux.

But the most serious charge against France was brought against her music.

Music had an important place in the education of gentlemen and poets throughout the Europe of the sixteenth and seventeenth centuries. A larger proportion of trained minds than before or since claimed intimate acquaintance with musical technique. The studies of philosophers as well as poets included ecclesiastical and secular song, the uses made of it being various, of course. Hobbes, says Aubrey, "had alwayes bookes of prick-song lyeing on his Table:—e.g. of H. Lawes &c. *Songs*—which at night, when he was abed, and the dores made fast, & was sure nobody heard him, he sang aloud, (not that he had a very good voice) but to cleare his pipes: he did beleeve it did his Lunges good, and conduced much to prolong his life." Poets drew much of their best knowledge and inspiration from musicians, so that any alteration in musical modes was certain to affect the styles of verse.

The seventeenth century in England was a century of secularization, first under Italian and then under French influences. In former times, when music had been bound to the service of the church, clear-cut rhythms had been avoided as recalling too much the motions of the body in the dance, and composers of madrigals had been confined to the learned contrivances of counterpoint. John Dowland, the Oxford and Cambridge lutanist, Thomas Campion, magical both as poet and as composer, and Henry Lawes, the friend of all good versifiers, three seventeenth-century native geniuses who were also disciples of Italy, introduced in succession new and individual song rhythms which were so compelling that by the time of the Restoration there had come into being an excellent body of sweet and simple secular airs with just enough strains of the older, more intricate harmonies lingering in them to remind of the golden age. Even in church and chamber music there had been a tendency to substitute songs for madrigals and dance-tunes for choral measures.

The Restoration saw complete and rapid changes. Charles II, who insisted on easy rhythms at his devotions to which he could beat time with his hand, sent his choir-boys to France to school, and encouraged his musicians to replace the lute and the viol with the guitar and the violin. The violin or fiddle, which John Playford called "a cheerful and sprightly instrument," was as old as the Anglo-Saxons, but it had been used before only for dancing, not in the church or the chamber. It was the rhythm of the dance that now pervaded theater and chapel and all the world of lyric poetry. There was hearty objection to the new mode. Playford began the preface to his *Musick's Delight on the Cithera* (1666) with the remark: "It is observed that of late years all solemn and grave musick is much laid aside, being esteemed too heavy and dull for the light heels and brains of this nimble and wanton age." The preface to the sixth edition of the same author's *Skill of Musick* in 1672 continued the complaint: "Musick in this age . . . is in low esteem with the generality of people. Our late and solemn Musick, both Vocal and Instrumental, is now justled out of Esteem by the new Corants and Jigs of Foreigners, to the Grief of all sober and judicious understanders of that formerly solid and good Musick." John Norris of Bemerton, in the preface to his *Poems* (1678), declared that music like poetry had degenerated "from grave, majestic, solemn strains . . . where beauty and strength go hand in hand. 'Tis now for the most part dwindled down to light, frothy stuff." Henry Purcell objected on the whole with greater effect than the others against what he called "the levity and balladry of our neighbours"; for his attack upon French opera in favor of Italian opera was in the end entirely successful. Yet even Purcell was well aware that French music had "somewhat more of gayety and Fashion" than any other, and he was not so insensible to current demands as to compose songs for the stage that were lacking in vivacity.

Dryden, who had secured the services of a French musician, Grabut, for his opera *Albion and Albanius* in 1685, was considered in 1690 a convert to "the English school" when in the dedication of *Amphitryon* he wrote of "Mr. Purcell, in whose person we have at length found an Englishman, equal with the best abroad. At least my opinion of him has been such, since his happy and judicious performances in the late opera (*The Prophetess*), and the experience I have had of him in the setting my three songs for this 'Amphitryon.' " Before Purcell died in 1695 he had not only written the accompaniment for an opera of Dryden's, *King Arthur*, but set to music the songs from *Cleomenes*, *The Indian Emperor*, an adaptation of *The Indian Queen*, *Aureng-Zebe*, *Oedipus*, *The Spanish Friar*, *Tyrannic Love*, and *The Tempest;* so that Dryden had the full advantage of an association with this powerful composer who, as Motteux put it in the first number of his *Gentleman's Journal* in 1692, joined "to the delicacy and beauty of the Italian way, the graces and gayety of the French."

It is debatable whether the musical personalities of Purcell and other contemporary composers were in general a good or a bad influence on Restoration lyric style. It is at least thinkable that as the new rhythms asserted themselves more powerfully the writers who supplied words for songs were somehow the losers in independence and originality. There was complaint at the end of the century that jingling music from France had won the field and was domineering over poetry. Charles Gildon in his *Laws of Poetry* (1721) pointed to a degeneration in song, attributing it to "the slavish care or complaisance of the writers, to make their words to the goust of the composer, or musician: being obliged often to sacrifice their sense to certain sounding words, and feminine rhymes, and the like; because they seem most adapted to furnish the composer with such cadences which most easily slide into their modern way of composition." Others besides Gildon felt with justice that genius was being ironed out of lyric verse; song was becoming sing-song. Relations between poets and composers were now the reverse of what they had been in the time of Henry Lawes. Lawes had been content to subordinate his music to the words; for him the poetry was the thing. If it seemed difficult at first glance to adapt a given passage to music, the difficulty was after all the composer's, and the blame for infelicities must accrue to him. "Our English seems a little clogged with consonants," he wrote in the preface to the first book of *Ayres and Dialogues* (1653), "but that's much the composer's fault, who, by judicious setting, and right tuning the words, may make it smooth enough." Milton was acknowledging the generous, pliant technique of his friend in the sonnet of 1646:

> Harry, whose tuneful and well-measured song
> First taught our English music how to span
> Words with just note and accent, not to scan
> With Midas' ears, committing short and long;
> Thy worth and skill exempts thee from the throng,
> With praise enough for Envy to look wan;
> To after age thou shalt be writ the man
> That with smooth air could humour best our tongue.

It was the delicacy and justness of Lawes that won him the affection of the most gifted lyrists of the mid-century; it will always be remembered of him that he loved poetry too well to profane the intricate tendernesses of songs like Herrick's to the daffodils.

Whatever conditions imposed themselves upon English song in the Restoration, Dryden for his own part was inclined to welcome swift, simple, straight-on rhythms, and he was destined to become master of the lyric field solely by virtue of his speed. His range of vowels was narrow; his voice was seldom round or deep, limiting itself rather monotonously to soprano sounds. Nor was the scope of his sympathies wide; a number of contemporaries sang more human songs. Rochester's drinking-pieces, like that which begins,

> Vulcan, contrive me such a cup
> As Nestor used of old,

Sedley's love-lines,

> Not, Celia, that I juster am,
> Or better than the rest,

And Dorset's playful flatteries,

> To all you ladies now at land,
> We men at sea indite,

are likely to touch nerves which Dryden leaves quiet. Congreve's diamond-bright cynicism and Prior's ultimate social grace exist in worlds far removed from his own. It was sheer lyrical gusto and momentum that carried Dryden forward, that drew to him the attention of the Playfords as they published their new collections, that made the editor of the *Westminster Drolleries* of 1671 and 1672 hasten to include his six best songs to date in those "choice" volumes.

Dryden's first song had something of the older Caroline manner in that its stanzas were tangled and reflective. It was sung in *The Indian Emperor*, and began:

> Ah fading joy, how quickly art thou past!
> Yet we thy ruin haste.
> As if the cares of human life were few,
> We seek out new:
> And follow fate that does too fast pursue.

Dryden passed swiftly from this to a more modern, more breathless world of song, a world where he fell at once, in *An Evening's Love*, into the dactylic swing that was to win him his way into the irrepressible *Drolleries:*

> After the pangs of a desperate lover,
> When day and night I have sighed all in vain,
> Ah what pleasure it is to discover,
> In her eyes pity, who causes my pain.

Another song in *An Evening's Love* ran more lightly yet; it was marked by the anapestic lilt which on the whole is Dryden's happiest discovery:

> Calm was the even, and clear was the sky,
> And the new-budding flowers did spring,
> When all alone went Amyntas and I
> To hear the sweet nightingale sing.
> I sate, and he laid him down by me,
> But scarcely his breath he could draw;
> For when with a fear, he began to draw near,
> He was dashed with "A ha ha ha ha!"

This lilt is heard in Dryden as many as fifteen times, being at its best in *Marriage à la Mode:*

> Why should a foolish marriage vow,
> Which long ago was made,
> Oblige us to each other now,
> When passion is decayed?
> We loved, and we loved, as long as we could,
> Till our love was loved out in us both;
> But our marriage is dead, when the pleasure is fled;
> 'Twas pleasure first made it an oath.
>
> If I have pleasures for a friend,
> And farther love in store,
> What wrong has he whose joys did end,
> And who could give no more?
> 'Tis a madness that he should be jealous of me,
> Or that I should bar him of another;
> For all we can gain is to give ourselves pain,
> When neither can hinder the other;

in *Amphitryon,* where Dryden for once is very much like Prior:

> Fair Iris I love, and hourly I die,
> But not for a lip nor a languishing eye:
> She's fickle and false, and there we agree,
> For I am as false and as fickle as she.
> We neither believe what either can say;
> And, neither believing, we neither betray.
>
> 'Tis civil to swear, and say things of course;
> We mean not the taking for better or worse.
> When present, we love; when absent, agree;
> I think not of Iris, nor Iris of me.
> The legend of love no couple can find,
> So easy to part, or so equally joined;

and in *The Lady's Song,* a piece of Jacobite propaganda which represents Dryden's long, loping jingle in its most gracious and mellow aspects:

A choir of bright beauties in spring did appear,
To choose a May-lady to govern the year;
All nymphs were in white, and the shepherds in green;
The garland was given, and Phyllis was queen;
But Phyllis refused it, and sighing did say:
"I'll not wear a garland while Pan is away."

While Pan and fair Syrinx are fled from our shore,
The Graces are banished, and Love is no more;
The soft god of pleasure, that warmed our desires,
Has broken his bow, and extinguished his fires;
And vows that himself and his mother will mourn,
Till Pan and fair Syrinx in triumph return.

Forbear your addresses, and court us no more,
For we will perform what the deity swore;
But if you dare think of deserving our charms,
Away with your sheephooks, and take to your arms:
Then laurels and myrtles your brows shall adorn,
When Pan, and his son, and fair Syrinx return.

The Lady's Song calls to mind two iambic pieces of a graver sort. The song from *The Maiden Queen* is subdued to a plane of elegy which Dryden seldom visited:

I feed a flame within, which so torments me,
That it both pains my heart, and yet contents me;
'Tis such a pleasing smart, and I so love it,
That I had rather die than once remove it.

Yet he for whom I grieve shall never know it;
My tongue does not betray, nor my eyes show it:
Not a sigh, nor a tear, my pain discloses,
But they fall silently, like dew on roses.

This to prevent my love from being cruel,
My heart's the sacrifice, as 'tis the fuel;
And while I suffer this, to give him quiet,
My faith rewards my love, tho' he deny it.

On his eyes will I gaze, and there delight me;
Where I conceal my love, no frown can fright me;

To be more happy, I dare not aspire;
Nor can I fall more low, mounting no higher.

The "Zambra Dance" from the first part of *The Conquest of Granada* begins with two stately stanzas that shed a soft Pindaric splendor:

Beneath a myrtle shade,
Which love for none but happy lovers made,
I slept; and straight my love before me brought
Phyllis, the object of my waking thought.
Undressed she came my flames to meet,
While love strewed flowers beneath her feet;
Flowers which, so pressed by her, became more sweet.

From the bright vision's head
A careless veil of lawn was loosely spread:
From her white temples fell her shaded hair,
Like cloudy sunshine, not too brown nor fair;
Her hands, her lips, did love inspire;
Her every grace my heart did fire;
But most her eyes, which languished with desire.

Dryden has used the iambic measure only slightly more often than the anapestic, but he has used it more variously. The two poems just quoted are far removed from the Cavalier conciseness of these lines in *An Evening's Love:*

You charmed me not with that fair face,
Tho' it was all divine:
To be another's is the grace
That makes me wish you mine;

or from the lively languor of these in *The Spanish Friar:*

Farewell, ungrateful traitor!
Farewell, my perjured swain!
Let never injured creature
Believe a man again.

The pleasure of possessing
Surpasses all expressing,

But 'tis too short a blessing,
And love too long a pain;

or from a pretty, rocking conceit like this in the *Song to a Fair Young Lady Going Out of Town in the Spring:*

Ask not the cause, why sullen Spring
So long delays her flowers to bear;
Why warbling birds forget to sing,
And winter storms invert the year.
Chloris is gone, and fate provides
To make it Spring where she resides.

The trochaic pieces, such as that in *Tyrannic Love,*

Ah how sweet it is to love!
Ah how gay is young desire!

and that in *King Arthur,* sung in honor of Britannia,

Fairest isle, all isles excelling,
Seat of pleasures and of loves;
Venus here will choose her dwelling,
And forsake her Cyprian groves,

attack the ear with characteristic spirit.

The songs of Dryden never go deeper than the painted fires of conventional Petrarchan love, but in a few cases they go wider. The "Sea-Fight" from *Amboyna,* the incantation of Tiresias in the third act of *Oedipus,* the Song of Triumph of the Britons and the Harvest Song from *King Arthur* are robust departures in theme from the pains and desires of Alexis and Damon. The incantation from *Oedipus* brings substantial relief, promising cool retreats:

Choose the darkest part o' the grove,
Such as ghosts at noon-day love.
Dig a trench, and dig it nigh
Where the bones of Laius lie.

The one hymn known to be Dryden's, the translation of *Veni, Creator Spiritus* which appeared under his name in the third *Miscel-*

lany of 1693, is in a certain sense a rounder and deeper utterance than any of the songs. The vowels are more varied and the melody has a more solid core to it; the bass of a cathedral organ rumbles under the rhythms. Scott on poor authority printed two other hymns as Dryden's, the *Te Deum* and what he called the *Hymn for St. John's Eve;* but it has been convincingly denied that, with the exception of *Veni, Creator Spiritus,* any of the hundred and twelve hymns which made up the Catholic *Primer* of 1706 had been translated from the Latin by the great convert between 1685 and 1700.[1] Dryden was a born writer of hymns, though the hymns he wrote were never, save in this one case, labeled as such. Praise with him was as instinctive as satire; he delighted as much in glorious openings and upgathered invocations as in contemptuous "characters." The King's prayer in *Annus Mirabilis,* Achitophel's first words to Absalom, the beginning of the *Lucretius,* the beginning of the *Georgics,* and the prayers in *Palamon and Arcite* are his most godlike pleas. "Landor once said to me," wrote Henry Crabb Robinson in his *Diary* for January 6, 1842, "Nothing was ever written in hymn equal to the beginning of Dryden's *Religio Laici,*—the first eleven lines."

> Dim as the borrowed beams of moon and stars
> To lonely, weary, wandering travellers,
> Is Reason to the soul; and, as on high
> Those rolling fires discover but the sky,
> Not light us here, so Reason's glimmering ray
> Was lent, not to assure our doubtful way,
> But guide us upward to a better day.
> And as those nightly tapers disappear
> When day's bright lord ascends our hemisphere;
> So pale grows Reason at Religion's sight;
> So dies, and so dissolves in supernatural light.

Dryden's operas, as poetry, are unfortunate. Here for once, partly from apathy towards a form of writing which the prologues and epilogues show did not command his respect, partly from a sense of obligation or dependence, he capitulated to the composer; thinking to produce new musical effects with his pen, he succeeded in bringing forth what was neither poetry nor music. The result in each of two cases, at least, was what St. Evremond defined any opera to be, "an odd medley of poetry and music wherein the poet and the musician, equally confined one by the other, take a world of pain to compose a wretched performance." *The State of Innocence,* which was never performed but which was first published as "an opera" probably in 1677, is not one of the two cases. It is an independent poem of some originality and splendor. *Albion and Albanius* (1685), however, and its sequel *King Arthur* (1691) deserve a fair share of St. Evremond's disdain. Dryden has taken the trouble in connection with them to describe his labors as a poet-musician. In the preface to *Albion and Albanius* he says he has been at pains to "make words so smooth, and numbers so harmonious, that they shall almost set themselves." In writing an opera a poet must have so sensitive an ear "that the discord of sounds in words shall as much offend him as a seventh in music would a good composer." "The chief secret is the choice of words"; the words are "to be varied according to the nature of the subject." The "songish part" and the chorus call for "harmonious sweetness," with "softness and variety of numbers," but the recitative demands "a more masculine beauty." The superiority of Italian over French or English as a musical language is heavily stressed; and it is plain that throughout the opera Dryden has aimed at an Italian "softness" through the use of feminine rhymes and dissyllabic coinages similar to those which were to mark the *Virgil.* The work as a whole is inane, and often it is doggerel; it is at best a welter of jingling trimeters and tetrameters, tail-rhyme stanzas, heroic couplets, and tawdry Pindaric passages. One song by the Nereids in Act III begins better than it ends:

> From the low palace of old father Ocean,
> Come we in pity your cares to deplore;
> Sea-racing dolphins are trained for our motion,
> Moony tides swelling to roll us ashore.
>
> Every nymph of the flood, her tresses rending,
> Throws off her armlet of pearl in the main;
> Neptune in anguish his charge unattending,
> Vessels are foundering, and vows are in vain.

King Arthur is in blank verse, with many departures into song and dance. The dedication praises Purcell and admits that the verse has in certain cases been allowed to suffer for the composer's sake. "My art on this occasion," says Dryden, "ought to be subservient to his." "A judicious audience will easily distinguish betwixt the songs wherein I have complied with him, and those in which I have followed the rules of poetry, in the sound and cadence of the words." The "freezing scene" in the third act does neither the poet nor the composer any credit; the effect of shivering, even if legitimate, is not exactly happy. The best songs are those in which, as Dryden says, he has "followed the rules of poetry": those like "Fairest isle, all isles excelling," the "Harvest Home," and the song of the nymphs before Arthur:

In vain are our graces,
In vain are our eyes,
If love you despise;
When age furrows faces,
'Tis time to be wise.
Then use the short blessing,
That flies in possessing:
No joys are above
The pleasures of love.

The short *Secular Masque* which Dryden wrote for a revival of Fletcher's *Pilgrim* in 1700 is the least objectionable of the pieces which he designed to accompany stage music. The masque celebrates the opening of the new century. Janus, Chronos, and Momus hold a sprightly review of the century just past and come to the conclusion that the times have been bad. Diana, representing the court of James I, is the first to pass in review, singing as she goes a hunting song which long remained popular:

With horns and with hounds I waken the day,
And hie to my woodland walks away;
I tuck up my robe, and am buskined soon,
And tie to my forehead a wexing moon.
I course the fleet stag, unkennel the fox,
And chase the wild goats o'er summits of rocks;
With shouting and hooting we pierce thro' the sky,
And Echo turns hunter, and doubles the cry.

The three gods agree with her of the silver bow that

Then our age was in its prime,
Free from rage, and free from crime;
A very merry, dancing, drinking,
Laughing, quaffing, and unthinking time.

Mars next thunders in and recalls the wars of Charles I. But Momus is a pacifist:

> Thy sword within the scabbard keep,
> And let mankind agree;
> Better the world were fast asleep,
> Than kept awake by thee.
> The fools are only thinner,
> With all our cost and care;
> But neither side a winner,
> For things are as they were.

Venus now appears to celebrate the softer conquests of Charles II and James II. But she also is found wanting, and so Dryden's poem ends with a sweeping dismissal of three Stuart generations:

> All, all of a piece throughout;
> Thy chase had a beast in view;
> Thy wars brought nothing about;
> Thy lovers were all untrue.
> 'Tis well an old age is out,
> And time to begin a new.

The force which drove Dryden forward through the somewhat foreign waters of song plunged him into a native ocean in the ode. His greatest lyrics are odes. He was constitutionally adapted to a form of exalted utterance which progressed by the alternate accumulation and discharge of metrical energy. The study of his utterances in this kind begins not with his first formal ode, but with the first appearance of swells in the stream of his heroic verse. That first appearance, as has been suggested before, is in the heroic plays, where the thump and rattle of the couplets is relieved from time to time by towering speeches like that of Almanzor to Lyndaraxa. *The State of Innocence* is virtually one protracted ode. Partly in consequence of a new and close acquaintance with Milton's blank verse, partly as the fruit of his experience among rhythms, Dryden here has swollen his stream and learned to compose with a powerful, steady pulse. Milton's paragraphing, whether or not it has been an important inspiration, is after all Dryden's greatest example in this instance, though Milton's metrical progression is little like that of his junior. Milton relies chiefly upon *enjambement* to give roll to his verse; as can best be seen for the present purpose in the *Vacation Exercise* of 1628, which is in heroic couplets. The bond of the couplets is broken only once, and then by drawing the sense variously from one line into another. The poet is addressing his native language:

> Yet I had rather, if I were to choose,
> Thy service in some graver subject use,
> Such as may make thee search thy coffers round,
> Before thou clothe my fancy in fit sound.
> Such where the deep transported mind may soar
> Above the wheeling poles, and at Heaven's door
> Look in, and see each blissful Deity
> How he before the thunderous throne doth lie,
> Listening to what unshorn Apollo sings
> To the touch of golden wires, while Hebe brings
> Immortal nectar to her kingly sire;
> Then, passing through the spheres of watchful fire,
> And misty regions of wide air next under,
> And hills of snow and lofts of piléd thunder,
> May tell at length how green-eyed Neptune raves,
> In heaven's defiance mustering all his waves;
> Then sing of secret things that came to pass
> When beldam Nature in her cradle was;
> And last of Kings and Queens and Heroes old,
> Such as the wise Demodocus once told
> In solemn songs at King Alcinous' feast,
> While sad Ulysses' soul and all the rest
> Are held, with his melodious harmony
> In willing chains and sweet captivity.

Dryden relies less on *enjambement,* though occasionally he relies on that too, than on sheer rhythmical enthusiasm, an enthusiasm that expresses itself first through a series of rapidly advancing couplets and last in a flourish of triplets or Alexandrines. One example has been given from *The State of Innocence.* Another is the speech of Lucifer at the end of the first scene:

> On this foundation I erect my throne;
> Through brazen gates, vast chaos, and old night,
> I'll force my way, and upwards steer my flight;
> Discover this new world, and newer Man;
> Make him my footstep to mount heaven again:
> Then in the clemency of upward air,

We'll scour our spots, and the dire thunder scar,
With all the remnants of the unlucky war,
And once again grow bright, and once again grow fair.

Eve's account of Paradise in the third act is more elaborately heaped:

Above our shady bowers
The creeping jessamin thrusts her fragrant flowers;
The myrtle, orange, and the blushing rose,
With bending heaps so nigh their blooms disclose,
Each seems to swell the flavor which the other blows;
By these the peach, the guava and the pine,
And, creeping 'twixt them all, the mantling vine
Does round their trunks her purple clusters twine.

The State of Innocence was only a beginning. Dryden's proclivity towards the ode grew stronger each year. His addresses, his invocations, his hymns were only odes imbedded in heroic verse. Even a prologue might end with a lyrical rush, as for instance that "To the Duchess on Her Return from Scotland" (1682):

Distempered Zeal, Sedition, cankered Hate,
No more shall vex the Church, and tear the State:
No more shall Faction civil discords move,
Or only discords of too tender love;
Discord like that of Music's various parts;
Discord that makes the harmony of hearts;
Discord that only this dispute shall bring,
Who best shall love the Duke and serve the King.

It is perhaps a question whether the poem on Oldham is an elegy or an ode. The "epiphonema" of the *Eleonora* is surely an ode of a kind; and the *Virgil* is one long Pindaric narrative.

Dryden's habit of dilating his heroic verse with Alexandrines not only grew upon him so that he indulged in flourishes when flourishes were not required, but it became contagious. Poetasters like John Hughes who lacked the impetus of Dryden learned his tricks and abused his liberties. There was something tawdry, in fact, about all but the very best of even Dryden's enthusiastic rhythms. It seemed necessary at least to Edward Bysshe in 1702, when he was compiling some "Rules for making English Verse" for his *Art of English Poetry*, to warn against license and to place restrictions on the use of long lines, allowing them only in the following cases:

1. "When they conclude an episode in an Heroic poem."
2. "When they conclude a triplet and full sense together."
3. "When they conclude the stanzas of Lyrick or Pindaric odes; Examples of which are frequently seen in Dryden and others."

Regardless of form, there always have been two distinct modes of utterance in the ode, two prevailing tempers. The Horatian temper is Attic, choice, perhaps didactic, and is stimulated by observation of human nature. The Pindaric temper is impassioned and superlative, and is inspired by the spectacle of human glory. In English poetry the Horatians have been Ben Jonson, Thomas Randolph, Marvell, Collins, Akenside, Cowper, Landor, and Wordsworth in the *Ode to Duty;* the Pindars have been Spenser, Milton, Cowley, Dryden, Gray, Wordsworth in the *Intimations,* Coleridge, Byron, Shelley, Keats, Tennyson, and Swinburne. Cowley is included among Pindaric writers of odes more by courtesy than from desert, for he was mortally deficient in afflatus; his importance is that of a preceptor and experimentalist, not that of a creator. His *Pindaric Odes* of 1656, with the preface and the explanatory notes that accompanied them, constituted a kind of charter for a whole century of English *vers librists* who sought in the name of Pindar to become grand and free. A parallel movement in France involved a gradual departure from the rigors of Malherbe and enlisted such men as Corneille, La Fontaine, Molière, and Racine; Boileau making himself the spokesman in 1693 when in his *Discours sur l'Ode* he defended Pindar against the current charges of extravagance and declared for the principle of enthusiasm in lyric poetry. Cowley considered that he was restoring one of the "lost inventions of antiquity," restoring, that is, what he believed was Pindar's art of infinitely varying his meter to correspond to the involutions of his theme. It was his notion that Pindar had been lawless in his splendor, or at the most only a law to himself; that he had proceeded without a method, now swelling, now subsiding according as his verse was moved to embrace great things or small. Cowley's *Praise of Pindar* began:

> Pindar is imitable by none,
>   The Phoenix Pindar is a vast species alone;
> Whoe'er but Daedalus with waxen wings could fly
>   And neither sink too low, nor soar too high?

What could he who followed claim,
But of vain boldness the unhappy fame,
And by his fall a sea to name?
Pindar's unnavigable song
Like a swoln flood from some steep mountain pours along;
The ocean meets with such a voice
From his enlarged mouth, as drowns the ocean's noise.

So Pindar does new words and figures roll
Down his impetuous dithyrambic tide,
Which in no channel deigns to abide,
Which neither banks nor dykes control;
Whether the immortal gods he sings
In a no less immortal strain,
Or the great acts of God-descended kings,
Who in his numbers still survive and reign;
Each rich embroidered line
Which their triumphant brows around
By his sacred hand is bound,
Does all their starry diadems outshine.

Cowley had an interesting theory that the Hebrew poets were sharers with Pindar of the great secret. In his preface he remarked: "The Psalms of David (which I believe to have been in their original, to the Hebrews of his time . . . the most exalted pieces of poesy) are a great example of what I have said." And one of his *Pindaric Odes* was a version of Isaiah xxxiv. "The manner of the Prophets' writing," he observed in a note, "especially of Isaiah, seems to me very like that of Pindar; they pass from one thing to another with almost Invisible connections, and are full of words and expressions of the highest and boldest flights of Poetry." Gildon followed Cowley in his *Laws of Poetry* (1721) when he cited among the great odes of the world the psalm that begins: "By the waters of Babylon we sat down and wept when we remembered thee, O Sion."

Congreve wrote a *Discourse on the Pindarique Ode* in 1706 to prove that Cowley had violated the first law of Pindar when he discarded shape; he explained the rigid strophic structure of the Greek ode and deplored the "rumbling and grating" papers of verses with which Cowley's loose example had loaded the England of the past half century. He was not the first to make this point; Edward Phillips in the preface to his *Theatrum Poetarum* (1675) had observed that

English Pindaric writers seemed ignorant of the strophe, antistrophe, and epode, and that their work seemed rather on the order of the choruses of Aeschylus; while Ben Jonson had left in his ode on Cary and Morison a perfect specimen of Pindar's form. But Congreve was the first conspicuous critic of Cowleian *vers libre,* and it was not until after him that Akenside and Gray and Gilbert West demonstrated on an extensive scale what could be done with strophe and antistrophe in a Northern tongue. Yet the difference between Cowley and Gray was far more than the difference between lawless verse and strophic verse. Cowley's crime had been not so much against Pindar as against poetry: he had written and taught others to write what metrically was nonsense. The alternation of long with short lines in itself does not of necessity make for grandeur; often, as Scott suggests, the effect of a Restoration ode was no different rhythmically from that of the inscription on a tombstone. Cowley was out of his depth in the company of Pindar; he was constituted for wit, for "the familiar and the festive," as Dr. Johnson said, but not for magnificence. The passage which has been quoted from the *Praise of Pindar* is not equaled by him elsewhere; most of the time he is writing like this, at the conclusion of *The Muse:*

And sure we may
The same too of the present say,
If past and future times do thee obey.
Thou stop'st this current, and does make
This running river settle like a lake;
Thy certain hand holds fast this slippery snake;
The fruit which does so quickly waste,
Man scarce can see it, much less taste,
Thou comfitest in sweets to make it last.
This shining piece of ice,
Which melts so soon away
With the sun's ray,
Thy verse does solidate and crystallize,
Till it a lasting mirror be!
Nay, thy immortal rhyme
Makes this one short point of time
To fill up half the orb of round eternity.

The trouble here is simply that there are no "numbers"; the stanza is not organic; there are no involutions which the ear follows with the kind of suspense with which it follows, for instance, an intricate passage in good music. Cowley has thought to forestall such an objection in the general preface to his folio of 1656. "The numbers are various and irregular," he says, "and sometimes (especially some of the long ones) seem harsh and uncouth, if the just measures and cadences be not observed in the pronunciation. So that almost all their sweetness and numerosity (which is to be found, if I mistake not, in the roughest, if rightly repeated) lies in a manner wholly at the mercy of the reader." But the most merciful and best of readers must fail to make certain of the odes of Cowley sound like poetry. Cowley had not a dependable ear.

It was Dryden's "excellent ear" which saved the Pindaric ode for Gray. Dryden diagnosed the ills of contemporary Pindarism with lofty precision in the preface to *Sylvae* in 1685. "Somewhat of the purity of English, somewhat of more equal thoughts, somewhat of sweetness in the numbers, in one word, somewhat of a finer turn and more lyrical verse is yet wanting. . . . In imitating [Pindar] our numbers should, for the most part, be lyrical . . . the ear must preside, and direct the judgement to the choice of numbers: without the nicety of this, the harmony of Pindaric verse can never be complete; the cadency of one line must be a rule to that of the next; and the sound of the former must slide gently into that which follows, without leaping from one extreme into another. It must be done like the shadowings of a picture, which fall by degrees into a darker colour." This is by far his most significant statement on the ode: it is not only an accurate analysis of the errors of others; it is an intimation of his own ideal, and incidentally it embodied a forecast of his best accomplishment. For his peculiar contribution was none other than the shading and the "finer turn" of which he speaks here. He let his ear preside; he let his cadences rule and determine one another in the interests of an integral harmony. He placed his words where they would neither jar nor remain inert, but flow. His best Pindaric passages are streams of words delicately and musically disposed.

The earliest instance of all, the "Zambra Dance" [2] from *The Conquest of Granada,* is fine but slight. The first ambitious effort is the translation of the twenty-ninth ode of the third book of Horace in *Sylvae*. "One ode," explains Dryden in the preface, "which infinitely pleased me in the reading, I have attempted to translate in Pindaric verse. . . . I have taken some pains to make it my master-piece in English: for which reason I took this kind of verse, which allows more latitude than any other." The combination of Horatian felicity with

Pindaric latitude is the happier for Dryden's excellent understanding of the bearings of each. Creech's *Horace,* published the previous year with a dedication to Dryden, had shown, as certain pieces from Horace in the first *Miscellany* (1684) had shown, what might be done in the way of running the Stoic odes into elaborate stanzaic molds; but Creech was most of the time perilously near prose. His version of the present poem, not particularly spirited but solid and just, may have suggested further possibilities to Dryden, who indeed did appropriate his predecessor's best phrases. As for the language of Horace, says Dryden, "there is nothing so delicately turned in all the Roman language. There appears in every part of his diction . . . a kind of noble and bold purity. . . . There is a secret happiness which attends his choice, which in Petronius is called *curiosa felicitas.*" As for his own versification, which of course is anarchy compared with Horace, he hopes that it will help to convey the Roman's "briskness, his jollity, and his good humour." The result is as nice as anything in Dryden. The ear has presided, and the shading is almost without flaw. Only five lines disappoint; four of these are Alexandrines (lines 33, 38, 59, 64) and one is a fourteener (line 39). Dryden has not learned as yet in this least rigid of all forms to dispose his long lines so well that none of them will halt the movement and kill the stanza; in the present instance it is significant that all of the five dead lines are attempts at reproducing effects of Nature. The first, second, third, fourth, sixth, eighth, ninth, and tenth stanzas are unexceptionable. The poem begins with a passage of remarkable carrying power; something somewhere seems to be beating excellent time:

Descended of an ancient line,
That long the Tuscan scepter swayed,
Make haste to meet the generous wine,
Whose piercing is for thee delayed:
The rosy wreath is ready made,
And artful hands prepare
The fragrant Syrian oil, that shall perfume thy hair.

The eighth stanza is in a way the most distinct and final writing that Dryden did:

Happy the man, and happy he alone,
He, who can call today his own;
He who, secure within, can say:

"Tomorrow, do thy worst, for I have lived today.
Be fair, or foul, or rain, or shine,
The joys I have possessed, in spite of fate, are mine.
Not Heav'n itself upon the past has power;
But what has been has been, and I have had my hour."

This is brisk yet liquid. The current of the stream widens and accelerates swiftly, but there is no leaping or foaming. The "cadency" of each line noiselessly transmits energy to the next. Alliteration helps to preserve an equable flow, while varied vowels heighten the murmur. And the monosyllables now have their revenge; for fifty-nine words of the sixty-eight are monosyllables.

The next Pindaric ode of Dryden's, the *Threnodia Augustalis,* is rambling and arbitrary in its rhythms; there is little or no momentum. A few passages, however, shine in isolation. At the news that Charles had rallied and might live, says Dryden,

Men met each other with erected look,
The steps were higher that they took,
Friends to congratulate their friends made haste,
And long-inveterate foes saluted as they passed.

There is a pride of pace in these lines that suits the sense. When Charles was restored from France, continues Dryden,

The officious Muses came along,
A gay harmonious choir, like angels ever young;
(The Muse that mourns him now his happy triumph sung.)
Even they could thrive in his auspicious reign;
And such a plenteous crop they bore
Of purest and well-winnowed grain
As Britain never knew before.
Though little was their hire, and light their gain,
Yet somewhat to their share he threw;
Fed from his hand, they sung and flew,
Like birds of Paradise, that lived on morning dew.

The ode *To the Pious Memory of the Accomplished Young Lady, Mrs. Anne Killigrew,* written in the same year with the *Horace* and the *Threnodia,* while it is sadly uneven is yet the most triumphant of the three. For although its second, third, fifth, sixth, seventh, eighth, and ninth stanzas are equal at the most only to Cowley and are indeed a good deal like him, the first, fourth, and tenth are emancipated and impetuous. The first stanza, which Dr. Johnson considered the highest point in English lyric poetry, rolls its majestic length without discord or hitch; its music is the profoundest and longest-sustained in Dryden, and its grammar is regal. The fourth stanza hurls itself with violent alliteration down the steep channel which it describes:

> O gracious God! how far have we
> Profaned thy heavenly gift of poesy!
> Made prostitute and profligate the Muse,
> Debased to each obscene and impious use,
> Whose harmony was first ordained above
> For tongues of angels and for hymns of love!
> O wretched we! why were we hurried down
> This lubric and adulterate age,
> (Nay, added fat pollutions of our own,)
> To increase the steaming ordures of the stage?
> What can we say to excuse our second fall?
> Let this thy vestal, Heaven, atone for all.
> Her Arethusian stream remains unsoiled,
> Unmixed with foreign filth, and undefiled;
> Her wit was more than man, her innocence a child!

The last stanza is a musical and grammatical triumph like the first, but one of a lesser magnitude. The triplet in the middle of it is something of an obstruction, and three near-conceits give the effect of a melody scraped thin. The *Ode on the Death of Mr. Henry Purcell* (1696) also suffers from conceits, being nowhere remarkable save perhaps in the first stanza, which aims at prettiness:

> Mark how the lark and linnet sing;
> With rival notes
> They strain their warbling throats
> To welcome in the spring.
> But in the close of night,
> When Philomel begins her heavenly lay,
> They cease their mutual spite,
> Drink in her music with delight,
> And listening and silent, and silent and listening,
> and listening and silent obey.

It seems now to have been almost inevitable that there should grow up at the end of the seventeenth century a custom of celebrating St. Cecilia's Day with poems set to music; so close were poets and musicians together, and so worshipful of music in that age were men as different from one another as Milton, Cowley, Waller, Marvell, and Dryden. During half a century before 1683, when the first Feast was celebrated, Orpheus and Amphion had been among the mythological personages most affectionately cultivated in English verse; and a whole splendid language had been constructed for the praise of the powers of harmony. Dryden's *Song for St. Cecilia's Day* in 1687 and his *Alexander's Feast* in 1697 were the most distinguished performances of the century, each making fashionable a new and sensational method. There was something sensational and monstrous, it must be admitted, about the whole series of music odes from Fishburn, Tate, Fletcher, and Oldham before Dryden to Bonnell Thornton in the eighteenth century, whose burlesque ode called into service of sound and fury such implements as salt-boxes, marrow-bones, and hurdy-gurdies. There was very little excellent poetry on the whole laid at the feet of St. Cecilia, and there was a deal of cheap program-music offered to her ears, even by Purcell and Handel. But the music had always a saving vigor; sixty voices and twenty-five instruments, including violins, trumpets, drums, hautboys, flutes, and bassoons, could make amends of a kind for the paltriest verse. Dryden's odes, if artificial and sensational, were the last thing from paltry; they are among the most amazing *tours de force* in English poetry.

The *Song* of 1687 established a new kind of imitative harmony in which verse became for practical purposes an orchestra, the poet drawing upon his vowels and his phrases as a conductor draws upon his players. Dryden had toyed with somewhat similar devices before. The song from *The Indian Emperor* had ended with the noise, he thought, of gently falling water:

> Hark, hark, the waters fall, fall, fall
> And with a murmuring sound
> Dash, dash upon the ground,
> To gentle slumbers call.

Oldham in his Cecilia Ode of 1684 had employed some such scheme as Dryden was soon to make famous. And of course it had been almost a century since Spenser had performed his miracles of sound with verse. But Dryden now was the first to declare a wholly orchestral purpose and to rely upon a purely instrumental technique. The first stanza is a rapid overture which by a deft, tumbling kind of repetition summons and subdues to the poet's hand all the wide powers of harmony. The second stanza slips through liquid cadences and dissolves among the sweet sounds of a harp:

> What passion cannot Music raise and quell!
> When Jubal struck the corded shell,
> His listening brethren stood around,
> And, wondering, on their faces fell
> To worship that celestial sound.
> Less than a god they thought there could not dwell
> Within the hollow of that shell
> That spoke so sweetly and so well.
> What passion cannot Music raise and quell!

A suggestion for this may have come from Marvell's *Music's Empire:*

> Jubal first made the wilder notes agree
> And Jubal tunèd Music's Jubilee;
> He called the echoes from their sullen cell,
> And built the organ's city, where they dwell;

although Marvell has only hinted of the possibilities that lie in the figure of Jubal and in the "-ell" rhymes; while Dryden has extracted the utmost, whether of drama or of sound, from both. The third, fourth, and fifth stanzas secure by obvious but admirable means the effects of trumpets, drums, flutes, and violins. From the sixth there ascend the softly rushing notes of the organ. The "Grand Chorus" which closes the poem is cosmically pitched:

> As from the power of sacred lays
> The spheres began to move
> And sung the great Creator's praise
> To all the blest above;
> So, when the last and dreadful hour
> This crumbling pageant shall devour,
> The Trumpet shall be heard on high,
> The dead shall live, the living die,
> And Music shall untune the sky.

Dryden, as has been said, seems always to have been moved by the idea of universal dissolution. The Hebrew notion of the Day of Judgment had reached him through the Bible and Joshua Sylvester. The Lucretian theory of disintegration had fascinated him when he was at the university if not before. He must have long been acquainted with Lucan's rehearsal of the final crumbling in the first book of the *Pharsalia.* His concern was with the physics rather than the metaphysics of a disappearing world. Milton's *Solemn Musick* and *Comus* spoke of a mortal mold which original sin had cursed with discord but which on the last day would melt into the great harmony of the invisible spheres. Dryden is not theological; his finale is the blare of a trumpet, and his last glimpse is of painted scenery crashing down on a darkened stage. His ode on Anne Killegrew and his *Song* of 1687 end hugely and picturesquely, like Cowley's ode on *The Resurrection,* where Dryden had read:

> Till all gentle Notes be drowned
> *In the last Trumpet's dreadful sound*
> That to the spheres themselves shall silence bring,
> *Untune* the universal string. . . .
> Then shall the scattered atoms crowding come
> Back to their ancient Home.

On the third of September, 1697, Dryden informed his sons at Rome: "I am writing a song for St. Cecilia's Feast, who, you know, is the patroness of music. This is troublesome, and no way beneficial; but I could not deny the stewards of the feast, who came in a body to me to desire that kindness." There is a tradition that he became agitated during the composition of this song, which was to be the *Alexander's Feast,* and that Henry St. John, afterwards Lord Bolingbroke, found him one morning in a great tremble over it. It is likely that he worked coolly enough at all times; yet he may well have exulted when the idea for this most famous of his lyrics first took shape in his mind. The idea of casting a music ode into narrative or dramatic form was itself a new and happy one. The materials for the story of Alexander probably came harder and were only gradually pieced together in Dryden's imagination. It had been a commonplace among classical, post-classical, and Renaissance writers that ancient Greek music, especially "the lost symphonies," had strangely affected the spirits of men; Pythagoras had cured distempers and passions by the application of appropriate harmonies. Longinus had written (XXXIV): "Do not we observe that the sound of wind-instruments moves the souls of those that hear them, throws them into an ecstasy, and hurries them sometimes into a kind of fury?" Athenaeus had cited Clitarchus as authority for the statement that Thais was the cause of the burning of the palace in Persepolis. Suidas, quoted by John Playford in his *Skill of Musick,* had related that Timotheus moved Alexander to arms. "But the story of Ericus musician," added Playford, "passes all, who had given forth, that by his musick he could drive men into what affections he listed; being required by Bonus King of Denmark to put his skill in practice, he with his harp or polycord lyra expressed such effectual melody and harmony in the variety of changes in several keyes, and in such excellent Fugg's and sprightly ayres, that his auditors began first to be moved with some strange passions, but ending his excellent voluntary with some choice fancy upon this Phrygian mood, the king's passions were altered, and excited to that height, that he fell upon his most trusty friends which were near him, and slew some of them with his fist for lack of another weapon; which our musician perceiving, ended with the sober Dorick; the King came to himself, and much lamented what he had done." Burton, after Cardan the mathematician, had said in *The Anatomy of Melancholy* that "Timotheus the musician compelled Alexander to skip up and down and leave his dinner." Cowley's thirty-second note to the first book of the *Davideis,* a veritable discourse on the powers of harmony, had contained the remark: "Timotheus by Musick enflamed and appeased Alexander to what degrees he pleased." Tom D'Urfey's ode for St. Cecilia's Day in 1691 had run merrily on through change after change of tempo, somewhat in the manner which Dryden was to employ:

> And first the trumpet's part
> Inflames the hero's heart; . . .
> And now he thinks he's in the field,
> And now he makes the foe to yield, . . .
> The battle done, all loud alarms do cease,
> Hark, how the charming flutes conclude the peace . . .
> Excesses of pleasure now crowd on apace.
> The ravishing trebles delight every ear,
> And mirth in a scene of true joy does appear. . . .
> Now beauty's power inflames my breast again,
> I sigh and languish with a pleasing pain.
> The notes so soft, so sweet the air,
> The soul of love must sure be there,
> That mine in rapture charms, and drives away despair.

In Motteux's *Gentleman's Journal* for January, 1691–2, was written: "That admirable musician, who could raise a noble fury in Alexander, and lay it as easily, and make him put on the Hero, or the Lover, when he pleased, is too great an Instance of the power of Music to be forgotten." And only three months before Dryden was writing to his sons at Rome, Jeremy Collier, who is seldom thought to have been a benefactor of Restoration poets, had published in the second part of his *Essays upon Several Moral Subjects* an essay *Of Musick* wherein it was told how "Timotheus, a Grecian, was so great a Master, that he could make a man storm and swagger like a Tempest, and then, by altering the Notes, and the Time, he would take him down again, and sweeten his humour in a trice. One time, when Alexander was at Dinner, this Man played him a Phrygian Air: the Prince immediately rises, snatches up his Lance, and puts himself into a Posture of Fighting. And the Retreat was no sooner sounded by the Change of Harmony, but his Arms were Grounded, and his Fire extinct; and he sate down as orderly as if he had come from one of Aristotle's Lectures." Such were the scraps that lay at Dryden's disposal in September of 1697.

"I am glad to hear from all hands," he wrote to Tonson in December, "that my Ode is esteemed the best of all my poetry, by all the town: I thought so myself when I writ it; but being old I mistrusted my own judgment." It is a question whether *Absalom and Achitophel* and the *Oldham* are not better poetry than *Alexander's Feast*, which perhaps is only immortal ragtime. Some of the cadences are disappointing; lines 128, 139, 140, and 145 puzzle and lower the voice of the reader. Yet few poems of equal length anywhere have been brought to a finish on so consistently proud a level and in such bounding spirits. Here is brilliant panorama; here are responsive, ringing rhythms; here is good-nature on the grand scale.

> And thrice he routed all his foes, and thrice he slew the slain.

The enormous vitality of this ode not only has insured its own long life; for a century it inspired ambitious imitators and nameless parodists. John Wilkes in 1774 [3] and the Prince of Wales in 1795 [4] found themselves hoisted in mockery to the highest throne that pamphleteers could conceive, the imperial throne of Philip's warlike son.

NOTES

[1] *Hymns Attributed to John Dryden.* Edited with an Introduction and Notes by George Rapall Noyes and George Reuben Potter. (Berkeley, California: University of California Press, 1937.)

[2] See page 394.

[3] W——s's Feast, or Dryden Travesti: A Mock Pindaric Inscribed to His Most Incorruptible Highness Prince Patriotism. (London, 1774.)

[4] Marriage Ode Royal After the Manner of Dryden. (1795.)

RUTH WALLERSTEIN

On the Death of Mrs. Killigrew: The Perfecting of a Genre

It is often said of Dryden, especially if we are speaking of those poems to which we are least sympathetic, that his frigidity is due to the conception of rhetoric which thought of an art of expression essentially divorced from substance. Or more recently, that to Hobbes's divorce of fancy from judgment may be attributed Dryden's false lights. And the use of the word *colors* in the famous and ubiquitous comparison is adduced as evidence of his view. But in Dryden's day the use of such a word is no clue to meaning. For the seventeenth century in its criticism still very largely followed the mediaeval pattern of thought in one important respect. It did not start its definitions afresh but accepted the terms of definition handed on by tradition, and altered them by criticism and redefinition from within. Accordingly, in writers of that age, it is particularly important to understand every individual term in the whole context of its use, rather than the reverse. Only so can we grasp both one basic point of view which determines the primary meaning of each term and at the same time that complex of meanings which in the Rénaissance adheres around each term and which allows different contexts to attract meanings to different facets as a result of the endeavor to fuse many systems of analysis. But it is not my purpose here to define what the term *color* or any other term

From *Studies in Philology*, XLIV (1947), pp. 519–28. Reprinted by permission of the publishers.

connoted to Dryden. Rather, I wish to ask what we can learn of his method and aims not from his criticism but by a necessary parallel method, by a close consideration of two related poems, his earliest, the elegy on Hastings, and one from his ripest maturity, his ode "To the Memory of Mrs. Killigrew." Taken together, these poems show us Dryden's evolution out of the dying metaphysical age into full neo-classicism without, however, any dimming of his sense of the English tradition. They also show, I think, throughout his art the continuity of an ideal of a poem which we may surmise to have taken shape in his schooldays under Busby's eye.

The music of his elegy on Hastings is so toneless to our ears, its imagery falls with such dusty dryness upon our imaginations, what is worse, the bones of its theology and of its social sentiment rattle so deadly in our thought, that we have been content to dismiss it with the term "metaphysical," using that term in a more than usually ill-defined sense. Yet it is an astounding achievement in structure for a boy of eighteen, highly revealing of Dryden's training. And if we consider it in its context, it is a valuable harbinger of the ode which succeeded it nearly forty years later. I propose to sketch the character of this elegy very briefly, with due apology for the dogmatism such brevity seems to give my comment, and then against this background to show how the ode on Mrs. Killigrew evolved.[1]

In his "Elegy upon the Death of the Lord Hastings," Dryden sought to integrate three types of elegy, pruning them to the compass of his own feeling, all three being part of the living tradition just before him or contemporary with him. *Lacrymae Musarum,* the volume in which the poem appeared, falls in its pagination into two parts. There were, first, a number of elegies by mature poets and poetasters, among them Sir John Denham, Robert Herrick, Andrew Marvell, the latter just coming into print, but ten years Dryden's senior. Second, several sets of verses by older hands which had presumably come in late to the printer and with them a group of laments by Hastings' schoolfellows. Of these last the others are very brief exercises, of the sort Busby would commonly have exacted from his students; Dryden's is a full scope endeavor in the elegy as then practised by England's leading poets.

Internal evidence makes it probable that the boys had seen the elegies by maturer hands before they composed their own; Dryden touches most of the themes sounded in them and hardly any theme not among them. But besides these immediate models, he had the larger background of elegies which had formed one of the most significant and characteristic types of seventeenth century poetry, such as the numerous poems on the death of Prince Henry in 1612,[2] and those of the *Lycidas* volume. Among these elegies, two forms dominated, pastoral allegory and what we may call the theological or devotional elegy.

Of the latter Donne had created the form and set the themes. But while his own elegy on Prince Henry is in the strictest religious sense a meditation or devotion, cast in the form of a thesis and its resolution, the elegies which followed him were often merely theological reflections, lacking both the metaphysical scope and the prayer form of his "Elegie upon the Death of Prince Henry" and of his "Anniversaries." Yet the form he had created was a powerful and a flexible one. And Denham's elegy on Hastings is the genuine heir of Donne's, though its religious emotion is turned outward upon the state and the martyred king, its verse regularized, and its ordonnance and imagery classicized. Marvell's is classicized in another direction, retaining the contemplative view and the emblem imagery, but arresting itself in a classical appeal to Fate.

Besides the organic forms defined in these two types of poem there still flourished the tradition of poetry-writing which taught the writer how to constitute a poem by aggregation of a selection of motives from a common store of themes suitable to one's subject. This method, which doubtless owed much to the tradition of invention as applied to poetry from the Middle Ages on down, had been clarified or given direction by the study of Quintilian. But it was still inorganic. Scholars have abundantly illustrated the process in relation to the pastoral.[3] Chapman's poem on Prince Henry well illustrates it in the non-pastoral elegy. For the seventeenth century, this method had been restated, and its motives and its devices of style classified by the Jesuit rhetorician Pontanus.[4] Though Scaliger is Pontanus's professed Bible, the work is distinctly what we should call a rhetoric and not a poetic. In tone and teaching it is thoroughly rational. Among the motives which Pontanus most strongly recommends in the funerary elegy is a description or *prosopopoeia* of the death of the subject, a precept abundantly heeded by the elegists on Hastings, who ring the changes on the smallpox, as eleven years earlier had been done on the watery death of Edward King. In style the Jesuit teaching fosters a witty ingenuity which should be carefully distinguished from the ampler symbolic and metaphysical vein of Donne and the religious poets of the seventeenth century in general except where the two touch in such a poet as Crashaw.

Now, how does Dryden combine the three? Like all the other contributors to the volume, Dryden turns his back upon the pastoral allegorical elegy which had begun in England with Spenser and which Milton had perfected only eleven years before. But though he discarded the allegory and the naturalism of "Lycidas" he kept the rational classical parts of its design. These steps clearly constitute its form: a lament for the particular death; a questioning of the nature of life; an expression of grief, including a lament for the state of the world; a consolation. Within this structure, he combines the theological elegy in the tradition of Donne with inventions taken from rhetoric of the Jesuit kind, they supplying the substance of the classical parts. To Donne belong the discussion of Hastings' character and his significance and the lament for the state of the world; to Pontanus the *Death,* the most universally used of the inventions and of course frequent in a less rigid form also in the pastoral; the comparison to the great dead; and the social reflection which Dryden draws on both for the lament of the mourners and for the consolation. Of Dryden's schoolboy treatment of these grand themes, I shall take time to say only a word on his handling of faith. It is characteristic of the changing age. The tide of seventeenth-century religious emotion which lifts the wave of Donne's prayer

Look to me faith! and look to my faith God!

has fallen. That man's knowledge and virtue are the marks in him of the image of God in which he is created has ceased to be the spur to the most daring contemplative and epistemologic speculation and has become the timid staple of current rational theology. Dryden asserts this truth objectively, as he heard it in sermon and treatise, with a naïvely fresh and honest application of it to his schoolmate. After the theological speculation, we should have expected a consolation in the beatific vision, where instead we find a promise that Hastings will live in the memory of his beloved. But Denham and Marvell have the same classical orientation.

A close study of seventeenth-century poetry shows that particular types of imagery or expression, not mere *degrees* of elaboration, were often held to belong by decorum to particular types of subject matter. The Donnian theme is expressed in accord with this seventeenth-century decorum in an emblematic image. The sickness, by the same decorum, in the type of witty ingenuity which Jesuit elegy and epigram had spread across Europe for such themes.

Perhaps the most notable aspect of the poem, if we look to the future of Dryden's poetry, is its fine ordonnance. Jesuit rhetoric contains no structural principle. Dryden's opening question and fine peroration rising in and returning to a single theme replace Donne's thesis and resolution, classical rhetoric replacing mediaeval dialectic. They draw his disparate materials together into a single perspective, the chief light falling on that aspect of Hastings' death which was probably most significant to his fellows, his snatching away just as he was leaving his childhood and entering into the full responsibilities of his place and name.

> Must noble Hastings immaturely die,
> The honor of his ancient family,
> Beauty and learning thus together meet,
> To bring a *winding* for a *wedding* sheet?
>
> . . . his best
> Monument is his spouse's marble breast.

Between this callow poem on Hastings and Dryden's ode "To the Memory of Mrs. Anne Killigrew" thirty-seven years had elapsed, but the two are bound together by their relation to a tradition, and by Dryden's unremitting endeavor to realize and redefine structural forms in terms of the new attitudes he molded to expression in them. Meanwhile, he had been studying Milton and Donne, among others, unsparingly. The study of Donne may be related to Dryden's conversion and to the fact that he was at this time giving serious attention to religious thought and to Catholic themes of devotion. Donne offered Dryden the sole great models in English of solemn verse of compliment in the religious field; and not only great models, but models Catholic in theme and spirit. Between the two poems had come also the major part of Cowley's work, and in particular the establishment by Cowley of the Pindaric ode as the form for high occasional poetry. The salient points of an ode upon which Cowley had seized had been its enthusiastic attack upon great concepts and intellectual events, the bold play of figures and ideas, and the large and varied metrical structure. He believed in embellishing high poetry; and he gathers about his central theme a play not only of witty figures but of scholastic concepts such as Donne had loved to bring to bear on his experience; but to Cowley they are now obsolete as thought and exist only as the material of sheer intellectual play, useful for poetic amplification.[5] Such was the embellishment suited to his extremely secular, rationalistic, and Epicurean temper; and the undisciplined energy of his meter perhaps does not come amiss to it.

Very different is Dryden's conception of the Pindaric ode as a genre, though he acknowledges Cowley as his authoritative predecessor in the form. Dryden sought to find its most universal forms both of thought and of structure, and he regarded the "embellishment" as a branching out of these. He has left on record his criticism of Cowley's Pindaric measures, namely that Cowley failed to study the organic relation of his varied line lengths to each other.[6] It is clear from his own odes that he did not believe that Cowley had adequately studied the structure of the ode any more than its meter. Such a form he himself seeks to perfect in his ode on Mrs. Killigrew.

In his poem he unites once more the tradition of the Greek and Latin elegy with the tradition of Donne, more particularly the Donne of the "Anniversaries," combining them within the form of a Pindaric ode. The classical lament supplies the main invention, Donne the philosophical meditation on man's fate. He does not, of course, return to the pastoral allegory. Both the descriptions and the personification of nature would have been alien to his taste as to that of his age, and alien to the Pindaric ode. More significantly, that conception of the relation between natural man and man as the creature of grace which enabled Milton to pass so triumphantly from the pagan grief of man and nature to Christian vision is a distinctive attitude of Renaissance Christian humanism, of Platonic humanism, outside the range of Dryden's thought. But the more immediate human grief for human loss which is another treatment of death in central classical poetry had from the time of Jonson taken its appointed place in that sense of order and of the bounds which define order that is the very heart of classicism in Dryden's age. In Dryden's ode, if we compare it with the elegy on Hastings, we find the theme deepened by a closer study of "Lycidas," and, seemingly, of the Sicilian odes themselves. Perhaps also Cartwright offered some suggestions.[7] To this classical theme we are first awakened by echoes of Milton and of the Greeks, echoes as deliberately suggested to our ear as Virgil's of Homer or Milton's of both.

> Whether adopted to some neighboring star,
> Thou rollst above us in thy wandering race, . . .
> Cease thy celestial song a little space . . .
>
> But thus Orinda died . . .

If we look at the structure of the ode with "Lycidas" in mind we see clearly these following parts: The statement of the theme of death, here an address to the dead; the praise of the dead; a lament for the times (stanza IV); the admission of the ineluctable claims of fate, closing with a reference to an earlier poetess; the lament of the mourners (stanza VIII); the consolation. But in actual development Dryden's poem has nothing of Milton's sense of the mystery of death and decay; rather Dryden evokes that other classical humanist theme of the Renaissance, only partially submerged by the great impulses of the religious revival and of Platonism, the theme of a great society and of art as the ornament of that society. This difference between Dryden and Milton renders easier and more decorous Dryden's transformation of the pattern of the elegy into the form of the Pindaric ode. On a close consideration of the transformation Dryden's critical and social temper stands forth clearly. The Pindaric was a poem celebrating some great idea. And for this Cowley had used it. In Cowley's Pindarics, however, there is little movement aside from the development of this idea itself, no great lyric structure. Dryden imitated the structural parts of Pindar's odes more closely, adapting the parts of the elegy with amazing neatness to that form. The elegiac praise of the dead transforms itself into what is in the *epinicea* the praise of the victor. The lament for the times opens out in stanzas V, VI, VII into the celebration of the idea —in this poem a critical definition of the new principles of painting of which Mrs. Killigrew was one of the first practitioners.

Thus in general Dryden follows the invention of the classical elegy. The theme of contemplation, however, is drawn from Donne and from the theological elegy.

The poem opens with a vision of Mrs. Killigrew among the blessed, in which there is an echo of Milton, but which is also probably reminiscent of the ascent of the soul of Elizabeth Drury. It closes with a Last Judgment and with a Renaissance and classical coda on fame. Cowley had written a Pindaric on the Judgment, but Dryden is closer to Donne in his development of the theme than is Cowley. And yet despite the resemblance to Donne the two scenes might be taken as typical of the difference between the ages of Donne and of Dryden.

> At the round earth's imagin'd corners, blow
> Your trumpets Angells, and arise, arise
> From death, you numberlesse infinities
> Of soules, and to your scattered bodies goe, . . .

But let them sleepe, Lord, and mee mourne a space,
For, if above all these, my sinnes abounde, . . .

When in mid-air the golden trump shall sound
To raise the nations underground;
When in the valley of Jehosephat
The judging God shall close the book of fate,
And there the last assizes keep
For those who wake and those who sleep;
When rattling bones together fly
From the four corners of the sky:
When sinews o'er the skeletons are spread,
Those clothed with flesh, and life inspires the dead;
The sacred poets first shall hear the sound . . .

Donne evokes in the first eight lines of his Judgment sonnet the experience of every single soul surprised by the trumpets blowing at the round earth's imagined corners. In Dryden, the whole outline of the Judgment scene is blocked in, but the description is impersonal, general, not carrying us inward to one individual soul facing itself, but diffusing outward to social comment and so by an easy step to a defense of poesy.

For Donne and for Milton, in different ways, the world is symbolic. For Dryden it is, despite his conversion, the essential imaginative reality. This is the fact which underlies or gives meaning to Dryden's imagery and to any theory of elocution that helped to shape it. The ode might well have been a reflective poem. But the poet has chosen to deal with the general idea of death, and accordingly to throw his thoughts into the form of the Pindaric. He must, therefore, develop the poem in the high style especially suited to the Pindaric ode, a style which will harmonize all the parts, and which by its imagery will startle and command our passion suitably to the greatness of the theme. The stanzas dealing with the thought are sustained by the elaborate statement of that thought and do not need additional color. It is different with stanzas I, III, and IX, expressing the lament. Since the lament is a ritual, these are the stanzas which in Dryden's view, as we may surmise, needed most amplification to sustain their passion and to elevate it to the level of the thought of death. Dryden, therefore, replaces the natural description which he has discarded by imagery drawn from elementary science and cosmic lore. These are just such amplifications as he had used many years before in his formal praise of Cromwell. Only the palms of Cromwell are become the palms of heaven. The image of the clustering bees had appeared in Beaumont's elegy on King James, a fact which reminds us of the deliberately traditional character of these adornments. Moreover, the play of ideas shown in amplification constituted the special character of the Pindaric. The ideas which Dryden brings into play are, unlike those of Cowley, of genuine interest to him and integrally related to his theme. He believed, at least at the end of his life, in judicial astrology; and the discussion of the origin of the soul had still a recognized place in orthodox treatises on the immortality of the soul. But still they are the outpourings of a discursive thought, not the substance of a concentrated intuition that draws thought and feeling inward towards a center.

The music of Dryden's ode, like its invention and its imagery, is true to neo-classical principles of formal design. Its beauty is inherent in the pure metrical pattern of the ode itself, objectively conceived, in the varied cadences of the lines within the stanza. It is conceived and managed with perfect artifice. To my ear, despite its fine numerousness, it never, like his lines on Oldham, takes emotion from its theme.

The ode on Mrs. Killigrew is at once illustrative of the grandeur of Dryden's analysis and reconstitution of the great formal genres of literature, and of the thin spiritual air he often had to breathe in his perennial struggle between the fading mediaeval world and the rising world of science and social enlightenment, in the midst of the disillusion of the first Stuart courts. Sometimes he failed to find a soul to inform what he designed, leaving it as yet only a bodily essence. But he maintained in England the tradition of high poetry. And it was by no trivial ideal of expression but by a profound sense of the forms of great poems that, even where he could not succeed himself he had left so much ready to the imaginations of those who followed.

NOTES

[1] I hope shortly to publish a detailed analysis of the elegies against the background of which I am here considering Dryden's poems.

[2] For the complete list the reader may refer to Mr. E. C. Wilson's volume, published since I made this study, *Prince Henry in English Literature* (Ithaca, 1946).

[3] See, for instance: Merritt Y. Hughes, "Spenser and the Greek Pastoral Triad," *Studies in Philology*, XXX (1923), 184–215; T. P. Harrison, Jr., "Spenser and the Earlier Pastoral Elegy," *University of Texas Studies in*

English, XIII (1933), 36–53; Don Cameron Allen, ed., *Meres on Poetry* (Cambridge, 1938).

[4] Jacobi Pontani De Societate Jesu, *Poeticarum Institutionum Libri III.* I am familiar with *Editio Secunda Emendatior* (Ingoldstatii, MDXCVIII). Pontanus in the digest of Buechler was certainly widely current, and it is to be presumed that the full book was well known. Dryden certainly used Pontanus's edition of Virgil, which might well have contributed more than has been made account of to his conception of the emotions and of the heroic treatment of character.

[5] See Cowley's notes to his Pindarics. Cowley's figures in the odes had of course been defended against the charge of fustian and praised for the beauty of their singular strength by Dryden in his *Apology for Heroic Poetry and Poetic License* in 1677.

[6] Preface to the *Sylvae; Essays,* ed. Ker, I, 267–8.

[7] As is suggested to me by Mr. Gwynne Blakemore Evans, who is shortly to bring out an edition of Cartwright.

IAN JACK

Mock-Heroic: *MacFlecknoe*

Il n'y a rien . . . de plus ridicule que de raconter une histoire comique et absurde en termes graves et sérieux.

Boileau [1]

I

"More libels have been written against me," Dryden remarked in the *Discourse concerning the Original and Progress of Satire*, "than almost any man now living. . . . But let the world witness for me, that . . . I have seldom answered any scurrilous lampoon, when it was in my power to have exposed my enemies: and, being naturally vindicative, have suffered in silence, and possessed my soul in quiet." [2] If we accept Johnson's definition of a lampoon as "a personal satire; abuse; censure written not to reform but to vex," we must admit that the fundamental impulse behind *MacFlecknoe* is that of the lampooner. It is so evidently inspired by no wish to reform Shadwell, or to reform anyone, that it sets a problem for the moral apologist for satire. Dryden felt this difficulty when he came to write his own essay on satirè, and was forced to conclude that a lampoon is "a dangerous sort of weapon, and for the most part unlawful. We have no moral right on the reputation of other men. 'Tis taking from them what we cannot restore to them." [3]

From *Augustan Satire: Intention and Idiom in English Poetry, 1660–1750* (Oxford, 1952; 1957), pp. 43–52. Reprinted by permission of The Clarendon Press.

The immediate occasion of *MacFlecknoe* is uncertain. No doubt Dryden felt that he had been "notoriously abused"—which he allows as a partial exculpation for writing a lampoon. All that is definitely known is that during the year 1678 something acted as a match to the heaped-up straw of Dryden's contempt for Shadwell and set him writing the only poem in his work which is wholly devoted to satirizing a private enemy. It is noteworthy that Dryden confines himself to Shadwell's literary character; in spite of the misleading sub-title, *A Satyr upon the True-Blew-Protestant Poet, T. S.*,[4] nothing is said of Shadwell's religious or political opinions; nor is his moral character seriously attacked. Dryden confines himself to portraying him as a literary dunce. The words "wit," "sense," "art," "nature," "nonsense," "tautology," and "dulness," which had been the current coin of Dryden's prolonged critical warfare with Shadwell, sound through the poem like a fanfare.

In its original impulse, then, *MacFlecknoe* may be considered as a lampoon. Dryden also described it as a Varronian satire, a category for which its primary qualification seems to be that it is based on a story of the poet's own invention. But the most helpful classification of the poem, as well as the most familiar, is that of the mock-heroic. Faced with the task of making Shadwell ridiculous, Dryden chose as his method the ironical politeness of the mock-epic.

MacFlecknoe is highly original. There are several English poems, of which the *Nun's Priest's Tale* is the least unlikely, which may have given Dryden a hint. But there is no earlier poem in the language which is at all comparable with it as a whole. The manner of the greatest satirist of the previous age, already cheapened by a host of imitators, was unacceptable to Dryden. When he remarks that Boileau "had read the burlesque poetry of Scarron, with some kind of indignation, as witty as it was," [5] the parallel with his own attitude to Butler is unmistakable. Dryden aspired to write "manly satire" and felt that the style of *Hudibras* "turns earnest too much to jest, and gives us a boyish kind of pleasure." [6] Believing satire "undoubtedly a species" of heroic poetry,[7] he had to look elsewhere for a model which would teach him how to give weight to his censure. He found what he wanted in *Le Lutrin*. "This, I think . . . to be the most beautiful, and most noble kind of satire," he was later to sum up. "Here is the majesty of the heroic, finely mixed with the venom of the other; and raising the delight which otherwise would be flat and vulgar, by the sublimity of the expression." [8]

II

Fully to appreciate the use of a mock-heroic idiom for highly uncomplimentary purposes it is necessary to be familiar with the panegyrical use of the heroic style. Fortunately the approach to *MacFlecknoe* is rendered easy by the fact that many passages of *Absalom and Achitophel* exemplify the use of the heroic style for panegyric which is here parodied. Any misconception of the modern reader's that a mock-heroic poem is designed to ridicule the heroic genre, or that it will be written in a bombastic, ranting style, is removed by a glance at *MacFlecknoe.* Dryden does not, like Pope's Blackmore,

> Rend with tremendous Sound [our] ears asunder,
> With Gun, Drum, Trumpet, Blunderbuss & Thunder.[9]

On the contrary a reader who did not know both poems well would be at a loss to say which of the following passages belonged to the heroic poem, which to the mock-heroic:

> (a) This aged Prince now flourishing in Peace,
> And blest with issue of a large increase,
> Worn out with business, did at length debate
> To settle the Succession of the State.

> (b) With secret Joy, indulgent *David* view'd
> His Youthful Image in his Son renew'd;
> To all his wishes Nothing he deni'd
> And made the Charming *Annabel* his Bride.[10]

The style of many passages in *MacFlecknoe* is identical with the polished heroic idiom of *Absalom and Achitophel.* The joke that makes it "a poem exquisitely satirical" [11] consists in using this style, which was soon to prove a perfect medium for a poem about the King and weighty matters of State, to describe Shadwell and his insignificant affairs. Nor is Shadwell so insignificant before Dryden gets to work: it is the elevated style that makes him so. A small man is not in himself a ridiculous object: he becomes ridiculous when he is dressed up in a suit of armour designed for a hero. The discrepancy between the important matters that the style is continually suggesting and the question of Flecknoe's successor is so marked that a shock of laughter ensues.

The purpose of such a poem must be made clear, as wittily as possible, right from the start. Here Dryden succeeds perfectly, striking the full mock-heroic note with a grave *sententia:*

> All humane things are subject to decay,
> And, when Fate summons, Monarchs must obey.

These lines might form the opening of a panegyrical funeral elegy on a royal personage; but the direction of the *prosecutio* which follows indicates the mock-heroic intention beyond all doubt:

> This *Fleckno* found.[12]

Right from the start, too, we have "the numbers of heroic poesy," which emphasize by their harmonious dignity the ludicrousness of the matter. Triplets, usually a sign of increased elevation in Dryden, are used with similar effect:

> For ancient *Decker* prophesi'd long since,
> That in this Pile should Reign a mighty Prince,
> Born for a scourge of Wit, and flayle of Sense.[13]

The skilful manner in which Dryden mingles direct and oblique attack is particularly clear in Flecknoe's speeches, which are introduced and terminated with due heightening of style and make up more than half of the poem. In a direct lampoon the lines

> The rest to some faint meaning make pretence,
> But *Shadwell* never deviates into sense,[14]

would be severe enough. They are rendered lethal by being uttered as an encomium.

One of the characteristics of the heroic idiom which Dryden adapts to his own purpose is the dignified *descriptio* of time and place. The great event is ushered in by a formal passage:

> Now Empress Fame had publisht the renown
> Of *Shadwell's* Coronation through the Town.
> Rows'd by report of Fame, the Nations meet,
> From near *Bun-hill* and distant *Watling-street*. . . .[15]

The scene of the solemnity is described with equal pomp:

> Close to the Walls which fair *Augusta* bind,
> (The fair *Augusta* much to fears inclin'd)
> An ancient fabrick rais'd t'inform the sight,
> There stood of yore, and *Barbican* it hight.[16]

In these passages the mock-heroic application of methods of description familiar in classical literature to scenes of contemporary "low" life is a reminder of the realistic bias of Dryden's mind—a bias characteristic of much of the best Augustan poetry.[17] He is very successful in his delineation of the "low" quarters of the town, "brothel-houses," and the haunts of "the suburbian Muse." The whole background of the poem (and not least the trap-door at the end, which parodies the heavy humour of Shadwell's play *The Virtuoso*) is reminiscent of the setting of a low comedy or farce. To remember Shadwell's dramatic propensities is to relish the poetic justice of the joke.

"As Virgil in his fourth Georgic, of the Bees, perpetually raises the lowness of his subject, by the loftiness of his words," Dryden observes in his remarks on *Le Lutrin*, "and ennobles it by comparisons drawn from empires, and from monarchs . . . we see Boileau pursuing him in the same flights, and scarcely yielding to his master." [18] The mock-heroic imagery of *MacFlecknoe* is no less brilliant. The joyful business of comparing small men to giants and making pygmies of them in the process begins in the third line of the poem, where we hear that Flecknoe,

> . . . like *Augustus*, young
> Was call'd to Empire and had govern'd long.[19]

The unfortunate Shadwell is compared in turn to Arion, to "young *Ascanius* . . . *Rome's* other hope and Pillar of the State," to Hannibal, and to "*Romulus* . . . by *Tyber's Brook*." [20] The tendency to blasphemy which is never far away in Dryden, whether in satire or panegyric, becomes very marked in the account of the signs and omens which foreshadowed Shadwell's coming. Flecknoe's speech parodies John the Baptist's:

> *Heywood* and *Shirley* were but Types of thee,
> Thou last great Prophet of Tautology:
> Even I, a dunce of more renown than they,
> Was sent before but to prepare thy way:

And coarsely clad in *Norwich* Drugget came
To teach the Nations in thy greater name.[21]

The manner in which the mantle of Flecknoe falls on the shoulders of Shadwell recalls the case of Elijah, who left the earth in the other direction.

It is not only in mock-heroic imagery (imagery which diminishes by irony) that *MacFlecknoe* excels. Brilliant examples of direct satirical imagery may also be found, notably in the latter part of Flecknoe's second speech, which makes relatively little use of irony and is written in a style closer to that of direct satire than most other parts of the poem:

When did his Muse from *Fletcher* scenes purloin,
As thou whole Eth'ridg dost transfuse to thine?
But so transfused as Oyls on Waters flow,
His always floats above, thine sinks below.
This is thy Province, this thy wondrous way,
New Humours to invent for each new Play:
This is that boasted Byas of thy mind,
By which one way, to dullness, 'tis inclined,
Which makes thy writings lean on one side still,
And, in all changes, that way bends thy will.[22]
Nor let thy mountain belly make pretence
Of likeness; thine's a tympany [23] of sense.
A Tun of Man in thy large Bulk is writ,
But sure thou'rt but a Kilderkin of wit.[24]

In such a passage the satire is wholly conveyed by the images. Starting with the simple object of name-calling, the poet chooses an image: as he gives expression to it another starts up in his mind, and the new image is tossed about until a third presents itself to his attention. The result is satire of great power: satire which differs completely—one may note in passing—from anything in *Le Lutrin*.

III

One of the passages in the *Discourse concerning . . . Satire* most frequently quoted and applied to Dryden's own satiric method occurs in the section devoted to complimenting the Earl of Dorset and Middlesex.

> How easy is it to call rogue and villain, and that wittily! But how hard to make a man appear a fool, a blockhead, or a knave, without using any of these opprobrious terms! To spare the grossness of the names, and to do the thing yet more severely, is to draw a full face, and to make the nose and cheeks stand out, and yet not to employ any depth of shadowing. This is the mystery of that noble trade, which yet no master can teach to his apprentice. . . . There is . . . a vast difference betwixt the slovenly butchering of a man, and the fineness of a stroke that separates the head from the body, and leaves it standing in its place. A man may be capable, as Jack Ketch's wife said of his servant, of a plain piece of work, a bare hanging; but to make a malefactor die sweetly was only belonging to her husband.[25]

In spite of this praise of indirectness in satire, however, Dryden cannot conceal the fact that he prefers the direct Juvenal to the indirect Horace. Admitting that "the manner of Juvenal" is inferior to that of Horace, he claims that "Juvenal has excelled him in his performance. Juvenal has railed more wittily than Horace has rallied."[26] Indirectness is not the most striking characteristic of Dryden's own satire. While "raillery" is perhaps a better word to describe *MacFlecknoe* than "railing," the obliquity of the attack can easily be exaggerated. The fundamental irony is the mock-heroic conception of the whole, and the brilliant heroic idiom in which it is written. The ridicule is much more direct than that in *A Tale of a Tub* or *Jonathan Wild the Great*. Qualities in fact ridiculous are nominally praised; but they are given their true names, "dulness," "nonsense," "tautology." Dryden does not tell us that Shadwell is a great poet, as Fielding tells us that Wild is a great man. Instead, and with the greatest gusto, he hammers out his lines of magnificent abuse:

> Success let others teach, learn thou from me
> Pangs without birth, and fruitless Industry.[27]

That Dryden is at liberty to speak out in this way is largely due to the fact that the heroic idiom is continually asserting that the hero is a great man, in a manner in which no prose style would be powerful enough to do. Helped by the "ostentation" of the verse (to borrow a good term from Charles Williams), Dryden is at liberty to use direct abuse without being inartistic. This is particularly evident in the speeches. The reader enjoys hearing Shadwell being abused without feeling that he is assisting in an unmannerly brawl; and the elevation of the verse adds authority to the condemnation. This mingling of irony with direct abuse is more effective than pure irony.

In writing *MacFlecknoe* Dryden had no intention of ridiculing his own heroic style, of which the greatest example still lay before him, or the heroic poem as a genre. If "parody" is taken, as in modern usage it often is, to mean a composition which ridicules the style of a given poet or poetic kind by exaggeration (as in Swinburne's self-parodies), then *MacFlecknoe* is innocent of parodic intention; except that one or two touches—principally the conclusion, and the archaisms "whilom," "hight," and "yore"—ridicule the manner of Flecknoe, Shadwell, and bad poets in general. But if by parody is meant "a kind of writing, in which the words of an author or his thoughts are taken, and by a slight change adapted to some new purpose," [28] several parodic passages may be found. They are not intended to ridicule their originals, but merely—as in the lines about the "Mother-Strumpets," [29] which parody Cowley—to amuse the reader by the allusion, and by the contrast between the original subject of the passage and that to which it is now applied. The elements of parody in *MacFlecknoe* are simply specific instances of the mock-heroic conception of the whole poem.[30]

Appreciation of the devastating satire of *MacFlecknoe* should not be allowed to blind us to its sheer comedy. It is one of the few poems that Dryden wrote for his own satisfaction, and there is no doubt that he enjoyed himself. His delight is evident everywhere, in the brilliant imagery lavished on Shadwell—

> His goodly Fabrick fills the eye
> And seems design'd for thoughtless Majesty:
> Thoughtless as Monarch Oakes that shade the plain,
> And, spread in solemn state, supinely reign [31]

—or in the hilarious couplet of advice which Flecknoe bestows on his successor:

> Let Father *Flecknoe* fire thy mind with praise
> *And Uncle Ogleby thy envy raise.*[32]

Throughout the poem there is an element of imaginative fantasy surpassed in *The Rape of the Lock* but lacking in many parts of the *Dunciad*. Shadwell is a *creation* in a sense in which Cibber is not. *MacFlecknoe* is not only a satire: it is also a comedy. Mere scorn withers. It is the ironic sympathy in Dryden's poem, the mischievous joy in contemplation, that gives life to a creature of the comic imagination. Shadwell takes his place as a member of the same company as Sir John Falstaff himself.

NOTES

[1] *Dissertation sur Joconde* (1669).
[2] *Essays*, ii, 80.
[3] Ibid., ii, 79.
[4] This was no doubt added by the publisher of the first edition, which seems to have been pirated. See Hugh Macdonald, *John Dryden: A Bibliography* (1939), p. 30.
[5] *Essays*, ii, 107.
[6] Ibid., ii, 105.
[7] Ibid., ii, 108.
[8] Ibid. For an examination of Dryden's debt to *Le Lutrin* see A. F. B. Clark's *Boileau and the French Classical Critics in England* (1925), particularly pp. 156–8.
[9] *The First Satire of the Second Book of Horace*, ll. 25–6.
[10] (a) *MacFlecknoe*, ll. 7–10; (b) *Absalom*, ll. 31–4. All quotations in this chapter and the next are from *The Poems of John Dryden*, Oxford edition, ed. John Sargeaunt (1913).
[11] Johnson's *Lives*, i, 383.
[12] Compare the much "lower" sententious passage, 36 lines long, followed by the usual *prosecutio* ("This Hudibras by proof found true"), with which Hudibras, II, iii begins.
[13] ll. 87–9.
[14] ll. 19–20. Here and elsewhere Sargeaunt follows the early editions in reading "*Sh*———."
[15] ll. 94–7.
[16] ll. 64–7.
[17] This device became essential to the "Augustan Eclogue," a descriptive piece modelled on the classical eclogue which dealt with the urban scene in a highly realistic manner.
[18] *Essays*, ii, 107–8.
[19] ll. 3–4.
[20] ll. 43, 108–9, 112–13, 130–31.
[21] ll. 29–34.

[22] As has often been pointed out, these lines parody a passage from the epilogue to Shadwell's *The Humorists:*

> A Humor is the Byas of the Mind,
> By which with violence 'tis one way inclin'd:
> It makes our Actions lean on one side still,
> And in all Changes that way bends the Will. (15–18.)

The parody is particularly appropriate because Ben Jonson was the focus of most of the disputes between Dryden and Shadwell.

[23] "A kind of obstructed flatulence that swells the body like a drum." Johnson.

[24] 183–96 ("Kilderkin" = a small barrel of wine, contrasting with "Tun").

[25] *Essays,* ii, 92–3.

[26] Ibid., 94–5.

[27] ll. 147–8.

[28] Johnson's *Dictionary.*

[29] ll. 72–3.

[30] "Parody" is only one of the critical terms which have changed their meaning since the Augustan age. To investigate the meaning of some of these words is one of the objects of this study.

[31] ll. 25–8.

[32] ll. 173–4. (My italics.)

Lindsay, A. D.	*The Modern Democratic State*	GB86
Litz, A. Walton, ed.	*Modern American Fiction*	GB100
Lowrie, Walter, tr.	*Kierkegaard: Christian Discourses*	GB49
Livingstone, Richard, ed. & tr.	*Thucydides: The History of the Peloponnesian War*	GB33
MacNeice, Louis, tr.	*Goethe's Faust*	GB45
Malinowski, Bronislaw	*A Scientific Theory of Culture*	GB40
Matthiessen, F. O.	*The Achievement of T. S. Eliot,* third edition	GB22
Matthiessen, F. O.	*Henry James. The Major Phase*	GB103
Matthiessen, F. O., and Murdock, Kenneth B., eds.	*The Notebooks of Henry James*	GB61
Mills, C. Wright	*The Power Elite*	GB20
	White Collar	GB3
Montagu, Ashley, ed.	*Culture and the Evolution of Man*	GB88
Muller, Herbert J.	*The Uses of the Past*	GB9
Murray, Gilbert	*The Rise of the Greek Epic*	GB41
Nisbet, Robert A.	*Community and Power*	GB91
Otto, Rudolf	*The Idea of the Holy*	GB14
Peterson, Merrill D.	*The Jefferson Image in the American Mind*	GB71
Price, Don K.	*Government and Science*	GB72
Radhakrishnan, S.	*Eastern Religions and Western Thought*	GB27
Roberts, David E.	*Existentialism and Religious Belief,* edited by Roger Hazelton	GB28
Rostovtzeff, M.	*Greece*	GB98
Rostovtzeff, M.	*Rome*	GB42
Russell, Bertrand	*The Problems of Philosophy*	GB21
	Religion and Science	GB50
Schelling, Thomas C.	*The Strategy of Conflict*	GB101
Schorer, Mark, ed.	*Modern British Fiction*	GB64
Schumpeter, Joseph A.	*The Theory of Economic Development,* translated by Redvers Opie	GB55
Shapiro, Harry L., ed.	*Man, Culture, and Society*	GB32
Shaw, T. E., tr.	*The Odyssey of Homer*	GB2
Sinclair, John D., ed.& tr.	*Dante's Inferno*	GB65
	Dante's Purgatorio	GB66
	Dante's Paradiso	GB67
Slonim, Marc	*From Chekhov to the Revolution*	GB92
Tillich, Paul	*Love, Power and Justice*	GB38
Thomson, George	*The Atom*	GB95
Toynbee, Arnold J.	*A Study of History, Volume 1*	GB74
	A Study of History, Volume 2	GB75
	A Study of History, Volume 3	GB76
	A Study of History, Volume 4	GB77
	A Study of History, Volume 5	GB78
	A Study of History, Volume 6	GB79
	A Study of History, Volume 7A	GB80
	A Study of History, Volume 7B	GB81

Toynbee, Arnold J.	*A Study of History, Volume 8*	GB82
	A Study of History, Volume 9	GB83
	A Study of History, Volume 10	GB84
Turberville, A. S.	*English Men and Manners in the Eighteenth Century*	GB10
Wagenknecht, Edward, ed.	*Chaucer*	GB24
Ward, John William	*Andrew Jackson: Symbol for an Age*	GB73
Wedgwood, C. V.	*Seventeenth-Century English Literature*	GB51
Wheare, K. C.	*Legislatures*	GB104
Whitehead, Alfred North	*An Introduction to Mathematics*	GB18
Wilson, Edmund	*The Triple Thinkers*	GB96
Woodward, C. Vann	*Tom Watson: Agrarian Rebel*	GB102
	The Strange Career of Jim Crow	GB6
Wright, Austin, ed.	*Victorian Literature*	GB52
Young, J. Z.	*Doubt and Certainty in Science*	GB3
Zaehner, R. C.	*Mysticism Sacred and Profane*	GB
Zimmern, Alfred	*The Greek Commonwealth*	GB

HESPERIDES BOOKS

Bridenbaugh, Carl and Jessica	*Rebels and Gentlemen*	HS7
Clifford, James	*Young Sam Johnson*	HS5
Einstein, Alfred	*Mozart: His Character, His Work*	HS8
Falls, Cyril	*The Art of War from the Age of Napoleon to the Present Day*	HS3
'erguson, George	*Signs and Symbols in Christian Art*	HS1
ry, Christopher	*Three Plays: The Firstborn; Thor, with Angels; A Sleep of Prisoners*	HS4
sen, Henrik	*An Enemy of the People; The Wild Duck; Rosmersholm*	HS2
stoy, Leo	*What is Art? and Essays on Art*	HS6